SPORT F

Sports, and the fans that follow them, are everywhere. *Sport Fans: The Psychology and Social Impact of Fandom* examines the affective, behavioral, and cognitive reactions of fans to better comprehend how sport impacts individual fans and society as a whole. Using up-to-date research and theory from multiple disciplines including psychology, sociology, marketing, history, and religious studies, this textbook provides a deeper understanding of topics such as:

- the pervasiveness of sport fandom in society
- common demographic and personality characteristics of fans
- how fandom can provide a sense of belonging, of uniqueness, and of meaning in life
- the process of becoming a sport fan
- sport fan consumption
- and the future of sport and the fan experience.

The text also provides a detailed investigation of the darker side of sport fandom, including fan aggression, as well as a critical look at the positive value of fandom for individuals and society.

Sport Fans expertly combines a rigorous level of empirical research and theory in an engaging, accessible format, making this text the essential resource on sport fan behavior.

Daniel L. Wann is Distinguished Professor of Psychology in the Department of Psychology at Murray State University.

Jeffrey D. James is the Mode L. Stone Distinguished Professor of Sport Management in the Department of Sport Management at Florida State University, and also Chair of the department.

SECOND EDITION

Sport Fans

The Psychology and Social Impact of Fandom

DANIEL L. WANN
JEFFREY D. JAMES

NEW YORK AND LONDON

Second edition published 2019
by Routledge
711 Third Avenue, New York, NY 10017

and by Routledge
2 Park Square, Milton Park, Abingdon, Oxon, OX14 4RN

Routledge is an imprint of the Taylor & Francis Group, an informa business

First edition published by Routledge, 2001

Library of Congress Cataloging-in-Publication Data
Names: Wann, Daniel L., author. | James, Jeffrey D. (Jeffrey Dalton) author.
Title: Sport fans : the psychology and social impact of fandom / Daniel L. Wann, Jeffrey D. James.
Description: Second edition. | New York, NY : Routledge, 2019. | Includes bibliographical references and index. | "Earlier edition entered under title."
Identifiers: LCCN 2018016207 | ISBN 9781138683150 (hb : alk. paper) | ISBN 9781138683167 (pb : alk. paper) | ISBN 9780429456831 (ebook)
Subjects: LCSH: Sports spectators—Psychology. | Sports spectators—Social conditions. | Sports—Social aspects.
Classification: LCC GV715 .W36 2019 | DDC 306.4/83—dc23
LC record available at https://lccn.loc.gov/2018016207

ISBN: 978-1-138-68315-0 (hbk)
ISBN: 978-1-138-68316-7 (pbk)
ISBN: 978-0-429-45683-1 (ebk)

Typeset in Sabon
by Apex CoVantage, LLC

From Dan:

To mom and dad, who always were there;

To Michelle, who always will be there.

From Jeff:

To Valerie, Kylie, and Kenzie, what I "do" may not always make sense, so I am very thankful you love me enough—and are patient enough—to let me "do my thing."

We are your biggest fans.

CONTENTS

ACKNOWLEDGMENTS

The authors wish to acknowledge the following individuals for their invaluable assistance throughout the writing of this book. First, we would like to thank Georgette Enriquez, Brian Eschrich, and the staff at Routledge Press for their tireless efforts throughout the various phases of this project.

Second, a special note of thanks must be given to Brian Gordon, Robert M. Carini Jr., Laurence DeGaris, and the other anonymous reviewers for their efforts as reviewers on earlier versions of this book. Your insights and suggestions were most useful and informative and served to strengthen this book.

Third, we would like to recognize the contributions of Merrill J. Melnick, Gordon W. Russell, and Dale G. Pease, coauthors on the first publication to this text. Their work on the original edition was invaluable in shaping the direction of this book.

Finally, we would like to express our gratitude to the following individuals who assisted with editing and other logistical tasks: Ashley Bieze, David Crittendon, David Castleman, Tommy Derossett, and Joanna Tweedie. We are so very grateful for your willingness to assist us; without your efforts, this project could not have been completed.

PHOTO CREDITS

CHAPTER 1

An Introduction to the Study of Sport Fans

When people are asked to imagine a typical "sport fan" or "sport spectator," their images can be vastly different. Some describe these persons as happy, well-adjusted individuals participating in a pastime that is important and beneficial to the structure of modern society. They imagine the strong social bonds that form among spectators—families coming together around a sporting event and groups of joyous fans storming onto the field to congratulate the victorious players. Others, however, hold a negative view of sport fans and spectators. They view them as beer-drinking couch potatoes possessing a pathological obsession with a trivial and socially disruptive activity. They conjure up images of the violent outbursts of sport fans, the strained marital relationships between fans and their spouses, lives that have been ruined because of sport gambling, and how sport directs attention away from life's more important concerns, such as religion, politics, education, and the betterment of humanity.

Thus, although some view sport fandom as a positive force for individuals and society, others feel it has a predominantly negative impact. Which of these divergent perspectives is correct? Is sport beneficial or harmful for society and its members? Are sport fans psychologically healthy or emotionally disturbed? Are fans harmless or harmful? And what are we to make of the seemingly endless amounts of time and money fans devote to the pastime? What drives their passion to consume sport? To answer these questions accurately, one must conduct a careful and thorough investigation of the personalities and characteristics of sport fans, the reasons underlying their decision to participate in the activity, and the relationship between sport fans and society. Such an investigation is the aim of this text. We attempt to answer these and similar questions by discussing and critiquing the current state of social scientific research and theory on sport fandom. The desired result is a better understanding of fans, their consumption habits, the meaning of sport in their lives, and the place of sport in contemporary society.

In this first chapter, we examine several basic topics relevant to the exploration of sport fandom, thereby setting the stage for the remainder of the text. We begin by defining, comparing, and contrasting sport fans, sport spectators, sport consumers, and highly identified fans. We then paint a picture of the typical sport fan by examining research on their demographic and personality characteristics. Next, to establish the necessity of the discipline, we provide a justification for the social scientific study of fandom. We conclude this chapter by previewing subsequent chapters and laying the groundwork for the remainder of the book.

Defining and Classifying Sport Fans

An important first step in understanding sport fandom involves defining and classifying persons involved in the activity. A number of different typologies and classification schemes have been proposed for segmenting sport fans (Bouchet, Bodet, Bernache-Assollant, & Kada, 2011; Giulianotti, 2002; Hunt, Bristol, & Bashaw, 1999; Koo, Andrew, Hardin, & Greenwell, 2009; Markovits & Albertson, 2012; Ross, 2007). Although the segmentation of fans into various groups is a relatively common practice, this process can be problematic. For example, the labels and categories used for classification can seem arbitrary, particularly when the scheme was developed though non-empirical methods. Crawford (2004) identified several additional pitfalls accompanying the classification of fans into discrete types. For instance, he notes that typologies often fail to consider the ever-changing nature of the fan experience and the fact that fans frequently move across categories.

Although there are drawbacks associated with segmenting fans into categories, there are advantages as well. Stewart, Smith, and Nicholson (2003) argue that segmentation can provide valuable information on the behavioral and attitudinal patterns of fans, particularly if the typologies are based on sound theory and are multi-dimensional in nature. They list a number of advantages to using classification schemes, including a better understanding of demographic and social/cultural groups which, in turn, can lead to a greater understanding of antecedents to and consequences of fan loyalty and commitment. They note further that information provided by segmentation procedures can be valuable to sport marketing and management professionals as they attempt to better understand and serve sport consumers. For example, classification schemes can provide data on interest in sport products, satisfaction with arenas and stadiums, and feedback on the effectiveness of marketing campaigns.

Given that the classification of fans can be beneficial, in the following paragraphs we examine three ways of classifying fans by focusing on the distinctions between sport fans and spectators, direct and indirect sport consumers, and various levels of team identification.

Distinguishing Between Sport Fans and Sport Spectators

The first important distinction to be made involves differentiating between sport fans and sport spectators (Sloan, 1989; Wann, 1997). **Sport fans** are individuals that are interested in and follow a sport, team, and/or athlete, while **sport spectators** are those who actively witness a sporting event in person or through some form of media (radio, television, etc.). Unfortunately, the terms "sport fan" and "sport spectator" are often used interchangeably, a practice that can lead to confusion and frustration for researchers and practitioners (Trail, Robinson, Dick, & Gillentine, 2003). The distinction between fans and spectators is important because some sport fans rarely witness sporting events in person, while some spectators have little interest in identifying with a favorite team or player. For instance, consider a person who attends a college basketball game simply because he was given a free ticket. This person may go to the contest even though he has no interest in the event itself or the teams competing (perhaps he simply wishes to be with his friends who are also at the game). Although this person would be classified as a sport spectator, he should not be considered a sport fan.

Although we believe the distinction between fans and spectators is an important one, maintaining a consistent use of these terms is difficult when writing a book such as this. A strict adherence to the "fan" versus "spectator" nomenclature becomes cumbersome and likely overstates the importance of the distinction. In this text we are, more often than not, focusing on individuals with an interest in a sport, team, or player (i.e., a fan) rather than those who are merely observing a sporting event (i.e., a spectator). To avoid confusion and an over-reliance on jargon, we have chosen to use the term fan throughout this book, unless the distinction of spectator is critical for the specific topic being discussed (e.g., the influence of watching sporting events on spectator violence).

Distinguishing Between Direct and Indirect Sport Consumers

Another important distinction involves the classification of sport consumers into two groups: direct and indirect (McPherson, 1975). **Direct sport consumption** involves one's personal attendance at a sporting event. **Indirect sport consumption** involves one's exposure to sport through some form of mass media, such as television, radio, or the Internet. Thus, an individual who attends the Super Bowl in person would be classified as a direct sport consumer, while someone watching the same contest on television would be classified as an indirect sport consumer. This distinction is important because the situational context in which one witnesses an event can impact his or her reactions (Brummett & Duncan, 1990; Hemphill, 1995; Wenner & Gantz, 1989). For example, consider the work by Wann, Friedman, McHale, and Jaffe (2003) on the consumption patterns of avid sport fans. Participants stated their preferences for consuming sport in person (i.e., direct consumption) and via television or radio (i.e., indirect consumption). The researchers found distinct differences between the various forms of consumption. For instance, only 2 percent of respondents indicated a preference for attending a sporting event alone. Conversely, 14 percent had a desire to watch sport on television by themselves and over 60 percent had a desire to listen to sport radio alone.

Wann and his colleagues (2003) offered two suggestions for the large proportion of persons preferring to consume radio sport programing alone. First, it could be that sport consumption via radio frequently occurs when driving, an activity that is often done alone. As a result, spectators may grow accustomed to listening to sport radio by themselves and develop a preference for this environment. Second, Wann and his associates suggest that, given the absence of verbal cues, consuming sporting events via radio may require greater levels of concentration than other forms of consumption. This greater level of focus may be disrupted by the presence of other persons, and, thus, fans may prefer to listen to sport radio broadcasts alone to better follow and comprehend the game action. Regardless of the reasons underlying the differences in consumption preferences, it is clear that such partialities do exist. Thus, it is important to differentiate between the two forms of consumption.

Distinguishing Among Fans Across Levels of Team Identification

A common approach to distinguishing fans is based on level of identification, or what has typically been referred to as **team identification**, although other terms (such as fan identification) have occasionally been used. Although researchers have utilized a variety of definitions of team identification, they often share commonalities (see Lock & Heere, 2017, for an insightful look at definitions of this construct). We will utilize an operational definition that is generally consistent with most others and view team identification as the extent to which a fan feels psychologically connected to a team (Guttmann, 1986; Lock & Funk, 2016; Wann, 2006a; Wann & Branscombe, 1993).

Although often thought to be a new term, references to team identification among sport fans can be found as early as the 1920s and 1930s. For example, consider the writings of Coleman Roberts Griffith (1938). Often viewed as the father of North American sport psychology (Green, 2009; Wann, 1997), Griffith was asked to consult with the Chicago Cubs Major League Baseball team. As part of a larger project to improve team performance and fan interest, he surveyed approximately 300 Cubs fans to gauge their motivations for following the team. The majority of respondents cited identification as a critical factor in fostering their interest in the team, leading Griffith to conclude that "interest in baseball was frequently based on the principle of identification" (p. 174). A few years earlier, Brill (1929) had also referenced the identification process among sport fans, arguing that fandom was a function of "the psychological laws of identification" (p. 430). Modern perceptions of identification within the realm of fandom typically have origins in general psychology (e.g., Kagan, 1958; Tolman, 1943) and, more particularly, **Social Identity Theory** (Tajfel, 1978; Tajfel & Turner, 1979).

Research suggests that a fan's sense of connection to a team is a highly stable trait. For example, team identification is not a function of the location or outcome of a team's most recent game (Wann, 1996, 2000; Wann, Dolan, McGeorge, & Allison, 1994; Wann & Schrader, 1996). Rather, fans tend to report consistent levels of identification from game to game and from season to season. Additional evidence of the stability of team identification was noted in the work of Boen, Vanbeselaere, Pandelaere, Schutters, and Rowe (2008). These authors investigated identification with a basketball team that had been recently merged with another team. Interestingly, they found that, "identification with the pre-merger club was the best predictor of identification with the new merger club" (p. 165).

Identification with a team is usually a lifelong love affair that fans take to their graves—literally, as fans often express their love for a team after death. For instance, they sometimes choose to be buried in team and sport-themed coffins and/or display team logos on their tombstones. Furthermore, people frequently feel compelled to describe the fandom of their deceased loved ones in the obituary section. For example, in an examination of over 1,800 newspaper obituaries, End, Meinert, Worthman, and Mauntel (2009) found that over 10 percent of the descriptions mentioned the deceased individual's fandom. Similarly, in his study of obituaries posted on legacy.com, Clotfelter (2015) found that 2 percent of the tributes specifically included mention of the person's loyalty to a college team.

For fans with a low level of team identification, the role of team follower is a very small part of their self-concept. As a result, these persons tend to exhibit mild reactions to team performances, if they react at all. However, for fans with a high level of identification, the role of team follower is a central component of their identity. They willingly present themselves as a fan of their team in their written self-descriptions and their choice of apparel (Derbaix, Decrop, & Cabossart, 2002; Wann, Royalty, & Roberts, 2000). Because of their close association with a team, highly identified fans often view it as a reflection of themselves. That is, the team becomes an extension of the individual (Smith & Henry, 1996; Tajfel, 1978; Tajfel & Turner, 1979). The team's successes become the fan's successes, and their failures become the fan's failures. Due to the increased importance highly identified fans place on their team's performances, their affective, cognitive, and behavioral reactions tend to be quite extreme. In fact, the responses of these fans are a consistent theme running throughout this book. Subsequent chapters will include information about a variety of fan reactions impacted by team identification, including consumption (Chapter 5), affect (Chapter 6), aggressive behaviors (Chapter 8), and the psychological health of fans (Chapter 10). A detailed discussion of team identification can be found in Chapter 3, including the origin of identification and the development of scales used to accurately measure this construct.

It is also important to note that, although most fans feel some sort of connection to a favorite team, there are other important points of attachment as well. That is, fans can identify with a variety of objects within sport. Consistent with work examining other social or organizational settings (Ouwerkerk, Ellemes, & De Gilder, 1999), sport researchers have reported that, in addition to a team, fans can feel a sense of identification with and connection to coaches, players, the fan community, the sport played by a team, conference affiliation, and the university linked to a collegiate team (Robinson & Trail, 2005; Spinda, Wann, & Hardin, in press; Trail et al., 2003). Researchers also suggest these points of attachment may be differentially important across levels of competition. For instance, Robinson, Trail, Dick, and Gillentine (2005) found that player, sport, and organizational attachment for college football varied as a function of NCCA division (e.g., player attachment was higher at lower levels of competition). Thus, although identification with a team may be a key predictor of fan responses (Kwon, Trail, & Anderson, 2005; Mahony, Nakazawa, Funk, James, & Gladden, 2002), other forms of identification are critical as well (see Chapter 3 for a detailed discussion of the various sport objects to which fans can feel an attachment).

Demographic and Personality Traits of Sport Fans

Now that we have classified the types of sport fans and spectators, it is appropriate to discuss the demographic and personality profiles of these individuals. However, prior to this discussion, a few points warrant mention. First, researchers have been inconsistent in their operational definitions of sport fandom. These inconsistencies render cross-study comparisons of fan characteristics more difficult. To aid researchers in acquiring a consistent and reliable assessment of sport fandom and therefore improve our profile of fans, Wann (2002) developed and validated the Sport Fandom Questionnaire (SFQ). The SFQ includes five items designed to measure level of identification with the role of sport fan (e.g., "My life would be less enjoyable if I were not able to follow sports"). By utilizing the SFQ when assessing sport fandom, investigators employ a more consistent operational definition of the construct, resulting in a greater ability to generalize across studies.

A second important point is that much of the research on the personality patterns of sport fans has been atheoretical. That is, similar to work on the personalities of athletes (Martens, 1981; Morgan, 1980; Silva, 1984), investigations of the personality profile of sport fans have not been guided by a theoretical rationale. Without theory, investigators are often left "fishing" for significant differences between fans and nonfans. Such findings are often difficult to replicate because they are the artifactual result of a single, unexpected observation. A more appropriate line of research would be to use relevant theory to predict specific differences between fans and nonfans and then test those predictions.

Finally, in the paragraphs that follow, we review the relationships between fandom and gender, age, race, involvement as a fan, socioeconomic status, and personality. This is certainly not an exhaustive list of research on characteristics associated with fandom, but we have limited our discussion to relationships that have been well-replicated. Additionally, even among the selected traits, there have been contradictory results. For instance, although researchers have found that age and socioeconomic status are positively correlated with fandom (see below), other work has failed to find these effects (e.g., Grove, Pickett, & Dodder, 1982; Lieberman, 1991; Wann, 2002). These contradictions are likely due to the differential methodologies employed by the researchers, the aforementioned inconsistencies in operationally defining sport fandom, and the atheoretical nature of the research.

Gender and Fandom

Gender is likely the most frequently investigated demographic trait associated with sport fandom. In the existing literature, a consistent finding is that males report a greater interest in sport fandom or indicate higher levels of team identification than do women. Additionally, End, Kretschmar, and Dietz-Uhler (2004) found that involvement in sport as a fan is believed to have a greater influence on the popularity amongst peers of adolescent males than females. These authors asked college students to rank seven popularity determinants for men and women. The determinants included physical attractiveness, sport participation, and sport fandom, among others. End et al. reported that following sport received the third-highest ranking for males (behind physical attractiveness and sport participation). Conversely, following sport as a fan was ranked as the *least* important predictor of popularity for females.

The volume of research indicating gender differences in sport fandom is quite impressive, and this literature is confirmed in national polling data (Jones, 2015). Although far from an exhaustive list, several of these studies are listed in Table 1.1. The studies highlighted in the table reflect the fact that gender issues in sport fandom have frequently been a topic of interest to sport scholars. In fact, discussions of gender will regularly appear in later chapters, including topics such as the processes of socialization into fandom (Chapter 2), motivational patterns (Chapter 4), and aggression (Chapters 8 and 9).

TABLE 1.1 A Partial List of Studies Indicating Gender Differences in Fandom and Team Identification

Anderson and Stone (1981)	Bahk (2000)
Bloss (1970)	Dietz-Uhler, Harrick, End, and Jacquemotte (2000)
Grove et al. (1982)	James and Ridinger (2002)
Judson and Carpenter (2005)	Lieberman (1991)
Groeneman (2017)	Mehus and Kolstad (2011)
Meier and Leinwather (2012)	Melnick and Wann (2004, 2011)
Murrell and Dietz (1992)	Norris, Wann, and Zapalac (2015)
Parry, Jones, and Wann (2014)	Prisuta (1979)
Roloff and Solomon (1989)	Sargent, Zillmann, and Weaver (1998)
Schurr, Ruble, and Ellen (1985)	Schurr, Wittig, Ruble, and Ellen (1988)
Tobar (2006)	Wann (1998, 2002)
Wann and Waddill (2014)	Yergin (1986)

Notes: The studies above found that males had a greater interest in sport or higher levels of team identification than females. Full citation information can be found in the Reference section.

Several researchers have investigated how the gender discrepancy in sport fandom might impact the experiences of female fans. For instance, authors have noted that women are often marginalized when they attempt to enter the male-dominated world of sport fandom (Esmonde, Cooky, & Andrews, 2015; Markovits & Albertson, 2012; Sveinson & Hoeber, 2016). Researchers have reported that individuals have different perceptions of the "typical" male and female sport fan. For instance, Dietz-Uhler, End, Jacquemotte, Bentley, and Hurlbut (2000) found that individuals believe males are more likely to be a sport fan, and they spend more time consuming sport. The differential perceptions of male and female fans were magnified by one's level of sexism; persons high in sexism were particularly likely to believe there are large differences in male and female fans. Dietz-Uhler and her colleagues argued that this pattern of effects suggests that men may feel threatened by female fans (see also Markovits & Albertson, 2012; McGinnis, Chun, & McQuillan, 2003). That is, given that they are threatened by female fans entering their space, male fans may have a preference for women who are not sport fans. However, this argument contradicts a large body of research indicating that individuals have a partiality for persons sharing similar attitudes (e.g., Byrne, Clore, & Smeaton, 1986; Caspi, Herbener, & Ozer, 1992). Based on this literature, one would expect male fans to report a preference for women who are also fans.

To determine whether male college students would be threatened by or attracted to female fans, Wann, Schinner, and Keenan (2001) asked male fans to read a description of a female college student. Some read that the target female frequently followed sport, while others read that she was not at all a sport fan. After reading the description, participants indicated the extent to which they had formed a positive impression of the target female. The results supported the importance of similarity, as male fans viewed the target female in a much more positive light when she was described as a sport fan. Thus, although some male fans may feel threatened by the entrance of women into the historically male-dominated arena of sport fandom, it is more likely men have favorable impressions of female fans.

A few final points about gender issues in sport fandom warrant mention. First, although males often report higher levels of team identification than women (e.g., Parry et al., 2014; Theodorakis, Wann, Lianopoulos, Foudouki, & Al-Emadi, 2017; see Table 1.1), this gender difference may be less likely for a local team. That is, a number of researchers have found that male and female fans report similar levels of identification for hometown college and professional teams (e.g., Mehus & Kolstad, 2011; Norris et al., 2015; Robinson & Trail, 2005; Wann, Brasher, Thomas, & Scheuchner, 2015). One conclusion from such a finding is that women may be more interested in and feel comfortable with becoming involved in teams with a local fan base. Interestingly, gender differences are also frequently absent when examining identification with a newly formed team (James, Kolbe, & Trail, 2002; Lock, Darcy, & Taylor, 2009). Such a finding could mean that women feel more accepted when joining a fan base that has yet to be fully established because such a group may not have developed the male-dominated nature of clubs with a longer history.

Second, **sex-role orientation** might be a better predictor of fandom than anatomical sex. Individuals can be viewed as possessing one of three gender roles: masculine, feminine, or androgynous (i.e., self-identifying with both masculine and feminine traits). Wann, Waddill, and Dunham (2004) found that, although anatomical sex did significantly predict levels of fandom, one's level of masculinity (regardless of biological sex) was a better predictor (femininity was not a significant predictor). McCabe (2008) also reported that gender-role orientation was a more effective predictor of fandom than anatomical sex. However, contrary to Wann and his colleagues, McCabe found that femininity (i.e., expressive traits) was the best predictor. Perhaps the inconsistency between these two studies lies in the assessments of fandom. Wann and his associates targeted general fandom, while McCabe assessed fandom specifically for women's professional basketball. Thus, it may be feminine gender roles are particularly important for understanding one's interest in women's sports. Taken together, the results of these studies indicate that simply utilizing anatomical sex as a predictor of fandom will result in an incomplete picture. Rather, researchers and practitioners alike should also assess gender-role orientation and consider its impact on interest in sport.

Third, there is some indication that the gender gap in sport fandom is shrinking (McGinnis et al., 2003). For example, in the 1990s there were reports of increased interest among females in several sports, including professional soccer, football, and hockey (Hofacre, 1994; Meyers, 1997; Mihoces, 1998). Perhaps as more women enter the realm of sport fandom, the perception of them as outsiders will diminish. Reductions in the marginalization of female fans should result in a more welcoming environment, paving the way for other women to become fans.

Finally, although research has frequently targeted the level of fandom for females, far fewer studies have examined the experiences of these persons. Although a few notable exceptions can be found (e.g., Farrell, Fink, & Fields, 2011; Markovits & Albertson, 2012; Pope, 2013; Toffoletti & Mewett, 2012), overall the affective, behavioral, and cognitive reactions of female fans is an understudied area of investigation (James & Ridinger, 2002; Sveinson & Hoeber, 2016). This lack of research is unfortunate given that women follow virtually all sports, including those that have historically been viewed as especially masculine in nature, such as rugby (Allon, 2012), hockey (Field, 2012), and rodeo (Thompson & Forsyth, 2012). Clearly, additional research on the experiences of female fans is warranted to better understand how their lives are impacted by their sport fandom.

Age and Fandom

Age is a second demographic variable that has garnered the interest of sport scholars interested in fandom. Although the breadth of work pertaining to age and fandom is not as extensive as work on gender, that which has been done illustrates age and fandom is a viable area of study. This body of work includes mixed results. Although some have reported that age and fandom were positively correlated (Lee & Zeiss, 1980; Murrell & Dietz, 1992), other researchers found that younger persons appeared to be more interested in sport (Lock et al., 2009; Tobar, 2006). Further muddying the water, others have failed to find age differences in fandom (James et al., 2002; McDaniel, 2002; Mehus, 2005). For example, in the initial validation studies of the Sport Fandom Questionnaire (Wann, 2002), levels of fandom and age were not significantly related across three different samples. Given these inconsistent findings, it is clear that additional work is needed to better our understanding of the relationship between age and sport fandom.

Although the relationship between age and level of fandom remains blurred, what has been established is that fans of varying age cohorts can exhibit differences in their fandom (Westerbeek, 2000; Yoh, Pai, & Pedersen, 2009). For instance, researchers have found that fans of varying ages report differential affective responses to sporting events. In a study of student and parent fans, Tobar (2006) noted that younger fans reported significant pre- to post-game mood changes, while older fans reported greater enjoyment of the sport viewing environment. Age differences in emotional responses were also documented by Rainey, Larsen, and Yost (2009) who found that younger fans reported particularly high levels of disappointment in their team's playoff loss.

Younger and older fans also differ in their agreement with old school values within the realm of sport. Sukhdial, Aiken, and Kahle (2002) define **old school sport ideology** as "old fashioned American notions of the team before the player, sportsmanship, loyalty above all else, and competition simply for 'love of the game'" (p. 73). These authors developed an Old School Scale assessing three components of old school ideology: materialism (e.g., modern athletes are greedy), role modeling (professional athletes have a duty to act as role models), and importance of winning (losing is unacceptable). In a series of studies, Sukhdial, Aiken, and their colleagues found consistent age differences in responses to the Old School Scale (Aiken, Campbell, & Sukhdial, 2010; Aiken & Sukhdial, 2004). Specifically, relative to those younger in age, older fans were far more likely to endorse old school values in sport, such as the belief that modern day athletes are too materialistic.

Race and Fandom

The relationship between race and sport fandom has also been investigated. In many ways, this research mirrors work on age and fandom, as the results have been inconsistent (Armstrong, 2002a). Earlier research by Schurr and his colleagues (Schurr et al., 1985, 1988) indicated that African Americans had significantly higher levels of fandom than Caucasians. However, subsequent work includes results showing either the opposite pattern (Brown & Bennett, 2015; Nelson & Wechsler, 2003) or a failure to find any differences by race (Armstrong, 2008; McDaniel, 2002). Furthermore, some researchers have found that the differences are sport specific (Groeneman, 2017). Thus, race and level of fandom is yet another area of research in need of further investigation to untangle the inconsistent findings from past efforts.

Similar to work on age and fandom, although work on race and degree of fandom is inconclusive, researchers have identified racial differences in fans' attitudes and behaviors (Armstrong & Peretto Stratta, 2004). For example, although large numbers of fans play fantasy sport games, participation is quite rare among African Americans (Drayer & Dwyer, 2013). Racial differences have also been found in the motivational profiles of fans (Armstrong, 2008; Wann, Bilyeu, Brennan, Osborn, & Gambouras, 1999). Because members of different races sometimes report different reasons underlying their interest in following and consuming sport, researchers have developed more racially inclusive measures of fan motivation (Armstrong, 2002b; Bilyeu & Wann, 2002).

Athletic Involvement and Fandom

Another individual difference variable positively correlated with level of sport fandom is past or present participation as an athlete. In fact, the volume of early studies indicating that fans are or were actively involved in sport suggests that this variable may be one of the best predictors of sport fandom (e.g., Bloss, 1970; Freischlag & Hardin, 1975; Grove et al., 1982). Work in subsequent decades has substantiated the positive relationship between fandom and athletic participation (Appelbaum et al., 2012; Inoue, Berg, & Chelladurai, 2015; Mehus, 2005; Shank & Beasley, 1998), leading some to suggest that hosting major sporting events may lead to greater athletic participation (Frawley & Cush, 2011; Mutter & Pawlowski, 2014). That is, the increased salience of and interest in fandom resulting from large-scale sporting events may increase sport participation rates among the population (but see also Murphy & Bauman, 2007). Interestingly, one of the more common criticisms of sport fandom is the belief that these individuals are passive, sloth-like creatures who rarely get off their couch. However, as will be discussed in Chapter 10, the high levels of physical activity among sport fans are frequently used to challenge this stereotype.

Socioeconomic Status and Fandom

As most fans are all too aware, following sport can be a costly endeavor. For example, in 2015–2016 the average ticket prices for the four North American professional sports leagues ranged from a not-so-low of $31 per ticket to Major League Baseball games to a potentially wallet-busting $93 per seat at National Football League contests; National Basketball Association and National Hockey League tickets averaged around $60 per event (Statista, 2016). And that is just the cost to get into the game. When you factor in other expenses such as travel costs, parking, food, and memorabilia purchases, the outlay of cash needed to attend sporting events can escalate quickly. Given this, it seems plausible that there may be a positive relationship between socioeconomic status (SES) and sport fandom. Indeed, researchers have found such an effect, as persons higher in SES report greater levels of fandom and sport consumption (e.g., Crawford, 2001; Lieberman, 1991; Mashiach, 1980; Pan, Gabert, McGaugh, & Branvold, 1997; White & Wilson, 1999; Yergin, 1986).

Personality and Fandom

A final individual difference variable concerns the personality characteristics of sport fans. **Personality** is commonly viewed as unique patterns of emotional, behavioral, and cognitive responses that endure across time and place (Phares, 1991; Wann, 1997). Work on the personalities of fans attempts to paint an accurate picture of the types of persons who gravitate toward this pastime. Given the large number of personality traits identified (one estimate included several thousand traits, Allport, 1937, 1961), it not surprising that researchers have examined a fairly wide range of personality characteristics of sport fans. This list includes, but is not limited to, locus of control (Miller, 1976), optimism (Wann et al., 2003), patriotism (McDaniel, 2002), empathy (Sun, 2010), curiosity (Park, Andrew, & Mahony, 2008), and assertiveness (Wann & Ostrander, 2017).

Although the list of individual personality attributes is quite long, in recent years psychologists have established that there are five core (i.e., Big 5) personality traits (McCrae & Costa, 1987, 2008). These core dimensions are **extraversion** (i.e., sociability and friendliness), **neuroticism** (i.e., emotional instability), **openness to new experiences** (i.e., flexibility and imagination), **agreeableness** (i.e., trustworthiness and cooperativeness), and **conscientiousness** (i.e., reliability and dependability). These traits have been examined in several studies in relation to team identification and sport fandom (Appelbaum et al., 2012; Donavan, Carlson, & Zimmerman, 2005; Sun, 2010; Wann, Dunham, Byrd, & Keenan, 2004). Taken together, the results of these investigations lead to a pair of conclusions. First, in the majority of cases, team identification was not significantly associated with the Big 5 personality traits. When significant correlations were found (e.g., a positive relationship between identification and extraversion, see Donavan et al., 2005; Wann et al., 2004), the magnitude of the effect was small. Second, other personality traits (e.g., empathy and need for affiliation) may mediate the relationship between core personality traits and fandom. These findings suggest that relationship between fandom and personality is complex, when it exists at all. Clearly, additional research is warranted in this area.

Justification for the Social Scientific Study of Sport Fans

After getting to this point, readers may be asking "Why bother? Why do we need to understand the psychology of sport fans? Why is it important to understand their place in society? Why should we care about fan motives and consumption practices?" Your authors believe these are fair questions, and we have certainly fielded inquiries such as these many times ourselves. It is our belief that there are a number of reasons for examining the psychological and sociological processes involved in sport fandom and spectating. In the paragraphs that follow, we highlight these justifications.

The Pervasiveness of Sport Fandom

Perhaps one of the most straightforward justifications for an empirical examination of sport fandom lies in the **pervasiveness of fandom** in modern society (as well as ancient civilizations; see Guttmann, 1986). However, prior to examining data on the pervasiveness of sport, it warrants mention that the impact of the proliferation of sport is not limited to fans but, rather, affects the lives of all members of society. Although most people have at least a moderate interest in following sport and/or teams, there are still some who do not feel or understand the passion fans have for sport. Referred to as the "sports agnostic" by Price (2016, p. 18), nonfans find themselves in a world driven by a pastime they have no interest in following. For these persons, it must seem as though half of their cable channels are useless, most of the conversations they overhear are spoken in a foreign tongue, and the Olympics last for three months *every* year.

Sport Fandom and Attendance Data The proportion of individuals who consider themselves to be sport fans and the number of persons attending sporting events can be mind blowing. As for fandom, based on polling results and laboratory data, it is estimated that roughly 60–80 percent of individuals self-identify as a sport fan, with different estimates likely attributable to varying operational definitions of "fan" (Groeneman, 2017; Jones, 2015; Luker, 2014; Wann, Melnick, Russell, & Pease, 2001). Although much of this work is based on samples from the United States, sport fandom is most certainly a worldwide phenomenon. For instance, it is estimated that there are 3.5 *billion* soccer fans globally (Topend Sports, n.d.; Sporteology, n.d.).

Statistics for attendance at sporting events are equally staggering (Gaines, 2015). For example, in the United States, well over 130 million spectators attended an NFL, NBA, NHL, or MLB game during the 2014–2015 seasons. Attendance for sporting events in other countries is just as impressive. For instance, leagues in 11 different countries average greater than 10,000 spectators per event. And these figures are simply for mainstream professional leagues. When one factors in attendance at less popular and minor league sports, school events (e.g., scholastic, collegiate), and youth contests, the number becomes almost incomprehensible. In fact, it seems as though sport fans are willing to watch any sport played at any level in any locale.

Sport on Television and Radio The pervasiveness of sport in the lives of fans and its important place in society are also evident in the extensive coverage of sport on television and radio. With respect to television coverage, one need only turn on the television and channel surf to see the pervasiveness of sport. For the major networks in the United States (ABC, CBS, NBC, and FOX), sport is a major component of their overall programming schedule. When one considers the addition of the Fox Sports Network, ESPN, professional and college league networks (e.g., NFL, SEC), WGN, TBS, TNT, HBO, and Showtime, specialty channels such as the Golf Channel and the Outdoor Channel, and pay per view events, two facts become abundantly clear: (1) network executives desperately want a piece of the sport programming pie, and (2) sport fans are rarely, if ever, deprived of opportunities to consume sport on television.

Viewership statistics indicate that spectators are flocking to their televisions to watch sport. For example, greater than 100 million viewers tune in to the Super Bowl each year (Statista, 2017c). That might sound like a lot of people until one learns that over three *billion* persons watched the 2014 FIFA World

Cup, and this many or more persons tune in to watch the Olympics every two years (FIFA.com, 2015; Statista, 2017b). The ratings of sport programs are equally impressive. For example, 44 of the top 50 most viewed primetime telecasts for 2016 were sporting events, including 19 of the top 20 (Porter, 2016). Networks are aware of these statistics and are willing to pay huge amounts for the right to air sporting events. For example, the right to air NFL games has escalated from $268 million ($67 million per year) in 1974 to an astounding $55.1 billion ($6.5 billion per year) in 2014 (Wolff, 2016).

Sport coverage on radio is also quite prevalent. Most professional and major college sport teams have their own radio network. Additionally, sport talk radio has become very popular. The first 24-hour-a-day sport talk radio station, WFAN in New York, was introduced in 1987 (Haag, 1996; Mariscal, 1999). As a testament to the popularity of this programming format, there were an estimated 150 such stations only ten years later (Goldberg, 1998; Mariscal, 1999). The number of sport-only stations continued to increase in the years that followed, reaching over 600 such stations by the year 2010 (Number of Dedicated, 2012). Referred to as "the church of athletic self-opinion" (Goldberg, 1998, p. 213), sport talk radio allows fans to express their views, release their frustrations, and (theoretically) demonstrate their sport acumen.

Sport-Related Movies and Videos Yet another example of the pervasiveness of sport is found in the large number of sport-related movies. Sport-themed movies are not a new phenomenon; athletic themes were common on film as far back as the 1910s. Several popular recent sport movies have been produced, including *Moneyball*, *Million Dollar Arm*, *The Rookie*, *Blindside*, *Secretariat*, *The Bench Warmers*, *Cars* (as well as *Cars 2* and *Cars 3*), *Fever Pitch*, *The Legend of Bagger Vance*, and *Miracle*, to name but a few. It is also interesting that movies not centered on sport often insert athletic competition into the film, apparently to arouse the passion of sport fans in the audience. Some notable examples of this practice include the pod races in the *Star Wars* series, quidditch matches in the *Harry Potter* films, and the chariot race in *Ben Hur*.

Sport in Print Media The pervasiveness of sport is also reflected in print media (i.e., sport-related books, magazines, and newspaper coverage). With respect to sport-related books, simply venture into a bookstore and you will quickly see the importance of sport, as most retailers have a special (and large) section for sport-related material. In fact, as of late 2016, searching for "sports books" on Amazon.com resulted in over 800,000 matches! There are also hundreds of sport-related magazines available, including periodicals with impressive subscription numbers such as *Sports Illustrated* and *ESPN the Magazine*.

Historically, newspapers have been the print media with the strongest connection to sport. It is likely that every major and minor newspaper contains a sport section. The "nation's newspaper," *USA Today*, includes a sport section as one of its four major components, and it is often the largest (how many of us have purchased a copy of *USA Today*, read the Sport section, and discarded the rest of the paper?). For example, in the Monday, March 13, 2017, issue of *USA Today*, the News section contained eight pages, the Money section four pages,

TABLE 1.2 Top 10 Sport Websites Ranked by Unique Visitors per Month

Website	Estimated unique visitors per month
1. Yahoo! Sports	125,000,000
2. ESPN	80,000,000
3. Bleacher Report	40,000,000
4. CBS Sports	30,000,000
5. Sports Illustrated	20,000,000
6. NBC Sports	19,500,000
7. SBNation	19,000,000
8. Fox Sports	18,000,000
9. Rant Sports	13,000,000
10. Deadspin	12,500,000

Notes: Data as of March 2017. Source: eBizMBA (2017).

the Life section four pages, and the *two* Sport sections sixteen pages. Thus, the editors allotted 50 percent of the newspaper's space to sport! This amount of coverage indicates that the editors understand the place of sport in today's society and its importance to their readers.

Sport-Related Internet Sites One of the greatest technological advances to impact modern society is the Internet. This impact most certainly extends to the lives and actions of sport fans (many of whom likely feel that the Internet was invented specifically for sport). Sport fandom has thrived on the Internet. Need proof? Consider that in March 2017 the keyword "sport" resulted in over 4 *billion* matches on Google. The keyword "football" resulted in 1.37 billion hits, while there were 1.2 billion matches for golf, 629 million for basketball, and 453 million for baseball. As shown in Table 1.2, the most popular sport sites have remarkable numbers of visitors. Truly, sport fandom has gone "high-tech."

Sport-Related Video Games The pervasiveness of sport in association with technology is also represented through the popularity of sport video games. The video gaming industry is big business. Very big, in fact; the video gaming market is expected to surpass $2 trillion annually by 2020. United States residents play video games an average of over 20 minutes per day and spend over $50 per year on games and accessories (Statista, 2017a). Sport video games have a large part of this market, as it has been estimated they account for roughly 20 percent of the sales (Entertainment Software Association, 2012). Many of the top-selling video games have sport themes, such as *Madden NFL*, *FIFA* (soccer), and the *NBA 2K* series (Kain, 2015).

Researchers have found that playing sport video games may actually influence the player's fandom (Crawford & Gosling, 2009). Kim and Ross (2015) randomly assigned participants to play a NASCAR-themed racing game either once, three times, or seven times. They found that increased exposure to NASCAR via video game play impacted participants' brand attitudes. Specifically, although there was little pre- to post-test attitude change for persons in the single exposure condition, those playing the game multiple times (i.e., three or seven) reported more favorable attitudes toward NASCAR after exposure to the game.

Sport as a Central Component in the Identity of Fans

Another important justification for an investigation of sport fandom concerns the importance of fandom in the overall identity of so many persons. For a large proportion of fans, the role of team supporter or follower of a particular sport is a highly central and important component of their sense of self. It plays a major role in how they perceive and define themselves. It is, in large measure, who they are. In fact, one's fandom can be more central than other important social institutions. Smith, Grieve, Zapalac, Derryberry, and Pope (2012) asked participants to complete measures assessing their level of identification with their favorite sport team, religious group, occupation, and school. The respondents reported a stronger sense of identification with their favorite team than they did for the other social institutions.

The importance of fandom is readily evident in the desire of fans for their favorite teams to succeed. Wann and his colleagues (2011) asked MLB fans to complete a measure assessing their identification with their favorite team and to complete a form gauging their willingness to consider a series of unusual behaviors if the acts would guarantee their team a World Series title. The researchers found that many persons were willing to consider engaging in the bizarre acts for the good of the team. A summary of these acts and percentages of fans willing to consider them is found in Table 1.3. Although the frequency data were interesting (and humorous), the predictors of willingness to consider the acts of desperation were particularly informative. Specifically, Wann and his colleagues found that two variables were associated with a greater desire to consider the unusual championship-guaranteeing acts. First, and most relevant to our current discussion, persons with higher levels of team identification were more willing to engage in the acts. This finding highlights the central nature of fandom in the identity of many persons. Because they care so deeply about their team, and because being a fan is so central to their self-concept, they are willing to do almost anything for the team's success. The second significant predictor was also interesting; supporters of teams who had experienced a longer passage of time since their last championship were especially likely to consider the acts. Thus, because the desperation of these fans was greater, they were more willing to consider the unusual acts.

The centrality of sport fandom and connections to teams is also revealed in the degree to which sport matters in the lives of fans (Mandelbaum, 2004). At

TABLE 1.3 Unusual Behaviors Fans Are Willing to Consider to Guarantee Their Team a Championship

Percent willing to engage in the following behaviors for at least a month

Behavior	Percent
Give up all drinks except water	58%
Give up all sweets	57%
Go without shaving	52%
Go without sex	51%
Go without watching television	35%
Stop talking to their best friend	18%
Wear the same underwear	17%
Go without talking	8%
Go without showering	5%

Percent willing to at least minimally consider the following behaviors

Behavior	Percent
Donate a paycheck to charity	75%
Get a permanent team-oriented tattoo	49%
Donate an organ	47%
Destroy their favorite keepsake	31%
Cut off one of their fingers	10%

Notes: From Wann et al. (2011).

the individual level, fandom impacts each of the "**ABCs of Psychology**": affect, behavior, and cognition. That is, fandom influences what people do, how they feel, and what they think. With respect to behaviors, there are innumerable ways in which sport impacts the actions of fans. Many of these behaviors will be detailed in this text, including consumption of sport (Chapter 5) and the aggressive actions of some fans (Chapters 7 through 9). As for affective responses, it is hard to imagine sport fandom without emotion. We will touch on emotional reactions to sport in several places throughout this text, but we give it our full attention in Chapter 6. And finally, with respect to cognition, sport fans frequently think about their favorite sports and teams (Griggs, Leflay, & Groves, 2012). This includes memories from the past (e.g., recalling the glory years), thoughts about the present (e.g., evaluating current performance), and hopes for the future (e.g., imagining championships yet to be won). As one might expect, because the role of team following is central to the identity of highly identified fans, these persons are particularly likely to allocate cognitive resources when confronted with team-relevant stimuli (Potter & Keene, 2012).

To simply and coldly conclude that fandom impacts individuals' affect, behavior, and cognition undervalues and underappreciates what sport means to fans. To many individuals, sport is more than this. Much more. Sport touches people's lives in ways that are both moving and profound. Although a seemingly countless number of examples can be used to illustrate the power of fandom (there are hundreds of such stories just from the Cubs' World Series title in 2016), we will limit our discussion to three. First, readers may find it interesting to learn that sport fandom (as well as participation) can become an invaluable resource and experience for persons with autism. Often times, individuals with autism struggle in social environments, finding these situations uncomfortable and difficult to navigate, and they may have a hard time connecting with others (Phetrasuwan, Miles, Mesibov, & Robinson, 2009; Waterhouse, 2013). However, as Wertheim and Apstein (2016) note, parents and therapists of children with autism often find that sporting events can provide a real-world environment for persons with autism to better hone their social skills and to better understand some social norms. Additionally, it provides those with autism an opportunity to share their love of sport with like-minded others and gain priceless social connections that might not occur without the unifying link of sport fandom.

A second example of the power of sport fandom comes from the country of Colombia in South America. Colombia has been a hotbed of violence, and the country had been in the midst of a civil war spanning several decades. In an attempt to expedite the end of hostilities, Colombian governmental officials devised several unique strategies (The New Colombia, 2016). This included sending lit messages of peace to "guerilla fighters" at night, placing messages on trees, and dropping Christmastime messages from family members over guerilla-fighter strongholds asking for peace. The architect for these programs was advertising specialist Jose Miguel Sokoloff. During an interview, Sokoloff was asked to name the most successful strategy. His response? "Football." Football (soccer in North America) is a passion of the citizens in Colombia, and this included the guerrilla fighters. During the 2011 Under 20 World Cup hosted by Colombia, Sokoloff had players, fans, and celebrities autograph thousands of soccer balls with the saying "Demobilize. Let's play again." The balls were dropped into locales held by the guerrilla fighters. When describing his explanation for the particularly high impact of this particular campaign, Sokoloff stated, "Football moves this country. Football is our passion."

A final example highlighting the centrality of fandom in the identities of fans is noted in the actions of politicians and world leaders. These individuals often present themselves as sport fans to establish a connection with voters. Two examples include President Barack Obama and Cuban dictator Fidel Castro (Price, 2016). Obama always had a passion for basketball (First Lady Michelle Obama commented that he would rather be a basketball player than a president). During college basketball's March Madness, Obama would frequently fill out his bracket predictions for the upcoming NCAA Tournament. By doing so, he could connect to millions of fans who were also caught up in the madness. (The first author fondly remembers when he predicted that

Murray State University would pull a first-round upset in the 2010 tournament.) As for Castro, he had long been a baseball fan and player (although his descriptions of his skill were likely overinflated). Castro used baseball both to connect to the masses and to bond them in a unified love for the game.

Sport Fandom Assists in Meeting Powerful Human Needs

Three critical dimensions of identity involve establishing and maintaining a sense of belonging with others, maintaining a sense of distinctiveness, and finding meaning in life (Thomas et al., 2017; Vignoles, Regalia, Manzi, Golledge, & Scabini, 2006). Another important reason to critically investigate sport fandom is because participation in this pastime has the capacity to aid in meeting each of these fundamental human needs.

The **need to belong** is an innate human drive (Pickett, Gardner, & Knowles, 2004) involving the desire to "form and maintain strong, stable interpersonal relationships" (Baumeister & Leary, 1995, p. 497). The importance of this motive cannot be overstated. Indeed, although the precise strength of this need may vary across individuals (Lavigne, Vallerand, & Crevier-Braud, 2011), the need to belong is "one of the most powerful, universal, and influential human drives" that "shapes emotion, cognition, and behavior" (Baumeister, 2012, p. 121). Quality social relationships even predict lower mortality risk (Holt-Lunstad, Smith, & Layton, 2010). Researchers from a wide variety of social scientific disciplines have found that individuals use sport fandom and their interest in a team to gain connections with others and, thus, assist in the quest to satisfy the need to belong (Bain-Selbo & Sapp, 2016; Clopton, 2008; Crawford, 2004;

Sport Fandom Can Assist in Meeting Our Innate Need to Belong

Elling, van Hilvoorde, & Van Den Dool, 2014; Groeneman, 2017; Lock & Funk, 2016; van Hilvoorde, Elling, & Stokvis, 2010; Wann, Waddill, Polk, & Weaver, 2011). For instance, Theodorakis, Wann, Nassis, and Luellen (2012) found that identification with a local sport team and the need to belong were positively correlated among samples of both U.S. and Greek college students. The relationship between fandom and belonging is examined in detail in Chapter 10.

The **need for distinctiveness** is a second basic human need to which sport fandom can contribute. Although humans want to feel a sense of belonging with those around them, they simultaneously have a need to be different and unique (Hornsey & Jetten, 2004). The fundamental need for uniqueness is best understood through Brewer's (1991) **Optimal Distinctiveness Theory**. According to this framework, individuals strive for two sometimes opposing social goals: inclusion and differentiation. These goals are best satisfied "through identification with distinctive groups that satisfy both needs simultaneously" (Brewer, 2012, p. 81). Given that brand consumption is associated with desires to be unique (Moon & Sung, 2015; Timmor & Katz-Navon, 2008), it seems reasonable that individuals use sport fandom as an opportunity to meet their need for distinction by selectively choosing to follow non-mainstream sports or less popular teams (Dimmock & Gucciardi, 2008; Goldman, Chadwick, Funk, & Wocke, 2016; Groeneman, 2017; Holt, 1995). For instance, individuals can partially meet their need for uniqueness by identifying with a distant team (Andrijiw & Hyatt, 2009; Hyatt & Andrijiw, 2008) or rooting for an underdog (Kim et al., 2008).

A third critical need impacted by fandom concerns the desire to experience **meaning in life**. The search for meaning involves gaining a sense of purpose and significance to one's existence (Frankl, 1963; Lambert et al., 2013; Steger, Frazier, Oishi, & Kaler, 2006). A life can acquire meaning when an individual attaches to something that is grander than the self (Angyal, 1941; Seligman, 2011). Given the centrality of sport fandom and team identification in the identities of fans, it seems reasonable that following sport and teams provides meaning to these persons and a connection to something larger than themselves. Indeed, researchers have found an association between fandom and meaning in life (Wann, Hackathorn, & Sherman, in press). For instance, in their interviews of Australian League Football fans, Doyle, Filo, Lock, Funk, and McDonald (2016) found that several participants described the meaning brought to their lives through their support of the team. Similarly, Keaton and Gearhart (2014) report that fandom can foster a sense of self-actualization (i.e., following sport "helps me to develop and grow as a person", p. 370).

Spectators Can Influence the Outcome of Sporting Events

A final justification for the study of sport fandom involves the influence spectators have on athletic performance. Although some sport audiences are inactive and do not interact with the performers, most would be classified as reactive because they respond to players and teams (Wann, 1997). When fans cheer, yell, boo, and scream, the verbalizations typically stem from their desire to influence the on-field action. Spectators think that these outbursts influence athletic performance (Wann et al., 1994; Wolfson, Wakelin, & Lewis, 2005), and both research and theory confirm their beliefs. Wann and Hackathorn (in press) discuss two empirically supported pathways through which spectators wield their influence: social facilitation and the home advantage.

Social Facilitation Theory originated with the work of Triplett (1898), who noticed that bicycle racers seemed to perform better when they rode against a competitor rather than alone. Triplett tested this effect by having children wind reels either alone or in pairs. Consistent with what he witnessed in the cycling races, the children wound the reels faster when in the presence of another child. As a result, Triplett concluded that audiences enhance performance, including actions of an athletic nature. Several decades later, Zajonc (1965) expanded on Triplett's original theory by incorporating the notion of social interference. Specifically, Zajonc theorized that although the performance of skilled individuals will be enhanced by an audience (i.e., social facilitation), performance may be hindered when the individual is not competent at the task (i.e., social interference). The large volume of studies supporting Zajonc's model (e.g., Davis & Harvey, 1992; Landers, Brawley, & Hale, 1978; Moore & Brylinsky, 1993) confirms the premise that sport spectators have the capacity to both positively and negatively influence individual athletic performance through the process of social facilitation.

A second process through which spectators impact athletic performance is the **home advantage**. The home advantage, or the tendency for home teams and players to outperform their visiting counterparts, is one of the most well-documented findings in sport psychology (Jamieson, 2010). A variety of explanations for the superior play of home teams have been suggested, including rules favoring home teams and the travel-induced fatigue experienced by visiting players (Carron, Loughhead, & Bray, 2005; Courneya & Carron, 1992). The influence of the audience has also been cited as a causal factor in the success of home teams, including the possibility that the home crowd positively affects the home team and negatively impacts the visiting team (Wann, 1997). Additionally, there is evidence that implicates the influence fans exert on officials and referees as the most powerful force behind the home advantage (Balmer, Nevill, & Williams, 2003; Dosseville, Edoh, & Molinaro, 2016; Moskowitz & Wertheim, 2011; Unkelbach & Memmert, 2010; see Wann & Hackathorn, in press, for a review). According to the results from this growing body of research, officials feel pressure from spectators and, as a result, make calls that are favorable to the home team (Jones, 2013; Nevill, Newell, & Gale, 1996; Pettersson-Lidbom & Priks, 2010). Regardless of which group is responsible for the home advantage (e.g., players or officials), it is clear that spectators are influencing someone and, consequently, the outcome of sporting events.

Overview of the Book

A lot has happened in the academic world since the first edition of this book was published in 2001. Research on fandom was somewhat rare in the decades prior to the publication of the first edition (Wann & Hamlet, 1995). However, since the late 1990s there has been an explosion of sport fan–related research from a variety of disciplines including psychology, sociology, leisure studies, general fandom studies, history, and business (e.g., marketing, management, consumer behavior, economics). In fact, it is likely that more empirical and theoretical work has been done in the years since the first edition was published than in all the years prior to that date. The proliferation of work in this area is evidenced by the fact that, in early 2017, entering "sport fan" into Google Scholar resulted in well over 400,000 hits.

Given the large increase in the sport fandom literature, the current edition contains new topical areas and expanded coverage of others. This includes (but is far from limited to) the emotional reactions of fans, the process of becoming a fan (including coverage of the Psychological Continuum Model, Funk & James, 2001, 2006), dysfunctional fandom, measurement issues for constructs such as fan motivation and team identification, and cross-cultural issues (such as cultural differences in the process of sport fan socialization). In fact, the current edition of this book contains approximately 600 citations that were written after the first edition was published, including well over 300 since 2010.

This text has been divided into three sections. The first section contains four chapters examining factors related to fan interest in and involvement with sports, teams, and athletes. Chapter 2, "The Process of Becoming a Sport Fan: The Psychological Continuum Model," includes an examination of the stages in becoming a sport fan. This chapter also contains a discussion of the sport fan socialization process. Chapter 3, "Points of Attachment: Understanding Connections to Teams, Players, and Beyond," is an examination of the process of becoming a supporter of specific sports, teams, players, and other points of attachment. This chapter includes a discussion of antecedents to team identification and the process of hero worship. Chapter 4, "Motivation and Sport Fandom," provides a detailed examination of factors underlying one's desire to follow sport. Chapter 5, "The Impact of Sport Fandom on Sport Consumption Behavior," is focused on the impact of fandom on sport consumer behavior.

The second section targets the affective and aggressive responses of sport fans. Chapter 6, "The Emotional Reactions of Sport Fans," includes an examination of the emotional responses of fans. Included in the discussion are both positive emotions (e.g., happiness and pride) and negative emotions (e.g., sadness and shame). Chapters 7 through 9 focus on fan aggression. Chapter 7, "An Introduction to Fan Aggression," provides a general overview of spectator violence. It examines definitional issues and forms of fan violence. Chapter 8, "Understanding the Causes of Fan Aggression," includes an examination of theory and research designed to account for fan violence, including discussion of both situational forces (e.g., modeling, temperature) and personal factors (such as team identification and gender). Chapter 9, "Sport Fan Riots," is the third chapter dedicated to fan aggression. This chapter is focused on large-scale fan violence as well as characteristics of persons typically involved in these disturbances.

The third section contains a pair of chapters dedicated to an examination of the pros and cons of sport fandom. Social scientists have debated the individual and societal costs and benefits of sport fandom for many years. Although some have argued that sport fandom can have a positive impact on individuals and society, others have contended that fandom has mainly negative effects. This section takes a critical look at both sides of the debate. Chapter 10, "The Psychological Consequences of Sport Fandom," focuses on the potential psychological costs and benefits of sport fandom. It begins with a critical examination of the argument that sport fandom has harmful effects on individuals. The chapter also examines the possibility that fandom has positive effects on fans. Chapter 11, "The Societal Consequences of Sport Fandom," addresses the larger societal implications of sport fandom. Similar to Chapter 10, Chapter 11 begins with an examination of sociological-based criticisms of fandom, followed by potential societal benefits of the pastime.

And finally, in Chapter 12, "The Future of Sport Fandom: Gazing Into the Crystal Ball," we summarize the text and consider the future of research on fandom. In this closing chapter, we offer suggestions for areas in need of additional research from sport scholars. So, settle in, and let's get started. On to the discussion of becoming a sport fan.

PART ONE

How and Why Fans Follow Sports, Teams, and Athletes

CHAPTER 2

The Process of Becoming a Sport Fan: The Psychological Continuum Model

In the first chapter, we discussed different ways to define and classify sport fans. We differentiated between sport fans and spectators, wrote about direct and indirect sport consumers, and examined the topic of sport team identification. However, an important point we have not yet addressed in depth is the notion of *how* people become sport fans, become sport consumers, and come to identify with particular teams. In this chapter, we examine the "how" of sport fandom by investigating fans' psychological connections with sport objects (e.g., a sport, team, or player) and the process through which such connections develop.

Think about the people you see when you attend a sporting event. It is not unusual to see people dressed in clothes (including costumes) portraying their favorite team's colors. For example, at Florida State University home football games there are two fans that cover their bodies with garnet and gold paint and glitter and refer to themselves as the "Garnet and Gold Guys." Perhaps you also frequently wear team apparel, paint your body, or have a tattoo of your favorite team's logo. Or maybe your fandom is a bit more subdued, and you simply have a favorite team jersey that you wear for special games. Such behaviors do not just occur spontaneously. A person does not just wake up one morning and decide to have the star symbolizing the Dallas Cowboys tattooed on his or her arm (or other body part for that matter). A person needing clothes does not randomly purchase multiple items of team apparel from among all the clothing choices available. Rather, a person *becomes* a sport fan and connects to sport objects through individual and social psychological processes. One theory that helps us better understand these connections is the **Psychological Continuum Model** (Funk & James, 2001, 2006, 2016). This framework and its application to the process of becoming a sport fan is the focus of the current chapter.

The Psychological Continuum Model (PCM) was introduced as a conceptual framework to organize and advance our understanding of the psychology of

TABLE 2.1 Psychological Continuum Model 2001 (Funk & James, 2001)

Stage of Connection	Key Psychological Characteristics
Allegiance	Intrinsic consistency Commitment to a sport (or team); persistent (positive) attitude toward a sport (or team); attitude resistant to change; attitude impacts cognition; intrinsic influences most important
Attachment	Intrinsic features Formation of a strong, positive attitude to a sport (or team); emotional complexity to a sport (or team); sport (or team) has personal importance and meaning
Attraction	Extrinsic and intrinsic features Selection of a favorite sport (or team); interest in sport (or team) impacted primarily by situational influences or dispositional influences
Awareness	Extrinsic features Knowledge that sport (or team) exists, but no particular interest; distinguishes between sports (and teams), but no particular interest; knowledge influenced by socializing agents and media

sport fans, particularly their interest in and connection with a sport object (Funk & James, 2001). The PCM contains four stages categorizing the connections people form within the realm of sport fandom: Awareness, Attraction, Attachment, and Allegiance. The PCM was conceptualized as a hierarchical model. Thus, people are expected to move through each stage (presuming there is movement), with each level representing a different degree of attitude formation and involvement toward a sport object. Psychological and sociological processes are thought to facilitate or inhibit movement among the stages. The PCM is illustrated in Table 2.1 as a bottom-up vertical progression. As a person advances to a higher stage, the psychological connection is expected to become stronger (i.e., stronger attitudes and greater involvement). In the paragraphs that follow, we take a brief look at the four stages. It should be noted that although the PCM explains connections to a variety of sport objects, for simplicity we will often frame our discussion around a fan's connection to a team.

Awareness

The first stage of the PCM, **Awareness,** occurs as an individual first acquires the knowledge that a sport object exists. For example, the second author knows that the Jacksonville Jumbo Shrimp minor league baseball team plays in Jacksonville, Florida. However, he has never attended a game and really does not have any other knowledge about or interest in the team. From a sport consumer perspective, he does not purchase merchandise, tickets, or consume the Jumbo Shrimp brand in any fashion. He is aware of the team but does not have any particular interest in it; he is simply not a fan of the Jumbo Shrimp. Similarly, although prior to reading the previous sentences you may have had no knowledge of the Jumbo Shrimp, you are now aware the team exists. At this stage, a person's connection with the sport object (the Jumbo Shrimp in our example) is essentially cognitive. That is, a person has knowledge and awareness of the focal object. This knowledge and awareness emanates from the sport fan socialization process, a topic that we will examine in much more detail in later sections.

Attraction

The second stage, **Attraction**, is reached when a person progresses from simply knowing that a sport object exists to learning details about the object, other sports and teams, the rules of play, and different levels of the sport and potentially making the conscious decision to view a team as a favorite (Funk & James, 2001). At this stage a person begins to develop positive thoughts and feelings toward the object that are triggered when the individual recognizes that hedonic and dispositional needs may be fulfilled through sport consumption behavior related to the object (Funk & James, 2006). For example, if you find yourself in Jacksonville, Florida, and you are seeking a fun activity, and if you happen to like baseball, you may think attending a Jumbo Shrimp game could be entertaining. You have positive thoughts and feelings about the sport of baseball and may view attendance at a game as an opportunity to have an enjoyable experience. Thus, at this point, you would be operating at the Attraction level, the second stage within the PCM.

Attachment

A person reaches the **Attachment** stage "when he or she has formed a stable psychological connection to a sport or team" (Funk & James, 2001, p. 132). A key distinction of the Attachment stage is that a person's connection to a team is based on the intrinsic importance of the relationship. That is, the team has a special, personal meaning to the individual. The difference between Attraction and Attachment stages can be illustrated in the following example. Imagine that a child's favorite sport team is The Ohio State University football team because her father is a fan of the Buckeyes. If the father were to suddenly decide that the Buckeyes were no longer his favorite team, it is possible the daughter might choose another favorite as well. For the child, there was an attraction to the team, but the connection was based on her relationship with her father, not with the team. However, if the Buckeyes take on personal importance to the daughter (beyond simply her relationship with her father), the team now has emotional and/or social psychological meaning to her, and she will have an attachment to the team regardless of her father's interest.

Here is a second example. Imagine that you have moved to a town that has a popular team, let's say an indoor soccer team. You may not enjoy indoor soccer, but decide to attend games and talk about the team as you make new friends and attempt to fit in to your new environment. As you become established and form relationships with others, you may no longer follow the team. You had an attraction to the team but never formed an attachment. Essentially, the team served its purpose (assisted in your acclimation to your new surroundings), and following the team is now no longer needed. Given the lack of attachment, the connection to the team can be easily severed. However, if you maintain your fandom for the team even after using it to gain connections with others, you are clearly attached to the team for intrinsic reasons beyond simply using the team as a catalyst to form relationships.

Allegiance

The final stage, **Allegiance**, represents the strongest psychological connection. According to Funk and James (2001), the term allegiance is used "to describe the construct of loyalty" (p. 134). At this stage an individual possesses an "attitude that is resistant to change, stable across context and time, influences cognitive processing of information, and is predictive of behavior" (Funk & James, 2016, p. 250). A fan at the allegiance stage invests significant emotional, psychological, financial, and temporal resources in the favorite team. From a sport consumption viewpoint, a fan at the allegiance stage will likely exhibit consistent and enduring behaviors such as purchasing team merchandise, attending or watching games, and talking positively about the team.

Understanding the PCM

In the paragraphs to follow, we provide a deeper examination of the PCM and its four stages. Such a presentation is designed to give the reader a deeper comprehension of the connections fans feel with sport objects. However, before continuing, it warrants mention that although the original presentation of the PCM provided a framework for understanding connections with a sport object (Funk & James, 2001), the authors soon revised the framework to provide additional information about movement among the stages, as well as inputs and outputs that operate within each level (Funk & James, 2006). The revision helps us better understand "how the psychological connection between an individual and a sport object progressively forms through particular internal social-psychological mechanisms" (Funk & James, 2016, p. 250). The revised PCM has the unique characteristic of integrating the advantages of a stage-based model and a continuum-style approach "to create a theoretical hybrid, a stage-based continuum model that serves as a framework to study the developmental progression of a psychological connection to a sport, sport-based object, or leisure activity" (Funk & James, 2016, p. 251).

Awareness

When thinking about the Awareness stage, Funk and James (2001) suggest two questions are likely to come to mind: (1) when and (2) how do people become aware of sport objects? The answer to the first question is that we become aware of sport and sport-related objects continually throughout our lives. From the very first years of life we are exposed to sport as part of the process of learning about the world around us. And we continue to learn about different aspects of sport at other times in our lives. For example, unless people were of Scottish descent, they were likely not familiar with the sport of curling prior to its inclusion in the 1998 Olympic Games. Furthermore, new sports emerge (e.g., indoor soccer, roller hockey, snowboarding, and many of the action/extreme sports), and new teams are added to existing leagues.

To answer the second question on the process through which people become aware of sport objects, think about the statement "learning about the world around us and our place in it" written in the previous paragraph. Such learning is referred to as **socialization**. Socialization is impacted by the cultural influences and environment in which a person resides. As a process, socialization involves learning the attitudes, values, and actions believed to be appropriate for members of a particular society (Kenyon & McPherson, 1974). Thus, **sport fan socialization** occurs as we learn about attitudes, values, and actions related to specific sport objects. This learning happens via **socialization agents**, that is, those individuals or institutions that expose us to the values, behaviors, and ideals of sport.

For example, think about your favorite team. Perhaps your family liked this team, and you were exposed to the team through family conversations. Or maybe you learned about the team from a close friend or peer, or as a child you played on a team with this name. Individuals like family members, friends, coaches, and others in our lives teach us about sports, teams, and sport fandom in general. Participating in organized sports through community leagues and school programs can also be informative. Additionally, teams engage in promotional activities to stimulate consumer awareness, that is, to ensure that consumers know about a sport product. Activities such as advertising, special promotions, and free admission for children are used to increase awareness. And we would be remiss if we did not mention the impact of media, particularly in the "digital age" with increasing access to sport news and information. Each of the aforementioned individuals (e.g., family and friends) and institutions (e.g., schools and the media) are important agents in the process of sport fan socialization. Sport socialization is a critically important process, and an impressive volume of research has been devoted to this topic. As a result, we will examine this issue in greater detail in a separate section following our discussion of the stages of the PCM.

Knowing that sports and teams exist is indicative of Awareness. At this stage, however, a person is not necessarily a fan of a particular sport or team. As one learns more about the sport object in question, he or she comes to recognize (consciously or otherwise) that hedonic and social needs may be fulfilled by supporting teams and by attending and watching sporting events. Such learning may result in movement to the next stage, Attraction.

Attraction

Once a person has learned about a sport object (i.e., Awareness), he or she may choose to follow it because he or she finds something pleasing about the activity and thus, move to the Attraction stage of the PCM. One interesting point about the Attraction stage is that the individual may or may not be a fan at this juncture. That is, we have to consider why the person is interested in the pastime. In essence, this stage focuses on factors that motivate fan interest in sports and the teams/athletes that play them. The motives that underlie fan interest are a critical piece of the puzzle for understanding one's connection to sports and teams. In fact, because of the importance of this topic and the large volume of research dedicated to it, we will address fan motivation in a future chapter devoted solely to this area.

At a more general level, two key processes associated with the Attraction stage involve experiencing the hedonic and social-situational aspects of sport (and team) consumption. That is, fans are motivated by and attracted to something pleasurable or socially stimulating about sport fandom.

Hedonic Need Fulfillment There are a number of potential elements of sport fandom that could be enjoyable for those interested in the pastime. There is excitement, drama, and aesthetically pleasing performances, and even the potential for escape, all of which may contribute to a pleasurable experience. Everyone (your authors included) prefers to have pleasurable experiences and to have fun. This desire is the essence of **hedonic need fulfillment**; one's attempt to satisfy a craving for pleasurable experiences. Sport fandom is one means through which people can satisfy their desire to have fun. For instance, think about the special events associated with sporting contests, such as pregame concerts and postgame fireworks shows, and the variety of promotional giveaways. Hey, *everyone* likes a free T-shirt (some people will seemingly do anything to catch one at a game). Such activities are enjoyable because they are fun, pleasurable experiences.

The preceding description illustrates that sport fandom can be a means through which people experience hedonic need fulfillment. However, this does not guarantee that someone seeking such fulfillment is connected to a particular team or other sport object. For example, imagine a person who attends a baseball game one night, yet the following day chooses to go to a movie or concert instead of another game. In this instance, the rationale for attending the game may have been to have a pleasurable experience more so than because of a connection to the team. If asked, such a person might say she or he is a fan of the team, but if there is not an abiding interest in following a specific team, the individual is really a mere spectator.

Social-Situational Aspects of Sport A second general driver of behaviors for those functioning at the Attraction stage concerns the **social-situational aspects of fandom**. Consider the earlier example of the child who roots for the same team as her father. Following the team, talking about the team, and watching games with her father are all useful ways for her to connect with him. In this instance, the father (or the relationship with him) is the focal point, not the team. Moving to a new location and supporting a local team as a way to fit in would be another example of social-situational attraction. In each of the aforementioned examples, the team is secondary to the focal point of establishing relationships with others. Once again, an individual may state that she or he is a fan of the team, but the question remains as to whether or not there is an abiding interest in following the team. If not, the connection to the team is still quite tenuous at this stage.

A large portion of work in sport marketing focuses on consumers at the Attraction stage and the ability to move people to this level. The special events, promotions, and price discounts associated with sporting events (particularly at the minor league level) are mechanisms for satisfying hedonic needs and the need to belong. However, when teams become the focal object and take on intrinsic importance to an individual, that person has progressed to the stage of Attachment.

Attachment

Once a person has reached the Attachment stage he or she has formed a meaningful psychological connection with a sport object, such as a particular sport or team (Funk & James, 2006). Of interest here is an understanding of what, precisely, is involved in a "meaningful psychological connection." As mentioned in our overview of the four stages presented above, at the Attachment stage a person's connection to a team is based on the intrinsic importance of the team rather than extrinsic factors such as satisfying hedonic and/or social needs. Intrinsic importance occurs when a team has a special meaning to the fan and becomes a part of the individual. You may be wondering how a team becomes "part of an individual." This occurs as a person assimilates the team within her or his self-concept. That is, the person derives value from thinking of her or himself as a fan of the team. It is at this point that a person comes to **identify** with the team. Being a fan of the team becomes more central to the individual's social identity, and he or she takes greater pleasure in being a supporter of the team (Doyle, Kunkel, & Funk, 2013).

For example, sport teams have particular characteristics that are thought to be representative of the team. One such team would be the Pittsburgh Steelers from the NFL, a team that has often been promoted as a hard-working, blue-collar team. For someone that values a strong work ethic and derives worth from being a "regular Joe," the Steelers may serve as a symbolic representation of those values. The team is thought of as a positive symbol, and through association with the team, a person derives positive self-esteem (Hogg & Abrams, 1988). Thus, one's connection with a sport object involves the person's social identity. Hogg and Abrams (1988) explain that social identity is "defined as the individual's knowledge that he belongs to certain social groups together with some emotional and value significance to him of the group membership" (p. 7). As a fan of a team, a person may view his or herself as a member of a group that supports the favorite team. That is, being part of the fan group provides a sense of belonging.

Recall what is happening at the Attraction stage. At this point in the process, the person is interested in following a team and attending games primarily due to the influence of hedonic need fulfillment and the psychological features of a social situation. When the individual has progressed to the Attachment stage, he or she likely still enjoys the hedonic need fulfillment and social pleasures accompanying sport fandom (e.g., still appreciates ticket discounts and special events). However, these elements are no longer the driver of attitudes and behaviors. Rather, the team has come to represent particular values or ideas that are important to the individual. From a sport consumer behavior perspective, individuals reaching the Attachment stage are quite likely to be consumers; they attend games, purchase merchandise and apparel, and engage in positive word of mouth when talking about the team (Funk & James, 2001). Additionally, as the connections and positive sentiments toward the team strengthen, a person may progress to the stage of Allegiance.

Allegiance

The Allegiance stage involves the notion of loyalty, that is, a commitment or devotion to a favorite team (or other sport object). At this stage of the PCM, a person's attitude toward a team is persistent, is highly central to one's social identity, influences cognitive processing, and is predictive of behavior (Doyle et al., 2013; Funk & James, 2016). Fans reaching this stage often attempt to promote the team to others (Lock, Taylor, Funk, & Darcy, 2012).

For fans at the Allegiance stage, the thoughts and feelings they have toward a sport object such as a favorite team are going to be quite strong. The concept of strength concerns the accessibility of the thoughts and feelings in one's memory. When a sport object such as a sport team is important to a person, she or he can easily access memories and feelings about it (Funk & James, 2001). For example, memories such as the team winning a championship or watching a memorable play are readily available in the person's memory. These cognitive and affective experiences stay with us, that is, they persist over time. As a result, attitudes toward the team become resistant and hard to change. When a person has a strong connection to a favorite team, it is difficult for the individual to change how he or she thinks and feels about the team because the role of team follower has become a central and valued part of the person's identity (Funk & James, 2001; Wann, 2006a). It seems that no matter what happens, be it poor team performance or unlawful acts by a player or coach, the individual does not waver in his or her allegiance (Kwon, Trail, & Lee, 2008; Spinda, 2011).

Fans are able to resist changing their attitude toward a favorite sport object (particularly a favorite team) in part due to biases in cognitive processing (Wann & Grieve, 2005; Wann & Schrader, 2000). For example, consider how you respond when your favorite team loses. Do you tend to blame your team or something else (e.g., the officials, bad luck, poor weather)? Researchers explain that most allegiant fans focus blame on objects other than the team in an attempt to protect the part of their identity built around the team (Wann, 2006c; Wann & Dolan, 1994a). When there is negative information reported in the media about your favorite team, how do you respond? Do you resist or reject these unflattering reports, reinterpret the information in a way that seems positive, or use selective perception to avoid information that conflicts with your thoughts and feelings? Again, researchers suggest that you are likely biased in your perceptions in a manner that favors your team as you attempt to cope with threats to your fan-related identity (Wann, 2006a, 2006c). For example, Funk

(1998) found that people with a strong attitude toward a team had more thoughts, recalled more facts, and demonstrated biased thinking when responding to prompts about a newspaper article compared to those having a weaker attitude toward the team. Sport fans develop and utilize an impressively wide range of these "mental gymnastics" to protect their fan-related identity. In fact, in Chapter 10 we will examine a number of strategies fans utilize to cope with team-related identity threats.

Another critical point about fandom at the Allegiance stage is that a strong positive attitude toward a team not only influences cognitions and perceptions but also has the capacity to influence behavior. It should seem logical that if a team is considered an important and central part of one's identity, then following the team should be a priority. Fans follow teams in many ways, including watching games in person or on television, reading information about the team, purchasing merchandise, and wearing team apparel. Importantly, these behaviors persist over time (for many, over a lifetime). In the context of sport consumer behavior, those characterized by allegiance are highly desirable to sport marketers because those reaching the Allegiance stage invest considerable amounts of monetary, temporal, and emotional resources to follow a team.

Summarizing the Psychological Continuum Model

The Psychological Continuum Model (PCM) is valuable as an explanatory framework for describing the process involved in becoming a fan. Additionally, the PCM is a useful model for describing the impact of connections with sport objects on thoughts, feelings, and behaviors. We will refer to the PCM throughout this book as we address other topics pertaining to sport fandom. For instance, in Chapter 5 we will return to a discussion of the PCM by focusing on how the framework has been used in the study of sport consumers, particularly the efforts that have been undertaken to develop a tool that may be used to "stage" (or position) individuals along the continuum.

Socialization Into Fandom

As noted earlier in this chapter, socialization is vital in the process of becoming a sport fan. We explained the pivotal role socialization is believed to play in the PCM, particularly at the Awareness stage. Beyond the parameters of the PCM, however, socialization merits further discussion in relation to sport fandom.

In Chapter 1, we presented information about the pervasiveness of sport, noting that its prevalence is evident in a variety of ways. For instance, the volume of fans that (repeatedly) attend sporting events at the professional, intercollegiate, and interscholastic levels is staggering. Additionally, sport is a primary source of programming for network, cable, and satellite television providers. The number of sport-related Internet sites, print media, and video games also illustrates the importance, and value, of sport in our society. Given the degree to which individuals are bombarded with sport, it seems reasonable that most persons end up being fans of the pastime. However, although survey data indicate that most individuals do indeed consider themselves sport fans (Jones, 2015; Luker, 2014), others have absolutely no interest. Some people seem immune to the influence of our sport-crazed society. How is it that so many persons come to love sport while others pay little or no attention to it (or, in the case of some people, actually loathe sport)?

Our starting point to answering this question is to acknowledge that the value attached to sport fandom is learned. A person does not simply wake up one morning and decide that she or he is a diehard fan of the Murray State Racers and thus proceed to spend $1,000 on team apparel and memorabilia. In this section our purpose is to illustrate that people learn to become sport fans through the process of sport fan socialization and, where possible, examine the role of various socializing agents.

As we move through the following sections, it will be useful to remember the general premise of socialization: it involves the process of learning to live in and understand a culture or subculture by internalizing its values, beliefs, attitudes, and norms. James (2016) articulated these concepts well when he wrote that socialization is "the process through which we learn what it means to be part of society and how to live and act within a given society" and that "individuals, groups, and institutions that are part of, and which create the social context in which we learn attitudes, values and roles are socializing agents" (pp. 264, 265). With respect to sport fandom, we are specifically concerned with the process by which individuals learn and accept the values, beliefs, attitudes, and norms of the sport fan culture (e.g., the notion of "never giving up," the jargon, terminology, rules of specific sports, players' statistics, and so forth). Examining sport fan socialization not only furthers our comprehension of how individuals become sport fans and form connections with specific sport objects, it also highlights the importance of cultural differences in fandom.

Research on North American Sport Fan Socialization

Much of the early work on sport socialization dealt with individuals becoming active sport participants. For example, in the 1970s scholars reported that during their elementary school years children learned about and were primarily influenced to participate in sport by family members (Kenyon & McPherson, 1974). As parents raise and teach their children, these interactions often include encouraging children to value sport and to become actively involved. However, as children grow, other socializing agents such as peers and the media become more influential (Kenyon, 1968; McPherson, 1968; Snyder & Spreitzer, 1973).

Social scientists began to show interest in the process of sport fan socialization in the 1970s. During this time period, although a small number of authors had written about the process (e.g., Kenyon & McPherson, 1974), few empirical studies were conducted. That changed when McPherson (1976) completed what is likely the first comprehensive examination of sport fan socialization. He believed that four sources (i.e., socialization agents) would be primarily responsible for teaching the values, beliefs, attitudes, and norms of sport fandom. These were family, peers (i.e., friends), schools, and community. To test the impact of these agents, McPherson asked Canadian adolescents to complete a questionnaire assessing the influence of each. The findings revealed that males and females reported different patterns of sport fan socialization. Specifically, males were most often influenced by their peers, followed by family and schools. The community did not appear to be a significant agent in the sport fan socialization of males (see also Smith, Patterson, Williams, & Hogg, 1981). As for female participants, family had the greatest influence, followed closely by peer groups. The community was also found to have a significant impact on the socialization of females, but to a lesser degree than family and peers. Schools did not appear to be a significant agent.

Although McPherson's (1976) work was valuable and shed light on the process of becoming a sport fan, it is quite dated. Cultures change with the passage of time, and so do the institutions and pastimes residing within them. To investigate the possibility that sport fan socialization had transformed in the years since McPherson's work, the first author and his colleagues conducted a replication and extension of McPherson's research, the results of which were presented in the first edition of this text (Wann et al., 2001). To maintain consistency with McPherson, we investigated the influence of the same four socialization agents. However, in our work, participants (United States college students) also answered an open-ended item in which they listed the person (e.g., father, aunt, etc.) or entity (e.g., school, media, etc.) that had the greatest single influence on their becoming involved with sport as a fan.

For males, the pattern of sport fan socialization remained consistent from the 1970s to the late 1990s. That is, similar to McPherson's (1976) findings, males were most strongly influenced by peers, and they were least likely to have been influenced by their community. Such was not the case for the female participants, however. Rather, although McPherson found that schools had the least amount of influence on female fans, respondents in our sample indicated this was the most powerful socialization agent. We surmised that this change for female fans may have been partially due to **Title IX**, a federal law that prohibits sexual discrimination in institutions receiving federal funding. Begun in 1972, Title IX has had a widespread impact on high school and college athletics because it requires that schools provide equitable opportunities to females. Consequently, the number of women's sport teams at the high school and collegiate levels increased dramatically (Oglesby, 1989; Snyder, 1993). Perhaps this increase in participation led to a greater prominence of female sports in school settings, thereby arousing greater interest in sport among the female student body. Thus, there may have been an added influence of Title IX, namely, the increased role of schools in the socialization of female sport fans.

Responses to the open-ended item on the single most influential agent were also quite informative. One's family was listed as exerting the greatest influence on socialization into fandom, as more than half of the male and female participants listed a family member as the individual who had the greatest impact. Within the family category, fathers were clearly the most influential agent (for males and females alike); they were named by over one-third of the sample (see also Thompson & Forsyth, 2012). However, although our data revealed the powerful

Family Members, and in Particular Fathers, Can Be Powerful Agents of Sport Fan Socialization

influences of family as a socializing agent, the impact of one's family (including parents) likely decreases as one transitions from youth to adolescence and adolescence to young adulthood (Casper & Menefee, 2010a; Yoh et al., 2009).

Another interesting result involved the gender of the socialization agents (Wann et al., 2001). Gender of the agent was detectible in slightly over half of the cases (e.g., father, sister, aunt, etc.). An examination of these agents revealed that they were far more likely to be male than female. Thus, it was evident that both male and female fans were more likely to be socialized into the sport follower role by males. Although one might believe that other women would have a stronger influence on the sport fan socialization for females, such was not the case. Similarly, Farrell et al. (2011) summarized their work on female sport fans by stating "the most robust theme to emerge was the profound male influence in the spectator lives of women" (p. 190). The fact that males wield such a dominant influence in the process of sport fan socialization should not be taken lightly. Rather, it likely aids in the persistence of the male hegemony associated with sport in general and sport fandom specifically, a topic that is examined further in Chapter 11.

Cross-Cultural Research on Sport Fan Socialization

Thus far, our investigation of sport fan socialization has focused on people from North America. However, sport fandom is a worldwide phenomenon. Thus, it is important to consider whether the socialization process varies among persons in different cultural groups. For instance, the values, beliefs, attitudes, and norms held by European soccer hooligans would almost assuredly differ from those held by North American golf fans. Given this, it is important for researchers to conduct cross-cultural work to determine how the sport fan socialization process differs across various sociocultural contexts. Fortunately, such a line of investigation has been undertaken. In fact, we now have information on the sport fan socialization process from persons living in a variety of regions, including Norway (Melnick & Wann, 2004), Greece (Theodorakis & Wann, 2008), Australia (Melnick & Wann, 2011), Qatar (Theodorakis et al., 2017), and the United Kingdom (Parry et al., 2014). To remain consistent with the work conducted by Wann et al. (2001), persons in each of the aforementioned studies reported on the influence of the four key socialization agents on their becoming a sport fan. Taken together, these studies highlight both cultural differences and similarities in the socialization process.

The influence of the four agents is depicted in Figure 2.1. Several points become apparent when looking at the figure. First, friends were consistently listed as a critical socialization agent across all cultures sampled. In fact, it was the highest rated agent for five of the samples and the second highest for the other. Second, there was little variability among agents in the Grecian sample, suggesting that each source had a roughly equal level of influence. Third, some countries differed markedly in the influence of communities and schools. For instance, although community was least important for the persons in the United States and United Kingdom samples, it was quite influential for those in Norway. Conversely, schools were far more powerful as socialization agents in the United States and United Kingdom than in Norway. As Melnick and Wann (2004) noted, this pattern of effects is reasonable when one considers the sport cultures

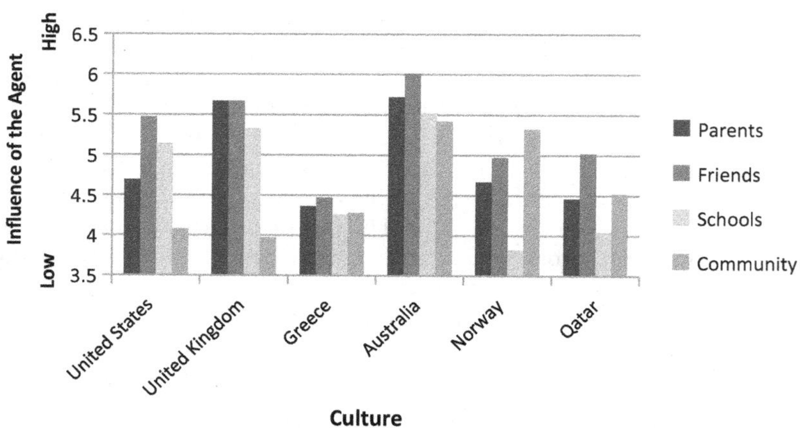

FIGURE 2.1 The Influence of Agents of Sport Fan Socialization Across Six Cultures. Scales Ranged From 1 to 8, with Higher Numbers Reflecting a Greater Influence for That Agent

in these locales. For example, the interscholastic model found in the United States likely results in greater attention being placed on school athletic teams, while the club model in Norway renders the community (and community-based teams) as superordinate.

Before leaving our discussion of cross-cultural work on sport fan socialization, a couple of points warrant mention. First, it should be noted that these projects utilized small convenience samples often comprised of university students. Thus, the results are limited in their generalizability. However, even with this limitation, this body of work provides a partial glimpse into the process of sport fan socialization for persons in the different countries.

Second, the work detailed above focused on only four socialization agents. Of course, there are many others. In particular, individuals learn about and may be socialized into sport fandom through media outlets such as team magazines, television programs, and the Internet. Socialization in this manner may be particularly common among displaced fans who are often far removed from other socializing agents such as friends and community (Farred, 2002). Interestingly, there is evidence to suggest that the impact of the media increases as people move from their early teens to early 20s (Yoh et al., 2009) and is particularly influential in the socialization of fans who did not play the sport in their childhood (Casper & Menefee, 2010b).

Some Final Thoughts

The current chapter focused on the process of becoming involved in sport fandom and attachments fans develop for various sport objects. Our presentation of this issue was divided into two sections: connecting to sport objects via the process described by the Psychological Continuum Model (Funk & James, 2001, 2006, 2016), and the process of sport fan socialization and the many agents that teach us what it means to be a fan. A few final thoughts warrant discussion before leaving these critical issues. First, the process of connecting with teams, players, and other entities within the realm of sport fandom is closely tied to the construct of involvement (Dimanche, Havitz, & Howard, 1993; Kerstetter & Kovich, 1997). **Involvement** is defined as a "state of motivation, arousal, or interest toward a recreational activity or associated product" (Iwasaki & Havitz, 1998, p. 260). Involvement is believed to be composed of five factors: attraction, sign, centrality to lifestyle, risk probability, and risk consequence (Funk & James, 2001). Table 2.2 includes a list of these factors and an explanation of each. The involvement factors are believed to differentially impact connections with a sport team, relative to the stage of connection. For example, at the stage of Awareness, a person would be expected to have low scores on the measures assessing each involvement factor. At the Attraction stage, a person would likely have a high score on the attraction factor as a function of anticipated hedonic need fulfillment. At the same time, we would expect scores on the sign and centrality factors to be lower. However, at the Attachment stage, a team may be viewed as representative of the self, and, therefore, scores on the sign factor would be higher. If following a team becomes important to an individual, then she or he would likely organize his or her time around watching

TABLE 2.2 Five Factors Comprising Involvement

Factor	Definition	Example
Attraction	The interest in an activity or product, and the pleasure derived from participation or use.	For example, the hedonic value associated with following a sport team.
Sign	The unspoken statement that purchase or participation conveys about the person.	For example, the Steelers are known as hard working; I am a Steelers fan, I am hard working.
Centrality to Lifestyle	Encompassing friends and families centered around activities and the primary role of the activities in an individual's life.	Following a particular team to feel accepted by family or friends. Organizing one's life around following the favorite team.
Risk Probability	The perceived probability of making a poor decision.	For example, what is the likelihood that choosing not to attend a game is a bad decision?
Risk Consequence	The perceived importance of negative consequences in the case of a poor decision.	What happens if I follow a losing team?

Note: Definitions are derived from the work of Havitz and Dimanche (1997), Iwasaki and Havitz (1998), Laurent and Kapferer (1985), and McIntyre (1989).

the team and attending the team's games. This greater degree of importance should be reflected in a higher centrality score. In Chapter 5, we examine further how the involvement factors can be used to determine stage of psychological connection.

As for the process of sport fan socialization, you may have noticed that the agents found to be most influential tend to be people (or persons). However, non-person factors can be important as well. For example, Kolbe and James (2000) found that the notion of a team representing a specific locale (e.g., "the hometown team") was an important influence on a person becoming a fan. Additionally, the media, promotions, and special events could also be considered non-person factors. It is likely that these non-person agents interact in some manner with one's personal experience as a fan. That is, one has to value the idea of a team being representative of one's hometown for that factor to be influential. The point we are drawing out here is that when we think about socialization, although we like to focus on "primary" influences or the person with the "most" influence, we must keep in mind that the process is not linear or even dichotomous. It might be more realistic to think of the sport fan socialization process as a wave, with various agents and factors flowing over and around an individual throughout her or his life. These waves likely include different agents and influential factors over time.

Thus, it is important to remember that sport fan socialization is a lifelong process. For example, consider the NHL fandom experience of the first author. Although I had routinely followed almost every sport, I made it into my early 50s before ever attending (or even casually watching or following) a professional hockey game. It was at this time that I found myself romantically involved with a Nashville Predators fan. Looking back, it seems as though my identification with the "Preds" paralleled my relationship with Michelle (now my wife). The more involved we became, the more I was socialized to follow hockey and support the Nashville team. We now attend 5–6 games per year and have even discussed purchasing a season ticket package. Similarly, it is possible (perhaps even common) for parents to be socialized to follow a new sport or team via their children. Referred to as **reverse socialization** (Hyatt, Kerwin, Hoeber, & Sveinson, 2017), this process can occur when a child becomes involved in a sport (or supports a team) with which his or her parents had yet to become acquainted (e.g., mom and dad now follow soccer because their child is on a school soccer team). Thus, it is critical not to view sport fan socialization as simply a top-down process. Quite to the contrary, socialization agents can and often do continue to exert influence throughout one's lifetime. As a consequence, fandom tends to be an ever-evolving and dynamic enterprise for those involved with the pastime.

CHAPTER 3

Points of Attachment: Understanding Connections to Team Players, and Beyon

I love football!
I am a diehard Cowboys fans!
I am a huge Stephen Curry fan!
I love Wrigley Field!

The preceding statements each convey some type of psychological connection common among sport fans. In Chapter 2, we examined the Psychological Continuum Model (PCM; Funk & James, 2001, 2006) as a framework for understanding the strength of connections people form with sport objects and the processes through which these connections develop. At the Awareness stage, the connection entails knowledge that a particular team exists, but the attitude toward the team remains ambiguous. Remember the Jacksonville Jumbo Shrimp discussion from Chapter 2? You are now aware of this team, but likely have no particular connection to it. At the Attraction stage, the connection is likely a hedonic motive (e.g., a desire to have fun) or a social-situational factor (e.g., a desire to spend time with family or friends). At the Attachment stage, the team (or other sport object) has become a person's favorite, and the connection has become intrinsically important. This may involve viewing the team's values as symbolic of one's own, and the fan may be developing a sense of identification with the team. At the Allegiance stage, the connection reflects a strong association with the self-concept. A person no longer regards herself or himself as just a fan of the team but, rather, views himself or herself as part of the team. The strong association found at the Allegiance stage influences the fan's affect, behavior, and cognition (i.e., how he or she feels, acts, and thinks).

The quotes used to open this chapter express a strong connection. Words and phrases such as "love," "diehard," and "huge fan" reflect a powerful attachment to a sport object. Importantly though, taken together these quotes convey something else as well. Sport fans may form connections to a variety of *different* sport objects. Although authors writing about the PCM typically use a sport team as the focal object, the reality is individuals form connections with many different components of the fan experience. The focus of the current chapter is on these different objects of connection.

It is also important to pay careful attention to the terms used in this chapter. Specifically, notice the phrase "**points of attachment**" in the chapter title. When they discuss the PCM, authors typically write about psychological connections. So, what is up with the phrase "points of attachment"? No, it is not simply the Attachment stage in the PCM (we agree that the use of the same term adds to the confusion). As explained, a *connection* with a sport object in the context of the PCM can range from simple awareness and knowledge to strong levels of allegiance. On the other hand, the phrase "points of attachment" typically refers to particular types of connections, namely, one's identification with sport objects.

The phrase and concept of "points of attachment" traces back to work from Trail et al. (2003). Of particular note is their introduction of the Points of Attachment Index (PAI), a scale used to measure connections with seven different sport objects: team, coach, community, university, players, level of sport (i.e., competition), and sport. Thus, the work by Trail et al. (2003), and much of the PAI work that has followed, dealt with an individual's strength of identification with different sport-related objects, whether it is a sport, team, player, or some other entity. In essence, research that includes the PAI involves measuring levels of identification with particular sport-related targets. This type of research aligns with some elements of, but is not as comprehensive as, the PCM, given that the PCM describes the process of connections rather than simply the type and magnitude of attachments.

Regardless of the nomenclature used, what is clear is that if we are going to better understand sport fans, we must pay attention to the sport objects with which they connect, how these connections form, and what influences the connections might have on fan affect, behavior, and cognition. In this chapter, we provide a review of the research involving points of attachment, then focus on the connections fans form with two particular objects: teams and players.

Points of Attachment

What are the sport-related objects to which people connect? As noted, a sport team is one such entity. By extension, fans may have an interest in one or more specific players on a favorite team. It is also possible fans have an interest in a particular player, but not a strong connection to the player's team. For example, some fans of LeBron James are interested in his performance as a professional basketball player, regardless of whether he is playing for Cleveland, or Miami, or Cleveland again (and whatever the next team may be).

We can also think from team back to sport. That is, a person may have a favorite team, but preceding their interest in the team may have been their connection with a particular sport. Indeed, James (1997) found most children he interviewed indicated they had a favorite sport prior to selecting their favorite team. The preceding highlights an important point: fans often identify with multiple sport objects. For example, it is hard to imagine someone announcing his or her love for a favorite basketball team but then claiming not to like the sport of basketball. Similarly, not everyone having a favorite team will have played that particular sport. Understanding that not all sport fans will have actively participated in a particular sport is important, especially for those interested in sport consumer behavior. Although many fans have participated in various sports (as noted in Chapter 1), having played a sport is not a necessary qualification for having a favorite sport or team. For example, consider that many women have a favorite NFL team. Although they may have played other sports, they likely had little to no opportunity to participate in organized football.

As the preceding paragraphs suggest, there are many sport objects with which fans can form an attachment. They can connect with sports, teams, players, and many other aspects of the sporting environment. Researchers have studied the extent to which fans connect with various sport-related objects. For example, Schurr, Wittig, Ruble, and Ellen (1988) studied connections with a university, players, and sport. Similarly, Murrell and Dietz (1992) also wrote about fans connecting with these same three sport objects. Matsuoka and Fujimoto (2002) proposed that fans may connect with players, coaches, other fans, or the hometown of a team (referred to as **place attachment**). Much of the previous work targeting points of attachment includes studying multiple objects (see Table 3.1 for examples of such work). Although that approach did not necessarily originate with Trail et al. (2003), it may have become the standard methodology in large part because of the development of the Points of Attachment Index.

Points of Attachment Research and the Sport Objects with Which Fans Form a Connection

As noted above, Trail et al. (2003) developed the Points of Attachment Index (PAI) to measure connections with different sport objects. In their work, five objects (team, coach, community, university, and players) were grouped as an assessment of organizational connection, while sport and level of sport were grouped as an indicator of overall sport connection. The organizational and sport connections were linked to various motives. For instance, vicarious achievement was associated with the organizational objects, while skill, aesthetics, drama, and knowledge were associated with the sport objects.

Shortly after the original work by Trail and his colleagues (2003), Robinson et al. (2004) continued work on points of attachment in their study of fans' connections to golf-related objects. Their work included testing connections with a specific golfer, the tour, one's community, the sport of golf, and a charity. Robinson et al. (2004) examined whether particular motives were associated with certain objects of connection, finding that vicarious achievement was significantly related to connections to a golfer and the tour. No other motive was strongly associated with a particular golf-related object.

TABLE 3.1 Points of Attachment Research

Citation	Points of Attachment
Ballouli, Trial, Koesters, and Bernthal (2016)	Team, Athlete, Place, Sport, Level of Competition, Community
Tokmak and Aksov (2016)	Team, Athlete, Coach, Level of Sport
Spinda, Wann, and Hardin (2016)	Team, Sport, University, Athlete, Level of Competition, Coach, Conference
Dwyer, Mudrick, Greenhalgh, LeCrom, and Drayer (2015)	Team
Keaton, Watanabe, and Gearhart (2015)	Team, Athlete
Reams, Eddy, and Cork (2015)	Sport, Level of Competition, Athlete, Sponsors
Yoshida, Gordon, Heere, and James (2015)	Community
Zembura and Zysko (2015)	Athlete, Organization, Sport
Shapiro, Drayer, and Dwyer (2014)	Sport, Team, Athlete, Community
Cottingham, Chatfield, Gearity, Allen, and Hall (2012)	Athlete, Sport, Community
Gencer, Kiremitci, and Boyacioglu (2011)	Team, Sport, Level of Competition, Community
Karg and McDonald (2011)	Sport, Team, League, Athlete, Coach
Woo, Trail, Kwon, and Anderson (2009)	Team, Coach, University, Athlete, Sport, Level of Competition
Dittmore, Stodt, and Greenwell (2008)	Team, Sport, Athlete
Robinson and Trail (2005)	Athlete, Team, Coach, Sport, Level of Competition, Community, University
Robinson, Trail, and Kwon (2004)	Athlete, Coach, Community, Team, Sport, Level of Competition, University
Murrell and Dietz (1992)	University, Athlete, Sport
Schurr, Wittig, Ruble, and Ellen (1988)	University, Athlete, Sport

The study of multiple points of attachment continued beyond the work by Trail and his colleagues. For example, Dittmore, Stoldt, and Greenwell (2008) measured connections with team, sport, and player among consumers of a weblog for a Major League Baseball team. They found that connections with the team was strongest, followed by sport, and then player. Karg and McDonald (2011) examined differences in connections to five sport objects among fantasy sport participants and non-participants. Specifically, they investigated connections to sport, league, team, players, and coach. They found that fantasy sport players reported a stronger connection with each object compared to persons not playing fantasy sport. The strongest connections were with team, sport, and players, respectively. Cottingham et al. (2012) studied points of attachment for wheelchair rugby. The objects of connection included player, sport, and disability community. Connection to sport and disability community were each significant predictors of future attendance intentions.

Although research on points of attachment typically targets sport, level of sport, team, player, university/school, and community, we would be remiss not to acknowledge that fans can connect to any sport-related object. For example, a fan could feel a connection to a particular piece of sporting equipment, such as a favorite football or baseball. Or maybe an autographed basketball from a favorite player has particular importance to the fan. Individuals may well go to extreme measures to take care of these items because of the strong connections they feel for the memorabilia. Likewise, a person could have a strong connection with a particular piece of sport apparel, such as a favorite jersey. Other sport-related objects to which individuals connect include sport conference (Spinda et al., 2016) and team sponsors (Reams et al., 2015).

A final sport object with which fans form a connection is a particular place (i.e., place attachment). For example, a major component of the attachment Nebraska Cornhusker fans feel for their football team centers on their connection with the state of Nebraska (Aden, 2008). Although place attachment is often a general locale such as a city or state, at other times the connection is with a specific facility. For some fans, a stadium, arena, or other sport venue is an object to which they form a strong connection. And we mean *really strong* connection. Remillard (2015) writes about sport venues that people consider sacred,

Sport Fans Often Become Attached to a Location, Such as the Strong Connection Fans of the University of Nebraska Cornhuskers Often Have With the State of Nebraska

viewing a place with a type of religious reverence (the link between sport fandom and religion is discussed in Chapter 11). For example, Remillard refers to an exhibit at the Baseball Hall of Fame in Cooperstown, New York, titled "Sacred Ground" that highlights noteworthy ballparks in the United States. We could write for several pages about college sport venues and the history and tradition associated with them. For instance, Delia and James (in press) document the importance of the Carrier Dome, a venue that is an integral point of connection for many Syracuse University fans.

Thus, fans may connect with any number of objects; no one is limited to having an interest in just one sport, one team, one player, or one anything sport-related. Fans can and often do connect with multiple sports, teams, players, and other sport-related objects. For example, Grieve and his colleagues (2009) found that fans averaged greater than a half dozen attachments just with different teams. Think again about our Lebron James example. Some people may have become Cleveland Cavalier fans simply because James was part of the team. When he left to play for Miami, some of these fans may have formed a new allegiance, becoming supporters of the Miami Heat. At the same time, other individuals may have been Cavaliers' fans prior to James becoming a member of the team. As a result of his playing for their favorite team, they could have become fans of James. When James changed teams, some may have continued to support him while also remaining fans of the Cavaliers. Clearly, fans can be complicated people.

Attachments to Teams: Team Identification

Identification with sport teams and the implications of these connections are one of the most oft studied topics among scholars of sport fandom since the 1990s. A literature search that utilized team identification as a primary variable of interest found over 100 journal articles published between 1980 and 2018. Furthermore, the topic of team identification has been cited in hundreds of additional articles. The study of team identification has been largely influenced by and generally originated with Wann and Branscombe's (1993) publication of the Sport Spectator Identification Scale (SSIS). However, the topic of identification among sport fans predates the work of Wann and Branscombe. As noted in Chapter 1, two of the earliest mentions of team identification come from the work of Brill (1929) and Griffith (1938). However, for all intents and purposes the "modern day" study of team identification began with the work of Wann and his colleagues.

In Chapter 1, we defined team identification as the extent to which a fan feels psychologically connected to a team. The impact of that connection is what has likely driven the interest in team identification as a topic of research. As we explained in Chapter 1, sport scholars usually study the strength of identification, ranging from low to high. Many scholars have examined the impact of "low" and "high" team identification on attitude, behavior, and cognition. A strong connection (i.e., high identification) is expected to result in consistent and enduring behaviors and attitudes towards a team (James et al., 2002). Such behaviors include purchasing event tickets (Wann, Bayens, & Driver, 2004), merchandise (Kwon & Armstrong, 2002; Lee & Ferreira, 2011), and team apparel (Kwon, Trail, & James, 2007), and positive word of mouth (Swanson, Gwinner, Larson, & Janda, 2003). In addition to marketing benefits, Wann (2006c) has discussed social psychological benefits of team identification, including enhancement of social well-being.

The range—not just the magnitude—of scholarly activity on team identification is indicative of its appeal to those who study sport fandom. It is somewhat ironic to note, however, that more than 25 years after the initial work by Wann and Branscombe (1993), sport scholars are just now giving proper attention to the theoretical underpinnings of team identification. Indeed, Lock and Heere (2017) point out that in the 1990s and early 2000s, the study of team identification often failed to include strong theoretical foundations. The authors did acknowledge that scholars had discussed team identification as a type of social identification (cf., Branscombe & Wann, 1991; Heere & James, 2007; Kwon et al., 2007; Madrigal, 1995), grounded in **Social Identity Theory** (SIT) (Tajfel & Turner, 1979). Fink et al. (2002) noted explicitly that "Team identification is based on social identity theory" (p. 196). There have also been some scholars (Trail, Anderson, & Lee, 2016; Trail & James, 2015) that have endeavored to study team identification using **Identity Theory** (Stryker, 1968) as a theoretical framework. Lock and Heere offer several insightful suggestions for improving the theoretical study of team identification.

According to the PCM, connections to a sport team progress from awareness, to attraction, to attachment, to allegiance. Where does identification fit in to such a progression? The Awareness stage simply involves knowledge that teams exist and learning about different teams, players, and coaches. The Attraction stage reflects an interest in attending a game played by a particular team. However, the connection is likely based on some social-situational (e.g., attending with family or friends) or hedonic (seeking a fun experience) factor. Thus, it is likely that identification with a team has not yet developed in either the Awareness or Attraction stages. Funk and James (2016) explain that as a team takes on intrinsic importance and meaning for a person, she or he has advanced to the stage of Attachment. Thus, identification is associated with this stage. Tajfel's (1978) definition that social identity is "that part of an individual's self-concept which derives from his knowledge of his membership of a social group (or groups) together with the value and emotional significance attached to that membership" (p. 63). Identification involves associating the team with one's self-concept or forming an attachment.

The Origins of Team Identification

Think for a moment about when you first started supporting your favorite team. Do you remember the reasons for your initial decision to follow this team? Now imagine asking your friends and family members who also support this team to recall the reasons they originally started following the team. In all likelihood, their explanations would not be the same as yours. In fact, you may be surprised to learn the factors leading to their support. Indeed, researchers have found there is a wide range of reasons that underlie fan's initial identification with a team (Wann, Tucker, & Schrader, 1996). And some of the reasons seem to lack reason. For instance, consider how actor Matthew McConaughey became a fan of the Washington Redskins even though he was born and raised in Texas, home of the rival Dallas Cowboys. When asked why he began to support the Redskins, McConaughey noted that his favorite food at that time was hamburgers and the Redskins had a player named Chris Hanburger (Steinberg, 2013). In a more personally relevant example, consider the experiences of the first author of your text. I am a diehard Cubs fan, a devotion that dates back to the late 1960s. Did I grow up in Chicago? Nope, not even in Illinois. Did my family follow the Cubs? Nope, and quite to the contrary, my father was a fan of the rival St. Louis Cardinals, having grown up in southeast Missouri. So why did I become a fan of the Cubs? Because my older brother decided to follow in our father's footsteps and also support the Cardinals (sport fan socialization in action). Consequently, in an attempt to drive my older sibling crazy, I decided to support a rival of the Cardinals and, hence, became a Cubs fan.

Many fans have similar stories of the strange circumstances that ignited their passion for a team. Listening to fans tell these stories may lead to the impression that the origin of team identification is a purely random process. However, this is not the case. Rather, a number of informative studies have been undertaken that shed light on the most common origins (also referred to as causes or antecedents) of identification. For instance, Wann and his colleagues (1996) asked 91 college students to state why they originally began to follow their favorite team. Participants generated a list of over 300 reasons, and one person reported 16 reasons for originally following a team! And to make matters even more complex, there was not a great deal of agreement among the participants. For example, no single factor was listed by more than 13 percent of the sample, and only two causes (characteristics of the players and one's family followed the team) were listed by as many as 10 percent of the respondents (Wann et al., 1996).

Because fans list such a wide variety of reasons for originally following a team, to describe them without some form or structure would be a logistical nightmare. Thankfully, a typology has been proposed to assist in our understanding of the variety of factors impacting the origination of team identification (Wann, 2006a). According to this perspective, the wide range of reasons fans originally begin supporting a team can be grouped into one of three categories: psychological, environmental, and team-related.

Psychological Origins of Team Identification Wann (2006a) lists two critical **psychological origins** of team identification: the need to belong and the need for distinctiveness. You may recall that these innate psychological drives were discussed at length in Chapter 1 and that sport fandom has the potential to assist individuals in meeting these needs (Goldman et al., 2016; Groeneman, 2017; Theodorakis et al., 2012).

As for the need to belong, individuals can satisfy their desire to gain connections to others by rooting for a sport team, particularly if that team has a strong local following. By supporting the local team, one can gain a sense of unity and cohesion with others (Gwinner & Swanson, 2003; Watkins, 2014). In fact, Sutton, McDonald, Milne, and Cimperman (1997) contend that a desire for "affiliation is the most significant correlate of fan identification" (p. 18). Wann et al. (1996) found that the desire to spend time with others was a fairly common antecedent for team identification, as this factor was listed third-most frequently. The need to belong may be a particularly powerful driver for identification with new teams because other potential links (e.g., players and team success) may not yet be in place (James et al., 2002; Lock, Taylor, & Darcy, 2011).

In addition, researchers suggest that the need to belong may be especially common among female fans (Aiken & Koch, 2009; Dietz-Uhler et al., 2000). For instance, consider a recent study by Koch and Wann (2016). In this research, fans completed a questionnaire assessing the extent to which the origin of their identification for a favorite team was based on a desire to establish relationships with others (e.g., "I became a fan of my favorite team to bond with family, friends, and/or peers"). They found that females were significantly more likely than males to originally identify with a team for **relationship-based** reasons.

In terms of the need for distinctiveness, one way for individuals to feel unique is to identify with groups that separate them from the mainstream. As it relates to fandom, persons may choose to support a team because the team is different in some way. For instance, one (albeit dangerous) way for persons in New York City to stand out and feel unique would be to begin supporting the Boston Red Sox.

The needs for belongingness and distinctiveness were the focus of recent work by DeRossett and Wann (2018). These authors asked United States college students to read a vignette describing a pair of equally successful Australian Professional Cricket teams (both teams were fictional). One team was described as being very popular and having a large fan base; the other was said to be less popular and had more of a cult-type following. Subsequent to reading the vignette, participants selected the team they would be most likely to support. Lastly, they completed scales assessing their need for belongingness and distinctiveness. The results indicated that persons who chose the more unique (less mainstream) team had higher levels of need for distinctiveness than those selecting the popular team. And which team did participants higher in need for belonging prefer? As you may have guessed, these persons were more likely to place their allegiance with the popular team.

For a third psychological origin of team identification, we need to return to the Koch and Wann (2016) project. In addition to investigating relationship-based origins of identification, this work also examined **recognition-based** antecedents (e.g., "I became a fan of my favorite team to be known as a fan of that team"). The authors found that participants were more likely to have begun following a team due to a desire to be recognized as a fan of the team than to establish relationships with others. It warrants mention that the desire to support a team to be viewed as a fan of that team is distinct from the desire to gain a sense of belonging. That is, belonging as an antecedent of identification involves using the team to establish social relationships. However, recognition-based origins involve a desire to manage one's impression by being perceived as a supporter of the team, a common practice among fans (Cialdini et al., 1976; Wann, 2006a).

A fourth psychological cause was noted by Dimmock and Grove (2006) in their research on uncertainty reduction. **Subjective Uncertainty Reduction Theory** (Hogg & Abrams, 1993) proposes that individuals possess a fundamental need for certainty because it provides meaning in life and an understanding of acceptable forms of behavior. One method of gaining certainty is via shared group membership (Grieve & Hogg, 1999). Given this, Dimmock and Grove hypothesized that team identification may assist in the need to reduce uncertainty. Consistent with expectations, they found that persons higher in the need for a structured life had higher levels of identification with their favorite team, leading the authors to surmise that "the desire for subjective certainty might influence the development of team identification" (p. 1209).

Environmental Origins of Team Identification One of the most critical **environmental origins** of team identification is the sport fan socialization process (Wann, 2006a). As was detailed in the previous chapter, socialization begins during the Awareness stage of the PCM (Funk & James, 2001) and involves exposure to a team via socialization agents. For example, if an individual's friends and/or family actively root for a team, this person may also begin to develop an affinity for the team (Crawford, 2003; Greenwood, Kanters, & Casper, 2006; Groeneman, 2017; Gwinner & Swanson, 2003; Keaton & Gearhart, 2014; Wann et al., 1996). Often, fans who are socialized to follow a team do so out of a sense of obligation to their family and friends (Koch & Wann, 2013). Your first author's youngest son, Kevin, witnessed firsthand a family's socialization of a child to support a specific team. While working at an arcade-style game room, Kevin was approached by a mother and her young child. The child had several hundred tickets he had won playing various games. The boy eyed a University of Louisville basketball and was overjoyed to learn that he had enough tickets to purchase the item. The joy quickly turned to sorrow (and many tears) when his mother refused to allow him to select the item, stating that they were University of Kentucky fans and definitely not supporters of Louisville. The child was informed that because they did not have a Kentucky basketball, he was not getting a basketball.

James (2001) noted the potential for socialization agents to have a combined impact on identification with a favorite team. For instance, although a person's father may have a strong influence on identification (particularly for younger fans, see Kolbe & James, 2000), it is likely there is a community influence as well, particularly if a fan grows up in the hometown of the favorite team (more about the impact of geography below). In essence, the importance of the team is reinforced through messages at home, interactions with peers, and messages through various media outlets. Additionally, the team is likely engaging in promotional activities to foster a positive connection with fans. Thus, fans are most likely socialized to follow a team by multiple sources.

Another environmental origin, and one that is likely related to socialization, involves **geographical nearness** to a team. Research suggests that growing up and/or living near a team can be a powerful force in facilitating team identification (Aiken & Koch, 2009; Greenwood et al., 2006; Kolbe & James, 2000), particularly for fans whose allegiance to the team was developed earlier in life (Popp, Barrett, & Weight, 2016). Although Wann and his colleagues (1996) found that a fair percentage (10 percent) of respondents listed geographical reasons for originally identifying with a team, subsequent work provides evidence this is more common than previously believed (e.g., Uemukai, Takenouchi, Okuda, Matsumoto, & Yamanaka, 1995). For example, in his work with English soccer fans, Jones (1997) found that over 60 percent of his sample listed geography as an antecedent. Likewise, Groeneman (2017) found that geography was listed by over 50 percent of fans of United States professional sports, the most frequent factor influencing the origin of identification. Interestingly, the impact of geography may be related to the type of sport in question. Specifically, Keaton et al. (2015) found that geography was more critical as an antecedent to identification with a team sport (i.e., college football) than to an individual sport (i.e., NASCAR).

Three additional environmental causes are interactions with players, the salience of rival teams, and a team's stadium (Wann, 2006a). As for **player contact**, the logic here is that exposure to and interactions with players leads to interest in the team (think Awareness and Attraction stages from the PCM) and such interest can facilitate the development of team identification. Direct contact with players via autograph sessions and other team events could be particularly influential.

In terms of **rival salience**, increasing awareness of a rival should result in greater levels of identification (Ashforth & Mael, 1989; Bass, Gordon, & Kim, 2013). This was the pattern of effects found by Luellen and Wann (2010). In their research, college sport fans completed a questionnaire assessing their level

A Stadium or Arena Can Be an Antecedent of Team Identification

of identification with the University of Kentucky men's basketball team. Participants completed the identification measure both before and after watching a rival team's highlight video or, for those in the control group, a generic sport highlight video (the rival team was not depicted in the control film). As expected, those exposed to the rival team video reported an increase in identification with the Kentucky team, a pattern of effects absent from those watching the control video.

Finally, fans may begin to identify with a team because of the team's **stadium** (Boyle & Magnusson, 2007; Underwood, Bond, & Baer, 2001; Watkins, 2014). Specifically, fans may develop a sense of pride for and attachment to a unique or historically relevant arena (e.g., Wrigley Field and Fenway Park in Major League Baseball). Lee, Heere, and Chung (2013) investigated how a fan's sensory experience at a stadium can impact team identification. They found that four stadium-related sensory experiences (sight, sound, touch, and smell) influenced team identification, with the visual sense having the greatest impact. The authors concluded that the "sport venue experience through consumers' senses can be an antecedent of team identity" (p. 209).

Team-Related Origins of Team Identification The third category contained in Wann's (2006a) typology involves **team-related origins** of identification, that is, issues directly related to the team itself. Wann further separates team-related causes into three categories: organizational characteristics, team performance, and player attributes. According to Sutton and his colleagues (1997), **organizational characteristics** involve "the 'off-field' image of ownership, decision making, and tradition of the franchise" (p. 15). This would include the team's history and rituals (Aiken & Koch, 2009; Boyle & Magnusson, 2007; Underwood et al., 2001), such as chanting "Rock Chalk, Jayhawk" at Kansas University basketball games and dotting the "i" in "Ohio" at The Ohio State University football contests.

As for **team performance**, it should come as no surprise that fans frequently begin to identify with a team due to the success of the franchise (Bass et al., 2013; Fisher & Wakefield, 1998; Wann et al. 1996). In fact, some work has found this to be the most influential factor (Aiken & Koch, 2009). End, Dietz-Uhler, Harrick, and Jacquemotte (2002) asked participants to list the teams with which they felt some level of identification and to rank the list from most preferred to least preferred. The authors then examined the success of these teams (e.g., winning percentage, Top 25 national ranking) and found that the teams listed were significantly more successful than one would have expected. For example, the teams listed had winning percentages far greater than .500. Additionally, those teams ranked higher in preference were more successful than those with a lower ranking. The authors concluded that fans utilize a team's past success as a criterion for determining which team (or teams) they choose to support. It warrants mention that non-performance factors can also serve as antecedents to team identification. For example, researchers report that trust in a team (e.g., belief that a team keeps its promises, Wu, Tsai, & Hung, 2012) and perceptions of a team's values (Groeneman, 2017) are also significant facilitators of identification.

In terms of **player attributes**, several investigators have found this to be a common antecedent of identification (Kolbe & James, 2000; Wann et al., 1996; Wu et al., 2012). Although player skill and ability are important (Aiken & Koch, 2009), non-performance characteristics matter as well (Nelson, 2004; Pritchard, Stinson, & Patton, 2010). For instance, it has been suggested that fans often begin to identify with teams composed of players that are attractive or similar to the fan (Fisher & Wakefield, 1998). However, in a direct comparison of these two traits, Fisher (1998) found that similarity was of greater importance than attractiveness in the development of identification.

Summary of the Origins of Team Identification Individuals may form a connection with a team at any point in time, and that connection may strengthen over the years. It is important to note that until a team takes on personal importance and becomes an element of one's self-concept, although the individual may have an attraction to the team, he or she likely does not feel a sense of identification. Rather, team identification is expected to form as individuals reach the Attachment stage of the PCM. For those interested in sport marketing and sport consumer behavior, we have to recognize that those at the Attraction stage are seeking satisfaction or fulfillment of particular needs (e.g., social-situational, hedonic), but the connection does not yet involve identification. Team identification concerns aligning the team with one's self-concept and, in so doing, engaging in behaviors such as buying tickets, buying merchandise, and attending games in a manner that is more easily predicted. These points matter, because those that study team identification "in the field," that is, in actual sport settings, must be careful about reporting whether fans are identified. As we explain in the next section, there have been some problems with the interpretation of whether people do or do not identify with a team.

Measurement of Team Identification

To aid in the assessment of team identification, Wann and Branscombe (1993) developed the Sport Spectator Identification Scale (SSIS). Investigators from several countries have successfully translated and used the SSIS in their work, including researchers in the United States (Gayton, Coffin, & Hearns, 1998), Germany (Straub, 1995), and Japan (Uemukai et al., 1995). Sample items from the SSIS are shown in Table 3.2.

Trail and James (2001) published a second measure of team identification that has had frequent use. Although the original work did not include a name for the scale, it has since been labeled the Team Identification Index (TII). The TII includes three items: (1) I already consider myself a fan of the [*team name*]; (2) I would feel a loss if I had to give up being a [*team name*] fan; and (3) Others recognize that I am a big [*team name*] fan. People typically have responded to the items on a seven-point scale anchored by "Strongly Disagree" and "Strongly Agree."

We have written specifically about the SSIS and TII because they have been utilized most frequently by sport scholars. This is particularly true for the SSIS. In fact, as of early 2018, Wann and Branscombe's (1993) article introducing the

TABLE 3.2 Sample Items From the Sport Spectator Identification Scale

1. How important is it to you that the [*team name*] wins?									
Not Important	1	2	3	4	5	6	7	8	Very Important
2. How strongly do you see yourself as a fan of the [*team name*]?									
Not at All a Fan	1	2	3	4	5	6	7	8	Very Much a Fan
3. How important is being a fan of the [*team name*] to you?									
Not Important	1	2	3	4	5	6	7	8	Very Important

Note: Wann and Branscombe (1993).

SSIS had been cited more than 1,000 times. In a review of more than 100 articles utilizing team identification as a focal variable, we found the SSIS was included in over half of the studies. However, there are other measures of team identification besides the SSIS and the TII. For example, Fisher (1998) reported use of an eight-item scale that was also included in Kim and Kim's (2009) work. Swanson and colleagues (2003) included a seven-item scale modeled on a measure of organizational identification originally published by Mael and Ashforth (2001) and similar in design to the scale reported by Bhattacharya, Rao, and Glynn (1995).

Regardless of whether researchers have used the SSIS, the TII, or some other measure of identification, one of the challenges with previous work is the lack of consistency in characterizing levels of identification. Those studying team identification often use some technique to place respondents into high, moderate, or low team-identification groups (James, Delia, & Wann, in press). Some common methods used include a median split (e.g., Madrigal & Chen, 2008; Wann et al., 2004; Wann, Ensor, & Bilyeu, 2001; Wann & Schrader, 1997), upper and lower percentiles (e.g., Dimmock & Grove, 2005; Parker & Fink, 2010), a midpoint scale split (e.g., Fink, Parker, Brett, & Higgins, 2009), and, in some instances, grouping individuals somewhat arbitrarily (e.g., Wann & Grieve, 2005). However, because different researchers have used different points along the identification continuum to divide fans into various groups, it can be difficult to compare across studies. For example, utilizing the SSIS, Wann and Schrader (1997) averaged the item scores and characterized an individual scoring 5.1–7.0 as high identification; low identification included those scoring 1.0–5.0. However, in the work done by Madrigal and Chen (2008), those scoring 3.4–6.8 were characterized as high identification, with those scoring 1.0–3.2 as low identification. In another example, Lee and Ferreira (2011) characterized those averaging 6.0 or 7.0 as high identification, and those averaging 1.0 or 2.0 as low identification.

Assessing Team Identification as a Unidimensional Versus Multidimensional Construct A common characteristic of most team identification measures is that they assess identification as a **unidimensional** construct. As you might guess from the prefix "uni," unidimensional means one. In this sense, team identification is just a single concept or component, a person's psychological connection to a team. However, think back to Tajfel's (1978) vision of social identity: "that part of an individual's self-concept which derives from his knowledge of his membership of a social group (or groups) together with the value and emotional significance attached to that membership" (p. 63). Given this, Dimmock, Grove, and Eklund (2005) proposed that social identifications such as sport team identification include three elements: cognitive (knowledge of group membership), evaluative (value of group membership), and affective (emotional significance of group membership).

As a **multi-dimensional** construct, team identification would be composed of multiple elements. Heere and James (2007) proposed that a unidimensional measure of team identification, such as the SSIS, provides a measure of an individual's sense of belonging (or connection) to a team. In other words, an assessment of whether a person feels a sense of connection with the team and the strength of that connection. Heere and James suggest further that a multi-dimensional measure of team identification allows for assessment of an individual's self-concept, knowledge, and value of membership in a group and the emotional significance attached to the membership. That is, viewed as a multi-dimensional construct, team identification would include different components and may provide a more complete picture of the basis for one's identification with a team.

Drawing from the work of Ashmore, Deaux, and McLaughlin-Volpe (2004), Heere and James (2007) reported their efforts to test a multi-dimensional measure of team identification they labeled the TEAM*ID. Following the standard scale development process established by Churchill (1999), Heere and James provided evidence of a six-dimension scale: public evaluation, private evaluation, interconnection to self, sense of interdependence, behavioral involvement, and cognitive awareness. Descriptions of these dimensions can be found in Table 3.3. Research conducted with the TEAM*ID scale has provided evidence of the reliability and validity of the scale (Heere & Katz, 2014; Katz & Heere, 2016; Yoshida, Gordon, Heere, & James, 2015). Thus, the TEAM*ID scale is a viable option for researchers interested in assessing team identification as a multi-dimensional construct.

The choice to measure team identification with a uni- or multi-dimensional scale should be based on the goal(s) of the particular research project. Both scales provide a measure of whether an individual has a psychological connection with a sport team. By extension, it is possible to characterize the strength of an individual's identification with a team. A unidimensional scale provides a simple, parsimonious measure of team identification. A multi-dimensional scale provides us with some understanding of what composes an individual's identification with a team. Thus, if the research goal is to better understand why a person identifies with a team (i.e., what drives team identification), then a multi-dimensional scale is likely the proper choice. On the other hand, if the goal is to capture whether there is a psychological connection (and the strength of that connection), a unidimensional scale is more than sufficient.

TABLE 3.3 Dimensions Comprising the TEAM*ID Scale

Dimension	Description
Public Evaluation	How favorably others are perceived to regard a particular social identity.
Private Evaluation	How favorably others are perceived to regard one's own identity.
Interconnection to Self	The cognitive merging of a sense of self and an ingroup.
Sense of Interdependence	An individual's recognition that he or she is treated the same as other group members.
Behavioral Involvement	The degree to which a person engages in actions that directly implicate the focal social identity.
Cognitive Awareness	The degree of knowledge a person has of a group that directly implicates his or her identity with the group as a whole.

Note: From Heere and James (2007).

Misinterpreting Team Identification

James and his associates (in press) noted that through the first three decades of team identification research, much of the work included an interpretation problem (your authors are included in the group of researchers responsible for the misinterpretation). To understand the misinterpretation, it will be helpful to refer back to the sample items from the SSIS listed in Table 3.2 (we will focus on the SSIS, but the problem with misinterpretation can occur with any measure of team identification). As researchers, we typically average or sum scores to the items and report a team identification score. Once we have a set of team identification scores, we generally categorize them as high or low identification via one of the methods mentioned above. However, whether we use a midpoint split, a median split, or a tripartite split or treat the responses as continuous data, we have misinterpreted participant responses by incorrectly labeling "not identified" individuals as those with "low" identification.

Here is how the misinterpretation happens. The SSIS (and likely all team identification scales) includes positive and negative anchors. Individuals who score all team identification items as "1" are disagreeing with the items and reporting they do not identify with the focal team. Yet we have consistently characterized these participants as having a low level of team identification (and remember, your authors are a part of this "we"). As James et al. (in press) explain, there is a fundamental problem when researchers use anchors that purport a "not," "never," or "strongly disagree" condition, yet they interpret this "no" condition as "low" identification. Consider item 2 in the SSIS, which is worded "How strongly do you see yourself as a fan of the [team]?" The anchors for the item are "Not at all a fan" and "Very much a fan." The individuals who read the anchors and choose "Not at all a fan" are reporting they do not identify with a focal team. Yet we have classified such individuals as having low team identification.

Consider the following examples presented by James et al. (in press).

> Example 1: In their research on spectating enjoyment, Wann and Schrader (1997) explained "A median split of 5.1 on the subjects' identification scores was used to divide the subjects into high (n = 58; M = 6.1, SD = 0.7, range = 5.1 to 7.9) and low (n = 56; M = 3.3, SD = 1.1, range = 1.0 to 5.0) groups" (p. 954). Notice the range for the low identification group, from 1 to 5.
>
> Example 2: Investigating individuals' causal attributions of game outcome, Madrigal and Chen (2008) noted "As expected, those in the high-identification group scored significantly higher on team identification (n = 61; M = 5.00, SD = 1.12, range = 3.4–6.80) than did those in the low identification group (n = 60; M = 2.08, SD = .67, range = 1–3.20), $t(119) = -17.33, p < .001$" (p. 725). Thus, in this study, the range for the low identification group was from 1 to 3.20.
>
> Example 3: Levin, Beasley, and Gilson (2008) studied the relationship between identification with NASCAR and intention to purchase products of NASCAR sponsors. They wrote "Total scores ranged from a low of 6 to a high of 42, with a mean of 32.4" (p. 199). The authors used a modified 6-item SSIS with scale range 1 to 7. Thus, some of those in the low identification group scored a 1 on each of the six items.

You may be thinking "So what? Why does this matter? Is this really just a problem of labeling?" Although some people might not think there is a problem here, or that it is a trivial concern at most, we believe the misinterpretation is much more than just a minor issue. Researchers have been reporting comparisons of high and low identified individuals which have in fact been comparisons of highly identified individuals and some combination of individuals with low and no identification. At the very least, our research has been plagued by a failure to recognize the not identified group.

Sport Spectator Identification Scale-Revised (SSIS-R)

Assuming that we have sufficiently convinced you that the misinterpretation issue is a problem worth addressing, you may now be wondering if there is anything that can be done to remedy the situation. Thankfully, the answer is a resounding "YES!" Because the problem of misinterpretation has arisen from how team identification is assessed, a reasonable solution is to revise the measurement tool. James and his colleagues (in press) reported on their effort to revise the SSIS (the new scale is referred to as the SSIS-R) in an attempt to eliminate the misinterpretation of team identification scores.

The screening question and sample items from the SSIS-R are shown in Table 3.4. The first portion of the SSIS-R is designed to determine whether or not a person is identified with a focal team. This is accomplished via a screening item asking, "Do you identify yourself as a fan of the [*team name*], even if just a little bit?" The purpose of the screening question is to determine whether there is any level of identification (that is, psychological connection) with a target team. If a person does not identify as a fan, she or he would be directed to the next section of the questionnaire. If a person does identify with the team, even if just a little bit, she or he would respond to the items in the SSIS-R.

Along with the addition of the screening item, the anchors with the SSIS-R are different from the original SSIS. Individuals responding to the SSIS-R items should have some level of connection with the team, given their affirmative response to the screening item. Accordingly, they should not disagree with any item. Thus, the anchors were revised to reflect the fact that participants should have at least a minimal connection with the target team (a comparison of Tables 3.2 and 3.4 will highlight the changes in anchoring). Preliminary work using the SSIS-R is quite encouraging (James et al., in press). It appears that with the SSIS-R, we seem to be able to capture those that are not identified and separate them from those that do identify with a team.

To close out this section, we return once more to the question of whether "low identification" versus "not identified" really matters. We wholeheartedly believe it does. For sport scholars, it does matter that we are performing research correctly, that we are accurately reporting results, and that we serve our peers in the industry without misleading them. And, it does matter that we do our science well and to the best of our ability. Misinterpreting data and mislabeling participants is simply not the best science available. Scholars interested in sport fandom can and must do better. We believe the SSIS-R (or another scale with similar modifications) can assist in this matter.

TABLE 3.4 Sample Items From the Sport Spectator Identification Scale-Revised

Do you identify yourself as a fan of the [*team name*], even if just a little bit?
Please circle the appropriate letter: A. Yes B. No

1. How important is it to you that the [*team name*] wins?

A Little Important	1	2	3	4	5	6	7	8	Very Important

2. How strongly do you see yourself as a fan of the [*team name*]?

Slightly a Fan	1	2	3	4	5	6	7	8	Very Much a Fan

3. How important is being a fan of the [*team name*] to you?

A Little Important	1	2	3	4	5	6	7	8	Very Important

Note: James, Delia, and Wann (in press).

Athletes and Players as Points of Attachment

In the previous sections, we have examined the strong connections sport fans develop and maintain with teams. However, if you were to wander into a sporting goods store and happen upon the team apparel section, another form of attachment would become apparent. Specifically, many of the team jerseys for sale would contain the names and numbers of popular local and national sport figures. This reveals the fact that fans frequently become attached to specific players (Robinson & Trail, 2005; Robinson et al., 2004) and often imagine having social encounters with them (Keaton, Gearhart, & Honeycutt, 2014). In many cases, these players become heroes to fans (Bain-Selbo & Sapp, 2016; Griggs et al., 2012; Mandelbaum, 2004; Peetz, Parks, & Spencer, 2004). In the paragraphs that follow, we review the process of attachment to athletes and the hero worship of these public figures by examining the prevalence of sport heroes, the process of selecting a sport hero, and the consequences of when sport heroes fall from grace.

The Sports World as a Source of Heroes: The Prevalence of Sport Heroes

Research suggests that the sports world is a fairly consistent source of heroes for children, although parents and other family members are more likely to be listed as a hero (Stevens, Lathrop, & Bradish, 2003; Wallis, 1999). Sport heroes were nonexistent among 12- to 14-year-old Americans prior to the 1900s, but by mid-century it had emerged as an important category, accounting for 23 percent of choices (Averill, 1950; Darrah, 1898). More recent data provide evidence to confirm that sport figures serve as a relatively common exemplar category for children, at least among those residing in North America (Giuliano, Turner, Lundquist, & Knight, 2007). Although percentages vary across studies, most suggest that between 15 and 25 percent of children list a sport figure as their greatest hero (Foundation for Child Development, 1977; Harris, 1994; Stevens et al., 2003; Wallis, 1999). However, much higher percentages have been found (Parry, 2009). As for adults, interviews with older respondents revealed that these persons seldom have sport heroes (Smith, 1976). Thus, it appears that the relationship between age and sport hero worship is nonlinear, specifically, the inverted-U curve depicted in Figure 3.1 (Harris, 1986).

Selecting a Sport Hero: The Importance of Similarity

Social psychologists have established that individuals tend to be attracted to others with whom they share traits, characteristics, backgrounds, and so forth (e.g., Byrne, 1971; Byrne et al., 1986). Consequently, it should not be surprising that sport fans tend to resemble their sport heroes on both sport-related and unrelated dimensions. As for sport-related dimensions, researchers have found

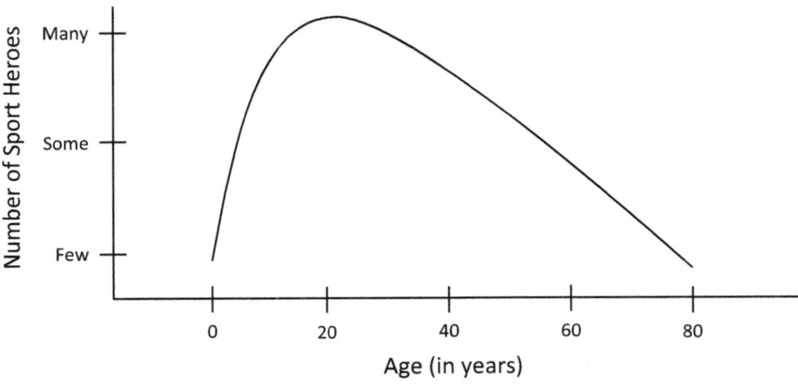

FIGURE 3.1 Hypothesized Relationship Between Age and the Number of Sport Heroes

that among children who identified an athlete as their hero, 59 percent chose a sport figure excelling at the youngster's favorite sport (Cooper, Livingood, & Kurz, 1981). Additionally, children tend to select a sport hero who plays a similar position within a sport (Castine & Roberts, 1974; Russell, 1979). Research on non-sport traits has typically focused on race and gender. This literature indicates that individuals often adopt sport heroes with whom they share a race and/or gender (Castine & Roberts, 1974; Parry, 2009; Vander Velden, 1986), although female children often choose male sport figures as well (Balswick & Ingoldsby, 1982; Harris, 1994). Of course, there are other important resemblance factors in addition to those noted above (e.g., nationality, see Parry, 2009). Because youngsters assign different levels of importance to the various components of the self (Harter, 1993), they may desire sport heroes who resemble themselves on a variety of traits and characteristics. One might speculate, for example, that left-handers tend to select other lefties, while disabled persons disproportionately select physically challenged athletes as their personal heroes.

When Sport Heroes Fall: The Impact of Athlete Transgressions

In the past few decades, a wide range of athlete transgressions have become public knowledge. These incidents have included a seemingly limitless variety of wrongdoings including marital infidelity, the use of performance enhancing drugs, and violent off-field actions involving rape and murder. For example, an archival investigation by Benedict and Yaeger (1998) revealed that 21 percent of players on NFL rosters had been charged with serious criminal offenses ranging from resisting arrest and armed robbery to kidnapping and homicide. And many of these players had multiple charges.

How do fans react when their heroes fall from grace? This is an important question given that athletes frequently serve as spokespersons (Ruihley, Runyan, & Lear, 2010), and athletes have the ability to develop their own brand image (Arai, Ko, & Kaplanidou, 2013; Arai, Ko, & Ross, 2014; Carlson & Donavan, 2013). Furthermore, given that trust in an athlete is a critical predictor of purchase intentions of the products he or she endorses (Tzoumaka, Tsiotsou, & Siomkos, 2016), an athlete's negative actions could potentially undermine his or her effectiveness as an endorser.

Although a variety of factors influence responses to athlete misdeeds, including intentionality (Sato, Ko, Park, & Tao, 2015) and locale (i.e., off-field versus on-field, see Sassenberg, 2015), research by Lee and his colleagues reveals that fans' **moral reasoning strategies** play a particularly important role (Lee, Kwak, & Braunstein-Minkove, 2016; Lee, Kwak, & Moore, 2015). Specifically, responses are impacted by the type of moral reasoning strategy utilized in response to the athlete's problematic behavior. Three moral reasoning strategies employed by fans are: **moral rationalization, moral decoupling,** and **moral coupling** (Bhattacharjee, Berman, & Reed, 2013). Descriptions of these strategies are found in Table 3.5.

Lee et al. (2015) primed participants in a manner consistent with one of the moral reasoning strategies. Respondents then read and reacted to a scenario describing a successful athlete whose career had been tainted by a tax-evasion scandal. The athlete was rated on a variety of dimensions such as attractiveness and trustworthiness. The results indicated that the moral reasoning strategies had a powerful impact on the participants' evaluations of the athlete. Specifically, ratings of the athlete were particularly negative when participants had adopted (via priming) a moral coupling approach. That is, when participants were less able to separate the athlete from the transgression, they were more critical of

TABLE 3.5 Moral Reasoning Strategies That May Be Used in Response to Athlete Transgressions

Strategy	Description	Sport Example
Moral rationalization	Evaluating immoral actions as less immoral; often involves justifying the actions or placing the blame on others	"Athletes can sometimes be excused from their immoral actions because they are under a great deal of pressure."
Moral decoupling	Separating the act from the actor; often involves criticizing the immoral behavior while simultaneously praising performance	"Fans should separate an athlete's off-field behaviors when judging his or her performance; rating should be based solely on how he or she plays."
Moral coupling	Difficulty in the justification (i.e., moral rationalization) or separation (i.e., moral coupling) of immoral act; likely results in attitudes toward transgressor	"Fans should consider an athlete's off-field actions when assessing their value and performance."

this person. In a second study, Lee et al. (2015) allowed participants to select their own moral reasoning strategy. The findings indicated that when an athlete's transgression was not related to his or her on-field performance, people tend to choose a decoupling (i.e., separating) moral approach to understanding the situation. Conversely, when the transgression was relevant to the athlete's on-field actions, individuals tended to choose either a moral coupling or rationalization strategy.

Lee and his associates further extended our understating of the impact of one's moral reasoning strategy in responses to athlete transgressions by examining the role of athlete identification (Lee et al., 2016). In this investigation, the authors utilized a real-life scandal involving NFL player Ray Rice (Rice had physically assaulted his fiancée). Participants completed an assessment of their estimated identification with Rice prior to the incident and were then exposed to a videotape of the assault. They then reported their emotional reactions to the images shown, their moral reasoning strategies, and their attitudes toward the transgressor. The results indicated that higher levels of identification with Rice were associated with fewer negative emotions about the event as "sport fans' identification functions as a suppressor in avoiding the expression of negative moral emotions" (Lee et al., 2016, p. 186). As a result, highly identified persons were able to select moral reasoning strategies that separated the athlete from the action (i.e., decoupling and rationalization). These strategies, in turn, helped fans with a strong attachment to the player to be more forgiving of the player's transgression and maintain a positive evaluation of the athlete.

Some Final Thoughts

One of the important takeaway points from this chapter is that sport fans can and do connect with a variety of sport objects. Although we are not quite sure which object may have the most influence on sport fans, if we had to choose, team identification would get both of our votes. But the truth is, we are still just learning about fans' attachment to all things sport, and, as a result, there are many interesting questions left to answer. For example, what is the impact of having connections with multiple objects? That is, are there differences between fans who simply connect with a team and those who feel an attachment to both a team and a star player on that team? What about connections to multiple teams in the same league? Or connections to players who perform for a rival team? Also, does forming a connection with one sport object lead to connections with other objects? For example, team identification may impact the other connections fans form. Heere and James (2007) address this idea in their work on group identification, explaining how attachment with a group such as a sport team may influence identification with other groups (e.g., university identification, city identification). As you can see, researchers should remain quite busy over the next few decades uncovering the impact of sport connections on fan affect, behavior, and cognition.

And finally, it warrants mention that forming attachments with a player can be risky in today's sport landscape given the large amount of player movement from team to team. That is, fans who establish a strong connection with a player for a favorite team may soon find that player on a different team. In fact, it is not unheard of for players to sign a new contract with a rival team (e.g., members of the Boston Red Sox who have chosen to play for the New York Yankees, and vice versa). Perhaps fans will eventually tire of identifying with a player only to have to root against that person in subsequent seasons. Ultimately, as the classic Jerry Seinfeld joke states, fans may end up cheering for uniforms rather than players in them. Research on player attachment should continue to investigate fan connections to athletes and, in particular, examine how player movement impacts the processes of connections and hero worship among fans.

CHAPTER 4

Motivation and Sport Fandom

When thinking about sport fans, an important question we should be asking is "Why are people interested in sport generally and sport teams more specifically?" Or, in the context of the PCM, "Why do people form psychological connections with sport objects?" Trail and James (2015) write about needs, values, and goals as drivers of sport consumer behavior, providing part of an answer to these "why" questions. They note that there are a variety of variables sport researchers have studied that are believed to help explain the connection people form with sport objects. We typically refer to these variables as **motives**, and although they likely could also be characterized as needs, values, or goals, we will continue to describe them as motives to remain consistent with the extensive literature on this topic.

In his chapter "The Motives of Sports Fans," Sloan (1989) described five categories of theories thought to be related to sport motivation: **salubrious effect** theories (those focused on pleasure and well-being), **stress and stimulation seeking** approaches (those related to the desire to experience positive stress or "eustress"), theories of **catharsis and aggression** (the reduction of stress through aggression), **entertainment** theories (approaches involving a desire for aesthetically pleasing experiences), and **achievement seeking** (those concerning a desire for prestige through victory). Although other approaches to sport fan motivation can be found (e.g., McDonald, Milne, & Hong, 2002; Sack, Singh, & DiPaola, 2009), Sloan's writing served as the foundation for the majority of work on fan motivation (e.g., Funk, Mahony, & Ridinger, 2002; Trail & James, 2001; Wann, 1995).

Common Sport Fan Motives

Trail and James (2015) reported that over 40 different motives have been included in the study of sport fan motivation. Although this is an impressive figure, it may be an underestimate. In truth, an entire book could be devoted just to the motives that influence a person's interest in sport fandom. However, our goal is not to provide an exhaustive treatise on all possible fan motives. We have focused instead on what are likely the eight most commonly investigated factors. Although there is some variation in labeling among different authors, these motives are commonly referred to as group affiliation, family, aesthetic, self-esteem, eustress, acquisition of knowledge, escape, and entertainment (a brief description of each can be found in Table 4.1). Our selection of these motives was based on their frequent inclusion in literature, and, as you will read later in this chapter, each of these factors has been incorporated into standard measures assessing fan motivation.

When reviewing research pertaining to sport fan motivation, it becomes readily apparent that a large volume of work examines this topic. In fact, a simple Google search for scholarly articles using the phrase "sport fan motives" produced almost 40,000 hits. Although we do not believe there are 40,000 discrete scholarly works, it is reasonable to conclude there has been, and still is, substantial interest in the study of sport fan motives. A key factor leading to this large volume of work is that fans of different sports exhibit differential motivational profiles (Wann, Grieve, Zapalac, & Pease, 2008). That is, researchers have examined how different motives can drive the interest of fans of different sports.

TABLE 4.1 The Eight Motives Included in the SFMS, MSSC, and/or the SII

Motive	Description
Group affiliation (social interaction; socialization)	Individual is motivated to consume sport because doing so provides an opportunity to spend time with others.
Family (bonding with family)	Individual is motivated to consume sport because doing so provides an opportunity to spend time with family members.
Aesthetic	Individual is motivated to consume sport because doing so provides an opportunity to enjoy the artistic beauty and grace of sport movements.
Self-esteem (achievement; vicarious achievement)	Individual is motivated to consume sport because doing so provides an opportunity to feel better about oneself through association with the success of others (e.g., an athlete or sport team).
Eustress (drama)	Individual is motivated to consume sport because doing so provides an opportunity to enjoy the excitement and arousal felt while consuming, particularly in relation to the excitement and uncertainty of outcome associated with sporting events.
Acquisition of knowledge (sport knowledge)	Individual is motivated to consume sport because doing so provides an opportunity to satisfy a desire to gain knowledge.
Escape	Individual is motivated to consume sport because doing so provides a diversion from the rest of his or her life.
Entertainment	Individual is motivated to consume sport because doing so provides an opportunity to be engaged in an enjoyable pastime.

In fact, researchers have investigated the motives of fans of traditional sports such as football, baseball, basketball, and ice hockey, as well as college-level, minor league, and women's sports. Researchers have even investigated the profiles for fan involvement in fantasy sports (e.g., Billings & Ruihley, 2013; Lee, Seo, & Green, 2013; Spinda, Wann, & Sollitto, 2012), use of sport-related mobile phone applications, (Kang, Ha, & Hambrick, 2015), consumption of sport online (Seo & Green, 2008), and communication via Facebook (Stavros, Meng, Westberg, & Farrelly, 2014). To make matters even more complicated, persons from different demographic groups often report different motivational profiles (e.g., Armstrong, 2002b; Bilyeu & Wann, 2002; James, Fujimoto, Ross, & Matsuoka, 2009; Ridinger & Funk, 2006). For example, female fans are more likely than male fans to be motivated by the opportunity to spend time with family, while males report higher levels of aesthetic, self-esteem, and eustress motivation (Wann, Schrader, & Wilson, 1999). To describe and explain the motivational profiles for each sport and demographic group would be a truly monumental task, one far beyond the scope of this chapter. However, to give the reader a sense of the breadth of this literature, several examples of sport-specific studies can be found in Table 4.2. This is by no means an exhaustive list; rather, it simply portrays the vast amount of work done.

TABLE 4.2 A Sample of Sport-Specific Investigations of Sport Fan Motivation

Focus	Reference
Minor league hockey	Andrew, Koo, Hardin, and Greenwell (2009)
Mixed martial arts	Kim, Greenwell, Andrew, Lee, and Mahony (2008)
Women's professional basketball	Funk, Ridinger, and Moorman (2003)
Women's professional tennis	Sack, Singh, and DiPaola (2009)
Professional baseball	Hong, McDonald, Yoon, and Fujimoto (2005)
Professional wrestling	Ashley, Dollar, Wigley, Gillentine, and Daughtrey (2000)
NASCAR racing	Roy, Goss, and Jubenville (2010)
Ski jumping	Mehus (2005)
College baseball	Allen, Drane, and Byon (2010)
College football	Pan and Baker (2005)
College basketball	Ridinger and Funk (2006)
College hockey	Ferreira and Armstrong (2004)
College wheelchair basketball	Cottingham, Phillips, Hall, Gearity, and Carroll (2014)
College wrestling	Cooper (2011)
Soccer	Correia and Esteves (2007)

Returning to our discussion of the eight common motives, we can now provide information about each. Remember, these are not the only motives of sport fans to consider. We have focused on the eight motives listed in Table 4.1 because they are included in the primary scales used by researchers to assess the motives of sport fans. After presenting information about these motives, we will turn our attention to the scales that have been used most often to study the motives of sport fans.

The Group Affiliation Motive

Sport fandom is a social activity. Whether it occurs at home, a restaurant, a bar, or the arena, sport tends to be consumed in a group environment. For instance, Schurr and his colleagues (Schurr et al., 1985, 1988) found that greater than 95 percent of spectators attending college basketball games purchased tickets next to friends. For some individuals, it is precisely the social nature of sport fandom they find attractive. Such people are driven by the **group** affiliation motive, that is, a desire to spend time with others in a fan environment (Guttmann, 1986; Kelley & Tian, 2004; Melnick, 1993; Sloan, 1989). Humans are social beings, a fact reflected in a number of classic theories of motivation (Alderfer, 1972; Fromm, 1941; Maslow, 1970). As noted in Chapter 1, sport fandom can help fulfill the basic human need for social interaction by providing a sense of belonging. The fact that most spectators consume sport as a member of a social group illustrates that fans do indeed use sport fandom to satisfy social interaction needs.

The Family Motive

The **family** motive concerns involvement as a sport fan because it provides an opportunity to spend time with family members (Evaggelinou & Grekinis, 1998; Gantz & Wenner, 1995; Guttmann, 1986; Weiller & Higgs, 1997). As one would expect, this motive is particularly common among fans that have children and/or are married (Wann, Lane, Duncan, & Goodson, 1998). Given this, it had been suggested that fans with high levels of family motivation may have a preference for nonaggressive sports, preferring not to expose their children or spouse to violent events (Wann et al., 1999). However, a series of studies failed to confirm a relationship between levels of family motivation and a desire to avoid aggressive sports (Wann & Ensor, 2001; Wann et al., 1998; Wann et al., 1999). Thus, it appears that persons motivated by a desire to follow sport to be with family members are just as likely to enjoy aggressive and combative sports as competitions that are nonviolent in nature.

The Aesthetic Motive

Another factor that can drive an individual's interest in sport fandom is enjoyment of the beauty and grace of sport movements. This factor is commonly referred to as the **aesthetic** motive (Guttmann, 1996; Hemphill, 1995; Rinehart,

Many Persons Are Driven to Sport Fandom Because the Activity Provides an Opportunity to Spend Time With Family

1996; Sloan, 1989). Stylistic sports such as figure skating, diving, and gymnastics are attractive to many fans because of their inherent beauty and the artistic expressions of athletes. However, it is important to note that the aesthetic motive is not limited to fans of stylistic sports (Sargent et al., 1998). Rather, persons interested in all sports may possess a high level of aesthetic motivation.

Similar to work on the family motive, investigators have examined the relationship between preferences for violent sports and aesthetic motivation. Wann and his collaborators (1999) suggested that fans with a high level of aesthetic motivation might prefer nonaggressive sports because the actions found in aggressive sports may "inhibit the graceful execution of sport movements" (p. 122) (e.g., hockey "goons" whose sole purpose is to disrupt the graceful flow of the other team's swifter and more athletic skaters). Wann and Wilson (1999) conducted a pair of studies designed to test this possibility. In the first study, participants completed questionnaires assessing their level of aesthetic motivation and the degree to which they enjoyed watching seven aggressive sports. Interestingly, and contrary to expectations, no significant relationships were found between the level of aesthetic motivation and enjoyment of the aggressive sports. In the second study, after completing an inventory assessing their aesthetic motivation, participants watched five violent football plays, rating their enjoyment of each. Surprisingly, there was no relationship between aesthetic motivation and enjoyment of the violent plays. Thus, it appears that sport fans who are motivated by the beauty and grace of sport enjoy both violent and nonviolent athletic events.

The Self-Esteem Motive

A fourth sport fan motive is **self-esteem** enhancement (Gmelch & San Antonio, 1998; Sloan, 1989; Weiller & Higgs, 1997; Wenner & Gantz, 1989). This motive concerns an individual's desire to participate in sport fandom because it provides a boost to the fans' self-concept. For instance, when a team is victorious, fans frequently join the players in a celebration of their achievement. Indeed, fans often increase their association with teams subsequent to successful performances in order to bask in the team's accomplishments and boost their own self-esteem (Cialdini et al., 1976).

The Eustress Motive

Several theorists have suggested that individuals fail to receive a sufficient amount of stimulation in their everyday lives (e.g., Elias & Dunning, 1970; Klapp, 1972; McNeil, 1968; Zuckerman, 1984). Consequently, people seek out other opportunities to gain excitement. One such opportunity can be sport fandom. For example, in one of the earliest observations of sport fans, Brill (1929, p. 434) stated,

> The life of man in America or in any of the industrialized countries today, laboring on the farm, in the factory, in the office, is not the natural life of man. He is still an animal formed for battle and conquest, for blows and strokes and swiftness, for triumph and applause. But let him join the crowd around the diamond, the gridiron, the tennis court or the ring. . . . Let him identify himself with his favorite fighter, player or team. . . . He will achieve exaltation, vicarious but real.

Brill's statement suggests that even though life often fails to meet our desire for excitement and stimulation, these needs can be partially fulfilled through sport fandom. Persons who participate in sport fandom to gain excitement and stimulation are motivated by **eustress** (Gantz, 1981; Gantz & Wenner, 1995; Sloan, 1989; Smith, 1988). Eustress refers to positive forms of arousal and stimulation (i.e., euphoria + stress). Fans motivated by a desire to experience high levels of eustress become involved with the pastime because they enjoy the excitement and arousal they experience by following sport.

It is important to note that although fans usually view the suspense of sport spectating as pleasurable (Bryant, Rockwell, & Owens, 1994; Schreyer, Schmidt, & Torgler, in press), these stressful reactions are not always positive. Some fans may not enjoy the anxiety associated with sport spectating and go to great lengths to avoid this anxious state. For these fans, the stress they experience watching their favorite team compete should be referred to as distress (i.e., negative stress). However, one of the advantages of sport fandom is that it is a voluntary activity. Fans who become uncomfortably aroused and excited (i.e., distressed) while watching a favorite team compete can simply remove themselves from the situation (e.g., leave their seat at the arena, turn off the television, etc.; cf., Eastman & Riggs, 1994).

The Acquisition of Knowledge Motive

Smith (1988) noted that many sport fans find great pleasure in reading box scores and examining statistics. For these persons, it is likely that much of the attraction of fandom involves the acquisition of knowledge about sport objects. This **acquisition of knowledge** is another sport fan motive. Trail, Anderson, and Fink (2005) noted that knowledge is acquired through various means, including social interaction and media consumption. For sport fans, this could include attending sporting events; reading about a sport, team, or player; or talking with others and sharing information. Trail and James (2015) explain that fans may desire sport-related knowledge so they can talk with others in situations where sport is the topic of conversation. Others may seek out sport knowledge as a way of taking a break from their daily routine by immersing themselves in the strategy of a game or becoming an expert in the statistics of a particular athlete or team. The latter notion is also associated with esteem enhancement; being perceived as one who is knowledgeable about a sport, team, and/or player can be a status symbol and perhaps confirm one's place as a true fan. In fact, as you will read in Chapter 10, it is important for fans to be accepted into their fan groups, and they may feel threatened when other fans do not accept them as supporters of the team.

A particular context for the knowledge motive may be found among fans participating in fantasy sports. Scholars researching both fantasy and daily fantasy sports have included knowledge as a specific motive (Dwyer & Kim, 2011; Spinda & Haridakis, 2008). For example, Suh, Lim, Kwak, and Pedersen (2010) reported that the acquisition of knowledge was one of the more influential drives of fantasy sport consumption. Kota, Reid, James, and Kim (in press) tested a scale to measure motives of daily fantasy sport consumers and found that knowledge was the third-highest-rated motive.

The Escape Motive

The **escape** motive is another popular reason people follow sport (Gantz & Wenner, 1995; Krohn, Clarke, Preston, McDonald, & Preston, 1998; Sloan, 1989; Smith, 1988). Sport fans participate in the activity because it provides a diversion. Individuals who seek a break from their home life, work, college experience, and so on are able to temporarily forget their troubles through sport fandom. The escape motive may be particularly prevalent during personally difficult and/or stressful times such as war or a natural disaster (Wann, 1997). For instance, President Roosevelt's decision to allow professional baseball to continue during World War II was an effort to provide an escape for North Americans. In explaining his decision, Roosevelt stated that Americans "ought to have a chance for recreation and for taking their minds off their work" (see McGuire, 1994, p. 66).

Although it is clear that sport fans use the pastime as an escape, one might wonder what it is about their lives they are attempting to escape. Sloan (1989) argued that sport could provide "an escape from work and the other tediums of life" (p. 183). Smith (1988) concurred, writing that "the search for excitement represents one of the most familiar means of escape" (p. 58). These statements suggest that individuals use fandom to escape from their under-stimulating (i.e., boring) lives. However, Heinegg (1985) argued that sport serves as "a flight from the pain of existence" and "worldly cares and crises" (p. 457). This perspective implies that sport fans use the pastime as an escape from their over-stimulating lives. Thus, it seems that fans can use sport as an escape from both over-stimulation and under-stimulation. For instance, consider two fans who meet at a bar each week to watch Monday Night Football. Although both may view the game as an opportunity to escape their daily routines, the reasons behind their desire for a diversion may differ. It could be that one individual is a police officer who considers her life very stressful, and thus she views the game as an **escape from over-stimulation.** Meanwhile, the other person works on an assembly line and finds her job extremely boring. She perceives the game as an opportunity to **escape from under-stimulation.**

Wann, Allen, and Rochelle (2004) attempted to determine if fans utilize sport as an escape from over- or under-stimulation. Participants completed scales assessing the extent to which they believed their life was stressful and boring as well as items assessing their level of escape motivation. Wann and his associates found positive relationships between level of escape motivation and perceptions of life both as boring and as stressful. That is, those who felt their life was stressful *and* those who believed their life was boring both reported using sport fandom as an escape. These findings substantiate the notion that fandom can and is used as a diversion from both over-stimulation and under-stimulation.

The Entertainment Motive

Social scientists (and, in particular, psychologists) have a tendency to overanalyze human activity. This can also be the case with the motives of sport fans. Yes, fans are often motivated by the factors described above. However, if you ask a fan "Why do you follow sport?", the most likely responses would be something along the lines of "I like it" or "It's fun." Thus, it is not surprising that many individuals are driven to sport fandom by the **entertainment** motive (Gantz & Wenner, 1995; Sloan, 1989; Smith, 1988). Here, one's motivation to engage in sport fandom is similar to other recreational pursuits (e.g., going to the theater, watching television, listening to music); individuals participate in the activity because they have fun doing it.

Measuring Sport Fan Motives

One of the takeaway points from the preceding sections is that sport fans are driven by a variety of motives. Accordingly, researchers usually assess multiple motives when conducting their research. Although there are now many different scales that may be used when studying sport fan motivation, this was not always the case. In fact, when the first edition of this text was published in 2001, there was only one primary scale, the Sport Fan Motivation Scale (Wann, 1995). Since the publication of the first edition of this text, other scales have been developed.

There has been a substantial amount of work dealing with the accurate measurement of sport fan (or sport consumer) motives in the last two decades (e.g., Funk, Mahony, Nakazawa, & Hirakawa, 2001; Trail & James, 2001; Wann, 1995). The focus of such work has been first to identify particular motives, then to develop tools (i.e., scales) to measure these motives. An extension of the scale development work has been the application of the measures to various sport fan settings. Certainly, a key reason to study motives is to acquire a better understanding of why people are interested in sport fandom and how this information could be useful to sport marketers (e.g., the various motives likely influence attendance decisions). In the following sections, we address the development of tools to measure sport fan motives. This examination includes a critical inspection of the scales and a summary of the current state of assessment of sport fan motivation. Implications from the study of sport fan motives are presented in Chapter 5.

Scale Development

Although Sloan (1989) set the stage by identifying and testing theories thought to impact sport fan motivation, he did not develop or present measures of specific motives. However, several other scholars have taken the initiative to develop such scales. It is beyond the scope of this chapter to examine every tool developed to assess fan motives. Rather, we have chosen to focus on three instruments that have been utilized extensively in the sport psychology, sport sociology, and sport marketing/management literatures.

The first measure, the Sport Fan Motivation Scale (SFMS), was developed by Wann and published in 1995. The next scale developed to measure sport fan motives was published by Trail and James (2001), an instrument they labeled the Motivation Scale for Sport Consumption (MSSC). Working at the same time as Trail and James (2001), Funk and his colleagues (2001) developed the Sport Interest Inventory (SII). In short order the SII was modified by Funk and his colleagues (2002) and then again by Funk et al. (2003). The latter effort resulted in a scale with 18 motives. The SFMS and MSSC assessed eight and nine motive constructs, respectively. Table 4.3 contains a listing of the motives from these scales.

It is important to note that the information included in Table 4.3 reflects the *original* work reported by Wann (1995) and Trail and James (2001) and the *revised* work from Funk et al. (2003). The original version of the SII only included ten factors (see note in Table 4.3). It should also be recognized that some motives capture the same idea but were labeled differently. For example, the notion that a sport fan is motivated by opportunities to spend time with others was labeled group affiliation by Wann (1995), social interaction by Trail and James (2001), and socialization by Funk et al. (2003). This illustrates one of the challenges within the study of sport fan motives, namely, that different scholars have used different labels to examine the same construct.

Another challenge to consider is whether one is interested in studying motives that are applicable across multiple sports or, rather, in determining if there are motives unique to a particular sport. An example of the latter would be support

TABLE 4.3 Comparison of Sport Fan Motivation Scales

Sport Fan Motivation Scale	Motivation Scale for Sport Consumption	Sport Interest Inventory
Self-Esteem	Achievement	*Vicarious Achievement*
Aesthetics	Aesthetics	*Aesthetics*
Escape	Escape	Escape
Group Affiliation	Social Interaction	Socialization
Family	Family	Bonding with Family
Entertainment		Entertainment
Eustress	Drama	*Drama*
	Acquisition of Knowledge	Sport Knowledge
Economic		
	Physical Attraction	
	Physical Skill	
		Interest in Player(s)
		Interest in Team
		Interest in Sport
		Role Model
		Bonding with Friends
		Excitement
		Wholesome Environment
		Community Support
		Support Women's Opportunity
		Customer Service

Notes: Italicized subscales were included in the original Sport Interest Inventory (Funk et al., 2001), along with *National Pride* and *Social Opportunities*. *Interest in Team* was labeled *Team Identification* in the original Sport Interest Inventory.

for women's opportunities as a motive for watching or attending a women's sporting event (Funk et al., 2003). Another example is physical attraction, that is, being motivated to watch particular athletes because of their physical appeal (Trail & James, 2001). Additionally, researchers may be interested in identifying motives that differentiate groups (e.g., men and women, fans in different age categories). For example, James (2002) reported that male consumers of college basketball enjoyed games to a greater extent than females because of their knowledge of basketball (e.g., the technical aspects and rules of the game). The point being made here is that when studying sport fan motivation, it is important to define the objectives or purpose of such work and to consider which scale(s) one should use to best meet the research goals.

Critiques of Existing Scales

Sport Fan Motivation Scale (SFMS) Trail and James (2001) raised concerns regarding the content validity of the SFMS. First, there were concerns about the lack of information about how the individual scale items were generated. A second criticism of the SFMS was the use of labels that may not accurately represent the items comprising a particular factor. For instance, Trail and James noted the use of "economics" as a label for items pertaining to betting or wagering on sports. A third and perhaps most pressing concern involving content validity was the wording of some of the SFMS items. As an example, Trail and James (2001) refer to the item reading "One of the main reasons that I watch, read, and/or discuss sports is that I get pumped up when I am watching my favorite teams." Note the inclusion of "watch, read, and/or discuss" along with the phrase "get pumped up when I am watching my favorite teams." Do fans watch games because they get "pumped up" when watching? That could be, but do they read to get "pumped up" when watching? Trail and James argued that the mixing of the two behaviors is awkward and potentially confusing. As a result, attempts to predict fan behavior might be difficult because it would be unclear what element was driving a particular action.

Motivation Scale for Sport Consumption (MSSC) The MSSC (Trail & James, 2001) was presented in an effort to improve on previous measures of sport fan motivation. In contrast to the concerns noted in their review of the SFMS (and other scales), Trail and James did report evidence of validity (construct, convergent, discriminant, and predictive validity).

Although there was reasonable evidence to support the MSSC, there were concerns with the scale (Trail & James, 2001). For example, some items did not reach statistical standards (i.e., psychometric cutoffs) for inclusion in a subscale. However, the individual item loadings did not result in substantive decline in other indicators. For example, the psychometrics for most subscales exceeded recommended cutoff levels (e.g., average variance extracted scores and reliability estimates). Also, as Trail and James (2001) noted, there appeared to be problems with the family subscale, as the psychometric indicators were below recommended levels, raising concerns about the validity and reliability for this subscale. Although the overall performance of the MSSC in the initial reporting was promising, Trail and James did indicate there was room for improvement.

A particular concern with the MSSC was the extent to which the items provide an assessment of motives rather than simply one's preferences for various characteristics of sport. For example, consider the items included in the knowledge subscale: "I regularly track the statistics of specific players," "I usually know the team's win/loss record," and "I read the box scores and team statistics regularly." When answering these items, a person is providing a description of her or his sport consumer behavior (e.g., how often he or she reads box scores), but not necessarily information about motivation for following a team. Similarly, examine the items in the achievement subscale: "I feel like I have won when the team wins," "I feel a personal sense of achievement when the team does well," and "I feel proud when the team plays well." When responding to these items, a person is providing information about a psychological and affective response based on a team's performance. Yet the items do not necessarily inform us about the individual's motive to follow or consume a sports team. Just because a fan feels proud when his or her team wins does not mean this experience is *why* they follow the team. A related idea was conveyed by Fink, Trail, and Anderson (2002) regarding the family construct. Spending time with one's family may be a reason influencing the decision to attend a sporting event, but it is unlikely that is the primary motive for sport consumption. In support of their argument, Fink and her colleagues reported the family motive was not significantly related to other sport consumer motives and only weakly related to team identification.

Additional concerns with the MSSC were highlighted in the work of James and Ross (2004) in their study of consumers of three non-revenue collegiate sports (baseball, softball, and wrestling). They concluded the knowledge subscale pertained to existing knowledge about the team/sport rather than as a motive to acquire additional knowledge. They also excluded the aesthetics motive due to its similarity to the physical skill motive and the high correlation between the two reported by Trail and James (2001).

Sport Interest Inventory (SII) The Sport Interest Inventory (SII; Funk et al., 2001) was developed at roughly the same time as the MSSC. The SII was initially developed to measure motivational factors associated with soccer spectators. The authors noted that although there were existing scales to measure sport fan motives, "one motivational scale for all sport events may not be possible" (p. 7). Noting that no existing scale (e.g., SFMS, MSSC) was universally accepted by sport scholars at that time, Funk and his colleagues tested ten motives purported to explain interest in attending the 1999 FIFA Women's World Cup. Although the authors argued that there may not be one motivational scale applicable to all sport situations, nine of the factors they tested were consistent with previous studies of sport fan motivation. The one unique factor they included was support for women's opportunities in sport.

The original project testing the SII included a comments section for respondents. After reviewing the comments, Funk et al. (2001) concluded that four additional motives should be considered: players as role models, entertainment value, bonding with family, and wholesome environment. Subsequently, Funk et al. (2002) "attempted to confirm and extend the Sport Interest Inventory by examining the level of continued interest in the U.S. Women's team subsequent to 1999 Women's World Cup" (p. 35). Their work included the original ten SII motives and the four additional factors derived from the participants' open-ended comments.

Reporting on the performance of the revised SII, Funk et al. (2002) noted low internal consistency for the socialization factor (also referred to as social opportunities). Overall, however, Funk and his associates reported satisfactory evidence of reliability and validity for the new 14-factor SII. However, there were still some potential concerns with the second generation of the SII. When reporting on how well a scale may "work," evidence of validity is critical; scale developers must demonstrate that items believed to assess a specific construct do actually measure said construct. For example, Funk et al. (2002) have items purported to measure national pride. Evidence of validity would include information that the items fit together and collectively do in fact assess national pride as a sport fan motive. Scholars typically provide evidence of validity for each specific motive. Curiously, Funk et al. provided information about all 14 factors as a group rather than reporting evidence of validity for each specific motive. Given that each motive is supposedly discrete, each should be evaluated on its own merit.

Perhaps as an acknowledgement of concerns with the second generation of the SII, a third effort was undertaken by Funk et al. (2003) to further develop the SII. A key point noted by Funk and his colleagues (2003) was that previous scales had been developed as comprehensive instruments for use across sports. They suggested that more attention was needed for contextual motives, that is, motives specific to particular sports. Funk and his fellow investigators sought to extend the SII by adding yet another four factors, bringing the total to 18. That is, in addition to testing the 14 factors from the second version of the SII (Funk et al., 2002), Funk et al. (2003) included four new factors based on responses from focus groups. The additional factors were: bonding with friends, knowledge of the sport, escape, and customer service. It is interesting to note that bonding with friends, knowledge, and escape are motives (or variations of such) that are included in the SFMS and/or the MSSC.

Funk and his coauthors (2003) tested the newest iteration of the SII with season ticket holders and those attending single games in the Women's National Basketball Association. The internal consistency measures for the third generation of the SII were all above recommended levels, providing evidence of reliability. There was also evidence of validity for each motive factor. Considering the information reported, there was reasonable evidence of reliability and validity for the third generation of the SII.

Summarizing the SFMS, MSSC, and SII At this point, someone interested in assessing sport fan motives may be wondering, "So which scale should I use?" Ultimately, what we have at our disposal are three different measures of sport fan motives, each with strengths and weaknesses. There is a great deal of overlap in the motives included in each scale, as well as motives that are unique to each instrument. Although certainly not an exhaustive list, the entries included in Table 4.4 demonstrate that each scale has been used in numerous studies of sport fan motives. They have been used in multiple settings, with student and sport consumer samples, and within the United States and in other countries. In some instances, the original scales have been used to develop other specialty scales. For example, Cottingham et al. (2014) modified the MSSC to form the Motivation Scale for Disability Sport Consumption.

Given the convoluted state of the measurement of sport fan motivation, one might wonder if the study of sport fan motivation could be simplified. As it turns out, the authors of the scales critiqued above (along with some additional colleagues) thought this might be possible. In the next section, we present our efforts to simplify the assessment of sport fan motivation.

TABLE 4.4 Examples of Research Utilizing the SFMS, MSSC, and the SII

Sport Fan Motivation Scale (SFMS)		Motivation Scale for Sport Consumption (MSSC)		Sport Interest Inventory (SII)	
Author(s)	**Title**	**Author(s)**	**Title**	**Author(s)**	**Title**
Wann et al. (2004)	Using Sex and Gender Role Orientation to Predict Level of Fandom	James and Ross (2004)	Comparing Sport Consumer Motivations Across Multiple Sports	Funk, Ridinger, and Moorman (2003)	Exploring Origins of Involvement: Understanding the Relationship Between Consumer Motives and Involvement with Professional Sport Teams
Madrigal (2006)	Measuring the Multi-Dimensional Nature of Sporting Event Performance Consumption	Ozer and Argan (2006)	Licensed Team Merchandise Buying Behavior: A Study on Turkish Fans	Neal and Funk (2006)	Investigating Motivation, Attitudinal Loyalty, and Attendance Behavior with Fans of Australian Football
Wann et al. (2008)	Motivational Profiles of Sport Fans of Different Sports	Lee, Trail, and Anderson (2008)	Differences in Motives and Points of Attachment by Season Ticket Status: A Case Study of ACHA	Wang, Zhang, and Tsuji (2011)	Examining Fan Motives and Loyalty for the Chinese Professional Baseball League of Taiwan
Theodorakis, Wann, Carvalho, and Sarmento (2010)	Translation and Initial Validation of the Portuguese Version of the Sport Spectator Identification Scale	James et al. (2009)	Motives of United States and Japanese Professional Baseball Consumers and Level of Team Identification	Wang and Matsuoka (2014)	Motives of Sport Spectators in China: A Case Study of the Chinese Super League

Lee, Shin, and Shinchi (2010)	Identifying Sociological Motivation of Hispanic/Latino Consumers Attending Sporting Events	Uhlman and Trail (2012)	An Analysis of the Motivators of Seattle Sounders FC Season Ticket Holders: A Case Study	Kang, Lee, and Bennett (2014)	Comparative Analysis of Sport Consumer Motivation Affecting Sport Consumption Behavior Between American and Asian International Students
Wiid and Cant (2015)	Sport Fan Motivation: Are You Going to the Game?	Cottingham et al. (2014)	Development and Validation of the Motivation Scale for Disability Sport Consumption	Gargone (2016)	A Study of the Fan Motives for Varying Levels of Team Identity and Team Loyalty of College Football Fans
Cohen (2017)	Fans' Identification with Teams: A Field Study of Israeli Soccer Fans	Monfarde, Tojari, and Nikbakhsh (2014)	Constraints and Motivators of Sport Consumption Behavior		

The Big 5

James, Trail, Wann, Zhang, and Funk (2006) reported on a project to determine whether the vast array of sport fan motives could be narrowed down to a more manageable number. Specifically, these authors sought to identify a core set of motives that would be small enough as to not require hours to complete when included in a questionnaire. It would be a daunting task to complete a scale that assessed 40 different motives. As Trail and James (2015, p. 194) noted:

> If we were very conservative and used three separate items (or questions) to represent each motive (trust us, we should have at least 3 questions per motive), the number of questions just testing the motives would be 120. That is before we add any other questions about demographic characteristics, attitudes, behavioral intentions, or whatever other topics in which we are interested.

People, particularly those in applied settings, are often reluctant to complete even the shortest of surveys. Given this, imagine how difficult it would be to convince them to answer a questionnaire that had hundreds of questions.

James et al. (2006) explained there was a need to bring parsimony to the study of sport fan motives. They highlighted three particular concerns inherent in having different sport fan motivation scales: the need for consistent wording of items; the need for consistent labels for the motives; and the ability to establish a core set of motive factors to recommend for use across multiple sports. In short, their project was an effort to offer "best practices" advice for the assessment and study of sport fan motivation.

In their work, James and his colleagues (2006) utilized the primary sport fan motive scales highlighted above (i.e., SFMS, MSSC, SII) as well as one additional instrument, the Spectator Motivation Scale (SMS; Pease & Zhang, 2001). They included motives that were assessed in two or more scales (some had different labels but represented the same construct). The researchers did not include factors that were end states (e.g., "I am a fan of the entire team") or interest variables (e.g., "I am a huge fan of soccer in general"). Furthermore, they omitted motives that were not applicable across a broad range of sports or sport consumers (e.g., economics/sport wagering, support women's opportunities). As a result, the researchers tested 34 sport fan motives (yes, the protocol packet was quite lengthy).

Questionnaires were administered to a sample of over 900 people. Through a series of psychometric tests and data analysis procedures (e.g., exploratory factor analysis to determine which items best fit together), five sport fan motives emerged: achievement seeking, aesthetics, drama, escape, and social interaction. The factors were referred to as **The Big 5**. The group completed two additional projects to provide evidence of the reliability and validity of The Big 5. The number of items for each factor was reduced to three, resulting in five motives represented by three items for each factor. Table 4.5 shows the wording of the individual items (all taken from the final project).

A concern with the wording of items in previous scales was a source of difficulty in assessing the relationship between motives and sport fan behaviors,

TABLE 4.5 The "Big 5" Sport Fan Motives

Please rate the extent to which you Disagree or Agree with each item below.

Think of each statement beginning, "I would be motivated to *watch a New England Patriots'* game because . . ."

Escape
. . . of the distraction that a game provided from my everyday activities.
. . . it provides me with a distraction from my daily life for a while.
. . . I could get away from the tension in my life.

Vicarious Achievement
. . . their successes are my successes and their losses are my losses.
. . . I feel like I have won when the team wins.
. . . I feel a personal sense of victory when the team wins.

Social Interaction
. . . of the opportunity to interact with other people.
. . . of the possibility of talking with other people.
. . . of the chance to socialize with others.

Aesthetics
. . . of the natural elegance of the game.
. . . of the gracefulness associated with the game.
. . . of the beauty and grace of sports.

Drama
. . . of the uncertainty of a close game.
. . . I like games where the outcome is uncertain.
. . . a close game between two teams is more enjoyable than a blowout.

psychological conditions, and other outcomes. As a solution to this problem, James et al. (2006) incorporated general wording in The Big 5 items. Such a strategy would allow The Big 5 to be used with multiple sports and settings and should avoid problems with assessing motives and their relationship to other constructs. As a second approach to solving this issue, the authors included a leading statement as part of the instructions so the wording of items could be more general (see Table 4.5). An additional advantage of using the leading statement is that researchers can specify that the items are assessing motives that pertain to a specific behavior or outcome, for example motives for attending a sporting event. As shown in Table 4.5, respondents were asked to think about the leading statement "I would be motivated to watch a New England Patriots' game because . . ." A different leading statement could be used to assess other behaviors such as attending games, talking about games, or wearing team merchandise. For researchers, such an approach aids their efforts to more accurately assess sport fan motives but does require *a priori* planning as to the type of behavior (or other outcome) that is of interest. Using this type of approach, researchers and sport marketers can simply insert other team names or sport objects as the focal target.

Funk, Filo, Beaton, and Pritchard (2009) completed a project using The Big 5 sport fan motives. Echoing the thoughts of James and his colleagues (2006), Funk and his colleagues stated that a primary reason for the project was to test a parsimonious set of motives in a survey that could be quickly and easily completed. They tested The Big 5 motives, along with a measure of past attendance (the focal behavior) and commitment to the focal team. It warrants mention that they only used two items for each sport fan motive, and they chose to use different labels for the motive factors. There was good evidence of reliability and validity, providing support for the approach for assessing sport fan motives initiated by James and his associates.

Some Final Thoughts

There has been and continues to be considerable interest in the study of sport fan motivation among sport scholars. Although a variety of scales have been developed to measure fan motives, most have their origins in the SFMS, MSSC, and/or SII. There have been concerns noted with each of the three main scales, and those working with the scales have contributed to improving each, providing us with reasonable tools to measure a vast array of fan motives. Even with the concerns noted throughout this chapter, the work completed to date has clearly advanced our understanding of sport fan motivation.

Thinking about future efforts to study sport fan motivation, the research by James and his colleagues (2006) illustrates the type of work needed. Although simply assessing five motives will be insufficient in some research settings, it is clear that inclusion of The Big 5 is warranted. Researchers can then determine additional motives that may be germane to particular sport or team settings that are relevant to their particular investigation. Researchers should also carefully examine the wording of items to avoid confounds with assessing relationships between motives and behavioral outcomes and psychological conditions.

And finally, for readers with a specific interest in sport marketing and sport consumer behavior, sport fan motives are of particular relevance given the volume of research indicating that motives may impact fan intentions and, ultimately, behaviors. In fact, these relationships are explored in more detail in the next chapter.

CHAPTER 5

The Impact of Sport Fandom on Sport Consumption Behavior

In previous chapters, we have discussed a variety of characteristics of sport fans and the responses they exhibit. For instance, people talk about sport, watch sport in person and through media sources, and use sport metaphors, and sporting events greatly impact our lives. We plan activities around watching March Madness, the College Football National Championship, the Super Bowl, and other major sporting events. Furthermore, during periods of crisis, people use sporting events as a means of coming together to experience a sense of "healing" after tragic events. For example, following the events of September 11, 2001, sport was a platform that brought people together, both to share their difficulties and to demonstrate their resolve to move forward. Additionally, the enduring interest people have in sports and teams can help them satisfy their needs for belonging and distinctiveness, and fandom can add meaning to their lives. In other words, an interest in and connections to sport influences what a person does, how they feel, and what they think (about sport, themselves, and the world around them).

At this point you may be thinking, "This is all well and good, but is there anything *practical* we can do with information about sport fans?" In fact, there is! We are referring here to **sport consumer behavior**, a growing sub-discipline and industry, and the focus of the current chapter. **Sport marketers** are professionals and academicians focused on factors that influence sport consumers to select and use particular products. They utilize research and theory to better understand how fans think and act and then put this information to practical use to predict and influence a wide variety of behaviors. A commonly utilized definition of **consumer behavior** is, "The study of individuals, groups, or organizations and the processes they use to select, secure, use, and dispose of products, services, experiences, or ideas to satisfy needs and the impacts that these processes have on the consumer and society" (Hawkins, Best, & Coney, 2004, p. 7). Extending this definition to sport fandom, those studying sport consumer behavior investigate sport-based products, services, experiences, and ideas. Sport consumer behavior involves the examination of the types of actions exhibited by fans as well as the frequency (or intensity) of these behaviors. Examples of sport consumption behavior include watching a sporting event in person (i.e., direct consumption); watching an event through some form of media broadcast (i.e., indirect consumption); reading about a sport, team, or athlete; and wearing team apparel.

Decisions, Decisions: An Introduction to Sport Consumer Behavior

Similar to most social scientific topics, sport consumer behavior is complex, and the decision making and consumption processes can be challenging to understand (Guttmann, 1986; Trail & James, 2015). For instance, consider what is typically involved in a sport consumption event, such as your decision to attend a baseball game. To begin with, there has to be an awareness that the baseball game will occur, and a wide variety of factors can impact this awareness (e.g., media outlets, pocket schedules, phone reminders, texts from friends). Once you are cognizant of the game, there needs to be one or more reasons for wanting to attend. Perhaps you like baseball or one of the teams playing. Or maybe there is some form of incentive (e.g., there is a promotional event at the game) or other influence impacting your attendance decision (e.g., your best friend wants you to attend with her). Assuming you do have an interest in attending, you still have many decisions to consider. How do you get tickets? How much do the

Sport Marketers Investigate Factors That Influence Sport Consumption Behavior to Help Teams and Leagues Increase Attendance and Avoid Empty Seats

tickets cost, and is the price worth it? When is the game being played, and do you have other commitments at that time? How will you get there, and where will you park? Should you eat at the ballpark? Can you stay for the entire game?

Personal Investment Theory

Are you starting to get the point? Sport consumer behavior involves a great many decisions. In the first edition of this text, we used **Personal Investment Theory** (PIT; Maehr & Braskamp, 1986) to frame our understanding of the seemingly countless number of decisions influencing sport consumption behavior. This theoretical approach allows us to critically examine factors underlying an individual's decision to invest time, energy, and personal resources to attend sporting events, observe games through the media, purchase merchandise, and engage in other sport consumer actions. PIT includes three dimensions that influence sport consumption decisions: (1) perceived options, (2) personal incentives, and (3) sense of self (see Figure 5.1).

Perceived Options The first dimension, **perceived options,** refers to one's recognition of the behavioral alternatives available in a specific situation. On any given weekend, a consumer has a number of recreational options. For instance, he or she could attend a sporting event, go to a movie, play a round golf or a set of tennis, have dinner out, see a nightclub show, and so on. If one chooses the sporting event, he or she is still faced with an important decision, namely, this person must choose between attending an event in person (direct consumption) or consuming sport via an indirect option. Given the number of direct consumption possibilities (e.g., Little League contests, junior and senior high school sports, collegiate and professional events) and the vast array of sport one can consume via television, radio, and the Internet, there can literally be hundreds of choices.

Once a consumer has identified his or her options, the next task is to determine the **viability** of each (Maehr & Braskamp, 1986). For example, although one may want to attend the Super Bowl, ticket availability and cost, travel

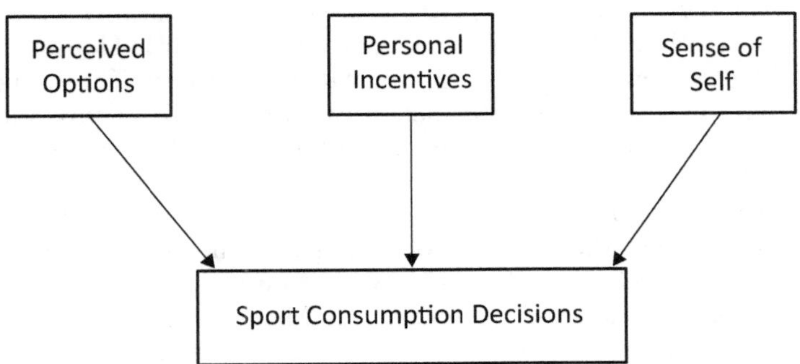

FIGURE 5.1 Personal Investment Theory Applied to Sport Consumer Decisions

requirements, and time away from one's family or job may make it an unrealistic option. The formula for estimating the viability of a sporting event option is **V = B – C**. In this formula, **B** refers to the benefits gained from the consumption (e.g., fun, time with friends), **C** refers to the costs associated with consumption (financial, time, etc.), and **V** refers to the viability of the option. If the benefits of consumption outweigh the costs, the individual will likely view the option as viable. If, on the other hand, the costs outweigh the benefits, the option will probably be perceived as nonviable.

A number of factors impact perceptions of the viability of a sport consumption option. These include driving distance to the event (Schurr et al., 1988), stadium/arena access and parking (Hay & Rao, 1982), and weather (Pan et al., 1997). One particularly critical factor involves the **financial cost** of attending a sporting event (Hansen & Gauthier, 1989; Schofield, 1983). Costs can range from no financial outlay (e.g., attending children's Little League competitions), to moderate costs for pay-per-view events and premier sport channels, to the exorbitant costs of attending professional sporting events. Of course, tickets are not the only expense associated with sport consumption. Additional costs that must be considered include food, beverages, parking, memorabilia, and travel. And what might such an excursion cost a family of four? The **Fan Cost Index** (FCI) provides an average financial outlay for attending professional sporting events. The FCI is based on the cost of four average-priced tickets (two adult and two child), two small beers, four sodas, four hot dogs, parking for one car, two game programs, and two caps. In 2015, the average cost of such as outing was over $500 for NFL games, greater than $300 for NBA and NHL contests, and in excess of $200 for MLB games (Scibetti, 2017). Unfortunately, a weekly trip to the ballpark or arena for a professional sporting event may no longer be a viable option for many fans, at least not as a family outing.

A second particularly important factor impacting viability concerns the **availability** of an event and tickets to an event (Maehr & Braskamp, 1986). Event availability can have both positive and negative influences on attendance decisions. For example, attending an Olympic event may be a once-in-a-lifetime opportunity (i.e., low future availability), thereby increasing the attractiveness of attendance. However, in some instances, the lack of future options may actually decrease the likelihood of attendance. An example of this occurred when the Houston Oilers NFL team announced a year in advance that they were moving the franchise to Nashville, Tennessee. During their last year in Houston, attendance at Oilers' games dropped by approximately 50 percent. Those who chose not to attend may have reasoned that, because future attendance was not a viable option (i.e., it would take a great deal of time and expense to see the team play in Nashville), it made little sense to continue rooting for the team. In addition, the Nashville stadium was still under construction during the following season. Consequently, the team was forced to play its home games in Memphis, Tennessee, a three-hour drive from Nashville. As was the case with attendance in Houston the previous season, attendance in Memphis was well under expectations. Many persons likely reasoned that, because the team would not be competing in Memphis next season, why support the team by purchasing tickets?

As for the availability of tickets, Wann et al. (2004) studied the influence of ticket scarcity on interest in attending a sporting event. College students read one of two scenarios describing their opportunity to attend an NCAA men's basketball tournament game in a city two hours away. The two scenarios were identical except in one condition participants learned that there were only 25 tickets remaining (the scarcity condition), while others read that there were still 2,000 tickets available (the not scarce condition). The respondents then answered items assessing their desire to attend the contest. Wann and his colleagues found that those in the scarcity condition had a greater desire to attend the game, were more likely to miss work to attend, and were willing to spend more for a ticket, relative to those in the not scarce condition. Thus, fans may be more likely to consume sport when they believe that tickets will be hard to acquire.

Personal Incentives A second dimension incorporated into PIT involves **personal incentives** (Maehr & Braskamp, 1986). There are four different types of personal incentives: task, ego, social, and extrinsic. **Task incentives** involve the activity itself, that is, the individual engages in the activity simply because of the enjoyment derived from it. Applied to sport consumption behavior, task incentives refer to an individual's desire to consume a specific sport because he or she enjoys one or more components of that sport.

Ego incentives involve competition with others and demonstrating one's superiority at a task. Thus, with respect to sport fandom and the consumption of sport, ego incentives refer to the desire to watch a favorite team succeed. Several studies have documented the positive relationship between team success and attendance (e.g., Baade & Tiehen, 1990; Brooks, 1994; Hay & Rao, 1982; Laverie & Arnett, 2000; Pinnuck & Potter, 2006), leading some to suggest that team performance is the most important factor in attendance decisions (Guttmann, 1986; Zhang et al., 1996).

Social incentives refer to interpersonal relationships that result from participation in an activity. This incentive is related to the pleasure received from spending time with and/or gaining the approval of others (Pan & Baker, 1999; Pan et al., 1997; Wakefield, 1995). For instance, for some people the opportunity to spend time with family members serves as sufficient incentive for attending a sporting event. For others, the social setting may be used for business purposes or to gain social status by being seen in public.

Finally, **extrinsic rewards** involve direct benefits gained from participating in an activity. To attract fans, team marketing strategists dole out extrinsic rewards in the form of giveaways (e.g., autograph balls, hats, T-shirts—we just *love* those T-shirts!), free entertainment (e.g., fireworks shows, postgame concerts), and opportunities to interact with the players (e.g., autograph and photo opportunity days).

Sense of Self Although marketing ploys can increase consumption (at least temporarily), there is likely a point at which fans will no longer be motivated to attend games simply because of special promotions and/or giveaways. For example, an individual may attend a game or two because the ticket prices have been lowered or to see a fireworks display, but these and similar strategies are not likely to result in enduring sport consumption behavior. Rather, repeat consumption will be driven by the personal meaning a fan attaches to a sport, team, or event. As the sport object becomes more meaningful, takes on greater intrinsic importance, and is incorporated into one's self-concept, consumption should increase.

Within Personal Investment Theory, the relevance of consumption decisions for one's identity concerns the **sense of self.** According to Maehr and Braskamp (1986), sense of self involves a "more or less organized collection of perceptions, beliefs, and feelings about who one is" and how an "individual perceives himself or herself as associated with certain groups and holds selected others to be significant" (p. 59). In previous chapters, we have discussed three areas of research that involve fans' sense of self: the Psychological Continuum Model, fan motives, and team identification. Each of these critically important topics concerns one's perception of why he or she is a fan as well as his or her connection to and identification with sport objects.

In the following sections, we examine the impact of these three areas. You will likely notice that the coverage of these topics is more detailed than that for perceived options and personal incentives. This unbalanced coverage did not happen by accident. Rather, your authors believe that although options and incentives influence sport consumption decisions, the impact of connections, motives, and identification (i.e., one's sense of self) plays a much more significant role. And as you will read, research substantiates our position.

The Psychological Continuum Model and Sport Consumer Behavior

Recalling the stages of the PCM (Awareness, Attraction, Attachment, and Allegiance), it is important to consider the forms and levels of consumption that one would expect from fans operating at the different stages. Those characterized by awareness are not likely to engage in sport consumption behaviors. The logic here is that at the Awareness stage, although an individual has knowledge of a sport object, this does not necessarily equate to interest in that object. Consequently, it is unlikely those merely at an awareness level would engage in sport consumption activities (Funk & James, 2016). Granted, there may be situations in which persons at the Awareness stage consume sport, but it is likely at low frequencies and may simply be exploratory in nature (Funk, Beaton, & Pritchard, 2011; Funk & James, 2016). For example, when a child is taken to his or her first game by a parent, although they are technically a sport consumer, they are still functioning at the Awareness stage.

As a fan progresses through the PCM stages and the connections to sport objects intensify, increases in consumption are likely (Funk et al., 2011; Funk & James, 2016). This pattern of effects should not be surprising. As a strong, positive attitude toward a sport object forms and connections increase, there should be greater interest in consuming that object. For example, if the sport object in question was a team, the increased connection should result in a greater desire to discuss the team, watch them on television and in person, and purchase team apparel. These behaviors convey a person's interest in the team, and, as the connection strengthens, the team becomes personally meaningful and associated with the self-concept. Consequently, sport consumer behaviors such as attending and/or watching games, talking about a team, and wearing team apparel become important outlets of self-expression and identification.

Having read the previous paragraph, you may be tempted to view fandom and sport consumption as a form of escalating commitment. Indeed, if you have read a sport marketing textbook, you likely have been exposed to a **Model of Escalating Commitment.** This approach is a simplistic representation of movement from lower to higher levels of consumption. For example, sport marketers begin with someone that has purchased a single game ticket, work to "move" that consumer to purchasing a partial season ticket plan, then further "move" the individual to purchase a full-season ticket package. Although there is an expectation of intensification in consumer behavior from Awareness to Allegiance, simply perceiving consumption as a consequence of escalating commitment is an oversimplification of the process. That is, to focus solely on encouraging sport consumers to buy more does not consider the complexity of consumer decision making.

One concern with the escalation framework is that those writing from this approach may not explain the rationale for such behavior (Mullin, Hardy, & Sutton, 2014). That is, authors writing about escalating commitment and consumer behavior frequently use game attendance as evidence; there is a progression from not attending, to attending a single game, to attending a few contests, to purchasing a partial season ticket package, to purchasing full-season tickets. But is such a progression an escalation in *commitment*? Maybe, but examples of escalating commitment are typically just illustrations of consumer segments and not empirical evidence of increasing commitment (Irwin, Southall, & Sutton, 2007; Pritchard & Stinson, 2014). Additionally, examples of escalating commitment are frequently based on cross-sectional research (the academician's version of "one and done"). For example, Mullin and his colleagues (2014) write, "fans who currently attend three games per year typically include their intention to attend five or six games the next year" (p. 43). A single cross-sectional study of purchase intentions provides some information but is not evidence of an escalating commitment. Rather, longitudinal designs are required to provide support for a process of escalation.

An additional concern with escalating commitment is that such an approach fails to address what happens at the top of the escalator. There are a finite number of games to attend and a finite amount of merchandise to purchase. For example, consider ticket sales to a sporting event. If a goal of escalating commitment is to "move people up" and get them to purchase more tickets, at some point all the seats in a venue will be sold out as season tickets. Granted, this seems like a desirable outcome from a sport marketing perspective. And it would be, as long as all our consumers are alive. But in such a scenario, are we waiting for consumers to "die off" to attract new consumers? If all the seats in an arena are sold as season tickets, how would a marketer attract new consumers? Where would the new consumers come from to begin their trek up the escalator?

The point we are emphasizing is that fandom and sport consumer behavior involve much more than just getting sport consumers to increasingly buy more (e.g., tickets, merchandise, memorabilia). It is important to understand not just *what* sport consumers are doing (e.g., how much they consume) but also to understand *why* individuals consume (e.g., what influences sport consumption). We contend the impact of fandom on sport consumer behavior should be studied with a comprehensive theoretical framework such as the PCM, allowing for an understanding of the interaction between attitudes and behaviors (Funk et al., 2011).

Using the PCM to Study Sport Consumer Behavior

A limitation in the early development of the PCM was the lack of a mechanism or tool to place an individual into one of the stages (Funk & James, 2016). To help fill this research void, Beaton, Funk, and Alexandris (2009) developed and tested a PCM staging tool utilizing a three-step procedure. The first step involves measuring three facets of involvement (**pleasure, centrality,** and **sign**) and calculating mean scores for each facet (Funk & James, 2016; see Table 5.1 for definitions of the three involvement facets). The second step concerns the application of predetermined cutoff points to characterize an individual as having high, medium, or low levels for each involvement facet. In the final step, one applies a staging algorithm to select one of 27 unique profiles to slot an individual within a particular stage of the PCM.

The unique profiles represent the different combinations of the three facets of involvement, and there are unique profiles for each stage. For example, if a person's level for pleasure was "high," and the levels for sign and centrality were "medium" and "medium" respectively, the unique profile would be "Attachment: H-M-M." If a person's level for pleasure, centrality, and sign are each "low," the unique profile would be "Awareness: L-L-L." One more example: if a person's level for pleasure, centrality, and sign are each "high," the unique profile would be "Allegiance: H-H-H" (see Beaton et al., 2009, for a complete description of each profile). Investigators have successfully utilized the staging tool to position individuals along the PCM (e.g., Beaton, Funk, Ridinger, & Jordan, 2011; Funk et al., 2011; Kunkel, Doyle, & Funk, 2014; Nyadzayo, Leckie, & McDonald, 2016) and to examine differences in attitudes and behaviors based on strength of psychological connection.

Surprisingly, though, there is limited information about the utility of the PCM in furthering our understanding of consumer behavior among fans. This

TABLE 5.1 Defining the Facets of Involvement

Facet	Definition
Pleasure	The hedonic value derived from a sport object.
Centrality	The primary role a sport object has in an individual's life.
Sign	The symbolic value of the sport object.

Note: Adapted from Doyle et al. (2013).

model has been successfully used to frame results from a variety of other sport-related domains. For instance, researchers have utilized the PCM to better comprehend active leisure (Alexandris, Du, Funk, & Theodorakis, 2017; Brandon-Lai, Funk, & Jordan, 2015), brand development and trust (Filo, Funk, & Alexandris, 2008; Kunkel et al., 2014), website content and attitude change (Filo, Funk, & Hornby, 2009), and involvement with a destination (Filo, Chen, King, & Funk, 2013). But research that includes testing the PCM within the confines of sport fandom remains rare. Two notable exceptions can be found.

Doyle et al. (2013) used the PCM and staging tool in their examination of consumers of particular leagues and teams. Because the staging tool constructed by Beaton and his colleagues (2009) was developed for sport participants (the PCM applies to both participants and fans), Doyle et al. (2013) modified the wording of items to assess involvement with spectator sport. They found that "attitudes become increasingly strengthened across the awareness, attraction, attachment and allegiant stages" (p. 105). Consumption behaviors such as watching games played by teams in a favorite league and watching a favorite team play on television became more frequent as the strength of the psychological connection increased.

In a study testing the PCM within fan environments, de Groot and Robinson (2008) studied the attitude formation of a fan of the Australian Football League. The researchers conducted this case study to better understand "the turning points and underlying psychological factors that made this particular subject an attached and devoted fan" (p. 120). The investigation included multiple in-depth interviews with the fan, as well as discussions with the fan's family members and friends. The authors used the information to document the process of becoming a fan across the stages of the PCM. De Groot and Robinson established the influence of socializing agents (particularly family), dispositional influences (self-esteem enhancement), the personal importance of the team manifested through identification, and the persistent and consistent behaviors (getting a tattoo, attending games) and attitudes toward the team. The authors concluded (pp. 135–136):

> The PCM provides a useful tool to examine fandom through the integration of stage based connections. Within the stages processes can confine the complexity and non-linear element of human emotion. It has been helpful to structure the qualitative interviews along the PCM in order to determine the process of attachment and identify the critical turning points that mark the different stages. The framework helped to structure the data and identify the transitions in the process.

As researchers, we recognize the value of the PCM as a comprehensive understanding of the formation and continuation of fandom. However, the PCM can also be used to help us understand behaviors associated with and expected at the different stages. This would include actions associated with sport consumption. What does this mean for sport marketers? If we gain a better understanding of the factors influencing how and why people become fans, promotional strategies can be developed to augment these factors. Furthermore, as our understanding of the process through which one becomes a fan is advanced, such as the factors that influence movement among the PCM stages, sport marketers should be able to develop successful strategies to foster connections with a team (e.g., campaigns such as MLB's "Our Team, Our Town").

Early work applying the PCM to the study of sport consumer behavior (e.g., Doyle et al., 2013) is promising, but clearly more should be done. As Funk and James (2016) explain, the PCM is entering a "Contextual Period of examination." Specifically, these authors write (p. 258):

> The Contextual Period will embrace an exploration of the nuances of the consumer context. The Contextual Period will primarily focus on the environmental experience in order to better understand what influences stage placement as well as transitions between stages. This should be driven by a service experience design approach in which the consumer experience is considered a journey through which many interactions occur between an individual and a sport organization . . . This will require researching the experience as it happens, as the use of pose-event surveys or online panels about an experience can suffer from memory decay. Efforts will be needed to map out a behavioral system or sequencing of behaviors and testing prototypes of simulated behavior. Without this approach, it will be difficult for researchers to create a comprehensive and customized blueprint of consumption points to measure and capture the complexities of the experiential journey, which includes the service design.

Sport Fan Motives and Consumer Behavior

Specific fan motives are a second sense-of-self factor. Sport fandom can satisfy many different motives, several of which were covered in the previous chapter. Specifically, we examined fulfillment of the need for belonging (i.e., group affiliation), a desire to spend time with family, enjoying the beauty and grace of sport (i.e., aesthetics), enhancement of self-esteem, searching for excitement and stimulation (i.e., eustress), the acquisition of knowledge, fulfilling a need to escape, and a desire to be entertained. Sport marketers recognize (or they should) that promotional strategies could be developed to focus on one or more motives in an effort to stimulate sport consumer behavior. For example, consider the group affiliation/belongingness motive. Fans new to an area could be targeted in marketing campaigns designed to reach new residents, such as offering periodic "meet and greet" promotions. Similarly, promoting the opportunity to spend time with family (e.g., "Family Night at the Ballpark!") is a fairly common sport marketing tactic. Additionally, consider television commercials that promote and hype the excitement of a sport (e.g., basketball ads depicting images of players flying through the air and dunking). Through these advertisements, sport marketers convey the excitement and beauty of sporting events in an attempt to stimulate attendance or viewership by targeting the entertainment and aesthetic motives.

However, just because people notice and remember marketing campaigns touching on fan motives does not necessarily mean the advertisements influence behavior and increase sport consumption. Thus, it is critical to investigate the extent to which such tactics are successful. Do strategies focused on connecting to sport consumer motives result in or lead to sport consumer behavior? Referring back to the examples above, do new residents attend meet and greet parties at a sporting event? Are families attending baseball games together? Do people watch basketball games specifically to see dunks and highly skilled play? In the following section, we investigate research designed to answer these questions by determining the relationship between sport fan motives and consumption behavior.

The Relationship Between Motivation and Sport Consumption

In this section, we review a handful of studies to determine what has been learned about the influence of sport fan motives on consumer behavior. Of course, this is not an exhaustive coverage of the literature—such an analysis could require several volumes. Rather, our goal is to provide a representative overview of this work. We follow this with a discussion of how sport marketers might use this research to inform their marketing campaigns, as well as challenges to such applications.

Let us start at the beginning with Wann's (1995) early work. In his initial development of the Sport Fan Motivation Scale (SFMS), Wann reported correlations between motives (i.e., SFMS subscales) and interest in 13 different sports. Overall, the motives were significantly correlated with ten of the 13 sports. Particular motives were correlated with interest in some but not all sports. For example, escape was significantly correlated with interest in baseball, basketball, football, golf, and fishing. Thus, it can be concluded that people were interested in following these sports in part to experience some degree of escape from their day-to-day routine.

If sport marketers would like to better understand reasons why people may be interested in a particular sport, the work of Wann, Grieve, Zapalac, and Pease (2008) can be informative. These authors examined the motives included in the SFMS in relation to different sport types (i.e., stylistic/non-stylistic, aggressive/nonaggressive, and individuals/team). The results provide information about which motives are more or less associated with various sport types. Several motivational differences were reported. For example, consider the group affiliation and aesthetic motives. Figure 5.2 depicts levels of these motives for interest in stylistic (e.g., figure skating, gymnastics) and non-stylistic sports (e.g., hockey, baseball). As noted in the figure, higher scores for group affiliation motivation were found for non-stylistic relative to stylistic sports. The opposite pattern of effects was revealed for aesthetic motivation; this motive was particularly high for stylistic sports.

Moving beyond correlations between sport interest and sport motives, it can also be useful to examine relationships among motives and sport consumption

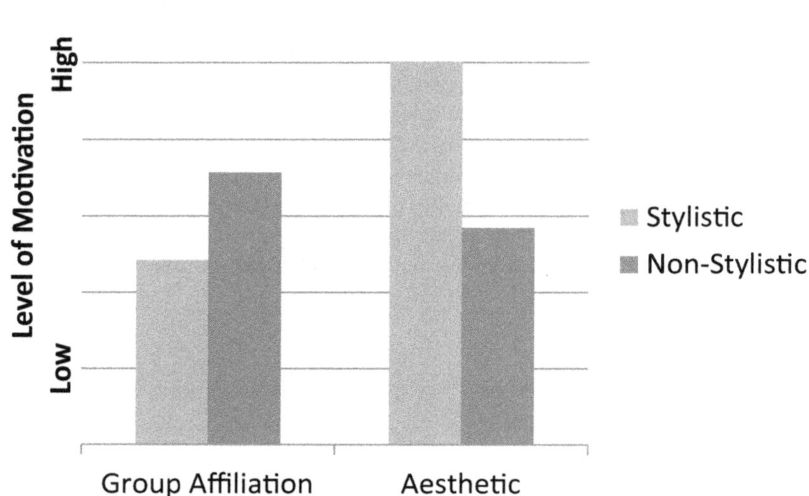

FIGURE 5.2 Group Affiliation and Aesthetic Motivation for Stylistic and Non-Stylistic Sports. Adapted From Wann et al. (2008)

behaviors. For example, in their work developing the Motivation Scale for Sport Consumption (MSSC), Trail and James (2001) examined behaviors associated with sport consumer motives. They found that various motives (although not always the same ones) were correlated with attendance, merchandise purchases, and media consumption. Thus, combining the work of Wann (1995) and Trail and James (2001), there is evidence that particular sport fan motives are correlated with interest in sport, as well as consumption behaviors such as attendance at contests, media consumption of games, and merchandise purchases.

Applying Information on the Relationship Between Motivation and Sport Consumption The studies outlined above reveal that fan motives are frequently correlated with sport interest and consumption. This pattern of effects has been documented in several additional studies (e.g., Fink & Parker, 2009; Funk, Beaton, & Alexandris, 2012; Funk et al., 2003; James, 2002; Kwon & Trail, 2001). However, simply acknowledging the relationship is of little use to sport marketing professionals. Rather, they must develop practical applications of this research and incorporate this information into their marketing and promotional campaigns. There are several ways marketers can use data on the relationship between sport fan motivation and consumption habits. One possibility is to utilize the information to develop motivation profiles of fans favoring certain types of sports (cf., McDonald, Milne, & Hong, 2002). For example, referring back to the work of Wann and his colleagues (2008) and the information presented in Figure 5.2, we would expect that marketing strategies incorporating aesthetic motivation to be particularly effective for stylistic sports.

Additionally, sport marketers could utilize the literature on fan motives and consumption to construct strategies for use in different settings. For example, Fink and Parker (2009) compared motivation patterns when individuals watched a televised contest involving a favorite team and when they viewed a game in which a favorite team was not competing. They reported significant differences for three motives: achievement, acquisition of knowledge, and physical skill. Each of these motives had higher ratings when watching a contest involving a favorite team. What might a sport marketer do with such information? Knowing that fans watching their team compete are particularly high in achievement motivation could lead to the development of marketing tactics highlighting this motive for these fans. That is, marketing campaigns for hometown fans (e.g., televising Philadelphia Eagles games in Philadelphia) could include statements highlighting the achievements and accomplishments of the team. Conversely, these statements could be replaced with content targeting different fan motives for campaigns presented to audiences outside the Philadelphia viewing area.

A third potential use of the data involves the development of strategies that resonate with particular groups of fans (Won & Kitamura, 2007). An example of this approach can be found in the work of Kwon and Trail (2001). They investigated differences in motives influencing the sport consumption of international and domestic university students. Kwon and Trail found one motive to be significantly different between the two groups; international students had higher scores for aesthetic motivation. Eustress was the highest-rated motive for both groups. Knowing this, sport marketers could develop campaigns that resonate with specific fan groups. Utilizing the results from Kwon and Trail as an example, marketing strategies emphasizing eustress could be developed and directed at both groups. Additionally, international students could be specifically targeted with promotions and slogans highlighting aesthetics.

Challenges With Applying Fan Motivation Results to Sport Consumption Although sport marketers may be able to use information on the relationship between motivation and consumption to structure and improve the effectiveness of their marketing tactics, this is a much more complicated process than most believe. In actuality, there are a number of issues that hamper the effectiveness of these endeavors.

One problem is that investigators often use motives to predict interest in sport, but interest may or may not translate into consumption (e.g., James, 2002). For example, as noted above, Wann (1995) found that a number of motives were significantly related to interest in certain sports. For the sport marketer, the challenge is that, although this helps us understand why people are interested in a sport product, it does not provide definitive answers as to whether such interests drive consumption behavior (Trail & James, 2015).

A second challenge in the applied use of research on sport fan motives is that much of this work assessed intentions rather than behavior (e.g., Byon, Cottingham, & Carroll, 2010; Kim, James, & Kim, 2013; Kim, Trail, & Magnusen, 2013; Koo & Hardin, 2008). That is, researchers have used motives to predict what fans *say* they would do, not their *actual behavior*. Granted, there are precedents for studying intentions based on the premise that intentions influence behaviors (Ajzen, 1985; Al-Suqri & Al-Kuarusi, 1980). Thus, we would expect that fans' intentions would correlate with their actions. However, there will be times when they fail to act on their desires. Thus, drawing conclusions based on intentions rather than actions can be problematic and lead to misguided assumptions (Sniehotta, Presseau, & Araujo-Soares, 2014; Zaharia, Biscaia, Gray, & Stotlar, 2016). For sport marketers, developing strategic campaigns based on intentions may not have the effectiveness they desire.

A third challenge concerns the fact that although researchers may provide evidence that motives are correlated with interest, intentions, and/or behaviors, there is not always conclusive information on cause and effect relationships. As professors remind their students on a daily basis (if they do not, they should), correlation does not equal causation. Definitive answers to cause and effect require experimental methods (e.g., random assignment), but these procedures are often difficult in applied disciplines such as the study of sport fandom.

When two variables are correlated, there are three possible causal patterns that could be at play. These possibilities are shown in Figure 5.3. For example,

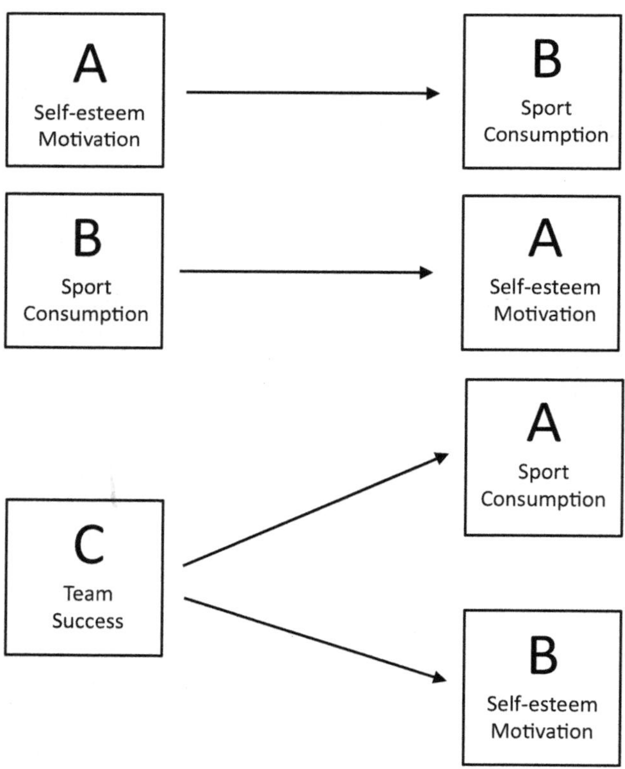

FIGURE 5.3 Potential Causal Patterns Involving Self-Esteem Motivation and Sport Consumption

consider if a researcher found that the self-esteem motive was positively correlated with sport consumption. With respect to causal relationships, one possibility is that a fan's motivation to enhance her self-esteem will lead (i.e., cause) her to consume sport (written generically as A→B). This causal pattern could be valuable to sport marketers; if they could devise strategies that tap into the self-esteem motive, they may be able to enhance consumption for a fan base. However, this is only one of three possible patterns. A second would reverse the variables. Written generically as B→A, for our example this would be that consumption causes changes in self-esteem. This pattern is also likely and, as you will read in later chapters, supported by research (Bizman & Yinon, 2002; Cialdini et al., 1976). And adding to the confusion, there may be one or more additional variables (i.e., "C") that are actually the cause of both A and B. For instance, perhaps a team's success drives both the fan's sport consumption and her self-esteem motivation. The existence of these additional variables can be problematic for sport marketers. Indeed, Trail and James (2015) note that one of the primary difficulties in studying sport consumer behavior in association with specific motives is that motives may be impacted by other factors (e.g., pricing, timing of sporting events, other life events). In fact, Trail and James write that "the influence of motives directly on sport consumption behavior is not very large" (p. 199).

Team Identification and Sport Consumer Behavior

Team identification is a third factor related to the sense-of-self component of Personal Investment Theory. As noted in Chapter 3, many scholars have examined the impact of team identification on the affective, behavioral, and cognitive reactions of fan. Historically, however, there seems to have been more work on identification in relation to attitudes and emotions than on sport consumer behavior, although this literature has begun to flourish in recent years. Overall, this growing body of work provides evidence that identification is a powerful predictor of a wide variety of sport consumption behaviors. This includes direct consumption via attendance (James & Trail, 2008; Matsuoka, Chelladurai, & Harada, 2003; Wakefield, 1995; Wann, Roberts, & Tindall, 1999), indirect consumption via the media (Bernache-Assollant, Bouchet, & Lacassagne, 2007; Suh, Ahn, & Eagleman, 2013), purchases of merchandise and apparel (Kwon & Armstrong, 2002; Kwon et al., 2007; Lee & Ferreira, 2011), and consumption of sponsor's products (Madrigal, 2004; Nassis, Theodorakis, Alexandris, Tsellou, & Afthinos, 2012).

Using Identification to Increase Sport Consumption: More Challenges for Sport Marketers

Team identification could have a greater impact on consumption than any other variable. Given this, the reader may conclude that to increase consumption, all marketers need to do is increase the identification of a fan base, and people will flock to the stadium; turn on their televisions, radios, and computers; and head to the team merchandise store. Although increasing identification to facilitate consumption seems like a simple task, in reality it is quite difficult. Some of the difficulty involves the same challenges found with sport fan motivation. For instance, as with research on fan motivation, work on team identification and consumption has often examined intentions rather than actual behavior (e.g., James & Trail, 2008; Matsuoka et al., 2003; Theodorakis, Kousetelios, Robinson, & Barlas, 2009). In addition, because the vast majority of research is correlational, we are left without definitive answers to causal patterns. Does identification lead to greater consumption, does consumption lead to increased levels of identification, or is there a third variable responsible for higher levels of both identification and consumption? Answers to questions regarding causal relationships are still largely unknown.

Additionally, sport scholars and marketing professionals need to think critically about how they assess team identification. As noted in Chapter 3, researchers have often misinterpreted their measurement of team identification by including persons not identifying with a team among those having low levels of identification (James et al., in press). This misinterpretation is problematic to sport marketers, given that those with no identification and those with low levels will almost certainly have dissimilar consumption patterns and respond differently to marketing campaigns. For instance, imagine an advertisement promoting an upcoming jersey giveaway. Those with a small connection to a team (i.e., those with low levels of identification) may at least notice the advertisement and have some interest in acquiring the jersey. However, persons with no connection to the team might completely dismiss the advertisement given that owning the jersey has no personal meaning to these individuals. Consequently, those examining the impact of team identification on consumption behaviors and the success of marketing tactics should use the revised SSIS (James et al., in press) or modify other measures of team identification to avoid the error of misinterpretation.

But perhaps the greatest challenge facing marketers hoping to impact consumption via team identification involves the difficulty in developing strategies to increase identification. For instance, consider the following antecedents to team identification: team success, living close to a team, and the socialization process. In addition to being important causes of team identification, these three factors share another thing in common: they are all difficult if not impossible to directly manipulate from a marketing perspective. That is, sport marketers are not able to influence how well a team performs, where someone lives, or how someone was raised. To illustrate this point, imagine that a sport marketer interviewed the authors of this text to gain information on how we became fans of the Murray State (Dan) or Florida State (Jeff) athletic teams. The marketer's plan is to use information gleaned from the interviews to develop strategies to enhance the identification of fans (or potential fans) of these schools. The interviews would likely be very short, and our answers would be quite similar. That is, when asked why we are identified with these teams, we would simply reply, "Because that's where I work." What could the sport marketers do with this information? Not much, really. Essentially, they would need to be able to dictate where someone gained employment, something they obviously cannot do.

So, does this mean we should abandon the notion of increasing sport consumption behavior via marketing strategies targeting team identification? Absolutely not! It simply means that one typically does not have the ability to reproduce the same set of environmental or psychological circumstances that served as antecedents to identification. But what marketers might be able to do is develop campaigns that highlight these antecedents. Using the example above, although marketers cannot choose who works where, they can develop tactics that focus on supporting teams that represent an employer. Similarly, although marketing professionals cannot impact the socialization process, they can highlight parents and children consuming sport together. By making these antecedents salient, marketers likely draw attention to the factors driving one's identification, which in turn may facilitate sport consumption (Laverie & Arnett, 2000). These strategies may also influence persons who are not yet identified with a team by highlighting positive aspects of identification. For example, stadiums have been implicated as an antecedent to team identification (Uhrich & Benkenstein, 2010; Underwood et al., 2001). Although sport marketers cannot decide what a stadium contains, they can focus on the stadium in their campaigns. This likely will impact those already identified with the team (i.e., remind them that they enjoy the stadium) as well as those not yet connected with the team (i.e., provide information on the positive attributes of the stadium to persons who have not yet attended a game there).

Post-Consumption: Still More Decisions to Be Made

By now it should be apparent that sport consumer behavior is influenced by a lot of variables, and fans are faced with many decisions when making consumption choices. In an attempt to apply structure to the complexity of this process, Trail and James (2015) proposed a comprehensive **Model of Sport Consumer Behavior** (see Figure 5.4). This approach incorporates many of the issues discussed in the preceding sections, such as cultural influences, awareness, person variables (e.g., motivation and identification), and behavioral intentions. However, looking closer at the final stage of the model, it becomes apparent that decisions do not end with consumption behavior. Rather, fans evaluate their experience and makes additional decisions based on those evaluations.

The Trail and James (2015) model incorporates three facets of an individual's sport consumption evaluation that impact his or her repatronage decisions: confirmation (or disconfirmation) of expectancies, affective responses, and self-esteem responses. **(Dis)Confirmation of expectations** refers to the extent that the game met the fan's expectations for the event. Perhaps the event was as exciting and enjoyable as expected. Or maybe the contest failed to meet expectations because the arena was in disarray and a star player did not play. **Affective responses** concern the consumer's emotional reactions to the event. As will be detailed in the next chapter, fans' emotional reactions to sporting events impact

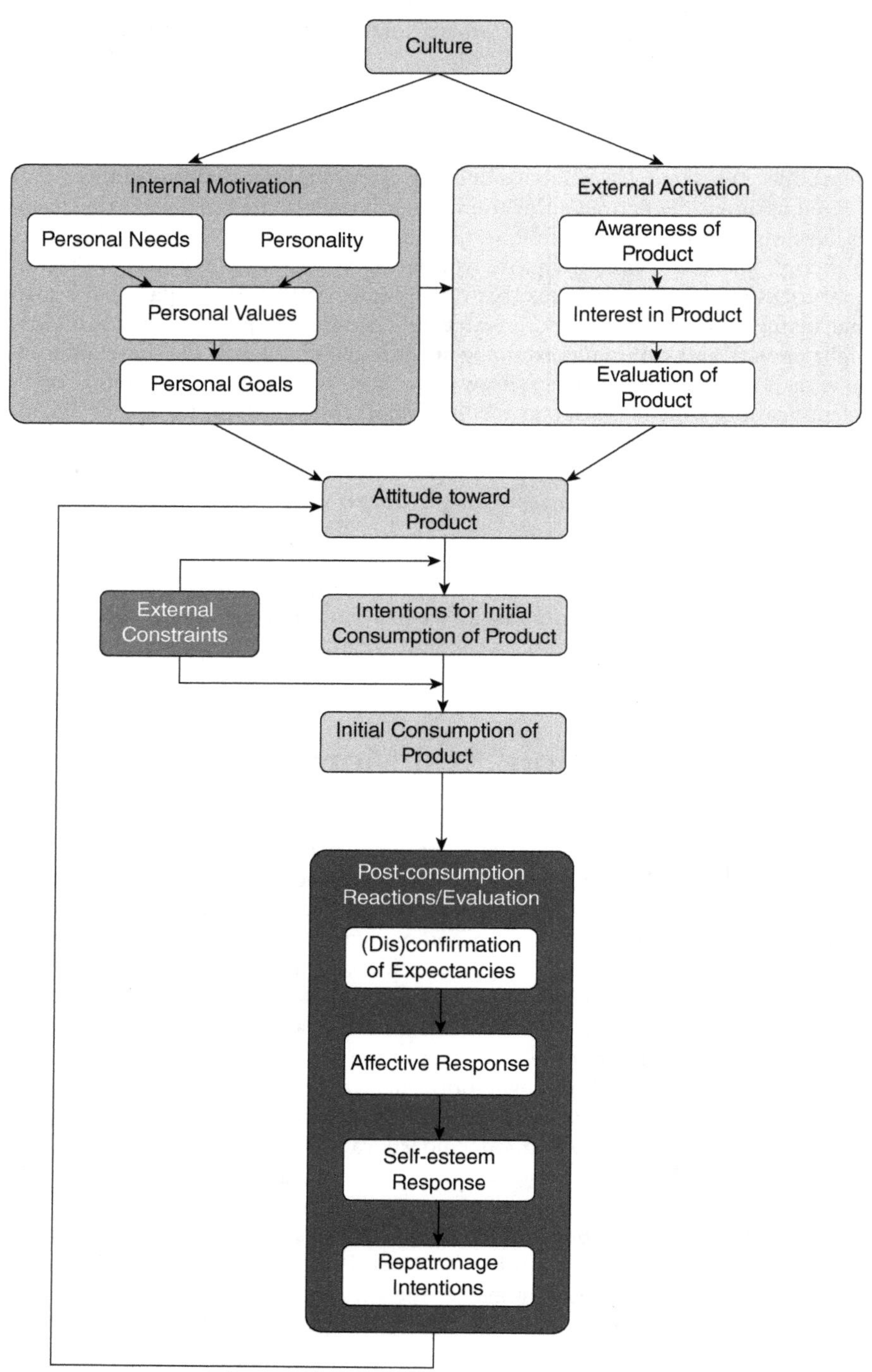

FIGURE 5.4 Model of Sport Consumer Behavior (Trail & James, 2015).

decisions for future consumption (Biscaia, Correia, Rosado, Maroco, & Ross, 2012; Jang, Ko, Wann, & Chang, in press; Yoshida & James, 2010). Fans who had a positive emotional experience are likely to choose to be repeat consumers. The third facet, the fan's **self-esteem response**, involves the extent to which an individual's consumption experience impacts her or his self-concept. One such response might be an increase in self-esteem (feeling good or confident about oneself) because a favorite team won a game. The psychological responses a fan experiences, including impact on self-esteem, are examined in more detail in Chapter 10.

Some Final Thoughts

We have learned a great deal about sport consumption behavior in the last few decades, and what has become quite clear is that there are a number of variables influencing a fan's consumption decisions. Moving forward, however, there are two important ways research on sport consumption could be improved. First, investigators need to conduct more field research, engaging with fans prior to, during, and after their consumption experience. Although valuable information can be acquired in the lab, acquiring data as fans live their experience will result in a more accurate picture of sport consumption. Admittedly, work has been done that involves sport consumers in live or "real" settings (e.g., Funk et al., 2012; James et al., 2002), but much more of this type of work is needed.

Second, although we presented the three PIT sense-of-self components separately, in reality, connections with sport objects, sport fan motives, and team identification interact in their impact on sport consumption behavior. For example, James and his colleagues (2002) studied reasons for purchasing season tickets for a MLB team, testing for differences in the motives underlying ticket purchases based on a fan's strength of psychological connection. James and his colleagues found that the number of motives influencing participants seemed to escalate with increases in psychological connection. Individuals with low levels of psychological connection were influenced by only one or two motives, while those with a moderate or strong connection were impacted by four or more motives. Thus, the sport consumer motivational profiles were different for individuals with varying degrees of psychological connection. Future endeavors should take into account the interrelationships among the three sense-of-self variables and incorporate them into assessments and analyses. Of course, this will add to the complexity of the process of sport consumption behavior and make life even more difficult for sport marketers hoping to develop theoretically and empirically sound marketing strategies. Thus, like the sport consumers they study, marketing professionals will face a lot of decisions when choosing the most effective plans.

PART TWO

The Emotional and Aggressive Reactions of Sport Fans

CHAPTER 6

The Emotional Reactions of Sport Fans

In the 2017 NCAA Men's Basketball Tournament, the Elite Eight contest between the University of Kentucky Wildcats and the University of North Carolina Tar Heels was March Madness at its best. A late surge by North Carolina gave them a seemingly insurmountable lead with under a minute left in the game, but a furious run by Kentucky found them with the ball and down by only three. The Kentucky comeback was complete when Malik Monk hit a game tying three-point basket with less than ten seconds remaining. However, much to the dismay of the Kentucky faithful, the Tar Heels raced back down the court and secured the victory when Luke Maye sank a game-winning jumper, sending North Carolina to the Final Four and Kentucky home for the season. Shortly after the conclusion of the game, video surfaced of Kentucky fans watching the last moments of the contest. The video depicted the wide range of emotions these fans experienced in only a few seconds. The Kentucky supporters, clearly anxious just prior to Monk's shot, erupted in euphoria when he tied the game. They were on cloud nine—happy, relieved, hopeful, ecstatic, and proud. And then it all came crashing down. The smiles, laughter, high-fives, and cheers changed, in an instant, to tears, screams, and faces in hands. Once on top of the world, they were now sad, disappointed, angry, depressed, and in disbelief.

The event described above is but one of a countless number of incidents highlighting the powerful impact sport has on the affective reactions of fans and spectators. Although fans do not always experience such a wide range of emotions in response to a single event, they likely can recall times when they felt almost every emotion imaginable. In fact, it would be difficult to describe one's fandom without incorporating the emotions that accompany the consumption of sport. The emotions fans experience as a consequence of their strong psychological connection to sports, teams, and players are an integral part of the pastime. Essentially, to be a sport fan is to be emotional.

In the current chapter, we examine the affective reactions of fans. What will become apparent is that the emotions of fans are intense and wide-ranging and impact many different aspects of their lives. In the first section, we examine research on the general positive and negative affective states of fans. Next, we review work on what may well be the most basic fan emotions: the happiness and sadness fans experience in response to their team's performance. After this,

Sport Fans Experience a Wide Range of Emotions When Watching Their Team Compete

we review other positive and negative emotions frequently reported by fans. And finally, we discuss a number of additional issues related to the affective experiences of fans, such as emotions stemming from non-performance events, behavioral and attitudinal consequences of fan emotions, and the impact of fan motivation on emotional responses.

General Positive and Negative Affective Experiences

Wann et al. (1994) conducted one of the first studies to target the general positive and negative affective responses of fans. These authors examined spectators' affective responses to an easy victory, a difficult victory, and a loss. Prior to the contest, the authors assessed participants' pregame positive and negative affective states as well as their level of identification with the home team. Participants also completed an assessment of their emotional state immediately following the contest. The results revealed that spectators experienced a small increase in positive affect after the easy win, a large increase in response to the difficult win, and a sharp reduction in positive affect following the loss. Responses for negative affect generally mirrored those for positive emotions as the respondents indicated a slight drop in negative affect following the easy win, a bit larger drop after the difficult win, and a sizeable increase in negative affect subsequent to the loss. Affect was also impacted by the spectators' level of identification with the home team. Specifically, the pattern of effects detailed above was magnified among those higher in team identification. A number of studies have replicated these effects, finding that fans experience positive affect after team success and negative affect after the team's failures and that these reactions are strongest for persons with stronger connections to the team (e.g., Bernache-Assollant, Laurin, Bouchet, Bodet, & Lacassagne, 2010; Bizman & Yinon, 2002; Gan, Tuggle, Mitrook, Coussement, & Zillmann, 1997; Jensen et al., 2016). As St. John (2004) writes of his journey into the world of college football tailgating, "One simple truth I've come upon is that the more you immerse yourself and identify with the team, the higher the payoff of a win, and the greater the cost of a loss" (p. 269). Interestingly, fans' positive and negative responses to wins and losses are detected by their relationship partners. That is, individuals report that their significant others are in negative moods after losses and positive moods after wins (End, Worthman, Foster, & Vandemark, 2009). This finding has implications for the impact of fandom on interpersonal relationships, an issue examined in Chapter 10.

The work detailed above reveals that to fully understand the emotional responses of fans, individuals need to consider the fans' psychological connection to the team (as well as the outcome of the contest). The impact of team identification on the affective response of fans will be a consistent theme running throughout this chapter, as identification plays a vital role in a number of different emotional responses. The **Disposition Theory of Sport Spectatorship** provides a theoretical framework for understanding the interrelationships among game outcome, team identification, and emotional reactions (Bryant, 1989; Izod, 1996; Sapolsky, 1980; Zillmann, Bryant, & Sapolsky, 1989; Zillmann & Paulas, 1993). This approach predicts that a spectator's affective response to watching a sporting event is a function of his or her disposition with the favored team, his or her dislike of the team's opponent, and the outcome of the competition (use of the term "disposition" in this theory is generally equivalent to team identification, see Bryant & Raney, 2000; Madrigal, 1995). Enjoyment of watching a team succeed is expected to increase with positive sentiments toward the team (i.e., identification) and decrease with negative sentiments. Enjoyment gained from watching a team lose is expected to increase with negative sentiments and decrease with positive sentiments. Therefore, spectators are predicted to be happiest (and experience lower negative affect) when their favorite teams succeed and when their least favorite teams fail. They should be least happy (and report more negative affect) when their favorite teams fail and when their least favorite teams succeed. In fact, some fans prefer rival failure *over* the success of a favorite team (Lehr, Ferreira, & Banaji, in press). Given these predictions, it follows that the greatest amount of positive affect should occur when a favored team defeats a rival while the greatest amount of negative affect would be experienced when a favored team loses to a rival. These patterns are depicted in Figure 6.1.

Specific Affective Experiences of Sport Fans

Although research on the general positive and negative affective reactions of fans is informative, a greater understanding can be achieved by investigating

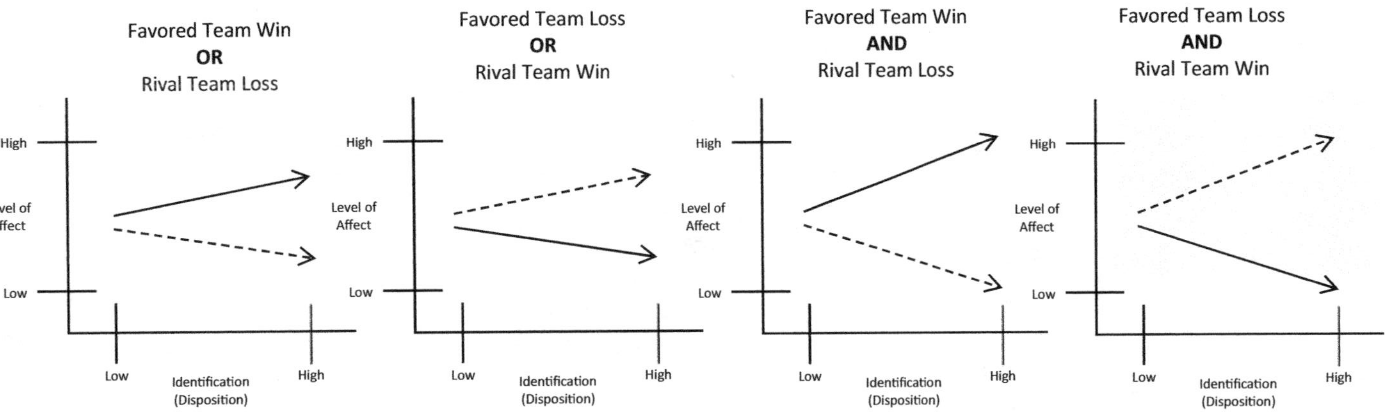

FIGURE 6.1 Disposition Theory of Sport Spectatorship and the Positive and Negative Affective Reactions to Favored and Rival Team Wins and Losses

specific emotions. For instance, consider the aforementioned study by Wann and his colleagues (1994). The negative affect index utilized in their research assessed a number of states, including frustration, anger, and sadness. Although these emotional reactions are correlated, and, thus, it is psychometrically appropriate to combine them into a single index, they are different. For instance, there are times when fans feel angry but not sad, and vice versa. In fact, this is precisely what Crisp, Heuston, Farr, and Turner (2007) found in their examination of the affective reactions of soccer fans. Their results revealed that, in response to poor team performance, low identified fans tended to respond with sadness while persons higher in identification reported greater levels of anger.

Thus, knowing the particular emotional responses to a team's performance sheds additional light onto our understanding of sport fandom. Thankfully, a number of studies have targeted specific affective responses. In the sections that follow, we examine this literature, beginning with what may be the most frequently studied fan emotions: happiness and sadness.

Happiness and Sadness of Sport Fans

> Sometimes you're crazy and you wonder why
> I'm such a baby 'cause the Dolphins make me cry

The lyrics above are from the 1990s hit song "Only Wanna Be with You" by Hootie and the Blowfish. The song references lead singer Darius Rucker's passion for the Miami Dolphins and, more particularly, the sadness he felt in response to their losing. Rucker's sorrow from following a struggling team is a plight shared by many fans (who can forget the video of the disgruntled fan referring to the Cleveland Browns' stadium as a "factory of sadness"). Of course, fan reactions to successful team performances bring about a vastly different affective response. When a team wins, the sky is bluer, the sun is brighter, and all is right with the world. These distinct responses underscore the powerful impact team performance can have on the happiness and sadness of sport fans.

A number of researchers have focused their attention on the happiness and sadness of fans. This research reveals that, just as physical activity is associated with greater levels of happiness (Wang et al., 2012), so too is involvement with sport as a fan and spectator (Wang & Wong, 2014). As one would expect, fans report happiness after successful team performance and sadness after poor performance (Gantz & Wenner, 1995; Sloan, 1989; Sloan & Van Camp, 2008), a finding that has been replicated at a variety of competition levels including collegiate (Jensen et al., 2016), professional (Koenigstorfer, Groeppel-Klein, & Schmitt, 2010), World Cup (Jones, Coffee, Sheffield, Yanguez, & Barker, 2012), and Olympic (Hallmann, Breuer, & Kuhnreich, 2013). Furthermore, consistent with the Disposition Theory of Sport Spectatorship detailed above, the experience of happiness and sadness is most intense among persons high in team identification (Jang, Ko, Wann, & Kim, in press; Keaton & Gearhart, 2014; Kwon, Lee, & Lee, 2008).

A series of studies conducted by Jang and his colleagues shed light on the processes through which sport consumption leads to happiness. Jang, Wann, and Ko (in press) investigated the impact of game process (i.e., a boring versus exciting contest) on fans' happiness. Participants were asked to either recall (Study 1) or imagine (Study 2) an exciting game that a preferred team had lost or a boring contest that their team had won. Subjects' identification with the preferred team was also assessed, as was their happiness in response to the game. The results indicated that highly identified fans were significantly happier after the boring but winning game relative to the exciting loss game. Low identified persons reported similar levels of happiness for both contests. Thus, it appears the combination of game process and outcome have differential impacts on fans high and low in identification (see Figure 6.2). Those with greater psychological connections to a team will be happiest after a win even if the game was boring. For these fans, the outcome was of greater value than the suspense and excitement of the game. Essentially, their happiness reflects former Oakland Raiders' owner Al Davis' famous line: "Just win baby!"

A second investigation conducted by Jang and his associates (in press) targeted the influence of vitality on fans' happiness. **Vitality** involves "one's conscious experience of possessing energy and aliveness" (Ryan & Frederick, 1997, p. 530). Given that vitality is related to positive psychological states (McNair, Lorr, & Droppleman, 1971; Stewart, Hayes, & Ware, 1992), Jang and his coauthors felt it may play a role in the happiness of sport fans as well. Research indicating that team identification and vitality are positivity correlated (Wann & Craven, 2014) provides additional evidence that vitality could be critical for understanding fans' experiences of happiness. In the Jang et al. study, participants watched a highlight video of a victory by the United States Men's National Soccer team. Subsequent to viewing the highlight video, participants completed a questionnaire packet assessing their happiness, vitality, and identification with the team. The results indicated that vitality mediated the relationship between identification and happiness. Thus, when watching one's team perform well, team identification influences vitality (i.e., energy) which, in turn, influences happiness.

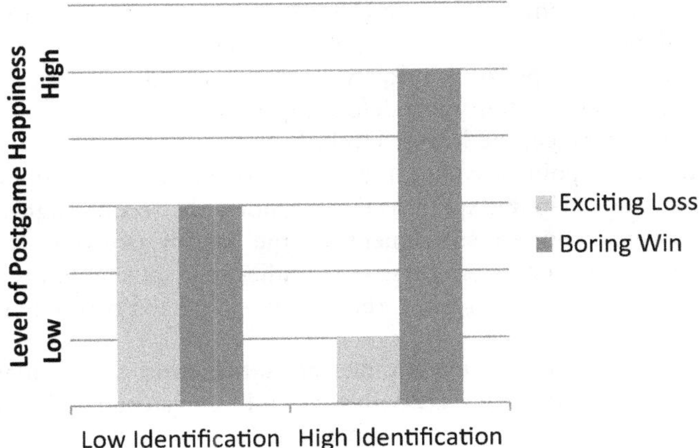

FIGURE 6.2 Postgame Happiness After an Exciting Loss and a Boring Win for Fans High and Low in Team Identification

Enjoyment and Satisfaction

Enjoyment and satisfaction are positive emotional responses that have gained the attention of sport scientists interested in fan affect (Gan et al., 1997). With respect to enjoyment, Tobar (2006) investigated the relationship between general sport fandom and enjoyment of watching the Super Bowl. Enjoyment of a number of different facets of the game was assessed, including athletic performance, the halftime show, and the broadcasters. These were summed to form an index of overall enjoyment. Persons with greater interest in sport reported more enjoyment from their viewing experience. Taking a somewhat different approach, rather than focusing on interest in sport, Wann and Schrader (1997) investigated the relationship between team identification and enjoyment of an athletic contest. Following two college basketball games (a win and a loss by the local team), spectators completed measures assessing their identification with the home team and their enjoyment of the contest. The greatest levels of enjoyment were reported by highly identified fans who had witnessed a victory by their team. Lower levels of enjoyment were found among highly identified fans watching a defeat and low identified persons watching either contest.

As for satisfaction, a pair of interesting studies included examination of fans' satisfaction with specific games. One of these investigations was conducted by Sloan (1989), who investigated affective reactions to three different athletic events: a loss, an easy victory, and a difficult victory. There was little pregame to postgame change in satisfaction following the easy win. However, the difficult win and loss conditions revealed drastic changes. Significant increases in satisfaction occurred after the difficult win, and large decreases were noted after the loss.

Madrigal (2003) conducted a second examination of satisfaction with specific sporting events. In this work, participants watched a live televised broadcast of one of six contests involving their university's men's basketball team (the home team's record was 1–5 in the contests). Following the conclusion of the games, participants completed a scale assessing their satisfaction with the event. Consistent with the findings of Sloan (1989), satisfaction levels were tied to the outcome of the games, with greater satisfaction reported after a win relative to a loss. However, a deeper look into the data reveals an interesting pattern of effects: satisfaction levels following defeat appear to be related to the magnitude of the loss. For instance, the lowest level of satisfaction was reported after the largest defeat (a 22-point loss) and the second-lowest level was found after the second-worst loss (11-point spread). Furthermore, the second-highest levels of satisfaction were reported subsequent to the team's overtime loss. Taken together, we can conclude from these two studies that satisfaction is not simply a function of wins and losses but, rather, is also impacted by the magnitude of the outcome.

A different approach to examining fan satisfaction was undertaken by Koenigstorfer and his colleagues (2010; see also Koenigstorfer & Uhrich, 2009). These researchers were interested in soccer fans' responses to the threat of their team being relegated to a lower division. Participants were supporters of one of four teams in danger of having their team relegated. At the conclusion of the season, two of the teams were indeed relegated, while the other two remained in the first division. Participants were asked to describe their feelings about the just completed season. The results revealed differences in satisfaction levels as a function of relegation. Specifically, a content analysis revealed a greater tendency for persons supporting a non-relegated team to mention feeling satisfied compared to persons whose team had been sent to a lower division. In fact, none of the persons whose team had been relegated reported satisfaction with the season.

A final investigation of fan satisfaction was conducted by Jang et al. (in press). In a pair of studies, these authors examined the impact of game characteristics and the spectating environment on fan satisfaction. The experiments employed methods similar to those utilized in the previously discussed work by Jang et al. (in press). That is, respondents recalled either an exciting game that their team had lost or a boring contest that they had won and reported their satisfaction with the game. In Study 1, the fans were more satisfied with the contest when their team won a boring game than if it was an exciting game but their team had been defeated. The second study extended these results by incorporating the viewing environment into the model. That is, in addition to recalling either a boring win or an exciting loss, participants targeted games they watched alone and those they watched with others. Consistent with Study 1, participants reported greater satisfaction after boring wins, and, for these games, the viewing environment did not influence satisfaction levels (i.e., they were equally high). However, an interesting pattern emerged for persons recalling an exciting loss. For these contests, game satisfaction was higher when they watched with others. Satisfaction was particularly low when persons watched exciting losses alone. Evidently, when individuals watch an exciting contest that is eventually lost by a favorite team, the ability to share in the excitement with others adds to their satisfaction of the event (although not to the levels felt when the team is victorious).

Tired and Fatigued

Researchers have also investigated the extent to which spectators feel tired and fatigued in response to watching sporting events. A consistent finding from such work is that fans watching their team lose report higher levels of fatigue/tiredness than those watching their team perform well. The previously reviewed study by Sloan was perhaps the first to examine the impact of competition outcome on the fatigue of fans. He found that spectators reported pre- to postgame increases in tiredness after a loss, while no such change was found following either an easy or difficult win. Wann and his colleagues (1994) replicated Sloan's work, but included an assessment of the participants' level of identification with the home team as well. Similar to Sloan's data, their findings indicated that feelings of tiredness increased from pre- to postgame for persons watching the team lose. However, highly identified fans tended to be especially tired following the team's defeat.

A final study on fatigue to consider was conducted by Jones and his associates (2012). These researchers investigated English and Spanish soccer fans' reactions to their team's performance during the 2010 Soccer World Cup. The English and

Spanish teams (and consequently, their fans) had drastically different experiences in this tournament. The English team failed to meet pre-tournament expectations, winning only one of the four matches they played. Conversely, despite an early loss, the Spanish team went on a six-game winning streak and won their first World Cup championship. For fans of both teams, post-match fatigue was tied to their team's performance. English fans expressed their lowest level of post-game fatigue following their team's lone win; Spanish fans expressed their highest level of post-match fatigue subsequent to their team's only loss. Furthermore, across all games, fatigue scores were higher among English fans than Spanish fans, a consequence of more losses by the English team.

Disappointment

Every sport fan likely experiences disappointment at one time or another. Thus, it is perhaps not surprising that a number of scholars have completed studies targeting this affective response, detailing those aspects of the fan experience that most frequently lead to feelings of disappointment. In particular, Rainey and his colleagues conducted a program of research using **Disappointment Theory** to guide their work (Bell, 1985; Loomes & Sugden, 1986). The argument is that individuals will be most disappointed in a losing outcome when success was particularly likely. For example, people express greater levels of disappointment when failing to win a "sure-thing" lottery (e.g., 90 percent likelihood of success) relative to situations in which winning is improbable (van Dijk & van der Pligt, 1997). A further prediction with this framework is that negative outcomes will be more disappointing for persons with higher levels of investment. As it relates to sport fandom, Disappointment Theory implies that fans should be particularly disappointed in a loss if they are highly identified (i.e., invested) with the team and if their team is expected to win (i.e., a win is viewed as a sure thing).

In their first study, Rainey et al. (2009; see also Yost & Rainey, 2014) investigated the experiences of Cleveland Indians fans following the team's loss in Game 7 of the 2007 American League Championship Series. This loss ended the Indians season and left them just one victory shy of the World Series. Participants completed a questionnaire assessing their disappointment in the team's loss, their dedication to the Indians (i.e., identification with the team), and the degree to which they had expected the team to win the series. Higher levels of disappointment were reported by persons with higher expectations and those with higher levels of dedication. However, dedication appeared to be especially important, leading the authors to conclude, "The most powerful predictor of fan disappointment was the self-reported measure of dedication" (p. 351). It warrants mention that the participants in this study likely had particularly high levels of disappointment, given that their team was so close to reaching the ultimate goal of winning the World Series. Research suggests that "near misses" (coming close to, but failing to reach a goal) lead to greater disappointment than losses that are farther removed from a goal (Clark, Lawrence, Astley-Jones, & Gray, 2009). For example, Olympic bronze medalists tend to be happier than

Disappointment Is a Common Reaction Among Sport Fans Whose Team Has Performed Poorly

silver medalists when appearing on the medal stand (Medvec, Madley, & Gilovich, 1995). For fans, this suggests that reaching the playoffs but exiting early may be particularly disappointing (Wann et al., 2017).

A second examination of fan disappointment by Rainey and his associates extended their previous work in several important ways (Rainey, Yost, & Larsen, 2011). First, they targeted fans of a different sport (NFL football). Second, rather than rely on retrospective beliefs about expectations, they assessed expectations prior to a season. And third, given the importance of dedication in their first study, the authors attempted to improve on the single-item measure of dedication they had previously employed by assessing team identification via the SSIS. Participants were fans of the Cleveland Browns, an NFL team who had experienced several years of losing. However, the previous (2007) season had been better than expected, as the team won 10 of 16 games and almost qualified for the playoffs. As a result, optimism for the 2008 season was quite high. Unfortunately, the team reverted to its former ways, ending the season with a 4–12 record. Just prior to the 2008 season, respondents completed a preseason measure assessing identification with the Browns and their expectations for the coming year. Following the season, they completed a questionnaire measuring their disappointment in the season. The findings replicated the data on Cleveland Indians fans, as both expectations and identification positively predicted greater levels of disappointment. Thus, Rainey and his associates found that for both baseball fans (Rainey et al., 2009) and football fans (Rainey et al., 2011), patterns of disappointment are consistent with the tenets of

Disappointment Theory. Specifically, higher levels of disappointment are found among those with greater levels of team identification and when expectations for success are highest.

Anger

Similar to disappointment, research indicates that fans often feel angry following their team's poor performance (Koenigstorfer et al., 2010; Sloan, 1989). For example, consider the aforementioned work by Jones and his colleagues (2012) on soccer fans' responses to their team's World Cup performance. The data revealed that post-match anger levels were a function of the team's performance. For supporters of both teams, the highest levels of anger followed losses, while the lowest levels were reported after wins. Interestingly, when fans were asked to report their anger after a tie (England's first and second games), levels of anger fell between those recorded after a win and those subsequent to a loss. In their investigation of sport fans' anger, Jensen and colleagues (2016) asked participants to watch a highlight video of a recent win or loss by a favored team. After viewing the video, the respondents wrote about the game and the team. The results indicated that not only did persons watching the losing video include more responses indicative of anger, they were also more likely to incorporate swear words into their writing.

Although the studies reported above provide valuable information on fans' postgame anger, they do not expose fluctuations that might occur during the contest. Sloan's (1989) work can be used to highlight this point. He found that people reported significant increases in pre- to postgame anger following a team's loss, but no such changes were found for those watching the team win. In fact, an examination of Sloan's data suggests that fans watching the winning game maintained a very low level of anger from the start of the game to the finish. However, this may lead to an overly simplistic perception of fan anger because those watching a winning contest may not have maintained low levels of anger throughout the course of the event. In fact, research suggests that this is indeed the case (Madrigal, 2003). For example, Kerr, Wilson, Nakamura, and Sudo (2005) assessed the affective reactions of fans attending either a winning or losing match involving a Japanese professional soccer team. Participants completed the affect scales before, during (halftime), and after the contests. Although fans watching the winning and losing contests had similar pregame anger levels, postgame anger was higher for those watching their team lose. Pregame and postgame anger scores differed very little for those watching the team win. However, these fans did report moderate increases in anger at halftime. Thus, fans supporting a winning team may show little change in anger from pre- to postgame, but this does not guarantee that their anger stayed consistently low throughout the contest. Rather, there are likely fluctuations in anger as a game is played.

The finding that fans feel greater levels of anger when their team performs poorly is consistent with the Disposition Theory of Sport Spectatorship (Zillmann et al., 1989; Zillmann & Paulas, 1993). However, this theory would predict that fans should also be angry when a rival team performs well.

Interestingly, this is precisely the pattern of effects found by Cikara, Botvinick, and Fiske (2011). In this research, diehard New York Yankees and Boston Red Sox fans viewed computer-generated plays in which their team either succeeded or failed. Participants then reported their level of anger in response to viewing the plays. As one would expect, they reported low levels of anger when the favored team succeeded and high levels of anger when this team failed. Furthermore, consistent with Disposition Theory, high levels of anger were also expressed after watching the rival team succeed, while low levels were reported after rival failure.

Fans appear to be most angry when their team fails and when a rival succeeds, a pattern consistent with the Disposition Theory of Spectatorship. However, recall that this framework also predicts that the greatest affective changes will be experienced by persons with high levels of team identification (i.e., a strong disposition toward the team). Research has consistently confirmed this effect as well. That is, similar to many of the previously discussed emotions, anger seems to be most intensely felt by those with higher levels of identification (Crisp et al., 2007; Keaton & Gearhart, 2014; Sumino & Harada, 2004).

Shame

Shame is yet another negative emotion experienced by sport fans (Lewis, 2007; Nathanson, 1992). Shame is a self-directed emotion that occurs when one feels his or her value has been diminished in a social setting (Elison, 2005; Tangney, Miller, Flicker, & Barlow, 1996). Although less frequently studied than other negative fan emotions, a handful of interesting studies have targeted this affective response. For example, Sloan and Van Camp (2008) examined the impact of game outcome on levels of pre- and postgame shame felt by fans at college athletic events. They found that, although fans witnessing an eventual win or loss reported similar levels of shame prior to the contest, shame increased for those watching the team lose but decreased for those viewing a win.

Partridge and her colleagues (Partridge & Wann, 2015; Partridge, Wann, & Elison, 2010) have taken a different angle in their work on sport fan shame. Rather than investigating levels of shame, these authors examined the maladaptive manner in which fans cope with shame. There are several **maladaptive coping strategies** fans could utilize to help them deal with their team-related shame (Nathanson, 1992; Partridge et al., 2010). Some fans cope by **attacking others**, choosing to direct their shame-generated anger toward other fans, coaches, players, or officials. Others may opt for **attacking self** in which they accept the shame as valid and, consequently, attack their allegiance to the team. **Avoidance** is a third option. Here, fans use denial to reject the shaming message or event, perhaps using humor to derogate the team. And finally, fans may choose **withdrawal**, preferring to avoid coverage of or discussions about the team.

Partridge and her associates were interested in determining which of the four maladaptive shame coping strategies were most common among sport fans. In their first study, Partridge et al. (2010) assessed the preferred coping strategy among college sport fans in response to their favorite team's actions. In a second project, they examined the shame coping styles of supporters of youth sport

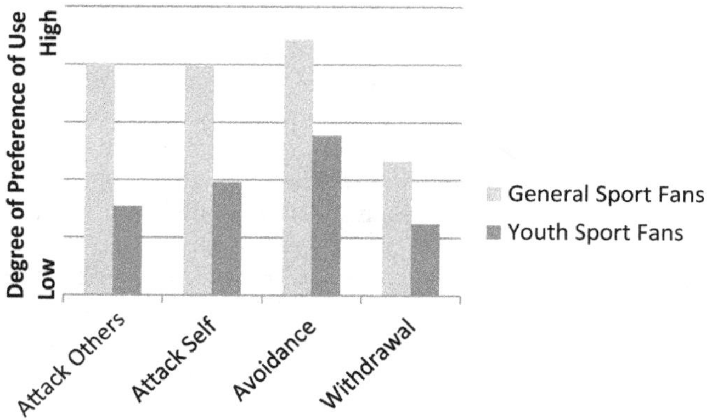

FIGURE 6.3 Degree of Preference for Use of the Four Maladaptive Shame Coping Strategies Among General Sport Fans and Youth Sport Fans

teams (Partridge & Wann, 2015). The results appear in Figure 6.3; patterns of preference were quite similar for the two groups. The most frequently utilized strategy was avoidance, while the least common was withdrawal. Thus, sport fans seemed to respond to team-focused shame via distraction or by denying the importance of the event (i.e., avoidance). They were less likely to seek solitude from others (i.e., withdrawal). This pattern of effects likely reflects the social nature of fandom, coupled with a desire to at least temporarily put the team's shameful actions out of mind.

Anxiety

Given that sport fans pour their heart and soul into their teams, it seems reasonable that many experience high levels of anxiety (e.g., worry, tension) before, during, and after games. Fans exhibit behaviors, such as pacing the floor, that are common among persons experiencing life's most anxious moments (Gantz & Wenner, 1995). Corbin (1973) conducted one of the earliest studies examining spectator anxiety. This investigator was interested in the impact of sport viewing on the physiological responses (heart rate) of persons varying in trait anxiety. Although the results did not provide evidence of differential response patterns for persons higher or lower in anxiety, sport viewing was associated with large increases in heart rate, suggesting that spectating could most certainly induce anxiety.

A number of more complex studies of fan anxiety followed Corbin's (1973) work. This literature indicates that fans often experience anxiety, worry, and tension when watching their team compete (Sumino & Harada, 2004). For instance, fans have been found to experience higher levels of anxiety after their team loses than after the team wins (Kerr et al., 2005). In his seminal work on sport fan affect, Sloan (1989) found several significant pre- to postgame changes in tension. Persons watching their team lose reported higher postgame tension while those watching the team win a challenging contest reported a reduction in tension. Spectators witnessing an easy win reported no change in tension from the beginning to the conclusion of the contest. Wann and his colleagues (1994) also found that witnessing a loss increased fans' tension. However, the effect was more pronounced among highly identified fans. Those low in identification indicated only minor increases in tension. This pattern of effects, which has been replicated elsewhere (Chien & Ross, 2012; Wann, Schrader, & Adamson, 1998), would be expected given that low identified persons have less interest in the outcome of the contest, and their sense of well-being is less likely to be impacted by team performance.

Other investigators have examined patterns of fan anxiety leading up to a sporting event. This work reveals that the anxiety experienced by fans is highly similar to that felt by athletes (Kelley & Tian, 2004). Players typically report steady increases in anxiety as a competition approaches, peaking just prior to the start of the event (Fenz, 1988; Wann, 1997). Wann et al. (1998) found roughly the same pattern of effects for highly identified college basketball fans. Participants completed an assessment of their anxiety for two games involving their college's men's basketball team. One game was against a highly inferior opponent, while the other was against a highly successful conference rival. Anxiety was measured at five points in time: three days before the game, 12 hours before, three hours before, immediately before, and at halftime. Two forms of anxiety were assessed: **cognitive anxiety** (mental anxiety involving worry and apprehension) and **somatic anxiety** (physical anxiety such as butterflies and jitters). For the difficult contest, both forms of anxiety slowly increased as the competition neared, spiking during the halftime assessment. Anxiety scores were lower for the contest against the inferior opponent relative to the difficult game. For the easier contest, increases in cognitive anxiety were not apparent as the game approached or at halftime. However, fans reported a slight increase in somatic anxiety as the game approached and a significant escalation at halftime. Thus, highly identified fans experienced increases in both cognitive and somatic anxiety as a challenging game drew near, but, for an easier contest, only somatic anxiety increased. For the nonthreatening game, highly identified persons became increasingly aroused, but not more apprehensive and concerned.

The anxiety experienced by sport fans and spectators should not be taken lightly, as a growing body of work suggests that their anxiety can be high enough to present serious health risks. In fact, several studies have found that viewing stressful sport contests is associated with stroke and myocardial infarction. Increased risk for these life-threatening, stress-induced events has been found among spectators watching soccer (Carroll, Ebrahim, Tilling, Macleod, & Smith, 2002; Kirkup & Merrick, 2003; Witte, Bots, Hoes, & Grobbee, 2000) and American football (Kloner, McDonald, Leeka, & Poole, 2009). For instance, consider the work by Wilbert-Lampen and colleagues (2008). These researchers examined emergency room (ER) visits to a German hospital involving cardiovascular issues (e.g., chest pain due to myocardial infarction and cardiac arrhythmia) on the seven days in which the German national team played in the 2006 World Cup. ER visits were markedly higher on game days relative to control days (i.e., other days during 2006, the same date in previous years). Based on their findings, the authors concluded that "it is clear that watching an important soccer match, which can be associated with intense emotional stress, triggers the acute coronary syndrome and symptomatic cardiac arrhythmia" (p. 477).

Additional Affective Reactions

Although the variety of affective reactions of fans described in the preceding paragraphs is impressive, it is far from a complete list. Rather, a number of additional emotions have also been investigated, although less frequently. Table 6.1 contains a sample of these additional emotions. This is not meant to

TABLE 6.1 A Sample of Additional Sport Fan Affective Reactions Targeted in Research

Emotion	Reference(s)
Admiration	Madrigal (2003)
Benevolence	Sloan (1989)
Boredom	Kerr et al. (2005)
Confidence	Sloan (1989) Wann and Wiggins (1999)
Curiosity	Park, Mahony, and Kim (2011) Park, Mahony, and Greenwell (2010)
Depression	Hirt, Zillmann, Erickson, and Kennedy (1992) Jones et al. (2012) Sloan and Van Camp (2008)
Discouragement	Sloan (1989)
Disgust	Keaton and Gearhart (2014)
Excitement	Sumino and Harada (2004)
Fear	Koenigstorfer et al. (2010)
Frustration	Madrigal (2003) Sloan (1989)
Gratitude	Kerr et al. (2005)
Humiliation	Kerr et al. (2005)
Love	Sumino and Harada (2004)
Placidity	Kerr et al. (2005)
Pride	Koenigstorfer et al. (2010) Madrigal (2003) Sloan and Van Camp (2008)
Provocativeness	Kerr et al. (2005)
Relaxation	Kerr et al. (2005)
Relief	Koenigstorfer et al. (2010)
Respect	Madrigal (2003)
Sullenness	Kerr et al. (2005)

be an exhaustive list but, instead, designed to provide the reader with information on a subset of other emotions that have been studied.

Additional Topics on the Affective Reactions of Sport Fans

The sections above detail research targeting what might be the most obvious issue for sport fan emotions, namely, their affective reactions to game outcome. But there is much more to fan affect than simply responding to team success and failure. In the following sections, we examine several additional topics related to the emotional reactions of sport fans.

Affective Reactions to Non-Performance-Related Events

Although fans become emotional in response to team performance, competition outcome is not required to elicit their affective reactions. In fact, fans can receive a positive emotional boost simply via their association with a team (Dwyer et al., 2015). Furthermore, fans' emotional responses are not limited to competitive environments. The list of non-performance events and situations that produce affective reactions from fans is quite impressive (Cottingham, 2012). For example, fans have been found to respond emotionally to reading about a disloyal fan (Wann & Branscombe, 1992), the potential loss of the team's name and mascot (Wohl, Branscombe, & Reysen, 2010), exposure to team-related photos (Hillmann, Cuthbert, Bradley, & Lang, 2004; Hillmann et al., 2000), stadium features such as the appearance of and the atmosphere within the arena (Uhrich & Benkenstein, 2010, 2012), player strikes/lockouts (Grieve, Shoenfelt, Wann, & Zapalac, 2009), changes in team coaching (Potter & Keene, 2012), and halftime shows (Tobar, 2006).

One emotional event that deserves elaboration concerns fans' reactions to player injuries. Although it seems reasonable that fans would respond with sadness, disbelief, and other negative emotions when their favorite players are hurt, research suggests that they also report positive affective responses to the injuries of rival players. Their reaction to the injuries to rival players involves **schadenfreude**, that is, joy in the suffering of others (schadenfreude is a German-based term combining "schaden" or harm, and "freude" or joy). Thus, the misfortune of rivals may lead fans to react with positive affect (Cikara et al., 2011; Dalakas & Melancon, 2012; Leach, Spears, Branscombe, & Doosje, 2003).

In fact, highly identified fans can even revel in the death of a rival (Dalakas, Melancon, & Sreboth, 2015). For example, consider the work by Wann and Waddill (2007) on fans' affective reactions to the crash and death of auto racing legend Dale Earnhardt. Earnhardt's fatal accident occurred on the last lap of the 2001 Daytona 500. A few months later, the researchers had participants complete a questionnaire assessing their responses to and memory of the incident. Participants also indicated if they had a favorite NASCAR driver and, if so, who that person was. Based on their responses to this item, participants were

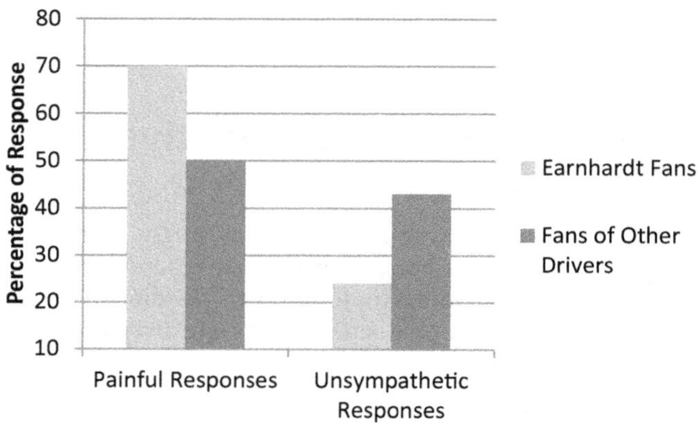

FIGURE 6.4 Reactions to the Crash and Death of NASCAR Legend Dale Earnhardt

classified as either Earnhardt fans or fans of a rival driver. Wann and Waddill conducted a content analysis of participants' responses to the crash, coding for answers reflecting painful emotional reactions (e.g., shock, loss) as well as those expressing indifference to Earnhardt's crash and death (e.g., "it's a dangerous sport and Earnhardt knew the risks"). The results, which are depicted in Figure 6.4, revealed that the majority of Earnhardt fans included painful remarks in their recollections of and reactions to the crash. Fewer fans of other drivers included painful responses. Rather, in line with schadenfreude, these persons were more likely to express a lack of sympathy and dismiss the event.

Unfortunately, if sport fans feeling gleeful (or at least less than sorry) about a fallen rival was not disturbing enough, research by Hoogland and his colleagues (2015) provides evidence that the negative affect continues when the rival athlete begins to recover. These investigators examined the process of **gluckschmerz,** a German term for feeling bad when a rival group member experiences a positive outcome. In their study, college students read an article describing an injury to a rival team's player and then answered questioned assessing their reactions to his injury. Participants then read a second article describing the injured player's quick recovery and answered items assessing their reactions to this report. As expected, fans higher in team identification reacted with schadenfreude when hearing of the player's injury, indicating pleasure in his (and his team's) misfortune. Furthermore, upon learning of his recovery, these fans reported displeasure and disappointment, a pattern consistent with gluckschmerz.

The Impact of Affective Reactions on Attitudes and Behaviors

Back in Chapter 1, we noted that sport fandom impacts the ABCs of Psychology, that is, affect, behavior, and cognition. This chapter has been dedicated to the affective responses of fans, documenting the variety of ways in which sport impacts the emotional states of fans. However, the ABCs do not operate in isolation. Rather, they frequently interact with one another. This is most certainly the case with sport fan affect. Not only does sport influence the emotions of fans, but these emotions, in turn, influence subsequent thoughts and actions.

Sport Outcomes Sport fan emotional responses may influence other sport-related outcomes, including thoughts and behaviors (or intended behaviors). With respect to cognition, researchers have found that fan emotions can influence both team loyalty and identification. In terms of loyalty, both positive (e.g., joy, excitement) and negative (e.g., worry, sadness) emotions have been shown to play a role in one's faithfulness to a team (Sumino & Harada, 2004; Trail, Anderson, & Fink, 2005). As for identification, although this tends to be stable (see Chapter 1), Yost and Rainey (2014) found that the disappointment of a poor season was associated with a decrease in identification, particularly for fans originally lower in their psychological connection with the team. Highly identified fans were "more resilient to the consequences of disappointment" (p. 415).

As for behaviors, research indicates that fans' emotional experiences can impact intentions for future attendance and positive word of mouth (Biscaia et al., 2012; Chen, Lin, & Chiu, 2013; Uhrich & Benkenstein, 2012; Yoshida & James, 2010). The list of emotions tied to increased future consumption and positive word of mouth includes satisfaction, pleasure, relief, and curiosity (Jang et al., in press; Kuenzel & Yassim, 2007; Lee & Kang, 2015; Park, Mahony, Kim, & Kim, 2015; Sarstedt, Ringle, Raithel, & Gudergan, 2014; Taute, Sierra, & Heiser, 2010).

Non-sport Outcomes Several interesting studies highlight the powerful effect fan-based affect can have on the lives of fans beyond sport. The negative affect accompanying the loss of a favorite team can lead fans to adopt a more pessimistic outlook (Schwarz, Strack, Kommer, & Wagner, 1987). Schweitzer, Zillmann, Weaver, and Luttrell (1992) found that supporters of a losing team were more likely to believe that the Gulf War was imminent, and these fans predicted a greater number of American casualties than did fans of a winning team. Fans supporting a winning team also report increased social interaction after the team's success (Jones et al., 2012). Additionally, the negative affect associated with supporting a losing team can spillover into the workplace. Researchers found that fans' dissatisfaction with their team's losses can lead to lower levels of job engagement and, as a result, poorer work performance (Gkorezis, Bellou, Xanthopolou, Bakker, & Tsiftsis, 2016).

Emotions stemming from sport viewing can also impact one's confidence in his or her abilities. Hirt et al. (1992) asked college students to report the extent to which they felt "depressed" or "elated" after watching a live broadcast of one of their university's men's basketball games. They were then asked to give estimates of their success on a pair of unrelated tasks. First, respondents were shown an example of a five-letter anagram in both the scrambled and unscrambled form. They then estimated the number of similar anagrams they could solve in five minutes (this was the "mental skills task"). Next, respondents were presented with a series of slides depicting members of the opposite sex. Subsequent to viewing each slide, participants estimated the likelihood that the individual depicted would accept the participant's invitation to attend a concert (the "social skills task"). The results revealed that team performance had a profound effect on the mental state of the participants. Spectators who watched the team lose were higher in depression (and, consequently, lower in elation) than those who watched the team win. These persons also reported significantly lower estimates of their mental and social skills (i.e., they estimated completing fewer anagrams and were less likely to believe their invitation to the concert would be accepted). These outcome-based differences in depression/elation and skill estimates were only found among participants with a high level of team identification.

The non-sport impact of fan emotions should not be taken lightly as research suggests they may even influence voting decisions and, hence, political elections. Noting that "people often transfer emotions in one domain toward evaluation and judgment in a completely separate domain" (p. 12804), Healy, Malhotra, and Mo (2010) investigated the link between the affective responses of fans and politics. They concluded that politicians may want to funnel money into improving the performance of local teams because the positive affect generated by local team success carries over into positive evaluations of currently elected officials. They examined election results spanning three decades and found that a win by the local college football team led to greater vote totals for the incumbent candidate. This was particularly true for high profile teams (e.g., a win by a championship-caliber team was associated with an increase of almost 2.5 percentage points for the incumbent). In a separate study of college basketball fans, greater success in the NCAA men's tournament was associated with more positive approval ratings for President Obama (Healy et al., 2010).

Economic Outcomes Economic outcomes are a final manner in which fans are influenced by their sport-generated emotions. Research indicates that happier consumers tend to spend more (Sherman, Mathur, & Smith, 1997; Spies, Hesse, & Loesch, 1997), and this pattern of effects has been documented among sport fans as well (Jones et al., 2012). For example, fans gaining a positive affective experience from their association with a team are more likely to purchase team-related apparel (Taute et al., 2010), spend more money at the sporting event (Uhrich & Benkenstein, 2012), and indicate a greater interest in purchasing sponsors' products (Wang & Kaplanidou, 2013). Additionally, pride from supporting a successful college team may lead to increased donations to the university (Daughtrey & Stotlar, 2000; Rhoads & Gerking, 2000). Furthermore, not only does positive affect facilitate spending, it also appears to positively impact the acquisition of money. For example, multiple studies have found that team success is associated with higher per capita personal income (Coates & Humphreys, 2002; Davis & End, 2010). Apparently, although disappointed fans exhibit lower job performance (Gkorezis et al., 2016), fans experiencing positive emotions are more productive and, as a result, earn greater amounts of money.

The economic consequences of sport fan affect are far from trivial, and the effect is not simply limited to "happy fans spend more money." Rather, the economic consequences of fan emotions are far-reaching. For example, Edmans, Garcia, and Norli (2007) investigated the affective consequences of performing poorly in national athletic competitions on a country's stock market. In an examination of almost 40 countries, they found "a strong negative stock market reaction to losses by national soccer teams" (p. 1991). The authors argued that poor stock market performance was a consequence of investors' negative mood stemming from their team's poor performance.

The Impact of Sustained Success

In 1991, the Atlanta Braves began an impressive string of success in which they made the postseason 14 times in 15 seasons, including 11 straight from 1995 to 2005. During the last several years of this successful run, the Braves fan base drew heavy criticism for low attendance at the team's home playoff contests. It was commonly argued that one factor leading to the poor attendance was the sustained success of the team. That is, fans had grown accustomed to the team's winning and, as a result, were not as excited about the team and their victories as one might have expected. Their emotional reactions to the team were becoming less intense with each passing successful season, which, in turn, resulted in less desire to attend games (as noted above, emotional reactions are frequently tied to attendance decisions).

Contrast the postseason attendance figures for the Braves with what was found in the fall of 2016 when, after over 100 years of futility, the Chicago Cubs finally won a World Series. Excitement for the Cubs and their newly found success was at an all-time high. Not only were the team's home playoff games sold out, but tickets were going for outrageous prices on the secondary market (some were sold for over $20,000). The joy and excitement continued after the World Series championship was secured, as evidenced by an estimated crowd of 5 million at the team's victory parade (believed to be one of the top ten largest gatherings in human history, Sadlock, 2016).

It appears that the sustained success and failure of a sport team can impact the emotional reactions of fans. Indeed, research on fans and work in general psychology lead us to conclude that it should. First, as we noted in Chapter 1, fans desperate for a championship respond differently from those whose team had recently been crowned (Wann et al., 2011). Additionally, based on Solomon's **Opponent Process Theory** (Solomon, 1980; Solomon & Corbit, 1974), repeated exposure to the same affective event can decrease the intensity of one's emotional response to that event. Thus, having one's team experience a sustained period of success may result in less extreme emotional responses relative to when success was new (Chang, Wann, & Inoue, in press).

Duration of the Affective State

In the Cubs example described above, Cubs Nation was on cloud nine after watching their beloved team's World Series victory over the Cleveland Indians. Given how the Series ended and their team's history of failure, it is likely Indians fans felt just as terrible as Cubs fans felt euphoric (in fact, their negative affect may have been more intense, see "Some Final Thoughts" below). But were Cubs fans still euphoric days or weeks later? Were Indians fans doomed to a winter of sadness because their team had lost in the fall? These questions point to an additional question concerning the affective reactions of fans, namely, the duration of their emotional response. The preceding sections of this chapter highlight the intensity in which fans feel emotional, but thus far we have yet to discuss the length of time fans remain in a positive or negative state. Although only a few scholars have examined the duration of fan emotions, their research does provide some valuable information.

Wann et al. (2003) examined the duration of fans' positive and negative affective reactions to sporting events, asking how long it took to "recover from a major loss" and "come down from game excitement" (p. 932). Almost half of the participants required a full day or longer to recover from a loss or calm down from game excitement. And almost 10 percent required more than a week to recover or calm down. In another study, Jones and his associates (2012) compared the postgame duration of positive and negative affect for fans of winning and losing teams. Interestingly, they found that the positive affect following team success persisted longer than the negative affect experiences in response to a team's defeat.

Motivation as a Predictor of Spectator Affect

In Chapter 4, we discussed a number of different motives that drive fans' desire to follow sport. Wann, Brewer, and Royalty (1999) reasoned that a fan's motivational profile may have implications for his or her emotional reaction to a sporting event. For instance, persons who are motivated by eustress may experience positive affect when watching an exciting contest, while those with higher levels of group affiliation motivation may become bored when watching a game alone.

To examine the link between fan motivation and affect, Wann et al. (1999) examined basketball spectators, assessing several fan motives prior to a contest and general positive affect after the game (positive affect was assessed because the home team won). The results revealed that two motives had a significant impact on postgame positive affect: entertainment was positively related, while family was a negative predictor. Given the parameters of the game, this pattern of affects is quite reasonable. First, the teams were evenly matched, and the game was a close and exciting contest. Thus, persons with high levels of entertainment motivation should have been pleased with the game's quality and been in a positive affective state after the event. However, because the teams were conference rivals and the game was of high importance, it was a standing-room-only crowd. In fact, the announced attendance was 511 spectators over arena capacity. Consequently, it was uncomfortably hot and crowded in the arena, the noise level made it almost impossible to converse with others, and almost all spectators stood throughout the contest. This combination of factors resulted in the environment being less than ideal for families. Thus, it seems logical that persons who attended this game to spend some quality time with his or her family would have been displeased after the event. Thus, Wann et al. (1999)

were able to confirm that fans' motivational profiles play an important role in their emotional experience when watching a sporting event, a finding that has been replicated elsewhere (Sloan & Van Camp, 2008; Wann, Royalty, & Rochelle, 2002). When the details of a contest match the motives driving a fan's interest in the game and sport, he or she is more likely to have a positive consumption experience.

Affective Forecasting

Affective forecasting concerns an individual's ability to predict the type and intensity of his or her emotional reaction to a future event. For fans, this involves their ability to accurately estimate their emotional responses to events such as a long-awaited championship, the retirement of a favorite player, or the opening of a new stadium. Research on affective forecasting reveals that, although individuals are quite successful in predicting which emotion they will experience (e.g., happy, sad, angry), they are generally poor at foretelling the intensity and duration with which they will experience the emotion (Gilbert, Driver-Linn, & Wilson, 2002). People tend to overestimate the impact of the emotive event, a phenomenon referred to as **impact bias** (Kermer, Driver-Linn, Wilson, & Gilbert, 2006; Wilson & Gilbert, 2005). This bias has also been found in sport settings (e.g., Van Dijk, 2009), including the affective predictions of football fans who, after a victory, were not as happy as they expected to be (Wilson, Wheatley, Meyers, Gilbert, & Axsom, 2000).

Researchers have identified some critical features leading to the impact bias outside of sport, such as **focalism**, or the tendency to focus specifically on the target event while ignoring other life events (Lam, Buehler, McFarland, Ross, & Cheung, 2005). However, investigators have yet to fully investigate factors that might impact the accuracy of emotional predictions among fans. Given the importance of team identification in the affective responses of sport fans, researchers should investigate how this variable impacts the degree to which fans exhibit the impact bias. Similarly, they should determine if long-suffering fans (i.e., those following teams who have not won a championship in many years) are more or less likely to exhibit the impact bias. By investigating these and other variables relevant to the affective responses of sport fans, researchers will extend our understanding of the unique emotional experiences of sport followers.

The Impact of Outcome Expectancy

A final topic that warrants mention involves the impact of **outcome expectancy** on sport fans' emotional responses. Research has found that people typically exhibit more intense affective responses to unexpected outcomes (Shepperd & McNulty, 2002). As applied to sport fans, unexpected wins and losses should result in greater levels of positive and negative affect, respectively (Simons, 2013). This pattern of effects is reasonable given that as unexpected sport outcomes unfold, this may lead to increased suspense, and suspenseful sporting events are associated with intense affective reactions (Knobloch-Westerwick,

David, Eastin, Tamborini, & Greenwood, 2009). However, similar to affective forecasting, little is known about factors that impact fans' perceptions of expectancy and how these perceptions influence their affective responses to sport competitions. Consequently, more research is needed in this area.

Some Final Thoughts

In the current chapter, we reviewed several common affective reactions of sport fans and ways that these emotions impact thought and behavior. This work illustrates that fandom serves as an emotional force in the lives of fans, and these emotions impact non-sport outcomes. The research reviewed in this chapter is further evidence of the powerful influence that sport has on the lives of fans.

Looking back on the emotions examined in this chapter, it is clear that considerably more time has been devoted to the negative emotional responses of fans compared to positive emotions (indeed, roughly twice as many pages in the current chapter are devoted to negative affective states). Two explanations could account for the differential coverage. First, perhaps researchers are succumbing to **negativity bias**, that is, the tendency for negative stimuli to be particularly salient and likely to gain our attention (Skowronski & Carlston, 1989; Vaish, Grossmann, & Woodward, 2008). It may be that the negative emotions of fans seem more common to researchers who, in turn, choose to study these reactions more often than less salient positive responses. However, another possibility is that fans do, in fact, experience negative emotions to a greater degree of intensity (and, perhaps frequency) than positive emotions. Interestingly, there is data confirming this explanation. Specifically, Sloan (1989) and Wann et al. (1994) found that pre- to postgame negative affective responses to poor team performance were of greater intensity than positive emotional responses to team success. Thus, perhaps Ian Fleming's James Bond is right; the British secret agent often remarked that the gain to the winner is typically less than the loss to the loser. That is, the positive affect we experience with successes does not match our negative reactions to failures. Regardless of the reasons underlying the overemphasis on negative emotional reactions, we would encourage researchers to expand their efforts in furthering our understanding of the positive affective consequences of sport fandom and spectating. Such an endeavor would likely paint a more accurate picture of the affective lives of fans.

And finally, this chapter was limited to a focus on micro-level fan emotions such as personal happiness and disappointment. However, research indicates that the outcomes of sporting events also impact fans' macro-level emotions. For example, the success and failures of national teams may enhance national pride, a well-replicated effect that has been found in several countries, including the Netherlands (Elling et al., 2014; van Hilvoorde et al., 2010), Hungary (Doczi, 2011), Germany (Hallmann et al., 2013), and the United States (Denham, 2010). Interestingly, feelings of national pride emanating from sport may be particularly common among residents of smaller nations (Evans & Kelley, 2002).

CHAPTER 7

An Introduction to Fan Aggression

I was surrounded by pimps, rapists, and murderers.
It was like being in the stands of an L.A. Raiders game.
Lieutenant Frank Drebin,
Naked Gun 33 1/3: The Final Insult

Although the *Naked Gun* line quoted above comes from a comedic film, there is sadly a lot of truth to it. Indeed, instances of fan and spectator aggression seem to be found everywhere one finds sport. This includes sporting events from the highest levels of competition, such as professional, international, and Olympic sports (Sivarajasingam, Corcoran, Jones, Ware, & Shepherd, 2004), to college sports (Rees & Schnepel, 2009), down to youth recreational sport contests (Wann, Weaver, Belva, Ladd, & Armstrong, 2015). Furthermore, acts of fan aggression are not confined to one country or continent. In fact, although North American sports often are viewed as immune to fan aggression, in reality examples of such behaviors are easily found (Young, 2002).

Although the overwhelming majority of sport fans are well-behaved and simply wish to observe an entertaining, well-played contest, a very small minority have a different agenda. It is this latter group that draws our attention because they can turn a day at the ballpark into a nightmare. The actions of this far-from-silent minority mandate the scientific investigation of sport fan aggression. Indeed, their actions have been an ongoing concern for academics, sport and civil authorities, and the general public for many years. Psychologists and sociologists alike have spent countless hours developing theories and conducting investigations with the goal of understanding acts of violence among those who follow sport. In the next three chapters, we take a critical look at this literature. In this short opening chapter, we introduce the topic of sport fan aggression. This includes discussions of basic topics such as operational definitions and various forms of aggression. The next chapter (Chapter 8) provides an examination of factors involved in the manifestation of sport fan violence. Then, in Chapter 9, we address large-scale fan aggression, focusing on fan riots and the characteristics of those participating in these aggressive encounters.

Definitions and Distinctions

As is often the case with social scientific phenomena, a number of different definitions of aggression have been adopted. When attempting to define a multifaceted construct such as aggression, it quickly becomes apparent that the task of crafting a suitable definition is difficult and fraught with complexities (see Baron & Richardson, 1994; Tedeschi & Felson, 1994, for an extended discussion of this issue). In this text, we have chosen to utilize Wann's (1997) definition stating that **aggression** is "the intent to physically, verbally, or psychologically harm someone who is motivated to avoid such treatment and/or the destruction of property when motivated by anger" (p. 257). Wann's definition extended a classic perspective offered by Baron and Richardson (1994) by including acts of destruction perpetrated against property. As Wann noted, the inclusion of the destruction of property is needed to fully account for acts of aggression found in sporting environments, including the violence displayed by sport fans. Examples of fan aggression include taunting opposing players, coaches, and fans; harassing officials; using profanity; throwing things on the field of play; vandalizing property; purposefully spilling a beverage on another fan; refusing to move out of someone's line of sight; obscene gestures; and pushing, shoving, or striking another person. Each of these acts fits Wann's conceptualization of aggression.

Sport Fan Aggression Is a Darker Side of Fan Behavior

Hostile Versus Instrumental Aggression

An important distinction should be made between hostile aggression and instrumental aggression (Buss, 1961; Wann, 1997). **Hostile aggression** refers to actions intended to harm another person who has annoyed or otherwise provoked an individual. With this form of aggression, the goal is simply the pain and suffering of the victim. By contrast, **instrumental aggression** involves acts that serve as a means to achieving some goal other than the victim's suffering (i.e., the violence is a means to an end). Although this dichotomy may be a bit overly simplistic and fail to reflect the multifaceted nature of aggression (Bushman & Anderson, 2001; Russell, 2008), it is a useful framework for differentiating fans' underlying motivation for exhibiting various acts of aggression. For example, consider a group of basketball fans heaping scorn on a rival player. Clearly, the abusive and obscene shouts would be consistent with our operational definition of aggression and should be classified as such. If the fans were responding to the player's poor sportsmanship and they wanted to inflict psychological pain on her, they would be displaying hostile aggression. However, if the rival player was standing at the free throw line and the intent was to impair her performance, their taunts would be considered an act of instrumental aggression.

When comparing the commonality of hostile and instrumental aggression among fans, most researchers have found the two forms of aggression are equally common when collapsed across other factors such as the aggressor's target (Wann, Carlson, & Schrader, 1999; Wann, Waddill, Bono, Scheuchner, & Ruga, 2017). However, fans are more likely to engage in instrumental fan aggression if they believe the actions will be successful. For example, Hennessy and Schwartz (2012) assessed respondents' beliefs in the utility of instrumental sport fan aggression (e.g., "yelling at others can sometimes help your child succeed in a game") and their tendencies to engage in these acts while watching youth baseball games. According to their results, belief in the success of instrumental fan aggression positively predicted the number of aggressive acts displayed by fans.

Forms of Fan Aggression

Using Wann's (1997) definition of aggression, there are many different aggressive acts exhibited by sport fans. However, most of these can be classified into one of five forms: verbal assaults, disrupting play, throwing missiles, fighting, and vandalism (Lewis, 1980; Young, 2002). In the following sections, we examine each of these forms of aggression.

Verbal Assaults

Perhaps the most common form of sport fan aggression, **verbal assaults** refer to the use of obscenities, vulgarities, and threatening words directed by fans at the targets of their derision (e.g., other spectators, players, coaches, and officials).

Common sense tells us that profanity and vulgarity have no place at the ballpark. Fans are obligated to exercise self-control, and when such is not the case, event managers should impose strong, negative sanctions upon those who are unwilling or unable to control their mouths. However, a visit to nearly any sporting event leaves one with the impression that an alarmingly large portion of fans left their verbal filters at home.

Opponents (i.e., players and coaches) and officials are two common targets of verbal assaults (Rudd & Gordon, 2010). Researchers have investigated which target is most likely to feel the wrath of fans. From studies conducted at youth baseball games (Hennessy & Schwartz, 2007, 2012; Wann et al., 2015) and at college basketball contests (Wann et al., 1999; Wann, Schrader, & Carlson, 2000), we find that officials are more likely to be targeted than are members of the opposing team. This finding substantiates work indicating that fans often possess negative impressions of sport officials, perceptions that could facilitate the verbal abuse officials frequently receive (Balch & Scott, 2007). Interestingly, the aforementioned work with college fans also found an interaction between aggression type (i.e., hostile versus instrumental) and aggression target (i.e., opponents versus officials). Specifically, officials were more likely to be the target of hostile aggression than instrumental aggression, while opponents appeared to be somewhat more likely to receive verbal taunts that were instrumental in nature. When fans yell at officials, they tend to be venting their anger rather than attempting to get the officials to favor their team in some manner. On the other hand, there is some indication that verbal aggression directed toward the opposition is designed to assist the fan's team and facilitate the players' performance. This pattern of effects is depicted in Figure 7.1. Finally, it warrants mention that the amount of verbal aggression found in these studies was rather low. Although

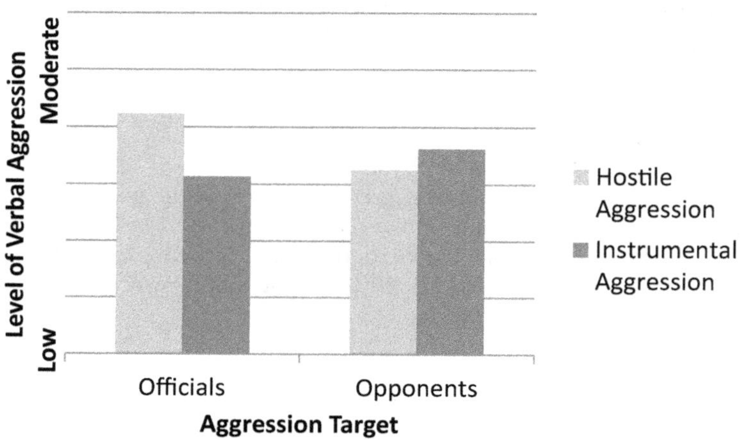

FIGURE 7.1 Spectator Aggression as a Function of Aggression Type and Aggression Target (a Combination of Results From Wann et al., 1999; Wann et al., 2000; Wann et al., in press)

some persons engaged in these behaviors, most did not. Indeed, it is important to remember that most fans are not aggressive in their vocalizations; rather, they yell positive comments in support of their team (Rudd & Gordon, 2010).

Throwing Missiles

Consider the following list of items: a softball, a shot glass, a Walkman, a golf ball, a plastic bottle, a beer can, a sanitary napkin dispenser, and a fortune in small change. Although this may read like the typical items found at a garbage dump, in actuality it is a list of objects New York Yankee fans hurled at the Seattle Mariners during the first two games of the American League Division Series in 1995. It seems as though garbage time has taken on a new meaning. Often used to refer to the final minutes of a basketball blowout when players seek to pad their scoring averages, garbage time has also come to mean the unseemly practice of fans throwing anything and everything at players, coaches, officials, and each other.

The danger of **throwing missiles** goes without saying. In fact, objects as seemingly harmless as snowballs can be quite dangerous when hurled from the stands. A particularly ugly incident occurred following an NFL game between the Oakland Raiders and Denver Broncos in which Broncos fans pelted Raiders players and coaches with snowballs, some of which were loaded with batteries (Gloster, 1999). The fight was so intense that players began throwing snowballs and punches back at the fans. Instances such as this in which the players return fire, so to speak, are rare, but they do happen. One such occasion involved Texas Rangers pitcher Frank Francisco and fans of the Oakland Athletics (Antonen, 2004). Upset over the abuse they had taken from fans seated near their bullpen, Rangers players began to argue with Athletics fans. The scuffle continued to escalate, culminating when Francisco hurled a chair into the stands, breaking one fan's nose. Francisco was charged with aggravated battery and the injured fan filed a lawsuit against the Rangers, which was eventually settled out of court (Lee, 2007).

Ice hockey fans are perhaps the most creative missile throwers. At Hamilton College in Clinton, New York, a game was delayed for several minutes because a traditional ritual had gotten out of hand. It had been custom at this school for fans to throw things at the opposing goalie after the home team's first goal of the season. But consider the articles attendants gathered up before play could resume: tennis balls, oranges, apples, melons, two live mice, a dead squid, and a life-sized, anatomically correct, inflatable doll. The school president did not find anything humorous about the incident and banned all attendees (except players' family members) from the next home game, stating "Extreme antisocial acts warrant censure" (Wolff & O'Brien, 1994, p. 19). Nashville Predators NHL fans also have a strange tradition involving throwing missiles, launching catfish onto the ice during home games. However, Pittsburgh Penguin officials were not amused when a Predators fan tried to extend the ritual to a road contest at Pittsburgh during the Stanley Cup Finals. In fact, the fan was identified, escorted out of the arena, and ultimately charged with "disorderly conduct, disrupting a meeting and possession of an instrument of a crime" (Jhaveri, 2017).

Disrupting Play

Although not frequently observed, fans occasionally decide to become "a part of the action" and run onto the field, thereby **disrupting play**. Usually without malevolence, they attempt to shake hands with a favorite player, request an autograph, demonstrate a sport skill (e.g., slide into second base), or simply seek attention. We see less and less of this behavior because it is now policy for broadcasters to refrain from showing those involved. When such disruptions occur, viewers are simply told that someone has run onto the field and security is trying to apprehend them. The applause viewers hear signifies that the individual has been caught and escorted out of the stadium. Stadium security officials treat this behavior very seriously. For instance, in 2010 a Philadelphia Phillies MLB fan was Tasered as he ran around the outfield trying to avoid security (Siemaszco, 2010). The players seemed to appreciate the conclusion to this event, as they appeared to be using their gloves to hide their smiles at the intruder's misfortune.

Fighting

Fighting among fans is an ugly, dangerous affair. Not only do the combatants risk serious injury, but oftentimes innocent spectators are injured as well. At the very least, these incidents are frightening and likely to ruin the game for those involved as well as those unfortunate enough to have witnessed the fight. It is not surprising that when these incidents are sorted out, drunkenness is often found to be a contributing factor. The surliness, belligerence, and bravado that oftentimes accompany excessive drinking can easily turn into fisticuffs following an unintentional push or shove (we will have more to say about the influence of alcohol in the next chapter). Frustration over a heartbreaking loss or a perceived mistake by an official can also cause opposing fans seated in close quarters to begin fighting.

Instances of fan fighting can also be found on the field of play where both players and officials can be targeted. With respect to players, although these events are rare, they do occur (Kessler & Brady, 2004), such as when two spectators ran onto the field at a Kansas City Royals MLB game and attacked Tom Gamboa, the Royals first base coach (Armour, 2002). Thankfully, attacks on officials are also not the norm, but they have been known to happen. Rainey and Duggan (1998) asked several hundred certified basketball referees, "Have you ever been physically assaulted while refereeing (including before or after the game)?" Approximately 14 percent of the sample reported at least one assault. Fans were the assailants in 15 percent of the cases.

Of course, fighting is not limited to incidents occurring inside a stadium. Rather, incidents involving serious (and even near-fatal) fan violence have been noted in other locales such as in a bar (Texas Football Fan, 2007), in a barber shop (Packers Fan, 1997), in the street (Schoetz, 2008), and in people's homes in the form of domestic violence (e.g., Gantz, Wang, & Bradley, 2006). Stadium parking lots, where a number of highly publicized and violent incidents have occurred, can be particularly dangerous (e.g., Galanis, 2015; Simon, 2016).

Vandalism

The willful or malicious destruction of public or private property is, on occasion, observed at sporting events. One of the most infamous instances of **vandalism** occurred on the campus at Auburn University. Toomer's Corner was the home of two large old-growth oak trees and a gathering place for Auburn fans for many decades. In November of 2010, an Alabama University fan named Harvey Updike poisoned the trees (Tomlinson, 2011). As a highly identified Alabama fan (he named his children Crimson Tyde and Bear Bryant), Updike was distraught over the recent success of Auburn, Alabama's greatest rival. Updike, who was tracked down after calling a popular sports talk radio show to brag about his actions, eventually pled guilty to a charge of unlawful damage to agriculture (Auburn Tree Poisoning, 2013). Both trees died, and Auburn officials have had difficulty in successfully planting new trees at the same locale due to the highly toxic soil.

Some Final Thoughts

Sport has a strong connection to violence, and, as scholars have noted, this connection is evident in the language of fandom (Segrave, 1997). For example, authors have noted that war terminology (e.g., "bomb" and "blitz" in football) is quite common in sport (Russell, 2008). Fans view the use of aggressive war terminology to describe sport as both acceptable and appropriate, and they feel that sport and war are quite similar (End, Kretschmar, Campbell, Mueller, & Dietz-Uhler, 2003; Wann & Goeke, 2017). Beyond the language of fandom, the very nature of many sporting activities involves violent, aggressive action. Contact sports involve players hitting one another in some way. As such, a link between fandom and aggression should not come as a surprise.

The reader may be curious about the prevalence of sport fan violence. That is, are fans more violent now, or were they more violent in past decades? We wonder about this as well. Unfortunately, comparisons of fan aggression across different time periods are extremely difficult. Several methodological issues render such comparisons problematic. First, more likely than not, researchers are forced to rely on secondary data sources. Use of archival data (e.g., encyclopedia, yearbooks, police reports, daily newspapers, popular magazines, sport news telecasts, etc.) raises questions about data availability, comprehensiveness, and media distortion. Second, investigators must select the appropriate time period for their research. For instance, they must decide if data should be gathered over the course of several weeks, months, or years. Similarly, researchers face a third dilemma, deciding on which sport or sports to include in their work. Should they monitor all popular sports, just those that are combative in nature, or a single sport? A further difficulty lies in the selection of a geographical area. The researcher could choose to focus on all of North America or limit the work to the United States, a specific region, a few states, or even a single state or town. Finally, researchers must choose their operational definition of fan violence. For example, they must determine the number of individuals that must be involved for an incident to qualify as a "riot," as well as the behaviors considered to be "violent." Given these formidable methodological barriers, it is difficult to say if fan violence has increased or decreased throughout the decades (Young, 2002). However, as you will read in the next two chapters, there are several data sets and theoretical frameworks to suggest that fan violence may be more common now than it was only a few decades ago.

CHAPTER 8

Understanding the Causes of Fan Aggression

In the fall of 2016, the Washington Post published the findings of an investigative study of spectator violence at NFL games (Babb & Rich, 2016). Upon reading this report, one thing becomes abundantly clear: fan violence has a wide variety of causes. For example, some of the many factors the report listed as playing a role in aggression included time of the game (e.g., day versus night), the opponent (e.g., rivalry games), and the score/outcome of the contest (e.g., losing a close game). And this barely scratches the surface; the list of factors impacting aggression (and sport fan aggression) is long and complicated. The complex nature of aggression is reflected in the history of social scientific work on the topic. In a word, it has been disjointed. Seemingly countless studies have been conducted and applied to a dizzying myriad of theories.

In an attempt to unify work on aggression into one comprehensive framework, Anderson and his colleagues developed the **General Aggression Model**, or GAM (Allen & Anderson, in press; Anderson & Bushman, 2002; Anderson & Carnagey, 2004; Anderson, Deuser, & DeNeve, 1995). The GAM has received widespread empirical support (although like most theories, it has been challenged, Ferguson & Dyck, 2012). One advantage of the GAM is the ability to explain real-world violence, such as relationship violence and the impact of global warming on aggression (DeWall, Anderson, & Bushman, 2011). Thus, it is perhaps not surprising that this theoretical approach has been successfully used to further our understanding of sport fan aggression (Anderson & Carnagey, 2009; Wann, 2006a; Wann, Haynes, McLean, & Pullen, 2003; Wann, Waddill, Bono, Scheuchner, & Ruga, 2017).

Although the exact composition of the GAM has changed a bit over the years (again, almost all theories do), a basic graphic presentation of key components appears in Figure 8.1. To reiterate, this diagram is not fully inclusive of all aspects of the current iteration of the model. However, the factors included here are sufficient to serve as a guide to unify the fragmented work on fan violence and incorporate key variables impacting the display of these problem behaviors.

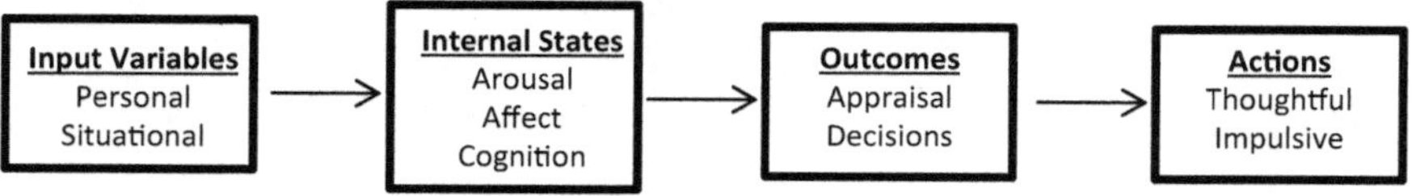

FIGURE 8.1 The General Aggression Model

The first stage of the model contains two types of input variables: personal and situational. **Personal input variables** involve "characteristics the person brings to the situation, such as personality traits, attitudes, and genetic predispositions" (Anderson & Bushman, 2002, p. 35). These variables would include gender, likes and dislikes, and individual tendencies. **Situational input variables** focus on the environment, such as a frustrating situation or the presence of others who are acting aggressively. The input variables are predicted to influence three key **internal states**, namely, **arousal**, **affect**, and **cognition**. That is, they may facilitate a heightened state of arousal, a negative affective state, and/or activate negatively associated cognitions. Next, the internal states impact the individual's **appraisal decisions**. This step, which includes both controlled and automatic processes, essentially involves a person's interpretation of a situation (e.g., did the other fan bump me intentionally) as well as an awareness of various features in the current environment (e.g., the presence of police). Finally, as a result of the earlier factors, the individual may respond in an aggressive fashion (which may be either thoughtful/controlled or impulsive/automatic).

Personal Input Variables

There are a number of personal input variables that play a role in sport fan aggression. In the sections that follow, we examine several of these individual difference variables.

Team Identification

Given our discussion of the impact of team identification in other chapters, it should come as no surprise that this variable is a powerful predictor of fan aggression (Amiot, Sansfacon, & Louis, 2014; Dietz-Uhler & Lanter, 2008; Fernquist, 2000; Wann, 2006a). Persons with higher levels of identification are more likely to engage in both hostile and instrumental aggression than are those with lower levels of identification. For example, Wann, Carlson, and Schrader (1999) found that persons higher in identification with a university basketball team were particularly likely to verbally assault others for both instrumental and hostile motives. This pattern of effects was found for aggression targeting both the officials and the opposition.

Team identification is also a strong predictor of verbal and physical aggression displayed by individuals attending youth sporting events (Wann et al., 2015). Unfortunately, these instances are all too common. Indeed, Pallerino (2003) found that over 80 percent of parents had witnessed a violent action from other individuals at youth sports contests. The high levels of identification family members feel for child athletes (it really *is* their flesh and blood competing), coupled with an overemphasis on winning (a situational input variable), lead to the perfect recipe for adult outbursts at youth sports (Wann, 2001).

The Self-Esteem Maintenance Model Wann (1993) developed the **Self-Esteem Maintenance Model** to shed light on the processes through which team identification facilitates fan aggression. According to this approach, those with strong team identification are predicted to respond differently to team losses than those with weak ties to a team. Wins by a favorite team tend to enhance one's social identity and self-esteem, both in the case of those with high and low levels of identification (i.e., **basking in the reflected glory** of the team's success, or BIRGing, Cialdini et al., 1976). However, team losses lead to quite different behaviors. Following poor team performance, some fans choose to engage in **cutting off reflected failure**, or CORFing (Snyder, Lassegard, & Ford, 1986). CORFing involves decreasing one's association with an unsuccessful team to protect one's psychological well-being. In essence, fans distance themselves from a losing team, thereby preserving a positive self-image and maintaining self-esteem.

Research suggests that CORFing is less available to highly identified fans (Hunt et al., 1999; Kwon et al., 2008; Spinda, 2011). From the perspective of the Psychological Continuum Model (Funk & James, 2001), fans that have reached the Allegiance stage may find it very difficult to dissociate from a team. The role of team follower has become central to their social identity, and simply turning off their affection for the team is not a viable option. As a result, their self-esteem suffers as a consequence of their team's poor performance. Because they are unable to cope with the team's failure via distancing (i.e., they do not CORF), they must choose and adopt a different strategy. Highly identified fans in this predicament often choose to engage in outgroup **blasting** (or derogation) as a means of repairing damage to their identity (Branscombe & Wann, 1992b; Foster, Hyatt, & Julien, 2012). Highly identified fans can derogate both threat-relevant and threat-irrelevant targets (Branscombe & Wann, 1992b, 1994). Threat-relevant targets would be those persons responsible for the team's loss, namely, the opposition. Threat-irrelevant targets would be other parties viewed as outgroups. This would include officials, such as the abuse Kentucky fans directed toward referee John Higgins after the Wildcats 2016 NCAA tournament loss to North Carolina (the game detailed at the start of Chapter 6, see Investigators, 2017). Importantly, identity restoration is only achieved via threat-relevant derogation; blasting threat-irrelevant outgroups is not successful in regaining lost esteem (Branscombe & Wann, 1994).

Dysfunctional Fandom

On occasion, an individual's level of identification with an organization or group can become obsessive (i.e., over-identified). At this point, the individual may become dysfunctional, exhibiting a number of problematic behaviors (Mael & Ashforth, 2001). Unfortunately, sport fandom is not immune from this process. The result is a second personal input variable with relevance for sport fan aggression, the extent to which one is a **dysfunctional fan** (Hunt et al., 1999; Wakefield & Wann, 2006). Dysfunctional fans are persons who chronically complain about team-related issues and who are highly confrontational with others (such as rival fans).

Recent work has made it possible to form an initial profile of these fans, and the picture being painted is not pretty. Dysfunctional fans are highly assertive (Wann & Ostrander, 2017), frequently commenting on sport talk radio and Internet discussion boards, voicing their "informed" opinions to anyone willing to listen (Foster et al., 2012; Wakefield & Wann, 2006). Furthermore, they were likely to have been a bully as a child (Courtney & Wann, 2010). But perhaps most illuminating is that highly dysfunctional fans are likely to believe that fan aggression is acceptable (Donahue & Wann, 2009). If you have ever sat near a loud-mouthed, vulgar, and rude fan that seems hell-bent on ruining your trip to the ballpark, the chances are good that he or she (but mostly he) was high in fan dysfunction. These individuals are obnoxious even before the beer begins to flow, but eventually it will flow as they drink more than their fair share (Wakefield & Wann, 2006).

Given the aforementioned description of dysfunctional fans, it should come as no surprise that they are particularly likely to act in an aggressive fashion. For example, Wakefield and Wann found that dysfunctional fans were more likely to verbally harass game officials than were persons with low levels of dysfunction. The difference in aggression between the groups was quite striking, as the highly dysfunction fans had an aggression rating nearly three times greater than the low dysfunction group.

Partridge and her colleagues (Partridge & Wann, 2015; Partridge. Wann, & Elison, 2010) examined the impact of fan dysfunction on fans' maladaptive strategies for coping with vicarious shame. Recall from our discussion in Chapter 6 that fans have several approaches they may utilize to deal with team-related shame. One of these options, attacking others, is aggressive in nature. Partridge and her colleagues found that fan dysfunction was a key ingredient in aggressive coping. For fans of college/professional teams and spectators at youth sporting events, fan dysfunction was a significant predictor of attacking others (Partridge & Wann, 2015; Partridge et al., 2010). From their work on youth sports, Partridge and Wann (2015) believed that there may be an additional maladaptive coping strategy used by fans. Specifically, they assessed the degree to which fans verbally attacked their child, a strategy that is also aggressive in nature. The researchers found use of this strategy was also positively correlated with fan dysfunction.

It is important to note that team identification was also a significant predictor of attacking others within the youth sport setting (Partridge & Wann, 2015). Thus, those higher in fan dysfunction as well as those with higher levels of identification were prone to coping via this aggressive response. This finding substantiates the inclusion of both identification and dysfunction as critical personal input variables in research pertaining to fan aggression. Such was the case in work conducted by Wann et al. (2017). These investigators examined the actions of those attending a college basketball game to determine the impacts of identification and dysfunction on their level of hostile and instrumental verbal aggression. An interesting pattern of effects was found. Higher levels of fan dysfunction were associated with higher levels of both hostile and instrumental aggression. On the other hand, although higher levels of identification predicted greater likelihood to be instrumentally aggressive, identification was not related to displays of hostile aggression. Wann and his associates concluded that "highly dysfunctional fans aggress both to help their team (instrumental aggression) and to inflict harm (hostile aggression)," while "highly identified fans reserve their aggressive actions for situations they believe will assist their team's performance" (p. 436).

Alcohol Consumption

What do the Colorado Rockies, Milwaukee Brewers, and Saint Louis Cardinals all have in common? Yes, the immediate response of "They are all Major League Baseball teams" would be correct. However, another common factor is they all play in home parks named after beer companies: Coors Field, Miller Park, and Busch Stadium, respectively. These stadium names reflect the long-standing relationship between sport fandom and alcohol. Although researchers have failed to establish a relationship between degree of alcohol consumption and level of sport fandom (End et al., 2009; Koss & Gaines, 1993; Wann, 1998), it is more than obvious that many fans consume alcohol while watching sporting events. Thus, by nature sport fans are not necessarily more likely to drink than nonfans. However, many fans drink when watching sporting events, and some drink heavily. In fact, one group of researchers found that 8 percent of individuals leaving a professional sporting event were legally intoxicated (Erickson, Toomey, Lenk, Kilian, & Fabian, 2011). Given a modest Saturday afternoon crowd of 25,000 spectators, this means that approximately 2,000 intoxicated individuals are roaming about the ballpark and parking lot. And perhaps most frightening is the realization that a substantial number of these individuals are climbing into the driver's seat. In a novel study, Wood, McInnes, and Norton (2011) examined the impact of game location and outcome on traffic fatalities following college and professional sporting events (football and basketball). The researchers found that close final score differentials were associated with greater frequencies of traffic fatalities. Interestingly, this effect was only found after close home wins. One suggestion for this pattern of effects was that fans supporting a team winning a hotly contested game will both increase their alcohol consumption and experience a raise in testosterone (we will have more to say about the impact of testosterone in a later section). The combination of elevated testosterone and intoxication may lead to unusually aggressive driving.

The preceding paragraphs (and our own experiences) indicate that alcohol flows freely at sporting events, parking lots surrounding stadiums, sports bars, and fans' homes during games. Many people consume alcohol when watching sport; there is nothing earthshattering in that revelation. Rather, the question is whether or not this consumption and the intoxication that may follow lead to greater levels of violence. Empirical work from a wide variety of disciplines

Alcohol Consumption and Sport Fandom Often Go Hand-in-Hand. Unfortunately, Research Indicates That Alcohol and Intoxication May Be a Key Contributor to Sport Fan Aggression

reveals that it does. Reviews using comprehensive meta-analytic methodologies highlight the causal role of alcohol consumption and intoxication in aggression (Bushman & Cooper, 1990; Foran & O'Leary, 2008; Ito, Miller, & Pollock, 1996; Russell, 2008).

Sport fans are not immune from these effects, and social scientific research implicates alcohol consumption as a key factor in fan violence (Ostrowsky, 2014). In fact, when teams stop selling alcohol, problematic behaviors decrease dramatically. Such was the case in 1996 when the University of Colorado ended beer sales at football games. In the seasons following the ban on beer sales, sharp declines were found in spectator ejections, arrests, assaults, and student referrals to the university's judicial affairs board (Bormann & Stone, 2001). Similarly, when the New England Patriots began to sell only low-alcohol beer at their concession stands, violence diminished noticeably. When the sale of regular beer was reinstated later in the season, the violence returned (Sullivan, 1986).

Of course, many college and professional teams rely on the revenue generated through alcohol sales, and given the gusto with which some fans drink, this revenue can be substantial (of course, the revenue is substantial in part because of the "captive audience pricing" used in most sport stadiums). Interestingly, it has been argued that this revenue may not outweigh the negative consequences of providing alcohol, at least at the collegiate level (Huang & Dixon, 2013). For example, although alcohol sales most certainly generate revenue, the total financial gain is likely an extremely small portion of an athletic department's overall budget, and thus selling alcohol may not be worth the hassles it brings.

Although our discussion thus far reveals that alcohol facilitates aggression, we have yet to examine why this occurs. As is the case with most psychological processes, there are multiple factors influencing the alcohol-aggression relationship (Berkowitz, 1993; Branscombe & Baron, 2017). There is far more involved than simply a lowering of inhibitions, and many people, sport fans included, consume alcohol without becoming aggressive. Whether or not alcohol increases aggression is in large measure determined by the social situation in which it is consumed (Berkowitz, 1993). We have all attended social functions where drinks flowed freely but tempers were not frayed and the guests did not come to blows. All in all, it was probably a congenial and nonthreatening environment in which alcohol acted as a social lubricant rather than a trigger for aggression. But other situations involving alcohol may be less friendly. Indeed, it is often the combination of intoxication and threat to one's personal or social identity that leads to aggressive responses (Baron & Richardson, 1994; Taylor, Gammon, & Capasso, 1976; Taylor & Leonard, 1983). The implications for fan violence are clear. Sport conducted in an atmosphere that is perceived as personally threatening (e.g., taunting from rival fans) is especially likely to invite hostile outbursts from intoxicated viewers.

An additional key factor implicated by a number of studies involves the reduced cognitive functioning that typically accompanies intoxication (Bartholow, Pearson, Gratton, & Fabiani, 2003; Leonard, 1989). With their cognitive abilities diminished, the social perception skills of inebriated persons are impaired, a state Steele and Josephs (1990) referred to as "alcohol myopia" (p. 921). An example of this process can been found in a study conducted by Begue, Bushman, Giancola, Subra, and Rosset (2010). These authors investigated the impact of intoxication on the **intentionality bias**, that is, the tendency to believe that others have acted deliberately (Rosset, 2008). For example, when we are bumped in a crowded room, we tend to believe that the act was purposeful, rather than accidental. Given that we are more likely to aggress when we have been provoked (Baron & Richardson, 1994), this bias has important consequences for how people respond in social situations. Importantly, Begue and his colleagues found that alcohol magnified the intentionality bias; inebriated individuals were especially likely to perceive the actions of others as intentional. Thus, for intoxicated sport fans, when they are accidently bumped while watching a game, they will be especially likely to perceive of the act as purposeful and, as a result, be more willing to respond in an aggressive fashion.

Additional Personal Input Variables

A few additional personal input variables warrant discussion. One such variable, which was mentioned briefly above, is testosterone. **Testosterone** can play a critical (albeit complicated) role in aggression, with higher levels of this hormone corresponding to higher levels of aggression (Baron & Richardson, 1994; Olweus, 1987; Russell, 2008). The relationship between testosterone and aggression has important implications for sport fandom because spectators often experience a rise in testosterone levels when watching sport (Bernhardt, Dabbs, Fielden, & Lutter, 1998; van der Meij, 2012). Highly identified fans feel vicariously challenged as they watch their team compete, and this challenge results in a rise in testosterone (Simons, 2013). Consequently, the increased testosterone could increase the likelihood of an aggressive response.

Another important personal input variable is **gender**. Researchers have consistently found that men are more likely than women to engage in physically aggressive acts (Baron & Richardson, 1994; Eagly & Steffen, 1986; Geen, 1990). If you watch a few YouTube clips of sport fan violence (there are, unfortunately, hundreds to choose from), it will appear that this sex difference extends to the realm of sport fandom. Indeed, researchers studying fan aggression frequently find male sport fans are more aggressive than their female counterparts (Russell, 2008; Wann & Waddill, 2014). For example, Lewis (2007) reports multiple data sets revealing that men are more likely to participate in a sport riot.

A third additional personal input variable is the extent to which a fan has a desire to watch violence. In Chapter 4, we examined a wide variety of motives that underlie fan interest in sport (e.g., entertainment, escape, group affiliation). Andrew et al. (2009) believe that a desire to watch aggressive and violent play should be added as another key motive, and their findings on minor league hockey fans suggest they are correct. They found that **attraction to violence** was the third-highest-rated motive, greater than more commonly tested motives such as group affiliation (social motivation) and escape. Males reported particularly high levels of the attraction-to-violence motive. Although researchers have yet to examine the relationship between this motive and levels of fan aggression, it stands to reason that those influenced to a greater extent by this motive would be more prone to violence.

We close this section by briefly noting a handful of other personal input variables found to facilitate fan aggression. First, Rudd and Gordon (2010) make a compelling argument that fans' lack of sportsmanship impacts the manifestation of aggression. That is, fans who have not internalized norms for sportsmanship have not learned what behaviors are acceptable. This lack of knowledge may lead to aggressive outbursts. Knecht and Zenger (1985) looked at a different aspect of knowledge, namely, knowledge of a sport. We have all heard spectators screaming at officials about a ruling the referees actually had correct, but the uninformed fan thought otherwise. Interestingly, Knecht and Zenger found that basketball fans with some knowledge were more likely to respond negatively to on-court events (i.e., plays favoring the opponent) than those with exceptionally low or high levels of knowledge. This illustrates the premise that a little knowledge can be a dangerous thing. And finally, Hennessy and Schwartz (2007) identified several personality traits that were associated with aggressive behavior at youth games. Specifically, they found that fans higher in vengeance, hostility, and trait anger were more likely to engage in verbal aggression.

Situational Input Variables

Although individual characteristics are important, the GAM includes the proposition that aggression is not simply a function of *who* someone is but also *where* someone is (Anderson & Bushman, 2002; Anderson & Carnagey, 2004). As the authors of this book so frequently tell their students: "The situation matters!" In the paragraphs below, we discuss a number of critical psychological and sociological situational factors and their impact on the violent behaviors of sport fans.

Observational Learning (Modeling)

One important situational input variable impacting fan aggression concerns the type of contest being witnessed. Several researchers have reported that fan aggression was more likely to occur when persons watched violent contests than when they viewed sporting events of a nonviolent nature (Arms, Russell, & Sandilands, 1979; Braun & Vliegenthart, 2008; Goldstein & Arms, 1971; Russell, 1981; Wann et al., 2000). The relationship between the consumption of violent sporting events and fan aggression is important because fans are frequently drawn to aggressive sporting events (Jewell, 2012; von Allmen & Solow, 2012), and they report particularly high levels of enjoyment for unscripted violence (Raney & Depalma, 2006; Westerman & Tamborini, 2010). Of course, the enjoyment of aggressive sports is not a recent trend. Rather, the earliest human competitions were characterized by high levels of violence, such as chariot races and gladiator tournaments (Jewell, Moti, & Coates, 2012). Some individuals are particularly likely to prefer aggressive and combative sports. This includes male fans, fans with a propensity toward violent behavior, and those with high levels of sensation seeking (Bryant, 1989; Bryant, Comisky, & Zillmann, 1981; Bryant & Zillmann, 1983; McDaniel, 2003). Advertising agencies often incorporate violence into their marketing campaigns to capitalize on fans' fascination with aggressive sports (Jackson & Andrews, 2004).

The facilitation of aggression as a function of viewing violent sports is best understood within the context of Bandura's **Social Learning Theory** (SLT; 1973, 1986). According to the social learning perspective, aggression is similar to other social behaviors in its acquisition and maintenance in that it is often learned through observation. SLT also considers the means by which aggression is regulated. Certainly, externally administered rewards and punishments influence one's aggressive behavior, as do self-regulatory mechanisms such as guilt. But equally important is the influence of reinforcements and punishments. The attentive observer takes note of whether a model is rewarded in some fashion for their aggression, such as with praise and wealth, or if the model is punished, for instance, with social disapproval. What does this mean for students of sport fan violence? It means that when a football fan sees his favorite player deliver an especially vicious hit and receive praise from his teammates for doing so, the spectator might be inclined, given sufficient provocation, to model the same behavior on the opposing team's fan seated a few feet away.

It is important to note that the research supporting SLT directly refutes **catharsis**, that is, the belief that one's aggressive impulses are released through the observation of or participation in violent activities (see Wann, 1997, for a detailed discussion of catharsis within sport). One of the major benefits believed to be gained from observing combat sports is that it allows spectators to discharge their pent-up aggressive impulses. Among U.S. college students, 39 percent believed that a cathartic purge of aggression results from watching violent sports in person, while 13 percent felt that similar benefits result from observing aggressive sports on television (Wann et al., 1999). Students who were most involved with violent sports expressed the strongest belief in catharsis. However, as popular as the notion of a catharsis may be (Alfred Hitchcock once stated that "Seeing a murder on television can be good therapy"), the construct simply does not stand up under careful scrutiny. Study after study has found that viewing aggression either does not affect the viewer's aggressive state or, even more likely, leads to an increase in aggression (Gilbert & Twyman, 1984; Goranson, 1980; Russell, 1993). It is pure fiction that individuals watching combat sports are miraculously drained of their aggressive impulses.

Thus, viewing of violent sports often facilitates the aggressive tendencies of those witnessing the events. However, the behavioral consequences of witnessing an aggressive sport can occur regardless of venue; it matters not whether sport fans view violence on television or from their seats in the stadium or arena (Gunter, 2006). Rather, the observation of violent sports has the capacity to serve as a trigger for violence among fans in all locales. In the paragraphs that follow, we examine evidence that watching violent sports enhances aggressive tendencies both at the arena and at home.

The View from the Stands Archival investigations provide evidence that violence among sport spectators is frequently tied to the actions of athletes. For instance, in one study 74 percent of instances of fan aggression were determined to have been "ignited by player violence" (Smith, 1976, p. 127). Equally suggestive is a finding by Semyonov and Farbstein (1989) that Israeli soccer teams whose rosters included the most violent players tended to have the most violent fans.

Goldstein and Arms (1971) provided evidence that the relationship between player violence and fan hostility is causal. Their classic field study was conducted on the occasion of the Army-Navy football game held annually in Philadelphia. Participants were approached on a random basis before and after the contest. Serving as a control, the same procedure was followed at an equally competitive but nonviolent sporting event (an intercollegiate gymnastics meet). Participants completed a hostility inventory and answered biographical and background questions (e.g., were they rooting for Army or Navy). The results were clear. Regardless of team allegiances, those witnessing the football game experienced an increase in hostility from before to after the game, whereas there were no changes at the gymnastics event. These findings are strong support for SLT and in direct opposition of any cathartic experience.

A few years later, Arms et al. (1979) replicated the earlier work by Goldstein and Arms (1971). In this project, university students were randomly assigned to view one of three events: ice hockey, professional wrestling, and a control event—a provincial swim meet. Pro wrestling was chosen as a violent sport because it represents a category of fictional (i.e., scripted) aggression. Once again, the results were straightforward. Participants showed increases in aggression at both the hockey game and the wrestling event with no changes reported at the swimming competition.

The View From the Couch Although fans often fill the stands at sporting events, greater numbers watch sport in public lounges, bars, and at home. Public health authorities and others have speculated that some individuals may be harmed as a result of televised images of violence. In fact, it has been claimed by some that domestic violence and even homicides can be traced to television programming featuring combat sports. As we will shortly see, there is merit in these speculations.

The possibility that televised aggressive sports may be associated with domestic violence has been a hotly debated topic for several decades (Adubato, 2016). However, a sufficient body of research has now been accumulated, with several studies linking the viewing of aggressive/combative sports with relationship violence (Brown, Sumner, & Nocera, 2002; Card & Dahl, 2011; White, Katz, & Scarborough, 1992). For example, Gantz et al. (2006) reviewed police records for multiple NFL cities spanning several years. The authors recorded the number of domestic violence incidents and examined predictors of their frequency. They found a small but statistically significant increase in domestic violence police dispatches on NFL game days, leading the authors to conclude that "the presence of an NFL game does slightly increase the number of domestic violence reports" (p. 374). Interestingly, domestic violence rates were highest when the game in question held greater significance, such as when a team was still in contention and there were only a handful of games left in the season (i.e., must-win games). Increases were also found on Super Bowl Sundays, suggesting that the impact was not limited to watching one's own team.

With respect to homicide, media coverage of combat sports can have lethal consequences for those in the viewing area. White (1989) tested the hypothesis that important football games are followed by an increase in local homicide rates. All NFL playoff games from 1973 to 1979 were examined, as were the homicide rates for the metropolitan areas in which the franchises were based. An increase in homicides was found, but the increase occurred six days after the playoff game and only in those cities whose teams were eliminated from the playoffs. The reason offered for the jump in homicides is intriguing. The sixth day following a playoff game falls on the eve of the next round of the playoffs. For fans of last week's winner, their team is still in contention. By contrast, fans of losing teams are forced to confront the realization that their season is over—there will be no game tomorrow. The investigators speculated that disputes arising from gambling losses might also have contributed to the increase in homicides.

Other evidence demonstrates that being physically distanced from the sport site fails to buffer the dangerous effects of witnessing violence. For instance, Phillips (1986) tested the possibility that heavyweight championship boxing matches are followed by a rise in national homicide rates. His assessment of lethal aggression was derived from the registry of U.S. national death certificates containing several key bits of information (e.g., age, sex, race, cause of death). Homicide rates were examined for ten days following all title bouts from 1973 to 1978. As predicted, homicides rose 12.5 percent on the third day following the fights and 6.6 percent on the fourth day. The impact of the media was evident, as the steepest increases occurred following the most heavily publicized fights.

It should be noted that the research conducted by White (1989) and Phillips (1986) are now several decades old. At the time this work was conducted, the Internet, cell phones, and other advances in communication and media consumption had yet to become a reality. Furthermore, interest in boxing appears to have been on the decline in recent decades, while consumption of Mixed Martial Arts events (perhaps even more violent than boxing) has increased in popularity. Given these factors, it would be wise for researchers to replicate this body of work to determine if the findings from the 1980s translate to today.

Frustration, Aggression, and Competition Outcome

As we discussed in Chapter 6, fans often become upset and angry when their team's performance falls short of expectations. Ultimately, frustration from a team's poor play has the propensity to lead to increased aggression. Thus, team performance (i.e., losing) is another critical situational input variable.

Understanding the process through which game outcome impacts fan violence is best understood within the framework of the **Frustration-Aggression Hypothesis** (FAH). Formulated in 1939 by a group of Yale psychologists, the authors of this framework originally proposed that when people are blocked or in some way thwarted in their efforts to attain a goal, aggression will inevitably result. Similarly, when we observe an act of aggression, the existence of a prior state of frustration is assumed (Dollard, Doob, Miller, Mowrer, & Sears, 1939). However, this sweeping view of frustration as the cause of aggression was not without its shortcomings. For instance, consider the hockey enforcer who obeys the orders of his coach to attack an opposing player. There is no clear sense that the goon's act of aggression originated with his being frustrated. Critics also observed that people do not always respond with aggression when they are frustrated. For example, some increase their efforts to attain their goals, others pursue alternate goals, and still others regress to behaviors that are typical of an earlier stage of their development (e.g., sulking and pouting). Miller (1941) subsequently proposed a less rigid formulation of the FAH. It allowed that "frustration produces instigations to a number of different types of response, one of which is an instigation to some form of aggression" (p. 338). This revised position accommodated many of the criticisms by providing for a number of nonaggressive responses to frustration. However, the dominant and most likely response to frustration remained aggression.

Applied to the realm of sport fandom, the FAH leads to the straightforward prediction that fans will be more violent after losses than following wins. However, when it comes to frustration and aggression, all losses are not the same. For instance, consider the fan bases of two college football teams, the Murray State Racers and the Florida State Seminoles (an example that hits home for both authors). The Racers play in college football's FCS Division (formerly I-AA), and no one would mistake them for a successful program. On the other hand, the Seminoles are an FBS team (i.e., I-A) and have a long tradition as a national power in football. If the Racers played at the Seminoles' home in Tallahassee, as they did early in the 2012 season, no one with any knowledge of college football would have expected the Racers to win. And they would have been correct; FSU won the contest in a 69–3 drubbing. After the game, were Racer fans frustrated by the loss? Nope, and quite to the contrary, most were happy that their team actually scored. Their team lost, but because the loss was expected there was no frustration and, hence, no enhanced likelihood of aggression. However, imagine a scenario in which the greatly out-manned Racers pulled of the upset of a lifetime. How would the Seminole fans have responded? It seems likely that, because the loss was unexpected (*highly* unexpected), they would have experienced a great deal of frustration and acted aggressively as a consequence.

The scenario above is precisely what is found in research. It is not simply a loss that drives frustration and, ultimately, aggression; rather, it is an unexpected loss. For instance, Rees and Schnepel (2009) examined data from the National Incident-Based Reporting System for over two dozen college communities. The data indicated that host communities experienced an increase in violent offenses on game days (e.g., assaults, vandalism, disorderly conduct arrests). However, a closer inspection revealed that violent incidents were especially common when the home team had been upset (i.e., an unranked visiting team defeated a home team ranked in the top 25). The unmet expectation of victory led to greater levels of frustration and, in turn, violent outbursts. In fact, Rees and Schnepel concluded that "our results clearly indicate that expectations, and what happens to fans' behavior when they are not met, should be explicitly built into future attempts to model the relationship between aggression and sporting events" (p. 80). Card and Dahl (2011) found a similar effect for family violence, as interpersonal violence directed toward women was most likely when the home team was defeated in a contest they were expected to win.

Aggressive Cues

A third important situational input variable involves the presence of **aggressive cues**, that is, people, events, objects, and so forth that have longstanding associations with aggression (Benjamin, Kepes, & Bushman, in press; Berkowitz, 1989). The presence of an aggressive cue can prime an individual to interpret their environment in aggressive terms, thus increasing the likelihood of a hostile reaction. Several studies have documented the impact of aggressive cues in sport (Frank & Gilovich, 1988; Wann, 1997). For example, Havard, Wann, and Grieve (in press) found that aggressively titled rivalry games (e.g., "Border War") may be priming the aggression of fans; aggressively named rivalry contests elicited more negative perceptions of rivals than did neutral names. Further, Wann and Branscombe (1990) found that fans watching an aggressive or combative sport (e.g., boxing, hockey) may be cued to behave aggressively simply by the name of the sport!

In recent years, investigators have documented that alcohol can also function as a powerful aggressive cue. Because alcohol consumption and intoxication are so frequently paired with violence, simply being in the presence of alcohol may facilitate aggression (Bartholow & Heinz, 2006). Their findings on the power of alcohol to function as an aggressive cue led Subra, Muller, Begue, Bushman, and

Delmas (2010) to the sobering (pun intended) conclusion that "People do not need to drink a drop of alcohol to become aggressive; exposure to alcohol cues is enough to automatically increase aggression" (p. 1052). Given the strong connection between sport viewing and alcohol consumption noted above, it is likely that alcohol serves as a particularly powerful aggressive cue for fans.

Environmental Factors: Heat and Noise

In the summer of 1998, Mark McGwire of the St. Louis Cardinals and Sammy Sosa of the Chicago Cubs embarked on a race to break the MLB home run mark of 61, set in 1961 by Roger Maris. In an attempt to see history broken, the first author and his family traveled to St. Louis to watch McGwire's assault on the record. We were there for an afternoon game on September 5th, and we were lucky enough to witness McGwire's 60th home run, a blast that landed less than five rows behind us in the left field stands. However, monumental (and, as we now know, tainted) as that moment was, that is not what I remember about that day. Rather, my recollection centers on how incomprehensibly uncomfortable I was. The stadium was packed, and there were many questionable odors emanating from the attendees. Furthermore, it was loud. And when McGwire came to the plate, it was deafening. And further still, it was hot. As in surface of the sun hot. My family still remarks about how it was the most uncomfortable any of them had even been. As I look back on that day, knowing what I do about precipitators of fan violence, I cannot help but wonder what would have happened if McGwire would not have homered. The crowd was not in a happy place, physiologically speaking, and it seemed as though the stage was set for violent outbursts in the stands.

The above experience highlights the potential for **environmental factors** to influence aggression. These factors constitute another set of situational input variables that can facilitate spectator violence. The viewing conditions such as those endured by spectators at the Cardinals game that day (e.g., noise, oppressive heat, crowding, uncomfortable seating, and noxious odors) are not uncommon in the experiences of many who attend sporting events. Importantly, research both from general psychology as well as work specifically testing sport spectators indicates that these aversive incidents can serve as a catalyst for aggressive actions (Russell, 2008). Below, we examine two environmental factors: noise and temperature (heat).

Noise An integral part of the spectator experience is extreme noise levels; capacity crowds in domed stadiums, arena sound systems, and the roar of engines at racing events create conditions that would be unwelcome in most non-sport contexts. Researchers have demonstrated that noise can contribute to aggressive behaviors (e.g., Geen & McCown, 1984) because it leads to heightened physiological arousal, a state shown to facilitate aggression (Baron & Richardson, 1994). Noise occurring at irregular intervals and noise over which the individual has no control produce the strongest effects. Further, the effects of aversive noise levels are more pronounced when the individual is already angered. For example, fans in the midst of a noisy environment and enraged by an official's controversial call would be especially likely to give violent expression to their feelings.

Temperature A wealth of archival and experimental evidence points to a positive relationship between temperature and interpersonal aggression (Baron & Richardson, 1994). For instance, researchers found that soaring temperatures in Texas are accompanied by an increasing incidence of rape and homicide (Anderson & DeNeve, 1992). Texas also provided the setting for a sport-related test of a heat-aggression hypothesis. Researchers examined MLB data on the number of batters hit by errant pitches over three seasons of play. As the temperatures recorded at game time rose, so too did the number of batters hit by pitchers (Reifman, Larrick, & Fein, 1991). Skeptical that hit batters can effectively be utilized as a measure of aggression? In actuality, it appears to be a valid reflection of a pitcher's aggression, as the researchers went to considerable lengths to statistically rule out rival explanations, such as fatigue or sweaty palms. Regarding those in the stands, there is every reason to believe that fans also become increasingly hostile as temperatures rise. Indeed, Dewar (1979) noted in his investigation of fan behavior at baseball games that violent outbursts were most likely to erupt during warmer weather.

Daily Hassles

Imagine a fan with tickets to an evening NCAA basketball game involving her favorite team and a conference rival. Likely, this fan would be excited about the contest, perhaps having had the date circled on her calendar for weeks. However, the day of the game was anything but smooth for her. In fact, it was one of those "nothing goes right" days. The alarm did not sound and she was late to work; a local bank refused to cash her check; her son came home from school with a less than stellar report card; and to top it all off, she got a flat tire on the way to the game. Clearly, as she enters the arena, she is not a happy camper.

Research suggests that the cumulative effect of the **daily hassles** in the example above may increase the likelihood that the fan will act aggressively at the basketball game, and, as a result, they can be considered as another situational input variable. Hennessy and Schwartz (2012) conducted an investigation of the impact of daily hassles on the aggressive responses of youth baseball fans and found that these negative life experiences were an important predictor. Specifically, parents with greater levels of daily hassles were more likely to exhibit verbal aggression toward their own child, the umpires, and other spectators. Thus, situational forces outside the sporting environment have the capability to facilitate aggression. That is, it is not only the game itself, the sport crowd, or other sport-related variables that influence fan violence. Rather, environmental forces beyond the realm of sport can also be impactful.

Game Opponents: The Influence of Rivals

Another situational input variable meriting discussion concerns the opposing team and, more specifically, if the competition involves a rival (Lewis, 2007). Just

TABLE 8.1 Understanding Perceptions of Rivalry: Subscales for the Sport Rivalry Fan Perception Scale (SRFPS)

Subscale	Description
Outgroup Competition against Others	Desire to support a rival team when that team is in competition against someone other than the favored team
Outgroup Academic Prestige	Fan impressions of a rival school's academic image
Outgroup Sportsmanship	Perceptions of the behaviors of rival fans (e.g., the extent to which these fans are well-behaved)
Sense of Satisfaction	The extent to which fans feel a sense of pride and accomplishment when a favored team defeats a rival

as fans often learn which teams to love via socialization (see Chapter 2), they are also frequently taught which teams to hate (Havard, 2014). A number of factors can facilitate rivalry between fans, including geographical proximity (closer fan bases often develop stronger rivalries) and a history of competitiveness, such as when two teams are equally matched (Kilduff, Elfenbein, & Staw, 2010; Wertheim & Sommers, 2016). Fans view rival teams (and perhaps their fan bases) as a threat to their status as the superior team (Tyler & Cobbs, 2015). Consequently, fans' dislike for rival teams runs very deep, particularly among highly identified fans (Wenger & Brown, 2014; Wann et al., 2016). In fact, the dislike can even be transferred to organizations related to the team. Bergkvist (2012) found that European soccer fans not only disliked their team's rivals, they also held negative attitudes about a beer company who was a major sponsor for the rival team. Havard, Gray, Gould, Sharp, and Schaffer (2013) developed a psychometrically sound instrument to assess perceptions of rival teams. This scale, called the Sport Rivalry Fan Perception Scale (SRFPS), can be used to examine several different perceptions sport fans have for rival teams. These can be found in Table 8.1.

Given that rival teams and fans are viewed as a threat and fans often have a strong dislike for rivals, it should come as little surprise that violence can be exacerbated by competitions against rival teams (Cikara et al., 2011). For example, as fans' perceptions of rivals become more negative, their consideration of acting aggressively toward them increases (Havard, Wann, & Ryan, 2013, 2017, 2018). Because fans are particularly likely to attend games involving their team and a rival (Havard, Shapiro, & Ridinger, 2016), opportunities for fan violence involving rival fans and players is certainly available.

Deindividuation

Although different theoretical models have been offered over the years (Vilanova, Beria, Costa, & Koller, 2017), generally speaking **deindividuation** is a mental state characterized by membership in a group and feelings of anonymity (Diener, 1980; Festinger, Pepitone, & Newcomb, 1952; Mann, Newton, & Innes, 1982). When individuals are in a deindividualized capacity, they focus their attention on the group, the result of which is diminished self-awareness. This loss of self-awareness, coupled with anonymity, allows some crowd members to give free reign to their otherwise inhibited aggressive inclinations.

Anonymity is a particularly critical component of the deindividuation process. Large crowds enhance a person's perception that he or she is anonymous by serving as a "human fog." Because the individual fan is just one among many at a sporting event, he or she is nameless, unknown, and less likely to accept ownership of his or her own aggressive actions. Anonymity also plays a key role in one's fear of retaliation. For instance, if a fan does engage in some type of antisocial behavior, there is often little reason for him or her to fear retribution given the difficulty of affixing individual blame (Gordon & Arney, 2017). For example, Dewar (1979) monitored fights at regular season MLB games and found that about 70 percent of the fights occurred during night games, when anonymity would be greater and fear of retaliation less.

Several researchers have examined how sport fans believe they would behave if their actions could remain completely unknown to others (i.e., they would be anonymous) and, as a result, there was no concern over retaliation from others (Havard et al., 2013, 2017; Wann et al., 2005; Wann et al., 2003; Wann, Peterson, Cothran, & Dykes, 1999; Wann & Waddill, 2014). The results of this work, which are presented in Figure 8.2, are a bit startling. As depicted, a sizeable minority of individuals admitted a willingness to consider engaging in a variety of aggressive acts if they could be guaranteed to not be caught and

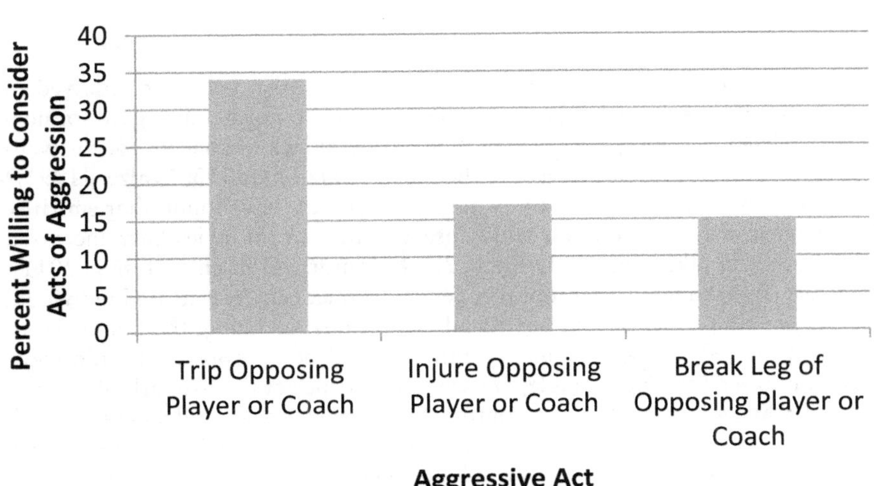

FIGURE 8.2 Sport Fans' Willingness to Engage in Various Forms of Anonymous Aggression (a Combination of Results From Havard et al., 2013, 2017; Wann et al., 2005; Wann et al., 2003; Wann et al., 1999; Wann & Waddill, 2014)

receive no punishment in return. In fact, a small number of persons (roughly 4 percent) indicated that they would consider murdering an opposing player or coach! Various factors did impact how likely the fans were to consider these acts. For instance, they were more likely to consider the hostile action following their favorite team's loss than after a win (Wann et al., 2005). Additionally, fans higher in team identification were more likely to consider the aggressive acts (e.g., Wann et al., 2003; Wann et al., 1999), as were those higher in fan dysfunction (Wann & Waddill, 2014).

Cultural Influences

Cultural influences play an important role in fan behavior and thus constitute another important situational factor for consideration in sport fan violence. Cultural changes across years and decades influence many forms of behavior within a given culture, and sport fans are not immune from this influence. Many societies (including the United States) are simultaneously becoming more violent and less civil. As a result, we should find that the institutions found in those societies are, likewise, becoming more violent and less civil. With respect to our violent society, the point being made here is that if we lived in a less hostile society, then we should see less violence at sporting events. Increases in disorderly behavior at sport venues simply reflect the fact that our society has become more violent. Sipes (1996) argues this point by observing

> We learn our individual patterns of behavior, and that our culture supplies us with these patterns . . . We can decrease unwanted violence and other aggressive behavior by reducing the aggressive component of culture patterns wherever this component is found.
>
> (p. 155)

As for incivility, it can be reasoned that the boorish behavior observed in some social settings, such as sporting events, is not so much a disregard for normative structures but, rather, stems from a general lack of concern for the well-being of others. Is civil society on the decline (Etzioni, 1993; Walzer, 1991)? Research suggests that it is. For example, researchers have found that empathy has waned in recent decades, while insecure attachment styles have increased (Konrath, Chopik, Hsing, & O'Brien, 2014; Konrath, O'Brien, & Hsing, 2011). Harris (1998) suggests that moral codes of conduct centered around individual self-interest have penetrated our social institutions, including the family, community, and education. For many fans, it would be appropriate to add sport fandom to the list. For example, one can see evidence at the ballpark of an individual ethos sometimes out of control. Some fans appear to deliberately seek their own personal pleasure and entertainment at the expense of others. They worry not that their cheering is too loud, their handmade sign is blocking the view of the person behind them, their sloppy drinking is objectionable, or their foul language is offensive to the ears.

Key Internal States: Arousal, Affect, and Cognition

According to the General Aggression Model, personal and situational input variables influence three key internal states: arousal, affect, and cognition. These states then impact the likelihood of violent action. For example, consider heat, an important situational variable discussed above (Anderson et al., 1995). When people find themselves in an uncomfortably hot environment (which is often the case when watching sporting events), the temperature can influence their level of physiological arousal, how they feel (e.g., negative affect), and what they are thinking (i.e., cognition). These psychophysiological processes then have the capacity to facilitate aggression.

Physiological Arousal

A number of studies have found that individuals are more likely to act aggressively when in a heightened state of physiological arousal (Baron & Richardson, 1994; Wann, 1997). And as fans can attest, watching sporting events can be intense and lead to high levels of excitation. This heightened state of excitation can have important consequences for fan aggression (Wertheim & Sommers, 2016). Branscombe and Wann (1992b) noted that both situational and personal factors can enhance fan arousal and, ultimately, fan aggression. As for situational variables, they point to factors such as noise, crowding, and heat (see also Russell, 2008). With respect to personal variables, they suggest that highly identified fans will be especially likely to become aroused due to their strong psychological connection to the team and the importance they place on team success. Indeed, researchers have found this exact pattern of effects (Harrison et al., 2000; Hillmann et al., 2000; Newell, Henderson, & Wu, 2001; Potter & Keene, 2012). For example, Branscombe and Wann (1992a) monitored the blood pressure of persons watching a boxing match involving a U.S. competitor. Highly identified fans exhibited increases in pre- to post-match arousal, a pattern not seen among those with low levels of identification.

Affect

With the GAM, Anderson predicts that situational and personal input variables have the potential to result in negative emotions, a second key internal state. Negative affect then facilitates aggressive responding. Research on sport fans has substantiated the link between input variables, negative affect, and aggression. For example, Bernache-Assollant and his associates (2010) asked French students to view a taped recording of the French national rugby team losing an important match (a rivalry game with England). The video clip was edited to highlight the success of the rival team and the euphoria of the rival fans. After watching the video, participants completed questions assessing their negative mood as well as items measuring outgroup derogation (e.g., blasting persons from England). As one would expect, team identification was positively correlated with both negative mood and amount of outgroup derogation. Interestingly, in a pattern wholly consistent with the GAM, negative affect mediated the relationship between identification and derogation.

Cognition

A third internal state incorporated into Anderson's General Aggression Model is cognition (Benjamin et al., in press). As it relates to sport fan aggression, this suggests that even before an aggressive sporting event takes place, the media have often unwittingly set the stage for interpersonal conflict (Russell, 2008). Pregame hyperbole intended to stimulate viewer interest in an event may prime stored memories and/or negative schema. References to "upcoming battles," "revenge," "taking no prisoners," and, as noted above, even aggressive sport names (Wann & Branscombe, 1990) can prime negative schema in some viewers. These, in turn, cause fans to judge others unfavorably and see them as personally threatening.

Appraisal of the Environment

The final stage in Anderson's General Affect Model involves one's appraisal of his or her environment (Anderson & Bushman, 2002; Anderson & Carnagey, 2004). As noted earlier, this concerns interpretations of the environment and features of the current situation. For example, consider a highly identified fan who has just watched his favorite NFL team lose a playoff game to a longtime rival. The loss occurred on the final play in which the outcome was decided by a referee's controversial call. Given the importance of the game and the fan's level of identification, there are several situational and personal input variables in play that would lead to a heightened level of arousal, negative affect, and aggression-based cognitions. The stage is clearly set for the fan to act aggressively. In fact, one might be willing to wager that this person would, at the very least, exhibit high levels of verbal aggression, yelling obscenities at the referee in question.

However, imagine further that the fan was seated next to a security guard or police officer. Would the fan be as likely to act violently? Likely, he would not, assuming that he had appraised his environment and realized the potential consequences of his actions. Such appraisals (if they occur) have the ability to act as a deterrent to aggression (Lewis, 2007). For example, Cleland and Cashmore (2016) found that increased policing was believed to be partially responsible for the decline in fan violence surrounding British soccer. Similarly, consider the novel approach adopted by the NFL Philadelphia Eagles management in an attempt to reduce the violence occurring at the team's home games. The city of Philadelphia, in cooperation with the Eagles, arranged for a court to be set up in the basement of the stadium to "mete out instant justice to the drunk, the disorderly and the vulgar" (McCallum & Hersch, 1997). The strategy seemed to have had some early success as arrests went from 20 persons the first game down to five in the second (NFL Notebook, 1997).

Police and Other Security Personnel May Reduce the Likelihood of Sport Fan Aggression

As an additional real-life example, consider the scary scene that occurred at a New Jersey youth hockey practice in the summer of 2000 (Hockey Dad Found Guilty, 2002). Two fathers attending a practice session began to argue about the overly physical play. The men came to blows, and, ultimately, the fight ended in the death of one of the fathers. The first author of this text was at a conference in which the chief of police in charge of the case was speaking about this incident. One of the more interesting comments made by Chief Silva was that the violence between the two parents may never have occurred had one of the other parents not left the practice a few minutes earlier. This third parent happened to be a police officer. It was Chief Silva's contention that the combative parents would likely not have come to blows had they been standing near a member of the police force. Essentially, Chief Silva was arguing that the angry parents would have noticed the off-duty policeman (i.e., they would have appraised the environment), and the dispute would not have escalated to the point of death.

A point for future researchers to consider is the extent to which technology may extend and impact environmental appraisals. With the likelihood that (seemingly) all actions are recorded on someone's phone or mobile device, are people less likely to engage in violent behavior? With the prevalence of Wi-Fi and digital signaling, might the presence of security cameras deter violence? The latter of course depends on sport venue managers making sure people are aware "big brother" is watching. Of course, it is also possible that persons may "show off" for the camera, and thus the presence of video recording devices may actually facilitate aggression. In this case, an appraisal of the environment would lead to higher levels of violence.

Some Final Thoughts

The ecological setting of a sporting event, while similar in many respects to other large gatherings, is also very different. These differences help us understand why individual misbehavior is more likely to occur at sporting events than at other large social gatherings. Today sporting events are presented and packaged as entertainment events. Management spares no expense to ensure that the spectator's arousal level is maximized. The "Cheer Meter," the wave, mascots of all kinds and descriptions, scantily clad cheerleaders, exhortations on the message board, fireworks, and loud rock music are all designed to excite and entertain the crowd. Management typically invites the fan to become an extra player—the 12th man (or woman) in football—and join the action. This strategy is not without problems because, if support for the home team is encouraged too strongly, it can engender very negative, potentially dangerous, feelings toward the opposing team and its supporters (Wann, 1993). Given sufficient provocation, what was an innocent rivalry between opposing teams and fans can give way to serious intergroup conflict (Lee, 1985).

CHAPTER 9

Sport Fan Riots

Moscow, Russia. Torino and Rome, Italy. Johannesburg, South Africa. Den Bosch, Netherlands. Zagreb, Croatia. Stockholm, Sweden. What do these locations have in common? Each was the site of a fan riot occurring during a five-year span from 1999 to 2003. And before readers from the United States begin to mock fans from other countries, during this same time period there were numerous sport riots in the U.S., including those taking place in Tucson, Arizona; Statesboro, Georgia; Durham, North Carolina; Huntington, West Virginia; Columbus, Ohio; West Lafayette, Indiana; and East Lansing, Michigan. And those are just riots occurring at college games! Indeed, the lists presented here are but a very small sampling of all sports riots. In fact, a Google News search of the phrase "sport fan riot" conducted during the writing of the book produced an astonishing 480,000 hits.

Although not the norm, sport fan riots do occur, and they result in tremendous physical, psychological, and economic costs. In this chapter, we take a critical look at the occurrence and form of these crowd disturbances. Our examination includes a look at collective behavior and a typology for classifying sport riots, a discussion of persons most likely to become involved in a riot, a look at those most likely to intervene, and a review of soccer hooliganism.

Definitions of Riotous Behavior

Similar to the construct of aggression, there is considerable diversity among definitions of riots. To illustrate, Darrow and Lewinger (1968) define riots simply as "aimless behavior involving disturbances or turmoil" (p. 2). Riots have also been described as "relatively spontaneous group violence contrary to traditional norms" (Marx, 1972, p. 50). Other scholars have attempted to define riots as they occur in the context of sport. For instance, Simons and Taylor (1992) define **sport riots** as "purposive destructive or injurious behavior by partisan spectators of a sporting event that may be caused by personal, social, economic, or competitive factors" (p. 213). But perhaps the most accurate and comprehensive definition of sport rioting was offered by Lewis (2007), a leading scholar in this area who has researched and written extensively on the topic. According to Lewis:

> A sports riot is defined as violence—vandalism, throwing missiles, rushing the field or court, committing arson, and or fighting—committed by

Although Not the Norm, Large-Scale Fan Violence in the Form of Rioting Does Occur, Frequently Resulting in Large Amounts of Property Damage, Injuries, and Even Fatalities

> five or more individuals in a crowd of at least one hundred people associated with a formally organized sporting event.
>
> (p. 7)

Theories of Collective Behavior and a Typology of Sport Riots

In the paragraphs that follow, we first examine several macro approaches to collective behavior that shed valuable light on sport riots. This discussion is followed by a review of a useful typology for classifying sport riots.

Theories of Collective Behavior

Several classic sociological viewpoints help to further our understanding of crowd misbehavior. These theories identify the dynamics of collective action, that is, how normally mild-mannered, non-demonstrative fans become involved in episodes of rioting. Although these approaches have their limitations, they provide a valuable introduction to concepts that underscore the importance of the larger social environment in explaining sport fan rioting (Jaffe & Yinon, 1983).

Contagion Theory Originating from the work of Le Bon (1946), **Contagion Theory** puts forth the notion that ideas, moods, attitudes, and behaviors can become rapidly communicated and uncritically accepted by crowd members (Polansky, Lippitt, & Redl, 1950). According to the theory, one aroused person in the crowd, by word or deed, arouses another who, in turn, arouses another, and so on. This circular action has the effect of stimulating the first person to an even greater extent, as well as other members in the circle of influence. Because the arousal has no specific focus or outlet, the collectivity is very suggestible and especially vulnerable to a leader's cues. Contagion Theory assists in our understanding of how both social (e.g., the wave, rhythmic clapping, organized cheering) and antisocial behaviors (e.g., booing, throwing missiles, invading the pitch) can take hold within a large crowd.

Convergence Theory Similar to contagion theory, **Convergence Theory** forwards the premise that "crowd behavior stems from the convergence of likeminded persons who are already predisposed to act in certain ways" (Simons & Taylor, 1992, p. 210; Wright, 1978). Increases in crowd homogeneity (i.e., similarity in values, norms, motives, and interests) lead to higher levels of arousal and lowered inhibitions. These states are expected to increase the likelihood of collective behavior.

Emergent-Norms Theory A third approach, **Emergent-Norms Theory,** involves group conformity, the process by which crowd membership influences individuals to conform to new norms developed within the group (Turner & Killian, 1972). Deviant behaviors such as spectator aggression become increasingly likely when crowds adopt antisocial standards of behavior they consider appropriate for a particular situation. Soon, members of the crowd are behaving in a particular way, leading others to join in as they assume that it is proper and acceptable. For example, if everyone in a crowd feels that an umpire missed a call, it takes only a few fans to express their displeasure by shouting obscenities before others are joining in the hostile behavior. In this situation, a norm has emerged encouraging abusive behavior.

Work on sport fans finds that those believing in a group norm encouraging derogatory actions are more likely to engage in the hostile acts themselves (Amiot, Sansfacon, & Louis, 2014), a pattern consistent with the emergent-norms approach. Interestingly, the authors found that the effect was strongest among those with higher levels of team identification. It was the combination of identification *and* internalization of the group norm for aggressive behavior that predicted hostile actions. This finding is important evidence that personal input variables (e.g., team identification) and situational input variables (e.g., norms for violence) may interact to produce particularly powerful effects.

Value-Added Theory No theoretical discussion of fan violence would be complete without mention of Smelser's (1968) **Value-Added Theory,** viewed as a "comprehensive approach to collective violence, particularly fan violence" (Lewis, 2007, pp. 8–9). In explaining an episode of collective behavior, Smelser identifies several **determinants**, each of which is viewed as a necessary but not sufficient condition for an episode to occur. However, when all are present, the probability of collective action occurring is far more likely. What follows is a brief discussion of each determinant, accompanied by appropriate examples. The reader is encouraged to consult Lewis (1989, 2007) for an informative real-world application of Smelser's theory to the Heysel Stadium riot that occurred on May 29, 1985, in Brussels, Belgium.

One important determinant, **structural conduciveness**, refers to the ecological setting in which the potential behavior may occur. Smelser's (1968) point here is that some structural factors facilitate aggressive responses (e.g., hot temperatures, noisy arenas). A second determinant—**structural strain**—refers to a generalized sense of deprivation or conflict. Structural strain may also involve hostile feelings provoked by an antagonistic group (e.g., rival fan base) or a particular situation (e.g., a general dislike for authority). The growth of a **generalized belief** is a third determinant. This factor refers to a perceived threat that has been exaggerated or is seen as being imminent. A sport-related example would include spectators' perceptions that the referee is biased toward the home team. A fourth determinant involves the **mobilization of participants** for action. This stage of the process typically involves the emergence of a leader who is able to incite others into action. For instance, in our previous example of the umpire's poor call, an individual may mobilize others by yelling "Kill the umpire!" while encouraging them to express their displeasure by throwing objects at the official. The operation of **social controls** (or the lack thereof) serves as the final determinant. This factor refers to strong threats of force discouraging the display of hostile actions. Thus, social controls function as a counter determinant. Staying with the previous example, this determinant is represented by stadium security/staff members who confront the loud fan and escort him or her out of the stadium before a collective action takes place.

Mann's FORCE Typology

Although the aforementioned sociological approaches to rioting are of value, it can also be useful to classify sport riots by type. Typologies assist in the recognition and categorization of particular kinds of collective behavior. A typology is also important because it has implications for understanding (1) the causes of hostile outbursts, (2) when they are most likely to occur (e.g., before, during, or after a game), (3) the types of individuals most likely to participate, and (4) those most likely to be targeted (Mann, 1979).

Mann (1979, 1989) developed a typology for classifying sport riots based on an analysis of case materials and archival records. Assigned the acronym **FORCE**, this typology identifies five types of riots, each based on the dominant characteristics of the rioters. A brief description of the riot categories included in this model is presented in Table 9.1. It should be noted that although other typologies have been constructed (e.g., Smith, 1983), we have limited our presentation to Mann's framework because it is highly comprehensive, and other models tend to contain a large amount of overlap with Mann's system.

Frustration Riots The **frustration riot** is caused by bitterly disappointed fans who wish to retaliate for what they regard as an illegitimate or unacceptable

TABLE 9.1 Mann's (1979) FORCE Typology of Sport Riots

Frustration riots	Riots caused by disappointed fans who wish to retaliate against the perceived source of frustration.
Outlawry riots	Riots caused by delinquent groups who assemble at sporting events for the purpose of engaging in threatening and destructive behavior.
Remonstrance riots	Riots that represent protests from groups who wish to use the sport stadium to express their political or ideological grievances.
Confrontational riots	Riots involving opposing fan groups with a history of hostility and resentment.
Expressive riots	Riots directly related to the euphoria or anger and depression spectators feel in response to the outcome of a sporting event.

action. The frustration riot can be precipitated when fans are deprived of a service (e.g., access to a sporting event) or when they perceive a gross injustice (e.g., a referee's bad call). For example, consider the dangerous situation that arose during the 1996 Summer Olympics held in and around Atlanta, Georgia (Wine, 1996). When a match involving fan favorite tennis star Andre Agassi was rescheduled, hundreds of frustrated fans become extremely hostile, forcing officials to call in almost two dozen additional police vehicles. Eventually, match officials reversed the schedule change as they "feared they (fans) would storm the gates" (Wine, 1996, p. 2B).

Outlawry Riots When the game becomes an opportunity for delinquent groups to assemble and engage in threatening or destructive acts, we have an **outlawry riot**. According to Mann (1979, 1989), the game and outcome are inconsequential to the violence, as the participants have neither an emotional nor a social attachment to the contesting teams or the sport itself. Rather, the event merely provides them with an opportunity to act out and cause others grief. Judged within the North American sport context, it is rare for youth gangs to seek out high school, college, or professional sporting events to engage in destructive behavior. But there are exceptions. For example, the principal of a suburban Los Angeles high school forfeited a football game to an urban school because he feared gang violence made the game too dangerous to play or watch (High School Team Opts to Take Forfeit, 1991).

Remonstrance Riots The **remonstrance riot** is essentially an ideological protest in which a group uses a sporting event to express a political grievance or advance a particular ideology. Hartmann (1996) notes that the popularity and availability of cultural settings like sport are especially appealing to powerless racial and ethnic minorities who wish to draw attention to a particular cause. For example, Aboriginal leaders in Australia warned Olympic officials that they were planning to wage violent protests during the 2000 summer games in Sydney to draw international attention to social injustices involving their people (Corder, 2000). In North America, Native American groups have frequently protested against teams (e.g., the NFL Washington Redskins, the MLB Atlanta Braves) whose symbols (e.g., the Tomahawk Chop, Chief Wahoo) are thought of as demeaning to their culture.

Confrontational Riots **Confrontational riots** involve opposing fan groups with a history of hostility and resentment toward each other. On this point, King (1995) observed that although a negative "historical background between two factions does not automatically cause disorder, this background nevertheless has a degree of determination over the actualization and interactional levels since it limits the horizon of possible practices, in which fans can engage" (p. 649). Basically, King is suggesting that, all things being equal, intergroup violence is more likely to occur between supporters of rival teams than between fan groups who have no history of confrontation. As our earlier discussion of rivalry suggests (see Chapter 8), King's point has merit. For example, an NFL game between the Chicago Bears and the Green Bay Packers is likely to place security on greater alert than a game between the Bears and the San Diego Chargers, a nonconference game involving two teams that seldom meet. The same can be said about a baseball game between the New York Yankees and the Boston Red Sox as opposed to a game between the Yankees and the Seattle Mariners. In the former instance, both teams are in the same division, play each other several times, and have a long history of an intense rivalry.

Expressive Riots The final type of riot found in Mann's typology is an **expressive riot.** These crowd disturbances are directly related to expressions of extreme euphoria or intense anger. Often referred to as **victory riots** and **sore loser riots**, respectively, these crowd disturbances are typically postgame phenomena. It is hypothesized that the emotional arousal engendered by the outcome of a game, be it joy and ecstasy or grief and anger, leads to a loss of normal restraint, or **disinhibition.** Disinhibition involves the expression of behavior "which is usually restrained by fear of adverse consequences mediated externally (punishment) or internally (guilt)" (Jaffe & Yinon, 1983, p. 267). The probability of expressive riots occurring at sporting events is more likely because of the emotionally charged atmosphere in which they are conducted, the fact that there are winners and losers, and the anonymity spectators enjoy in a large crowd.

Although there are certainly exceptions, fans of the losing team often respond with cold silence and a hasty retreat from the venue. Thus, victory or celebratory riots may be more common, at least in North America (Lewis, 2007). In fact, these crowd disturbances are often anticipated following a championship victory by the home team. In anticipation of a sixth NBA title, the city of Chicago used a computer mapping system that allowed police to identify trouble spots and quickly dispatch officers (Howlett, 1998). This was the same type of system used by the CIA, Scotland Yard, and U.S. Border Patrol. In addition, the police department's 13,500 officers were placed on alert, some freeway ramps were closed, traffic was rerouted away from trouble spots, and bar owners were asked to close early if they saw patrons getting rowdy.

Two Distinct Forms of Victory Riots • Mann's victory (i.e., celebratory) riot category should be subdivided because there appear to be two different forms of victory riots. The first typically takes place in the host city immediately after the game, usually under nightfall, and has little to do with sport fandom. The celebration merely provides a cover for individuals to loot, rob, and maim. The motive behind their actions is straightforward: destroy what's not valuable and steal what is. Celebratory riots also become an opportunity for the socially and economically disadvantaged to take out their frustration on a social system that they perceived as inequitable. For example, the riots associated with Chicago Bulls NBA championships may well have constituted a form of economic protest by socially and economically marginalized groups (Rosenfeld, 1997).

The second form of victory riot is closer to what Mann (1979) describes. These riots result from the sense of euphoria fans feel when their team has won a championship. For example, on October 30, 1993, seven people were critically hurt and dozens more were injured when thousands of celebrating fans poured onto the football field following Wisconsin's 13–10 victory over Michigan. Approximately 12,000 spectators among the sellout crowd of 77,745 scrambled out of five student sections in an attempt to reach the field. The injured fans were trampled in the rush (Telander, 1993). The euphoria of the surging crowd was understandable given the fact that it was the first Badger victory over Michigan in 12 years. More importantly, the victory raised Wisconsin's record to 7–1, giving the school an excellent chance to win its first Big Ten Conference championship in over 30 years and a trip to the Rose Bowl. Combine the crowd's excitement with weak, ineffective physical barriers separating the students from the end zone, a grossly undermanned security force, and Halloween weekend, and you have a potentially deadly situation.

Based on his own research (e.g., examinations of celebratory riots following victories by the Ohio State University football team and the Boston Red Sox), and the work of others, Lewis (2007) developed a framework that offers several predictions about when these disturbances are most likely to occur. These hypotheses, listed in Table 9.2, are consistent with research discussed in several sections in the current text. The model presented by Lewis is of great value to sport management and marketing professionals because it sheds light on the types of games and circumstances in which celebratory riots are most likely. As a result, team, league, and university officials should be able to better prepare.

Those Who Would Participate in and Escalate a Sport Riot

You may be surprised to learn that we know a great deal about those individuals who are at the center of a riot, trading punches, destroying property, and/or throwing missiles of one sort or another. Specifically, we know something about their demographics, the impact of group processes on their behavior, ways in which they process information, and personality profiles. Each of these topics is discussed in this section.

TABLE 9.2 Lewis's (2007) Theory of Celebratory Sports Riots

Hypothesis 1:	A celebration riot (e.g., rioting by fans of a winning team) is more likely than a sore loser riot (e.g., rioting by fans of a losing team).
Hypothesis 2:	A celebration riot is more likely to occur after a championship contest.
Hypothesis 3:	A celebration riot is more likely to occur if the winning team has not had a championship season within five years.
Hypothesis 4:	A celebration riot is more likely to occur as a championship playoff series continues (e.g., MLB World Series, NBA Finals).
Hypothesis 5:	A celebration riot is more likely to occur if the final game is close.
Hypothesis 6:	A celebration riot is more likely to occur if fans have easy access to urban gathering areas.
Hypothesis 7:	If a celebration riot has occurred, most individuals involved will be young, white, and male.

Demographic Characteristics of Rioters

Several decades of research present us with a picture of the typical rioter as a young, single male, a demographic profile fitting most rioters in North America and Europe (Kerr, 1994; Lewis, 2007; Pilz, 1989; Reiss & Roth, 1993; Russell & Arms, 1998; Zani & Kirchler, 1991). This work also suggests that rioters at European sporting events tend to be marginalized, poorly educated, unemployed, and alienated from the mainstream of society. These traits are less likely to be found among rioters at North American sporting events, given that many of these riots center around college sport and are populated by university students.

Group Processes and Riotous Behavior

Those bent on trouble run in packs. An official inquiry by Harrington into British hooliganism observed that "most misbehavior at soccer matches involves small or large groups; rarely does it involve a single spectator" (cited in Mann & Pearce, 1978). Evidence pointing to higher levels of aggression on the part of group members is seen in several studies. For example, Mann found that groups of spectators attending Australian football matches scored higher on a hostility measure than those attending alone (cited in Mann & Pearce, 1978). Also, not only do groups of young male hockey spectators score higher on anger and physical aggression scales, they also have a history of repeated and recent fighting (e.g., Russell & Arms, 1998). More to the point, men attending in the company of other men rate the likelihood of their escalating a riot higher than do solitary spectators.

Social Cognition and Riotous Behavior: The False Consensus Effect

Turning now to studies of cognitive processes, we are able to get a glimpse of how would-be rioters perceive events inside the arena or stadium. An important cognitive bias, the **false consensus effect**, may play a key role in the hostile outbursts of some spectators (Russell, 2008). This phenomenon involves the tendency of people "to see their own behavioral choices and judgments as relatively common and appropriate to existing circumstances while viewing alternate responses as uncommon, deviant, or inappropriate" (Ross, Greene, & House, 1977, p. 280). That is, persons believe their thoughts, choices, and actions are the norm and, therefore, acceptable. This perceptual bias is evident among hockey spectators. For example, those expressing a strong likelihood of joining a fight that erupts in the stands estimate that a higher percentage of others would do likewise compared to those who would not get involved. Similarly, spectators attending because they like to watch player fights often believe that a disproportionately larger number of other spectators attend for the same reason (Russell & Arms, 1995). These perceptions may set the stage for some spectators to engage in violence. That is, those wavering in their decision to join in a fight may be emboldened by their belief that an inflated number of other spectators would tacitly approve of their aggression and are poised to follow them into battle.

A Personality Profile of Rioters

In the 1990s, a series of field studies were undertaken in Canada, Finland, and the Netherlands using spectators attending ice hockey and, in the Dutch case, a football match (e.g., Mustonen, Arms, & Russell, 1996; Russell, 1995; Russell & Goldstein, 1995; see Russell, 2004, for a review of this research). An extensive battery of personality measures was administered to spectators over the course of nine studies. Participants were asked to indicate the likelihood they would join in a fight if one would break out near them. The results indicated that, to no one's surprise, men who were angry and physically aggressive were more likely than others to become involved in a riot.

However, the researchers found that other less obvious traits also characterized the potential rioters. Individuals apt to involve themselves in crowd disorders exhibit strong **sensation seeking** tendencies (Mustonen et al., 1996). For example, given choices between exciting activities (e.g., surfing and sky diving) and less exciting pastimes (e.g., chess or reading a book), they choose the former. Sensation seekers express a "need for varied, novel, and complex sensations and experiences and the willingness to take physical and social risks for the sake of such experience" (Zuckerman, 1979, p. 10). A crowd disturbance, containing as it does an element of risk, would understandably act like a magnet for these people.

Another interesting facet of the personality of would-be rioters was their tendency to act **impulsively** (Arms & Russell, 1997). Faced with a social situation that calls for action, they jump in without reflecting on the consequences. In the case of a nearby disturbance, they may well join in, giving little thought to the physical harm and legal consequences that might await them. The means by which impulsive individuals become involved in crowd violence was shown in an early experiment (Wheeler & Caggiula, 1966). Impulsive individuals were found to exhibit more aggression following exposure to aggressive models than were individuals lacking impulsive tendencies. Seemingly, they had fewer inhibitions against violating social norms and as a consequence were more easily influenced by peers to act on their deviant inclinations.

A final characteristic that appears related to riotous behavior is psychopathology, or **antisocial tendencies** (e.g., Russell, 1995). This syndrome involves a lengthy list of symptoms and is not adequately diagnosed by personality inventories alone (Hare, 1993). However, inventories do provide a rough approximation, capturing an individual's tendency to be manipulative, unremorseful, and deceitful. The motivation underlying the antisocial behaviors of these individuals is glimpsed in the inventory item "I often do things just for the hell of it" (Levenson, 1990).

The information provided above was an important step in furthering our understanding of the personality profile of sport rioters. However, it warrants reiteration that the aforementioned studies sampled would-be rioters, not persons who had necessarily participated in a riot. In a more recent investigation, Lanter (2011) surveyed individuals who had actually participated in a celebratory riot. Lanter conducted his investigation surrounding fan violence that occurred on the University of Maryland campus following their road victory over Duke University in a hotly contested men's basketball game. The victory was particularly empowering for the Maryland faithful because it snapped a number of winning streaks for the Duke team. For two days following the riots, the investigator interviewed persons who acknowledged participation in the disturbance. Lanter assessed their level of identification with the basketball team, if they had consumed alcohol, their reactions to the celebratory riot, and the various riotous activities in which they had engaged (e.g., vandalism, throwing items into a bonfire). The results were quite illuminating. First, highly identified persons reported participating in a greater number of riotous activities than those lower in identification. The highly identified fans also indicated having had more fun during the event and were more likely to desire participation in a future riot. As for alcohol, the findings revealed that persons who consumed alcohol during the game or riot were more destructive than those who had not consumed an intoxicating beverage. Thus, consistent with research detailed in Chapter 8, both team identification and alcohol consumption were key predictors of their aggressive actions.

Those Who Would Quell a Sport Riot: The Peacemakers

If you look closely at scenes of sport riots, you will see that only a handful of people are actually involved in the rioting. Most are milling around watching, apparently not centrally involved in the violence. Others seem not to be engaging in aggressive acts themselves but, rather, are encouraging the rioters to continue their destructive ways. And still others, upon seeing the riot, appear motivated to flee the scene as quickly as possible. Thus, there are several options open to spectators when a disturbance breaks out. They can join the fight, applaud and incite the combatants, leave the facility, or hang back and merely observe the proceedings. But those who exercise a final option are in many ways the most interesting of all. They are the **peacemakers,** the ones who intervene in a disturbance with the intention of verbally and/or physically dissuading those involved in the fight.

A Profile of Peacemakers

As with rioters, researchers have attempted to construct a profile of peacemakers. As one might guess, they are of greater stature than rioters, being generally taller and heavier. Regarding their personality traits, peacemakers are less angry, aggressive, and impulsive than those they try to restrain (Russell & Mustonen, 1998). Also in contrast to rioters, peacemakers are low on measures of sensation seeking. Their motives appear to stem from a high regard for the rule of law and the importance of orderliness in a civil society (Russell & Arms, 1999; Russell, Arms, & Mustonen, 1999).

Additionally, it is something of a truism that what people will do in the future is frequently indicated by what they have done in the past (social scientists often state that "the best predictor of future behavior is past behavior"). This pattern is also found among peacemakers. Those who have tried to stop fights in the past, especially those who see their efforts as having been in some ways successful, are foremost among those most likely to intervene in the future (Russell & Arms, 1999; Russell et al., 1999).

Peacemakers and rioters do share one commonality, though. They both display the false consensus effect (Russell & Arms, 1999; Russell et al., 1999). That is, similar to rioters, peacemakers also believe that a disproportionately large number of other spectators would act as they (i.e., as peacemaker) would when a disturbance erupts. Their interventions, although taken precipitously, are bolstered by the belief that others are poised to follow their lead.

Peacemakers as a Source of Crowd Control

If peacemakers are plentiful among the spectators at a sporting event, they represent a large, untapped force for crowd control. As noted elsewhere (Russell & Mustonen, 1998), they are already on the scene, often know the instigators, and are familiar with the events leading up to the hostile outburst. As a result, peacemakers are ideally positioned to assist in the control of a disturbance before it escalates. The potential for other spectators to play a role in crowd control during (or prior to) violent episodes presents a unique challenge to sport management professionals.

It is unfortunate that spectators with the most honorable of motives and acting on the best of intentions find themselves in physical and legal jeopardy. When security personnel and police eventually arrive on the scene, arrests are likely. And who gets arrested? Sadly, for peacemakers, they and the rioters will likely be sharing accommodations in the local jail, and there is little hope that the judge will be sympathetic to their explanation. Understandably, police are hard pressed to distinguish peacemakers from rioters in the dangerous and confusing turmoil that surrounds a riot. Indeed, Stott and Reicher (1998) noted that experienced and highly trained British police officers typically "perceive crowd members as homogeneous in terms of the danger that they represent to public order and to the officer's well-being" (p. 522). That is, police seemingly do not distinguish the various actors and the roles they play in a crowd disturbance. From the officers' perspective "it is impossible to distinguish crowd members from each other behaviourally or physically" (p. 522). A worthy challenge for crowd control specialists then is to devise means of mobilizing peacemakers in a preemptive capacity as an effective complement to existing security arrangements.

Soccer Hooliganism

Much has been written in recent decades about the exploits and violent behaviors of **soccer hooligans**. Consequently, no discussion of spectator riots would be complete without a brief discussion of these persons. The word hooligan traces back more than 100 years to London, home to a hoodlum named Patrick Hooligan. Sometimes referred to as "the English disease," hooliganism has come to be most closely identified with soccer-crazed English lads and their propensity for antisocial behavior, like lewd chants and songs, pitch invasions, and no-holds-barred battles with opposing fans and security personnel. There appear to be no temporal or spatial constraints on hooligan behavior; it can occur before (e.g., at a rest stop along a motorway), during (e.g., at a stadium concession stand), or after a game (e.g., when opposing fans are boarding their buses to return home). At the very least, hooligan behavior is distasteful, disruptive, and dispiriting for those who care about the game and civil order.

Although soccer hooliganism is commonly viewed as a predominately British phenomenon, the behavior can be found all over the world. For example, at the 1996 Soccer World Cup, French officials had to contend not only with overly rabid English fans but also with German neo-Nazi and French-Tunisian diehards. Scattered outbreaks of fan violence were everywhere. Riot troops fought pitched battles in Marseille, and newspaper headlines proclaimed "Hooligans Sour World Cup" (1998).

Where Are the North American Hooligans?

An interesting question regarding hooliganism concerns the apparent lack of such behavior among North American sport spectators. A quick scan of the North American sport scene reveals nothing even remotely resembling soccer hooliganism, European style. One of the best answers to the question "Where are the American hooligans?" can be found in the work of Roadburg (1980). Roadburg identified a number of precipitating factors associated with fan violence, noting their presence or absence at professional soccer games in Britain and the United States. Table 9.3 provides an adaptation of his findings applied to professional team sport in general. Although Roadburg's analysis is now

TABLE 9.3 Comparison of English Soccer and U.S. Sports

English soccer	U.S. sports (NBA, NFL, NHL MLB)
1. Most British stadiums were built at the end of the nineteenth century; amenities are very limited.	1. The vast majority of all stadiums and arenas were built since 1960; they are modern, clean, and comfortable.
2. Thousands of fans walk to the soccer grounds because they are centrally located and many fans lack their own transportation; there are many opportunities to engage opposing fans on the way to the game.	2. Spectators drive to games in small groups; they generally do not come into contact with one another until they are at the facility.
3. Strong feelings of solidarity, excitement, and anticipation build on the way to the game.	3. Lead-up activities to the game are not as conducive for generating arousal, excitement, and solidarity.
4. A large proportion of spectators stand on the terraces located at both ends of the pitch; more conducive to developing camaraderie and unity.	4. All spectators are seated with the exception of a few who purchase standing-room-only tickets.
5. Considerable amount of movement among standing fans; changing positions to get a better view of the action.	5. Fixed seats mean fans have no control over their space, hence, little movement among spectators.
6. The game is the culmination of an entire day of preparation, a single event in a sequence of events; anticipation level is very high.	6. The game is typically the only event of the day; when the game is over, the day is over.
7. Because of the relatively short distances between home grounds, large numbers of fans follow their favorite teams to rival grounds.	7. Few fans follow their favorite team to away games because of the great distance involved; presence of rival fans is unlikely.
8. Absence of women and small children in the crowd.	8. Although middle-class males are usually in the majority, many women and children are present.
9. Team identification runs deep because it is often based on religion and/or class; fans are much less likely to change affiliations because they are less geographically mobile.	9. Team identifications not as strong because they are based on proximity; affiliations susceptible to change because of greater geographical mobility.

(*Continued*)

TABLE 9.3 (Continued)

English soccer	U.S. sports (NBA, NFL, NHL MLB)
10. Fans have fewer sports and teams with which to identify.	10. The sport fan has well over a hundred professional teams from which to choose; interest in favorite team not likely to be as intense and passionate.
11. Fan loyalty confined to a single professional soccer team—the local side.	11. Loyalty diffused among several favorite teams within a single geographical region (e.g., the New York Knicks, Rangers, Islanders, Mets, and Yankees).
12. Sectarianism often plays a major role in team affiliation; games frequently pit teams representing different religions against one another.	12. No evidence of sectarianism in selection of favorite teams.

several decades old, its value has been retained because it provides an explanation of the continuing lack of North American hooliganism.

Based on the information presented in Table 9.3, it becomes evident that the typical British soccer fan's relationship to his (or her) favorite team and his actual experience at the sporting event are very different from those of his North American counterpart. Personal and psychosocial issues related to territoriality, possession, loyalty, and sectarianism, as well as class and cultural conflict, set the British soccer fan apart from the American baseball, hockey, football, or basketball fan. Why no American hooligans? Roadburg's (1980) answer almost four decades ago is still appropriate today:

> Due to differences in the historical development and present day physical and social conditions within which the game is played, soccer in Britain lends itself to crowd violence whereas soccer (as well as basketball, football, hockey, baseball) in North American does not.
>
> (p. 265)

Some Final Thoughts

Riots are perhaps the most unfortunate consequence of sport spectating. Almost anyone who has survived such a chaotic and terrifying experience is sure to be haunted by it for quite some time and may think twice before venturing into another sport stadium or arena. Most certainly, riots give sport fandom a black eye, tarnishing this leisure pursuit. Consequently, a firm understanding of the factors that precipitate these crowd disturbances is warranted. However, it is not enough to simply describe and explain sport spectating riots. Although these are valuable research goals, in the name of safety and civility, those interested in the sanctity of sport must also strive for the final goal, namely, control. Sport administrators and managers must begin to utilize the information generated by social scientists to reduce the occurrence of riotous behaviors among fans. Thankfully, some organizations have done just that. For example, in 2003 both The Ohio State University and the University of New Hampshire sponsored conferences on fan violence in response to riots that had recently occurred on their campuses. These summits led to working documents containing suggested policies and procedures for proactively reducing the likelihood of future disturbances (National Conference, 2003; Student Summit, 2003).

Another attempt to better prepare for sport rioting was initiated by coordinators of the 2000 European Soccer Championships, preparations that ended in a bizarre twist. Organizers staged a mock riot in Rotterdam in preparation for the upcoming matches involving teams followed by fans with a history of hooliganism and violence (Security Check, 2001). Alas, their efforts were thwarted, and they had to end the exercise when real hooligans arrived, armed with stones! It seems that this incident serves notice that the ultimate control of sport spectator riots will require a great deal of effort, patience, and persistence.

PART THREE

The Consequences of Sport Fandom for Individuals and Society

CHAPTER 10

The Psychological Consequences of Sport Fandom

Social scientists have debated the virtue of sport fandom for a very long time. For instance, consider the thoughts of Howard, who as early as 1912 stated that sport fandom was

> A singular example of mental perversion, an absurd and immoral custom tenaciously held fast in mob-mind, has its genesis in the partisan zeal of athletic spectator-crowds. I refer to the practice of organized cheering, known in college argot as 'rooting.' From every aspect it is bad.
>
> (p. 46)

Granted, this negative perception of fandom is over a century old. However, several more contemporary social scientists held similarly negative views of the pastime (e.g., Beisser, 1967; Lazarsfeld & Merton, 1948; Meier, 1989), including Reese (1994), who argued that "no human being on this Earth either has to or needs to attend any professional sports events" (p. 12A). In fact, Zillmann et al. (1989) wrote that there is "nearly a universal condemnation of sport spectatorship" on the part of social scientists (p. 246). Hughes (1987) agreed with this viewpoint and argued that everyone seems to like and enjoy sport except the social scientists who comment on it.

In contrast to the detractors, some earlier authors had a favorable view of sport fandom. And we mean *early*! In fact, around 500 BC the mathematician and philosopher Pythagoras argued that of all those who attended the Olympics (e.g., athletes and merchants), the spectators were the best because of their desire to simply observe and learn (Lenk, 1982). Expressing a similarly positive view of sport fans, almost a century ago Brill (1929, pp. 430, 434) stated:

> The average man, for perfectly simple psychological reasons, just will not muster much enthusiasm for the idea of getting out and playing instead of watching the game. On the other hand, through the

> operation of the psychological laws of identification and catharsis, the thorough-going fan is distinctly benefited mentally, physically, and morally by spectator-participation in his favorite sport. . . . I conclude that the national habit of watching rather than playing games, despite all of the head-shaking of physical culturists and economists, sociologists, and intellectuals, is a salutary habit.

More recent authors have also viewed sport fandom as a positive pastime (Guttmann, 1980, 1986; Hemphill, 1995; Lasch, 1989; Melnick, 1993; Smith, 1988, 1989).

So, which of these contrasting views is correct? Are sport fans violent beings engaged in a useless activity that has negative consequences for society and its members? Or are sport fans similar to nonfans in most respects, with the exception that they have an abiding interest in a worthwhile, socially acceptable pastime? In the next two chapters, we attempt to answer these questions by ascertaining the potential costs and benefits of sport fandom. Our analysis examines the debate from both psychological and sociological perspectives; that is, we review the positive and negative consequences of sport fandom for both the individual fan and for society as a whole. The current chapter focuses on the psychological consequences of fandom, while Chapter 11 analyzes its societal consequences.

We begin the current chapter with an examination of several psychologically based criticisms of sport fans and their pastime (i.e., positions arguing that fandom is harmful to individuals in some way). Each criticism will be critiqued within a framework of existing data when possible. We then examine the mental health of sport fans and the methods they employ to maintain their psychological well-being.

Psychologically Based Criticisms of Sport Fandom

Although a number of different psychologically based (i.e., individual level) criticisms of sport fandom have been raised, four arguments appear to be most common: (1) fans are lazy, (2) fans are aggressive, (3) sport encourages fans to adopt negative values and maladaptive behaviors, and (4) fans have poor interpersonal relationships. The merit of each of these alleged psychological costs of fandom are addressed in this section.

Are Sport Fans Lazy?

One of the most common criticisms involves the perception that **sport fans are lazy** (Lasch, 1989; Meier, 1989; Smith, 1988). Individuals who hold this belief view fans as little more than overweight couch potatoes. However, several decades back Guttmann (1980) offered an insightful challenge to this criticism. He suggested that "Although it is unusual to denounce museum-goers for not painting still-lifes and bad form to fault concert audiences for not playing the violin,

One Common Criticism of Sport Fandom Is That Fans Are Little More Than Lazy Couch Potatoes

it is quite common . . . to criticize spectators for athletic inactivity" (p. 275). Likewise, Hemphill (1995) noted that

> it would be absurd to insist that all spectators become players, just as it would be absurd to insist that everyone should stop reading books and start writing them, that ballet audiences should take up dancing, that movie goers should make their own films.
>
> (p. 52)

The criticism that sport fans are lazy has also not held up well to empirical investigation. This conclusion is drawn from three lines of research: the relationships between fandom and (1) athletic participation, (2) other pursuits, and (3) success/involvement in higher education. With respect to the relationship between fandom and athletic participation, recall from Chapter 1 that fans are particularly likely to participate in sport as athletes (e.g., Appelbaum et al., 2012; Inoue et al., 2015). If sport fans are lazy, one should find a negative correlation between sport and athletic participation. Clearly, this is not the case.

A second line of evidence standing in contrast to the notion that fans are lazy concerns the extent to which these individuals are involved in other pursuits (leisure, political, etc.). Rather than being single-minded people wrapped up solely in sport, research suggests that fans are involved in other life domains as well (Appelbaum et al., 2012; Clotfelter, 2015; Lieberman, 1991). For example,

Montgomery and Robinson (2006) found that rather than competing for audiences, fandom for sport and the arts were complementary activities. They concluded that "individuals who attend sporting events are likely to attend arts events as well" (p. 36). Additionally, Sun, Youn, and Wells (2004) found that sport consumers exceeded nonfans' interest in politics, world events, and working on a community project. These findings extend to non-North American cultures as well. For instance, Theodorakis, Wann, Akindes, and Chadwick (2017) found positive relationships between attendance at football (i.e., soccer) matches and visitations to museums among persons residing in the Middle East.

With respect to higher education, if sport fans are lazy, one would expect them to exhibit poorer academic performances and lower levels of involvement than nonfans. However, once again the data contradict this notion. Instead, research indicates that sport fans often outperform nonfans and are more involved with their university. For example, consider the work of Schurr, Wittig, Ruble, and Henriksen (1993), who compared the graduation rates and grade point averages (GPAs) of college student fans and nonfans. Using students' high school performance and college entrance scores, they found that although the two groups were similar in their predicted college performance, analyses of actual performance revealed that the fan group had a higher six-year graduation rate and higher GPAs. A second relevant project was completed by Wann and Robinson (2002), who examined the relationship between team identification and integration into one's university. They found significant correlations between identification with the school's teams and both graduation intentions and involvement with the university. That is, participants higher in identification reported greater levels of involvement with the school and were more likely to believe that they would graduate from that university. Katz and Heere (2016) noted a similar pattern of effects with the establishment of a new college football team. Specifically, they found that a "newly added football team appeared to be a powerful instrument to increase people's behavioral involvement with the university" (p. 143).

Are Sport Fans Aggressive?

Another common argument against sport fandom is that **fans are overly aggressive**. When examining the relationship between fandom and aggression, it is important to distinguish between violent actions and violent personalities, that is, the difference between state and trait aggression. **State** aggression involves temporary shifts in one's aggression. **Trait** aggression, on the other hand, involves an individual's dispositional level of aggression over a long period of time. Thus, trait aggression is similar to a personality variable. The finding that sport fans occasionally report high levels of state aggression and sporadically exhibit violent behaviors does not insure that these individuals also possess high levels of trait aggression (i.e., that fans have an inherently violent disposition).

To accurately critique the argument that sport fans are aggressive, one must conduct two separate analyses: one each for fans' state aggression and trait aggression. With respect to state aggression, on rare occasions sport fans do become violent (see Chapters 7, 8, and 9). But the fact that sport fans occasionally exhibit aggressive behaviors does not make them aggressive individuals *per se*. Rather, additional research assessing trait aggression is needed to justify this claim. In the past couple of decades, a number of such studies have been completed. This body of work has included attempts to operationalize fandom in a variety of ways including attendance at sporting events (Russell & Goldstein, 1995), level of team identification (Wann, 1994b; Wann, Peterson, Cothran, & Dykes, 1999), and level of fandom (Wann, Fahl, Erdmann, & Littleton, 1999). Although a few exceptions can be found (Wann, Shelton, Smith, & Walker, 2002), in the majority of these studies researchers failed to find a significant relationship between fandom and trait aggression. For example, Koss and Gaines (1993) examined predictors of sexual aggression among male college students, including the extent to which they followed sport news and watched televised sport. Although some predictor variables were positively related to self-reported sexual aggression (including membership in a fraternity, participation in a varsity sport, and alcohol consumption), there was no relationship between sport fandom and sexual aggression.

Thus, based on the research conducted to date, it is safe to conclude that although a handful of fans sometimes exhibit heightened levels of state aggression, there is little evidence suggesting they have unusually high levels of trait aggression. That is, most fans do not walk into a sport arena as aggressive creatures bent on wreaking havoc and destruction. Rather, the competitive environment fuels their state aggression. This conclusion is consistent with an interesting set of findings reported by Dimmock and Grove (2005). These researchers examined the attitudes of Australian sport fans as a function of their level of team identification. They found that high, moderate, and low identified fans did not differ in their acceptance of physical and verbal aggression, with each group reporting that such behaviors were not appropriate. However, the identification groups did indicate differential levels of behavioral control (i.e., their ability to manage their own actions). Highly identified fans felt significantly less control over their own behaviors than did persons low or moderate in identification. Thus, the highly identified participants were not more aggressive *per se*; rather, they were more likely to be influenced by the circumstances of the game and, as a result, lose control over their behavioral responses.

Does Sport Lead to the Adoption of Negative Values and Behaviors?

Another common criticism of sport fandom is that **following sport leads to the adoption of negative values and behaviors**. This criticism is based on the logic that sport fans may internalize the questionable values and actions sometimes displayed by athletes and sport administrators. For instance, it has been argued that sport fandom facilitates belief in winning at all costs, in strict authoritarianism, and that violence, corruption, cheating, sexism, and racism are acceptable (Brohm, 1978; Cullen, 1974; Hoch, 1972; Schwartz, 1973).

Does this criticism have merit? Does following sport promote the adoption of negative values and behaviors? Certainly, it is not difficult to find instances when athletes, coaches, and administrators have exhibited questionable behaviors (watching any episode of ESPN's *SportsCenter* typically results in multiple cases). To scientifically examine the possibility that sport encourages the adoption of negative values and behaviors, we must once again consult the available research. Unfortunately, this criticism is difficult to evaluate empirically because of a scarcity of relevant research. However, the results from two studies provide evidence that this criticism has merit. First consider the work of Wann, Hunter, Ryan, and Wright (2001). Adopting methods often used to examine fan aggression, these researchers asked college students to indicate their willingness to consider anonymously cheating to assist a team. The results indicated that a large minority of fans would consider engaging in the duplicitous acts, a sample of which can be found in Table 10.1. However, even more damaging evidence was the significant positive correlation between level of identification with a team and willingness to consider the dishonest actions. The more an individual supported a team, the more likely they were to consider cheating to assist that team. Among the participants in the Wann et al. (2001) study, following a team seemed to lead to the adoption of a win-at-all-costs attitude and the belief that cheating is acceptable.

A second study seemingly in support of this criticism was conducted by Vildiz (2016). This author examined Turkish soccer fans' beliefs that their team was involved in unethical behavior (e.g., match fixing) and the extent to which they would want the team penalized for the transgression. The results indicated that team identification and desires for penalization were negatively correlated; highly identified fans were least likely to want the team to be sanctioned if found guilty of wrongdoings. Vildiz concluded that unethical team actions can be acceptable to highly identified fans provided that the actions assist the team in meeting performance goals. These results parallel those reported by Wann and his colleagues (2001) and suggest that as fans become more attached to a team, they are more accepting of unscrupulous behaviors by the team and players.

TABLE 10.1 Percentage of College Student Fans Willing to Consider Anonymously Cheating to Assist a Team

Let a player cheat off you in class	41%
Write a paper for a player	27%
Steal an opposing team's playbook	18%
Steal a test for a player	14%
Take a test for a player	13%
Bribe game referees	13%
Contribute illegal funding for recruitment	13%
Falsify a player's drug test	8%
Help a player acquire illegal steroids	7%
Drug an opposing team's water	7%
Lie in court to protect a player	6%

Notes: From Wann et al. (2001).

However, if sport teaches negative values and behaviors, logic dictates that it must teach positive ones as well and assist in character building, such as the importance of fair play and adhering to the rules and the value of perseverance (Bain-Selbo, 2012; Kelley & Tian, 2004; Smith, 1988; Zillmann et al., 1989). For instance, consider the pattern of effects found by Brown, Basil, and Bocarnea (2003). These authors examined the impact of two public behaviors by MLB player Mark McGwire. Subsequent to his assault on the MLB home run record, the public became aware of his use of the muscle-building supplement Androstenedione. Although this drug was legal in MLB, many viewed his use as a form of cheating. However, McGwire was also well-known as an advocate for child abuse prevention programs, placing his image in a positive light that was contrary to his image as a cheater. Brown and his colleagues examined the extent to which knowledge of McGwire's behaviors influenced others. What they found was quite interesting, suggesting that sport and athletes can have an impact on both positive and negative attitudes and behaviors. Specifically, exposure to McGwire was associated with both a desire to take Androstenedione *and* a desire to speak out against child abuse.

Do Sport Fans Have Poor Interpersonal Relationships?

In an issue of *Reader's Digest* (Game Plans, 1997), a wife recounted a conversation she had had with her husband as he sat watching Sunday afternoon football. When she asked him what he intended to do the following evening, he said he would be watching *Monday Night Football*. When she reminded him that it was their anniversary, he simply said "Okay, we'll hold hands while we watch the game" (p. 91).

This story speaks to another common criticism of sport fans; their interest in **sport has disruptive consequences for interpersonal relationships**. The logic here is that fans devote so much time and energy following sport there is none left for meaningful relationships with family and friends. A number of studies have investigated this condemnation of fans to determine, empirically, the impact of sport fandom on relationship quality. For instance, Roloff and Solomon (1989) asked college students to list sports they enjoyed following that their partner did not, sports their partner enjoyed that they did not, and sports they enjoyed together. Participants also completed items assessing their relationship satisfaction. The authors found greater similarity than conflict in sport interest, as 63 percent of participants listed at least one sport they and their partner enjoyed watching together on television, and 72 percent listed at least one sport they enjoyed attending together. There was no correlation between the number of sports listed that only one partner enjoyed and relationship satisfaction. Roloff and Solomon concluded that there was "no support for the notion that conflict over sports adversely affects relational quality" (p. 308).

Gantz, Wenner, Carrico, and Knorr (1995a) also completed an investigation of the impact of sport fandom on interpersonal relationships (see also Gantz, Wenner, Carrico, & Knorr, 1995b). Participants in this study reported their perceptions of how their partner felt about the participants' sport television viewing. Only 2 percent of the participants believed that their partner was angry or frustrated by their viewing behavior. Similar figures were found when the individuals were asked to evaluate their partner's televised sport viewing as 93 percent reported that consumption of televised sport had either a positive (54 percent) or neutral effect (39 percent). Consistent with the conclusions drawn by Roloff and Solomon (1989), Gantz and his colleagues summarized their findings by stating that "televised sport viewing appears to be a minor and nondisruptive activity in most ongoing relationships" and that "our data appear to refute . . . the much publicized football widow phenomenon" (p. 371).

Based on the research detailed above, which has been replicated elsewhere (e.g., Russell & Arms, 2002; Wenner & Gantz, 1998), claims of sport fandom disrupting interpersonal relationships have been largely overstated. Instead, fandom tends to have either a positive or neutral impact. At this point, based on available empirical evidence, the most accurate conclusion to be drawn is that the vast majority of relationships are not adversely affected by a partner's interest in sport fandom. However, this does not mean relationships are never negatively affected by one (or both) partner's fandom. For example, End et al. (2009) investigated the impact of game outcome on romantic relationships and found that individuals perceived their partners to be more irritable after a loss. They also enjoyed being with their partner less after his or her team had been defeated. One conclusion from this work is that fandom may have a short-lived negative effect on some relationships, at least following a favorite team's poor performance.

Psychological Well-Being and Sport Fandom

In the previous sections, we examined a number of individually based criticisms of sport fandom. Although complaints about sport fans and their pastime are common, some social scientists have taken the opposite stance, arguing there may be psychological benefits associated with fandom (Giamatti, 1989; Iso-Ahola & Hatfield, 1986; Smith, 1989; Smith et al., 1981). For instance, almost a century ago Brill (1929) asked his readers, "Are you a fan? It is altogether to be hoped, for your psychic health and well-being, that you are" (p. 429). In the sections that follow, we examine theoretical and empirical support for the belief that fandom can have positive consequences for one's psychological health.

The Psychological Health of Sport Fans: Two Routes to Well-Being

There are two methods through which persons can improve their psychological health via sport fandom (Wann, 2006c). The first route involves the pride and happiness fans experience when a favorite team performs well. That is, when a fan's team succeeds, he or she gains a vicarious sense of accomplishment, boosting self-worth (Stieger, Gotz, & Gehrig, 2015).

The second route is not reliant on team performance (Wann, 2006c). Rather, this process involves a boost in well-being simply as a consequence of following a team, regardless of that team's success or failure. Psychological research has frequently found that group identification is positively associated with well-being (Compton, 2005; Crocker & Major, 1989; Ketturat et al., 2016). The argument here is that similar benefits should be available via sport fandom and team identification. Through their involvement with sport, fans gain valuable connections to those around them. These connections may prove beneficial to one's psychological health by serving as a buffer against depression and alienation while increasing self-esteem and self-worth (Aden & Titsworth, 2012; Smith, 1988, 1989; Wang & Wong, 2014). Furthermore, because sport fandom may be replacing traditional but declining social ties such as religion and the family (e.g., Bain-Selbo & Sapp, 2016; Branscombe & Wann, 1991; Melnick, 1993; Putnam, 1995), fandom may be a particularly important vehicle for gaining well-being via group memberships. In the following sections, we examine research investigating the relationships among team identification, sport fandom, and psychological health.

Team Identification and Psychological Health Perhaps the first work to investigate the relationship between fandom and psychological health was conducted by Branscombe and Wann (1991). In their first study, they found a positive correlation between level of identification with the local college's men's basketball team and self-esteem, as well as a negative correlation between identification and frequency of depression. In a second study, Branscombe and Wann found that higher levels of identification were positively correlated with experiencing positive emotions and negatively correlated with the frequency of negative emotions. In the years that followed, researchers were able to replicate the relationships documented by Branscombe and Wann (1991) using a wide variety of measures of psychological health (Wann et al., 2004; Wann et al., 1999). Table 10.2 provides a sample of this research. As revealed in the table, the positive relationship between team identification and psychological well-being is robust and the generalizability of this effect is quite impressive. For instance, the relationship holds in multiple cultures (Inoue, Funk, Wann, Yoshida, & Nakazawa, 2015; Wann, Dimmock, & Grove, 2003), in and out of a sport season (Wann, Keenan, & Page, 2009), for less popular teams (Wann et al., 2009), in a variety of settings (Wann, Walker, Cygan, Kawase, & Ryan, 2005), and with multiple age groups including adolescents (Wann et al., 2015) and the elderly (Wann, Rogers, Dooley, & Foley, 2011).

At this point, we need to pause to note that the studies cited above and those listed in Table 10.2 were correlational in design. As discussed in Chapter 5 (and in most likely every social science course), correlation does not equal causation. Although the argument is that fandom (in particular, team identification) leads to psychological well-being, correlational methodologies render it inappropriate to use this work to discuss specifics about causal patterns. However, it is important to note that research in social psychology has consistently found that membership in groups does indeed foster (i.e., cause) improved mental health (e.g., Baumeister, Twenge, & Nuss, 2002; Berkman & Syme, 1979; Jetten, Haslam, &

TABLE 10.2 Various Forms of Well-Being Correlated With Sport Team Identification

Forms of Well-Being	Reference
Personal self-esteem	Branscombe and Wann (1991) Wann, Inman, Ensor, Gates, and Caldwell (1999)
Collective (i.e., social) self-esteem	Lanter and Blackburn (2015) Wann (1994b) Reding, Grieve, Derryberry, and Paquin (2011) Wann and Pierce (2005)
Meaning in life	Wann et al. (in press)
Social integration	Wann and Weaver (2009)
Social coherence	Wann and Weaver (2009)
Trust in others	Wann and Polk (2007)
Community cohesion	Inoue et al. (2015)
Energy (i.e., vigor, vitality)	Wann et al. (1999) Wann and Craven (2014)
Extraversion	Reding, Grieve, Derryberry, and Paquin (2011)
Personal and social life satisfaction	Phua (2012) Inoue, Sato, Filo, Du, and Funk (in press) Wann, Waddill, Brasher, and Ladd (2015)
Collective happiness	Reysen and Branscombe (2010)
College student adjustment	Clopton (2012)
Social avoidance and distress*	Wann and Craven (2014)
Social isolation*	Wann et al. (2015) Wann et al. (2011)
Loneliness*	Wann, Polk, and Franz (2011) Wann, Rogers, Dooley, and Foley (2011)

Note: * indicates a negative relationship.

Haslam, 2012). In fact, his review of this literature led Sani (2012) to conclude that "Results such as these leave little room for doubt. Social integration has causal effects on mental and physical health outcomes" (p. 24).

Do these causal patterns extend to memberships formed through identification with sport teams? One empirical study provides evidence that they do (Wann, 2006b). This project utilized a cross-lagged panel design, a longitudinal approach in which participants are tested at multiple points. College students completed a questionnaire assessing their identification with their university's men's basketball team as well as their social psychological health (e.g., collective self-esteem, loneliness). The questionnaire was completed at two points in time: at the beginning of the college basketball season, and again three months later toward the end of the season. By comparing the Time 1 identification–Time 2 well-being correlation with that from Time 1 well-being–Time 2 identification (i.e., the cross-lagged relationships), there is an indication of the casual pattern. The results revealed that although the Time 1 identification–Time 2 well-being correlation was statistically significant (and positive), the Time 1 well-being–Time 2 identification relationship was not. This pattern of effects lends support to the notion that sport team identification leads to psychological health.

Understanding Relationships Among Fandom, Identification, and Psychological Well-Being

The previous discussion makes one thing quite clear: Sport fandom is positively associated with psychological well-being, and the association is likely causal. However, although research confirms the relationship, it does not describe *how* or *why* the relationship exists. Such an explanation can be found in the **Team Identification–Social Psychological Health Model** (TI-SPHM; Wann, 2006c). Depicted in Figure 10.1, this theoretical approach illustrates the processes through which fandom, and more specifically team identification, fosters well-being. Identifying with a sport team leads to social connections and relationships with other fans. Thus, as discussed in Chapter 1, identification assists individuals in their attempt to meet their innate need to belong (Baumeister, 2012; Pickett et al., 2004). The model also predicts that it is team identification, and not sport fandom *per se*, that results in connections with others. The logic employed here is that fans are for more likely to bond around their shared love for a team than for a sport.

Team identification is believed to result in two types of social connections: enduring and temporary. **Enduring social connections** occur when a fan resides where the team is located, such as a fan of The Ohio State Buckeyes who lives in Columbus, Ohio. In these instances, follow supporters of the team are easy to find, and they are highly salient. A Buckeyes fan living in Columbus would find herself constantly surrounded by other OSU supporters. **Temporary social**

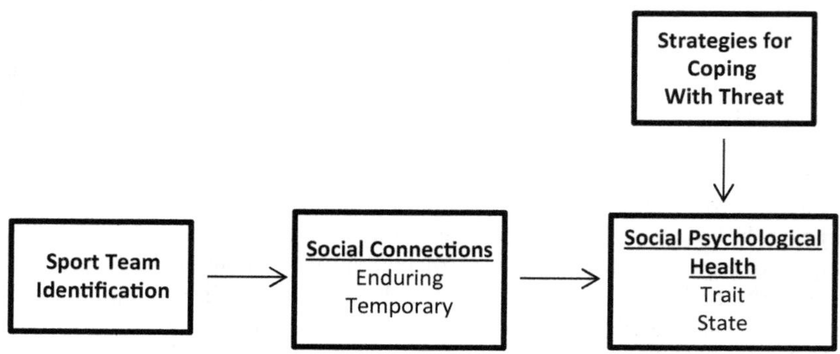

FIGURE 10.1 The Team Identification–Social Psychological Health Model

connections occur when a fan does not reside near the team but occasionally finds his or herself in the company of other like-minded fans. For instance, an Ohio State fan living in Tallahassee, Florida, would not have easy access to other fans. Walking the streets of this city, she might never see another OSU fan. However, if she meets with other similarly distant Ohio State alumni to watch the football team on television, she will gain temporary connections during those events. Although occasions such as this may seem rare, there are actually many opportunities to establish and maintain these short-term relationships, particularly for persons living in larger metropolitan areas. These encounters allow fans to congregate with fellow supporters of their team and rekindle memories of life back home (Thompson, 2011). For example, although it is located well over 600 miles from Green Bay, there are multiple "Packer Bars" in Nashville where hundreds of displaced Packer fans congregate each week to watch their team and socialize with fellow "Cheeseheads." A number of teams even have online directories providing information on watch sites in distant locales.

In the next phase of the model, the enduring and temporary social connections are expected to result in social psychological health. Both **trait well-being** (i.e., chronic, long-term) and **state well-being** (i.e., transient, short-term) should be impacted. Trait well-being is predicted to be the result of enduring connections, while boosts in state well-being are believed to occur when one gains temporary connections. Based on the TI-SPHM, one would predict that **social psychological health** is more likely to be impacted than personal well-being. Social psychological health involves those components of well-being that are group based, such as loneliness, isolation, and collective self-esteem.

Research Testing the Team Identification–Social Psychological Health Model

The Team Identification–Social Psychological Health Model (Wann, 2006c) has several components and leads to numerous predictions. In the sections that follow, we examine empirical support for the model, including a handful of recent studies that have attempted to simultaneously test several of the framework's "moving parts."

Team Identification, Rather Than Sport Fandom, Leads to Well-being

As noted above, one of the first predictions contained in the TI-SPHM is that team identification rather than sport fandom results in social connections and psychological well-being. Wann's (2006c) analogy here was that "Simply being an 'animal lover' is not likely to lead to valuable connections with other such persons. However, numerous groups have been established with the intent of bringing together fans of specific animals (cats, various breeds of dogs, horses, etc.)" (p. 276). A number of studies have tested the relationships among fandom, identification, and well-being, and many of these support Wann's logic (Theodorakis et al., 2012; Wann et al., 2015). For example, studies using both fandom and team identification as predictors of well-being found that although identification was a significant predictor, mere fandom was not (Wann et al., 2003; Wann & Runyon, 2010; Wann & Weaver, 2009).

However, contrary to expectations, a few studies have found that sport fandom was positively associated with well-being (Wann & Craven, 2014; Wann & Martin, 2008). For instance, Wann et al. (in press) found that sport fandom (as well as team identification) was a significant predictor of both a sense of belonging and meaning in life. Additionally, consider work by Schlegel, Pfitzner, and Koenigstorfer (2017) on the subjective well-being of inhabitants of Rio de Janeiro. The authors had one sample of residents complete a questionnaire assessing their subjective well-being a week before the 2014 World Cup (held in Rio), while a second sample answered the same questions in the middle of the tournament. Interestingly, those tested during the event reported higher subjective well-being. For instance, they believed they were more cheerful and active and that life was interesting. These benefits were not tied to any particular team but, rather, were a consequence of the festive nature of the event. Thus, modifications to the TI-SPHM may be needed to account for the possibility that, under certain circumstances, sport fandom may also play a role in facilitating social psychological health.

Team Identification Leads to Social Connections Social connections and relationships with others are strongly associated with psychological well-being (Lee & Robbins, 1998; Townsend & McWhirter, 2005). The Team Identification–Social Psychological Health Model (Wann, 2006c) includes the prediction that one of the greatest benefits of identifying with sport teams is that it has the capacity to facilitate these connections, and research confirms this pattern of effects (Inoue & Havard, 2014; Katz & Heere, 2016; Skinner, Zakus, & Cowell, 2008). For example, a pair of studies conducted by Wann and his colleagues found that team identification was associated with multiple assessments of social connectedness, including the percentage and number of friends who were fans of the team and beliefs that following the team helped establish and maintain friendships (Wann, Waddill, Brasher, & Ladd, 2015; Wann et al., 2011).

Although the work above supports the proposition that team identification can lead to social connections, the reader may be wondering about the level of relationship intimacy required for this effect to occur. For instance, returning to the Ohio State fan described earlier, imagine that she is shopping at a mall in Columbus, Ohio, while wearing her Buckeyes sweatshirt. She will encounter many other OSU supporters, also easily identifiable by their team apparel. As they pass, these persons may exchange a smile, a "Go Bucks!", or even a high-five. They may even strike-up a short conversation about the team. Can these brief, weak connections promote well-being? Research suggests they can. For example, Sandstrom and Dunn (2014a, 2014b) found that short social encounters with a barista (someone who prepares coffee) or college classmates led to increases in sense of belonging and positive affect. Thus, the social connections fans develop do not have to be intimate to have well-being benefits. Rather, the casual encounters that are so common among local fans are sufficient.

A final point concerns the notion of what comprises a local versus a distant fan. That is, should a fan living 50 miles from a university be considered a local or distant? Unfortunately, precise operational definitions of these terms have not been established. Yet this distinction is critical to the model, given that local fans are expected to gain enduring connections while distant fans are forced to seek out temporary ones. However, Pu and James (2017) found that distant fans can have very strong psychological connections to the favorite teams. This is in spite of the fact that they never lived in proximity to a favorite team and have never attended a game in person (they literally live in another country). The original formulation of the TI-SPHM began around 2000. At that time, social networking for fans was not available. Today, however, fans from across the globe can connect and "watch" a sporting event together, while not actually being together in a physical sense. This form of consumption could have important implications for the TI-SPHM (Phua, 2012). That is, perhaps one can gain enduring connections by connecting with other fans via social networking sites.

Team-Based Threats to Identity Thus far, we have provided ample evidence that higher levels of team identification are associated with psychological well-being and that this relationship is likely causal. However, if the reader were to turn back to Chapter 6, it is also clear that highly identified fans experience strong negative reactions to outcomes involving their team (e.g., Bernhardt, Dabbs, Fielden, & Lutter, 1998; Eastman & Riggs, 1994; Lisjak, Lee, & Gardner, 2012). Because the role of team follower is a central component of the social identity of highly identified fans, the performances and actions of the team and players have implications for the fans' self-worth. When the players and/or team perform poorly or engage in questionable behaviors, these actions serve as an **identity threat** to highly allegiant fans. Branscombe, Ellemers, Spears, and Doosje (1999) developed a typology of threats to identity, each of which has implications for sport fans. This typology is found in Table 10.3. As shown in the table, fans can feel threatened by far more than poor team performance.

A series of interesting studies by Xiao and Van Bavel (2012) suggest that threats to the identity of fans can be far-reaching, even powerful enough to alter perceptions of the physical world. Based on research finding that people view personal threats (e.g., spiders, cliffs) as closer than they actually are (Riskind, Moore, & Bowley, 1995), Xiao and Van Bavel predicted that similar distortions of physical distance could occur as a result of threats to social identity. Specifically, they expected that individuals would perceive a shorter distance between themselves and a rival outgroup. Several studies confirmed their expectations, including one testing the MLB rivalry between the New York Yankees and Boston Red Sox. Fans outside of Yankees Stadium completed a questionnaire assessing their favorite MLB team and their identification for this team. Additionally, the participants estimated the distances from Yankees Stadium to Fenway Park, home of the rival Red Sox, and Camden Yards, home of the Baltimore Orioles (Camden Yards is actually closer to Yankee Stadium by about 20 miles). The results were quite intriguing. Non-Yankees fans correctly estimated that Fenway Park was further away from Yankee Stadium than Camden Yards. However, Yankees fans incorrectly believed that the home of the rival

TABLE 10.3 A Typology of Threats to Social Identify

Threat	Description	Examples from Sport Fandom
Value-competence	Desire to view one's group as more successful than a rival	When a team loses a competition; when a team is faced with relegation to a lower division
Value-morality	Desire to view one's group as morally superior to a rival	When a player is accused of using performance-enhancing drugs; when a player is arrested for a DUI
Distinctiveness	Desire to view one's group as unique from rival groups	When one learns that an ingroup fan base is not unique from a rival's; when one is informed that sport fans are "all alike"
Acceptance	Desire to be viewed by ingroup persons as a member of the group	When one is accused of lacking team-related knowledge; when one is accused of supporting a rival team

Note: From Branscombe et al., (1999).

Red Sox was closer than the home park for the non-rival Orioles. Thus, the threat provided by the rival team led to an altered perception of physical distance. The saying "Keep your friends close and your enemies closer" appears to encompass our impressions of rival fans as well.

Coping With Team-Based Threats So we have an interesting paradox involving the behaviors and attributes of sport fans. On the one hand, there is evidence from research that highly identified fans (at least those identified with a local team) have a particularly healthy psychological profile. On the other hand, there is also evidence that these fans often experience negative affect, a poor outlook on life, and depression in response to team-relevant threats (e.g., subsequent to watching their team lose). To resolve this contradiction, one must consider the methods highly identified fans use to cope with the threats. **Coping strategies** involve "those responses that are effective in reducing an undesirable load (i.e., the psychological burden)" (Snyder, 1999, p. 5). Research indicates that these strategies are successful in alleviating the psychological distress caused by team-based identity threats (Bizman & Yinon, 2002; Delia, 2017; Diener, Suh, Lucas, & Smith, 1999; Wilson & Gilbert, 2005). In the following sections, we examine a wide variety of these tactics.

Strategically Manipulating Associations With the Team • One of the most common set of tactics used by fans to maintain their psychological health is to strategically adjust their associations with their team (Delia, Bass, & Wann, 2017). These strategies, some of which were mentioned in Chapter 8, are self-presentational in nature because they involve conscious attempts to alter one's public association with a team (Leary, 1992, 1995). Two of these strategies are found in response to successful team performance, while two are used in response to unsuccessful performance. These strategies are briefly described in Table 10.4.

The first strategy utilized after team success is **basking in reflected glory** (BIRGing; Cialdini et al., 1976). The BIRGing phenomenon was first identified in a series of studies conducted by Cialdini and his colleagues (1976). In one study, the experimenters recorded the proportion of college students who wore clothing that identified their university. As predicted by BIRGing, the proportion of students wearing university-identifying apparel increased following a win by the university's football team. In a second study, Cialdini and his associates telephoned respondents and asked them to describe a recent contest involving their university's football team. Again, consistent with the BIRGing phenomenon, participants were more likely to use the pronoun "we" to describe a recent win and "they" to describe a defeat. A number of authors have replicated Cialdini's work (Cialdini & De Nicholas, 1989; Delia, 2015; Jensen et al., 2016; Kimble & Cooper, 1992; McHoul, 1997).

Thus, one method fans use to maintain their psychological health is to increase their relationship with successful teams via BIRGing. However, given that the team was victorious, an astute reader may wonder how the fan was threatened. That is, if the team won, where is the threat and how is BIRGing used to cope? The answer lies in the fact that fans maintain multiple group identities (Delia,

TABLE 10.4 Self-Presentational Strategies Used by Sport Fans to Enhance or Protect Their Psychological Well-Being

Strategy	Description
Strategies following team success	
Basking in reflected glory (BIRGing)	Increasing one's association with a successful team to enhance psychological health.
Cutting off future failure (COFFing)	Decreasing one's association with a currently successful team to protect one's future psychological health should the team perform poorly at a later date.
Strategies following team failure	
Cutting off reflected failure (CORFing)	Decreasing one's association with an unsuccessful team to protect one's psychological health.
Basking in spite of reflected failure (BIRFing)	Maintaining an association with a team despite the team's failures.

2015), and they typically support many different teams (Grieve et al., 2009). What BIRGing allows fans to do is increase their association with teams that are successful to lessen the threat of teams they support that are not living up to expectations (Delia, 2017).

In some situations, supporters may be reluctant to bask in their team's victory. For instance, consider a fan that is highly identified with his university's men's basketball team. Imagine that this team has a history of poor performance and typically finishes last in its conference. However, this team somehow manages to gain a home court victory over the conference powerhouse. Research on BIRGing suggests that the fan would increase his association with his team, thereby enhancing his psychological well-being. However, what might happen if the two teams were scheduled to meet a second time at the rival school's home court? Would the fan be as willing to boast about his team's surprising victory? The is evidence that he may not. Rather, he may employ **cutting off future failure** (COFFing), a second strategy used following team success (Bernache-Assollant & Chantal, 2011; Wann, Hamlet, Wilson, & Hodges, 1995). This occurs when individuals resist the urge to bask in a team's success and, instead, distance themselves from the team out of concern that the team will be unsuccessful in the future (i.e., the team's future performance serves as the threat). Although individuals may maintain a private connection to the team, publicly they downplay their association. Thus, COFFing helps one maintain a positive psychological state by avoiding association with a potential loser, even though that team is currently experiencing success.

There are also two important self-presentational strategies fans use when faced with poor team performance (see Table 10.4). The first is **cutting off reflected failure** (CORFing; Snyder et al., 1986). You may recall that CORFing involves decreasing one's association with an unsuccessful team to protect one's identity. However, this option is far more common among persons with lower levels of identification with a team (Kwon et al., 2008; Spinda, 2011). For persons with high levels of identification (i.e., those reaching the Allegiance stage of the Psychological Continuum Model, see Funk & James, 2001), the centrality of the role of team supporter makes it difficult for them to renounce the team. Wertheim and Sommers (2016) argue that one cause of the tendency for highly identified fans to stick with their team is **cognitive dissonance** (Festinger & Carlsmith, 1959). Classic research on dissonance by Aronson and Mills (1959) found that the more individuals put time and effort into an act, the more they believed the act was worthwhile. Wertheim and Sommers contend that this process explains why so many fans are willing to remain associated with losers (i.e., not CORF). The effort and time they have put into following the team (e.g., ticket costs, years supporting the team) would result in cognitive dissonance should they abandon the team. As a result, they remain loyal. As a side note, it is interesting that Aronson was a diehard Boston Red Sox fan beginning in the 1940s. Thus, he should know a thing or two about both cognitive dissonance and how it drives persons to remain loyal to a chronically underperforming team.

The tendency for highly identified fans to remain loyal in the face of team failure is a second strategy following team loss. Referred to as **basking in spite**

of reflected failure (BIRFing), in this situation fans celebrate a team's ineptness (Aden & Titsworth, 2012). In describing this process, Campbell, Aiken, and Kent (2004) wrote "While the team may be losing, fans in this case are reveling in the loyalty, camaraderie, rebelliousness, and other alternative reasons for fandom" (p. 153). These fans are trying to avoid being perceived as disloyal (i.e., they are faced with acceptance threat). In fact, a team's losing ways may even become one of the team characteristics with which fans identify. For example, when the Chicago Cubs were close to ending their century-old championship drought, roughly 25 percent of Cubs fans reported that they would miss the Cubs losing ways (Hart, 2016). Furthermore, over 80 percent of respondents indicated that part of the camaraderie they felt with other fans was tied to the team's history of failure.

Cognitive and Perceptual Biases Related to Team Performance • A second set of coping strategies employed by sport fans involves **cognitive and perceptual biases.** With this strategy "identification predisposes sport consumers to engage in biased cognitive processes, enabling them to resist negative information about their favorite player and team" (Lee et al., 2016, p. 179). Viewed from the Psychological Continuum Model (Funk & James, 2001), fans who have reached the Allegiance stage have a strong desire to evaluate their team in a positive light. Cognitive and perceptual biases assist in this endeavor and allow fans to view their team in a favorable fashion, even when faced with evidence to the contrary.

One cognitive/perceptual bias involves use of **ingroup favoritism** (Brewer, 1979; Howard & Rothbart, 1980), that is, viewing favorite teams, players, and fans as superior to rivals. With respect to biased perceptions of teams and players, athletes are viewed in a more positive manner when believed to be on a supported team than on a rival team. For instance, Wann et al. (2006) asked fans to watch a videotape of a potential player for either their team or a rival team. They found that highly identified fans rated the player more favorably when he was described as a recruit for their team than for a rival school, even though all subjects watched the same video. As for biased perceptions of fans, a similar pattern holds true (Franco & Maass, 1996; Sabo, Jansen, Tate, Duncan, & Leggett, 1996). Fans may be able to deflect some of the negative impact of their team's losses by believing that "our team may have lost the game, but our fans are better than your fans." As one would expect, research suggests that highly identified fans are especially likely to possess a positively biased perception of fellow fans (Wann & Branscombe, 1995; Wann & Dolan, 1994c; Wann & Grieve, 2005; Wann et al., 2012).

Fans also protect themselves from threat via **biased attributions**. Attributions are causes individuals assign to behaviors. For example, a fan of a winning team may conclude that the team won because they possessed a high level of skill or exerted a high level of effort. Meanwhile, fans of the losing team may believe that their team lost because of bad luck or biased officiating. In these instances, the fans can improve their well-being after team success and protect it after team failure. Research for a number of decades has found that these **self-serving attributions** are common among fans as a method for handling threat (Hastorf & Cantril, 1954; Lau, 1984; Tanner, Sev'er, & Ungar, 1989). However, the self-serving bias is not found among all spectators. Rather, only those with a high degree of team identification utilize this strategy (Grove, Hanrahan, & McInman, 1991; Lanter, 2013; Sweeney & Nguyen, 2012; Wann & Dolan, 1994a; Wann & Schrader, 2000). Because the psychological well-being of highly identified fans is related to their team's performances, these fans have the most to gain through biased beliefs about the causes of an outcome.

A third perceptual bias fans exhibit involves **predictions and recollections of team performance** (Murrell & Dietz, 1992; Wann, 1996). Sometimes referred to as the **allegiance bias** (Markman & Hirt, 2002), fans can protect and enhance their psychological health by believing that their team performed well in the past and will continue this success in the future. Essentially, they remember the glory years as more glorious than they actually were, while the future is viewed as brighter than reality suggests it will be. Once again, these biases are more common among highly identified fans than those low in team identification (Dietz-Uhler & Murrell, 1999; Hirt et al., 1992). As Wann and his coauthors (2017) stated, "it is evident that as fans' identification with a team increases, so too does the rose-colored hue of the lens through which they perceive and evaluate their team" (p. 155). For instance, consider the research by Wann and Dolan (1994b; see also Wann, 1994a). College students completed a questionnaire assessing their identification with the university's men's basketball team as well as their estimates of the number of games the team had won during the previous year and the number they would win in the current season. As expected, highly identified fans were more biased in their estimates than were low identified persons. Those high in identification estimated that the team had won 20.4 games during the previous season and that they would win 19.1 games during the current season (both estimates were higher than the actual number of wins, as the team had won 17 games during the previous season and would win 18 during the current year). Those low in identification estimated the wins to be only 18.7 and 17.6 for the past and current seasons, respectively.

Outgroup Derogation (Blasting) • Another strategy highly identified fans employ to cope with threat involves **outgroup derogation** (i.e., **blasting**). Threats to social identity often lead to increases in deviant behavior (Belmi, Barragan, Neale, & Cohen, 2015), and for some sport fans this involves violent outbursts directed toward others (Wann, 1993). That is, as discussed in Chapter 8, because highly identified fans tend not to CORF, they may resort to hostility as a means of repairing their identity (Branscombe & Wann, 1994).

Pessimism • Sport fans also cope with threat via pessimistic appraisals of their team (Delia, 2017). Two forms of pessimism can be used by fans: proactive pessimism and retroactive pessimism. **Proactive pessimism** involves the adoption of an increasingly more negative outlook as an event draws near (Shepperd, Quellette, & Fernandez, 1996). By lowering expectations, individuals can proactively reduce the sting of poor performance. For fans, this could involve lowering expectations as a season approaches in an attempt to proactively decrease the threat of the team underperforming (Sloan, 1989). For example, Wann and Grieve (2007) asked individuals to indicate their favorite MLB team and their expectations for the upcoming season (e.g., the likelihood the team play in the World Series). Participants were tested four weeks prior to and immediately before the start of the season. As expected, highly identified fans became more pessimistic at Time 2 (i.e., reported lower expectations) relative to Time 1.

A second form of pessimism that can be used to cope with identity threat is **retroactive pessimism.** In this instance, individuals become more negative about their chances for success *after* the disappointing outcome has occurred (Tykocinski, Pick, & Kedmi, 2002). Essentially, they reevaluate their likelihood of success now knowing that they failed (e.g., "Now that I think about it, we never really had a chance"). Wann, Grieve, Waddill, and Martin (2008) found evidence of retroactive pessimism among college fans. Supporters of two college basketball teams completed questionnaires a few days prior to and again a few days after a men's game between the two schools. The pregame protocol included an assessment of their identification with their university's team as well as estimates of the game's outcome. The postgame questionnaire asked participants to retroactively estimate their team's chance of victory in the game. The results indicated that highly identified supporters of the losing team reported significant changes in their pre- to postgame evaluations, and the pattern of effects reflected retroactive pessimism. That is, strong supporters of the losing team reported more negative evaluations of their team's chances of victory subsequent to the team's loss.

Magical and Mystical Strategies • Another interesting set of coping tactics involves **magical and mystical strategies,** such as beliefs in curses and the use of superstition (Jones, Cox, & Navarro-Rivera, 2014). A number of **sport curses** have been propagated, particularly in baseball. One of the most often discussed is the Curse of the Bambino and the accursed Boston Red Sox (until 2004 when they won the World Series, hence "breaking the curse"). Wann and Zaichkowsky (2009) examined predictors of beliefs in the Red Sox curse, finding that level of identification with the Red Sox was a positive predictor of belief in the curse. Such beliefs function as a coping mechanism for highly identified Red Sox fans. That is, it's easier on their social identity to believe that the Red Sox lost because of a curse than due to poor pitching, hitting, and poor managerial decisions.

With respect to **sport fan superstitions,** the findings from several studies provide confirmation that highly identified fans are particularly likely to engage in superstitious acts (Wann & Goeke, in press; Wilson, Grieve, Ostrowski, Mienaltowski, & Cyr, 2013). Perhaps the most comprehensive examination of sport fan superstition was conducted by Wann and his colleagues (2013), who assessed the superstitions of over 600 fans. Several intriguing findings emerged, such as the most prominent types of superstitions (e.g., those involving apparel and vocalizations). Furthermore, many fans truly believed that their superstitious acts influenced the outcome of games involving their team, and because of this they expected to feel guilty if they stopped the superstitious behavior.

Schadenfreude and Glory Out of Reflected Failure • Another method sport fans use to deal with threats to their social identity is **schadenfreude,** a topic we briefly discussed in Chapter 6. Recall that schadenfreude is a German term meaning joy in the misfortune of others (Cikara et al., 2011; Dalakas & Melancon, 2012). Researchers have suggested that schadenfreude may be a popular coping mechanism among highly identified fans seeking relief from the distress of their team's poor performance (Dalakas et al., 2015). Essentially, fans may feel better about their team's struggles if they focus on the disappointments of rival teams, a process Havard (2014) refers to as **glory out of reflected failure** (GORFing; Havard et al., 2018). By focusing on a rival's failures, the poor play of one's own team may become less salient and less threatening.

Consumption of food • A final coping method involves the consumption of food. Given that some people deal with stress through unhealthy eating (Fischer, Anderson, & Smith, 2004; Lambird & Man, 2006), and watching a team compete can be quite stressful (see Chapter 6), it seems reasonable to expect sport fans to cope through consumption of food as well. Indeed, research does find this pattern of effects (Gantz & Wenner, 1995). For instance, consider the work of Cormil and Chandon (2013), who investigated the unhealthy eating habits of NFL fans. The authors used national survey data on consumption habits and found that on Mondays following games, saturated fat and caloric intake increased after a loss but decreased after a win. The increased saturated fat and caloric consumption was greatest after games involving evenly matched teams and those with a close final score. These results suggest that fans cope via unhealthy eating when they are most stressed, such as when the game in question is closely contested.

Trait and State Well-Being According to the Team Identification–Social Psychological Health Model (Wann, 2006c), connections generated via sport team identification impact both trait and state well-being. Trait well-being is thought to be associated with enduring connections, while state psychological health is expected to be impacted by temporary connections. Although multiple studies have included examination of trait well-being and found the expected relationships (e.g., Wann et al., 2004; Wann et al., 1999), empirical work examining state well-being is quite rare. However, work that has been done indicates that identification can be correlated with state well-being as well (Wann, Martin, Grieve, & Gardner, 2008). For instance, Wann et al. (2011) asked highly identified supporters of a distant university's men's basketball team to watch a basketball video either alone or in the presence of other fans. Participants viewed either a highlight video depicting the target team or a control video. After watching the video, participants completed an assessment of their state loneliness. As expected, and consistent with the TI-SPHM, persons watching the team highlight video in the presence of other fans of the team reported a significant decrease in loneliness, while no such effect was found for persons watching the control video or those watching either video alone.

Social Well-Being, Rather Than Personal, Is Impacted by Identification A final important component of Wann's (2006c) model is the prediction that the social connections accrued via sport team identification will be more likely to result in social (i.e., group) well-being than personal (i.e., individual) well-being. The logic employed here is that because identification with a team and the corresponding connections are group-level phenomena, the benefits should be social in nature. Research has consistently supported this proposition (Wann et al., 2015; Wann et al., 2003). For example, team identification appears to be more strongly associated with collective (i.e., social) self-esteem than personal self-esteem (Branscombe & Wann, 1991; Wann, 1994a). In fact, an examination of Table 10.2 reveals that the majority of psychological health benefits found to be associated with team identification are social in nature (e.g., social integration, community cohesion).

Testing the Paths From Identification to Connections to Social Well-Being As detailed in the previous sections, many of the individual components contained in the TI-SPHM (Wann, 2006c) have empirical support, and in some cases, the support is quite substantial. However, although it is useful to examine a theory piece-by-piece, a more appropriate method of analysis involves testing a model in its entirety by examining the various links and patterns of relationships predicted by the framework. Although there are several such relationships that could be tested, the critical pattern predicted by the TI-SPHM concerns the paths from team identification→social connections→social psychological health.

A handful of studies have tested the predicted causal paths among identification, connections, and well-being. These studies have had mixed results. Some work has found results that are consistent with the patterns predicted by the model (interestingly, this includes work on fans identifying with non-sport entities, see Reysen, Plante, Roberts, & Gerbasi, 2017). For example, Wann and his colleagues (in press) examined the interrelationships among identification with a local college basketball team, sense of belonging, and meaning in life. The results were consistent with the TI-SPHM, as sense of belonging mediated the relationship between team identification and meaning in life.

Other research, however, has failed to find the hypothesized links from team identification to social connections to well-being (Clopton, 2012). For example, consider a pair of studies conducted by Wann and his associates. In these investigations, high school (Wann et al., 2015) or college students (Wann et al., 2011) completed questionnaires assessing identification with one of their school's sport teams, connections gained via their support of team, and social well-being. As expected, team identification was correlated with well-being and social connectedness. However, social connections failed to mediate the relationship between identification and psychological health. Essentially, identification was found to have a direct effect on both social connections and social well-being.

To muddy the waters even further, other work supports the hypothesized pattern of effects predicted by the TI-SPHM, but with a different mediating variable. Specifically, recent work suggests that it is perceived emotional support from other fans, not social connections *per se*, that mediates the team identification—social psychological health relationship (Inoue, Sato, Filo, Du, & Funk, in press). For example, Inoue and his associates examined post-disaster responses to the Great East Japan Earthquake occurring in 2011. They found that identification with a hometown soccer team was positively correlated with post-disaster community cohesion (a measure of social well-being). Furthermore, this relationship was mediated by the degree of emotional support provided by the team.

Summarizing Work on the Team Identification–Social Psychological Health Model Based on work conducted to date, the following conclusions can be drawn about the Team Identification–Social Psychological Health Model (Wann, 2006c). First, it is clear that team identification and social psychological health are positively associated and that the relationship is likely causal. The amount of evidence amassed makes this proclamation essentially irrefutable. However, although identification and well-being are related, the exact processes through which identification aids psychological health remain somewhat of a mystery. Clearly, additional work is needed in this area.

There are several areas of the model that need further clarification and or refinement. One such area is the role played by sport fandom in the psychological health of fans. As noted above, although the TI-SPHM does not expect fandom to be related to well-being, a growing list of studies have found that these variables are related. A second area in need of further explanation concerns what is meant by a "local" versus a "displaced" fan and how consumption of sport via social media impacts the process. Clark, Loxton, and Tobin (2015) found evidence that loneliness is declining among American high school and college students, a result they believe is partially due to increased use of social networking. If the advancement of social networking opportunities has impacted loneliness in the general population, and sport fans frequently use social networking while consuming sport, then it is plausible that this form of consumption impacts the relationship between team identification and well-being. And third, as noted earlier, it is common for fans to identify with more than one team (Grieve et al., 2009). Given that possessing multiple identities can have important implications for psychological well-being (Brook, Garcia, & Fleming, 2008), future work should investigate the impact of following multiple teams on the well-being of fans. To date, only one such study has been conducted (Wann et al., 2009). This work found that fans who were highly identified with multiple teams reported particularly high levels of social psychological health. However, given that this was just a single study, more research in this area is needed.

Some Final Thoughts

In this chapter, we examined the psychological consequences of sport fandom. We began by critiquing four micro-level condemnations of fans. Using empirical analyses to evaluate the merits of these complaints, the following conclusions appear warranted. First, each criticism of sport fandom can be supported anecdotally. For instance, high levels of sport involvement have led to marital problems for a few fans, and a handful of fans do become violent when watching their favorite team compete. However, the existing data indicate that these problems are the exception rather than the rule—most fans do not have marital strife or violent tendencies. Thus, it appears that for the vast majority of fans, the pastime is a harmless leisure activity.

We also investigated the possibility that, rather than having a detrimental effect on a fan's psychological health, sport fandom (or, more specifically, team identification) actually facilitates one's psychological well-being. Indeed, there is evidence that strong attachments to a geographically close team is positively (albeit modestly) related to a number of forms of psychological health, including personal and collective self-esteem, affective expression, alienation, and vigor.

In light of the fact that sport fans are often disappointed by their favorite team's poor performance, the finding that highly allegiant fans generally possess a sound psychological makeup may well be the most compelling paradox in sport fandom. It would seem more logical for these persons to possess an unhealthy and perhaps fragile psychological profile. Clearly then, highly identified fans must find ways to protect and even enhance their psychological health in the face of constant threats to a highly valued and central component of their self and their social identity. Although we addressed a number of possible methods employed to maintain psychological well-being, more research is needed before we arrive at a complete understanding of the mechanisms through which highly identified sport fans ensure that their spectating activity is personally beneficial.

CHAPTER 11

The Societal Consequences of Sport Fandom

In the previous chapter, our examination of the utility of sport fandom focused on the personal level. That is, our concern was with the impact and meaning of sport fandom for the psychological well-being and mental health of fans—the extent to which this is a harmful or beneficial activity for the participant. In the current chapter, our focus shifts from the individual to society at large. For students of sport fandom, there is perhaps no more compelling or challenging question than "How does sport fandom impact society?"

Similar to issues surrounding the psychological impact of fandom, differences abound with respect to thoughts about the societal value of the pastime. Some critics are perfectly comfortable assigning sport fandom to the toy department of human affairs. Others see sport fandom as a valuable activity contributing to society in a multitude of ways. In attempting to address this debate, there are a number of theoretical perspectives available to help guide the way, each with its own particular strengths, weaknesses, and biases. In this chapter, we examine several of these theories to better understand the impact of sport on society at large. As with the previous chapter on the psychological impact of fandom, we will begin our analysis with several arguments suggesting that fandom has an overall negative influence on society. This will be followed by a discussion of the structural-functionalist viewpoint and the stance that sport serves society well.

Societally Based Criticisms of Sport Fandom

Similar to work on the psychological impact of fandom, some scholars have criticized fandom for its potentially negative impact on society. In the paragraphs that follow, we will examine four such criticisms, each of which is briefly summarized in Table 11.1.

TABLE 11.1 Critiques of Sport Fandom

Critique	Description
Conflict	Views sport fandom as maintaining and consolidating the interests of society's power elite.
Feminist	Views institutions such as sport fandom as supporting the gender order and masculine hegemony.
Cultural elitist	Views sport fandom as a superficial, inferior, brutal, lowbrow form of mass entertainment.
Moralist	Suggests that the moral fiber of society is in decline as evidenced by current television programming, movies, popular music, and spectator sports.

The Conflict Critique

According to the **conflict critique**, sport fandom is seen as maintaining the interests of society's power elite (Bain-Selbo, 2012; Danielson, 1997; Hoch, 1972). Shaped by the needs of capitalist systems, fandom serves vested interests as a type of opiate that distracts, diverts, and deflects attention from the pressing social problems and issues of the day (Howard, 1912; Lazarsfeld & Merton, 1948; Meier, 1989; Walker, 2012). This perspective argues that by exploiting spectator sports, members of the ruling elite are better able to consolidate their power and privilege. Literature enthusiasts may recall that this viewpoint is expressed in the novel *1984*, in which Orwell writes that the Proles were easily controlled by keeping their focus on mundane activities such as football.

The **sport fandom as opiate** thesis was strongly articulated by Harris (1981), who wrote:

> If Karl Marx, who died 100 years ago, were still alive today, he might be sorely tempted to revise his famous slur, "Religion is the opium of the people." It is no longer true, if it ever was, for something else has taken its place, at least in our country. Today, sport has become the opium of the people. . . . While it may be true that religion, in the past, narcotized many, it also awakened many others to their social and moral responsibilities. Sport has no such redeeming aspects in our society. . . . It has turned into a passion, a mania, a drug far more potent and widespread than any mere chemical substance.
>
> (p. 3B)

Those who agree with this line of reasoning can certainly find instances where sport appeared to be more important to members of the society than other civic responsibilities. For instance, consider the media coverage of Michael Jordan's (second) retirement, which occurred during the same time period as the impeachment trial of President Clinton. The television ratings for CNN's coverage of Jordan's retirement press conference received a rating of 1.6. The next day, during the same time slot, CNN's rating for the impeachment hearings was only 1.3 (Walters, 1999). Similarly, when the *Chicago Sun-Times* asked local residents to name the greatest Chicagoans of the twentieth century, Jordan placed number one on the list, ahead of several mayors, three governors, and five Nobel Prize winners (Cook & Mravic, 1999).

If, as the conflict critique purports, fandom functions as an opiate, fans should be generally apathetic and less involved in the business of society. However, quite to the contrary, research shows that fans often have broader general interests and more active lifestyles than nonfans. For instance, recall from Chapter 10 that, far from being lazy, sport fans are often involved in a variety of cultural and political activities (Appelbaum et al., 2012; Lieberman, 1991; Sun et al., 2004). Additional evidence is provided by the positive correlation between sport fandom and athletic participation (see Chapters 1 and 10). In his critique of the neo-Marxist indictment of sport, Guttmann (1980) concluded that there is no evidence to support the notion that sport fans are apolitical; to the contrary, sport fandom may actually heighten class consciousness.

The Feminist Critique

Shuster (1994) made an interesting observation when she noted that "it is fascinatingly coincidental how football has overtaken baseball as the preeminent TV sport for men at the same time women have begun asserting their rights in the arena of sports" (p. 3C). The suggestion that sporting events provide male viewers with something more than diversion and entertainment is worth serious consideration (Nelson, 1994). Judged from a **feminist critique**, it is through institutions like sport fandom that male hegemony is constructed and retained (Bryson, 1987; Esmonde, 2015; Mean, 2012). Far from an innocent and innocuous pastime, sport fandom is viewed as reproducing traditional ideas about masculinity and femininity, thereby helping maintain patriarchal rule in society at large. The net effect is to view females and their activities as inferior. Implicit in the feminist analysis is the notion that the celebration of hypermasculinity perpetuates gender inequality, reinforces sexual stereotypes, ensures patriarchal control, and ultimately acts as an agent of women's oppression (Theberge, 1985).

Empirical and theoretical examinations of the feminist critique suggest that these arguments have merit and that sexism, gender inequity, and the like are still problematic in sport today (Fink, 2016). For example, sexist attitudes still exist within many sports, including golf (McGinnis, McQuillan, & Chapple, 2005; Nylund, 2003), soccer (Jones, 2008), and hockey (Crawford & Gosling, 2004). Problematic portrayals of women may be particularly common in sport-focused social media where "the anonymity of the Internet permit hegemonic masculinity to flourish in specific locations, without contestation" (Kian, Clavio, Vincent, & Shaw, 2011, p. 680).

The Cultural Elitist Critique

Higgs (1982) noted "it is difficult to imagine Socrates, Jesus, Augustine, Leonardo, Newton, Beethoven, Tolstoy or Einstein in the stands cheering a team, which may tell us something about the phenomenon of mass spectacle" (p. 150). The stance implicit in this quote is consistent with the **cultural elitist critique** of fandom. As Smith (1988) noted, sport fandom has been traditionally viewed as an inferior, brutal, and lowbrow pastime because

> it is for the masses and therefore lacking in refinement. It follows then, that watching a sporting event is several notches below so-called more discriminatory leisure pursuits like visiting an art gallery, attending an opera, or listening to a symphonic concert.
>
> (p. 63)

Thus, the cultural elitist critique argues that the masses lack taste and refinement. If their tastes are to be satisfied, everything has to be reduced to the lowest common denominator (Strinati, 1995). Judged from this perspective, sport fandom is viewed as a standardized, repetitive, and superficial activity that celebrates the trivial. Because they lack intellectual challenge and stimulation, spectator sports are forced to cater to fantasy and escapism and the denial of thinking.

Elitists can certainly be challenged on their holier than thou attitude. However, more telling is the fact that, upon closer inspection, sport fandom is not the trivial, infantile, and superficial activity its critics claim. Rather, sport fans often turn out to be more knowing, active, and discriminating than people expect. Many fans take special pride in their knowledge of individual and team statistics and their ability to strategize. Far from being cultural dolts, the typical sport fan is cognitively engaged in the activity—analyzing individual performances, sharing sport nostalgia and history with others, mulling over game strategies, and critiquing coaching decisions. The intricacies and complexities of the game action allow fans to give expression to their creative and critical thinking skills.

The Moralist Critique

Those identifying with the **moralist critique** warn that the moral alarm clock is ticking away in the United States (and many other countries) and that the nation better pay attention before we are all plunged into a moral abyss. While television programming, movies, and popular music are frequently singled out for specific criticism, sport fandom has not escaped the moralist's critical eye. Boxing, football, ice hockey, and ultimate fighting are viewed as especially barbaric. For example, many decades ago Mumford (1937) observed:

> Sport, in the sense of a mass spectacle, with death to add to the underlying excitement, comes into existence when a population has been drilled and regimented and depressed to such an extent that it needs at least a vicarious participation in difficult feats of skill or heroism to sustain its waning life-sense.
>
> (p. 80)

Although moralists have been predicting the end of Western civilization for some time, American society continues to defy the predictions of gloom and doom. However, it would be irresponsible to make light of the moralist critique insofar as it is directed at blood sports such as boxing and mixed martial arts, sports that can have lifelong debilitating effects for some combatants (e.g., Muhammad Ali) and, on occasion, can even be deadly. Although it may be extreme to argue that spectacles such as the Super Bowl, Kentucky Derby, March Madness, and the World Series are debased and immoral, some sports are difficult to defend given their violence and total disregard of basic human values.

The Structural-Functionalist Perspective

The **structural-functionalist perspective** takes the position that for any social institution to exist, it must contribute to the maintenance or survival of society. If we accept, for argument's sake, that sport fandom satisfies the definition of an institution (Goodger & Goodger, 1989; Zurcher & Meadow, 1967), then the challenge is to discover which specific societal objectives are served by sport. This can be accomplished by examining various societal **imperatives** that are aided via sport fandom. That is, typical of structural-functionalist thinking is the specifying of several prerequisites (i.e., imperatives) that every society must successfully address if it wishes to remain a viable entity (Aberle, Cohen, Davis, Levy, & Sutton, 1950; Parsons, 1951; Stevenson, 1974). If sport fandom assists in the meeting of these imperatives, then one can reasonably conclude that the pastime has a positive impact on society as a whole (Delaney, 2015; Lewis, 2007; Shin, 2007).

In the sections that follow, several functions of sport fandom are identified, discussed, and critiqued (a brief description of each function can be found in Table 11.2). As you will read, the evidence for the societal benefits of fandom is quite strong. In fact, authors have even begun to develop psychometrically sound instruments to assess the positive social impact of fandom (e.g., Lee, Cornwell, & Babiak, 2013).

TABLE 11.2 Potential Functional Imperatives Associated With Sport Fandom

Sport fandom may:
1. Allow for affective expression.
2. Enhance communication.
3. Facilitate national identity.
4. Produce social capital.
5. Contribute to the socialization process.
6. Serve as a form of religion.
7. Enhance integration at all levels.

Sport Fandom and Affective Expression

Affective expression is part and parcel of being human. To smile, to laugh, to experience euphoria, and to be joyful is to be alive. Although society must guard against the unrestricted expression of some forms of affect, lest the social order be seriously disrupted, other emotional responses need to be encouraged and produced. For the structural-functionalist, society must provide its members with opportunities that produce positive affect to survive. Perhaps the ancient Roman satirist Juvenal said it best when he observed "Duas tantum res anxius optat, panem et circenses," meaning "Two things only the people anxiously desire—bread and circuses" (cited in Preston, 1978, p. 207). In sport fandom, we have an institutional structure with a Barnumesque quality, where marching bands, exploding scoreboards, inspirational music, cheerleaders, mascots, and colorful pageantry overwhelm the senses (e.g., think of the opening and closing ceremonies of the Olympics).

Sporting events provide an opportunity for fans to experience a wide range of both positive and negative emotions (Cottingham, 2012; Ferguson, 1981). Indeed, the affective experience of fans is rich and varied enough to warrant coverage in a full chapter in this text. By serving as a catalyst for the expression of affect, sport helps combat the pernicious effects of apathy and the cessation of motivation, a condition that can prove fatal to any social system. The importance of affect in the experiences of sport fans was captured by Bain-Selbo (2012), who noted that "When asked to rank a number of aspects of their lives (family, friends, church, work, hobbies, et cetera), fans ranked football immediately behind church as the place where they have 'the deepest and most positive emotional experiences' " (p. 71).

Sport Fandom and Communication

No society, however simple, can exist without shared, learned, symbolic modes of communication (Aberle et al., 1950). Communication is absolutely essential because it provides the basis for social interaction, helps maintain a society's common value structure, and is indispensable to the socialization and role differentiation processes. That **sport impacts communication** is not debatable. In fact, the discipline of sport communication studies has flourished in recent years with the publication of numerous texts and the establishment of several scholarly journals. In fact, many universities now offer a Sport Communication degree.

Sport fandom contributes to the communication process in two important ways. First, the language of sport, or "Sportugese" as it has been termed, finds its way into almost every aspect of life, be it the military, business, politics, advertising, or even sexual relations (Hardaway, 1976; Segrave, 1994; Tannenbaum & Noah, 1959; Wann et al., 1997). In fact, Palmatier and Ray's (1989) *Sports Talk: A Dictionary of Sports Metaphors* listed a total of 1,700 popular American English words and expressions derived from terms directly associated with sport, games, and recreation. Given that this list is now several decades old, the number of these metaphors is now likely much greater. Baseball, in particular, provides many popular metaphors, several of which are listed in Table 11.3. Thus, the lexicon of sport fandom makes an important contribution to the communication process. Through the sport metaphor we are able to share our ideas, desires, meanings, and experiences using words and phrases easily understood by others. When a friend asks, "Can you pinch hit for me tonight?", or when your boss instructs you to "Take the ball and run with it" we know precisely what these individuals mean.

A second manner in which sport fandom contributes to the communication process is by providing a topic of conversation. Although much of everyday conversation focuses on people, sport is also a popular topic, especially among those who follow sport on a regular basis. Because sport talk functions so well as small talk, it has become a very important vehicle for communication in modern society. Sport talk as small talk is more important than people think. Not only does it make individuals feel more comfortable in social situations, it also helps them establish new relationships as well as maintain old ones.

TABLE 11.3 Metaphors in Contemporary Language Directly Traceable to Baseball

1. He was born with two strikes against him.
2. He couldn't get to first base with that girl.
3. He sure threw me a curve that time.
4. I'll take a rain check on it.
5. He went to bat for me.
6. I liked him right off the bat.
7. He was way out in left field on that one.
8. He's a foul ball.
9. I think you're way off base on that.
10. It was a smash hit.
11. Let's take a seventh-inning stretch.
12. I hope you touch all the bases on this report.
13. Could you pinch hit for me?
14. He doesn't even know who's on first base.
15. I just call 'em like I see 'em.
16. He's only a bush-leaguer.
17. Major league all the way.
18. He was safe by a mile.
19. He has a lot on the ball.
20. No game's over until the last man's out.

Note: Adapted from Spink (1978).

Sport Fandom and National Identity

Because sport allows people to represent themselves or their social groups to others, national sports carry particular psychological and societal significance, even where there is considerable social and cultural heterogeneity (Goodger & Goodger, 1989). Hence, sport fandom can potentially be used to instill a sense of **national identity** (Bain-Selbo & Sapp, 2016; Bairner, 2001; Chalip, 2006; Doczi, 2011; Heere & James, 2007; Hong, 2011). For example, the following sports and their affiliated countries immediately come to mind: baseball in the Dominican Republic, rugby in New Zealand, bullfighting in Mexico, ice hockey in Canada, basketball in the Philippines, skiing in Norway, golf in Scotland, ice skating in the Netherlands, and sumo wrestling in Japan. Such is also the case with the NCAA men's college basketball championships, otherwise known as March Madness. In trying to account for the extraordinary attention and excitement this tournament engenders, Price (1991) suggested that the competition appeals to the American Dream—it's democratic (e.g., all teams start on equal footing), it appeals to the underdog mentality, it's monotheistic (i.e., the idea of a single champion is attractive), and it celebrates capitalist competition (i.e., survival of the fittest).

Although a strong case can be made for the close link between national sports and collective representation, Bairner (1996) made a very important point when he observed that this association is by no means straightforward. Rather, the exact nature of the relationship depends on the role of nationalism in each societal context. For example, in Scotland and the Republic of Ireland, because of the politics of nationalism, it has proved difficult to "construct a cohesive sportive nationalism" (p. 33). On the other hand, "in Sweden, where national identity is less of a political issue, the development of an inclusive sportive nationalism has been relatively smooth" (p. 332). Although some national sports contribute to collective representation and nationalism, others accentuate group differences, making it difficult to construct coherent and unified national identities (Bairner, 1996).

Sport Fandom and Social Capital

Social capital (or social currency, see Magdol & Bessel, 2003) involves features of social organization such as networks, norms, and social trust that facilitate coordination and cooperation within a culture. One of the more controversial and hotly debated social scientific essays published in recent decades was Putnam's (1995) *Bowling Alone: America's Declining Social Capital*, in which he offers the provocative thesis that social capital has declined over the past several decades. To bolster his argument, Putnam points to the fact that the average number of associational memberships (e.g., church-related groups, labor unions, fraternal-veteran organizations, and school-service groups) has fallen substantially over the last 25 years. Putnam also notes that, to make matters worse, the two most fundamental forms of social capital—the family and the neighborhood—no longer provide the rich social interaction and bonding opportunities they once did.

Sport Fandom Can Help Foster a Sense of National Identity

These disturbing trends in social connectedness and civic engagement, and their subsequent toll on social trust, cooperation, and communication, are blamed on several factors, including geographical mobility and technology. Putnam suggests the latter has been responsible for privatizing or individualizing our use of leisure time and thus disrupting many opportunities for the development of social capital. Although Putnam dismisses secondary and tertiary networks and associations (e.g., sport fandom) as effective venues for social capital formation, closer inspection of these "social worlds" (Unruh, 1983), "public scenes" (Irwin, 1977), and "third places" (Oldenburg & Brissett, 1982) reveals perhaps a hasty judgment on his part.

Although Putnam (1995) concedes that two fans may root for the same team, he argues that "they are unaware of each other's existence. Their ties, in short, are to common symbols, common leaders, and perhaps common ideals, but not to one another" (p. 71). But the fact is, traditional forms of sociability in American life have been changing for some time "from primary associations to secondary ones, from the more intimate to the less intimate, from the realm of stronger affect to weaker affect, and from less monetized forms of social interaction to more monetized ones" (Melnick, 1993, p. 48). Empirically, a number of researchers have found that leisure activities can and often do lead to an increase in social capital (Glover, Parry, & Shinew, 2005; Perks, 2007; Warde, Tampubolon, & Savage, 2005), and this includes work on sport fandom (Palmer & Thompson, 2007; Phua, 2012; Swyers, 2005). For instance, as discussed in Chapter 10, team identification is associated with increased social connectedness (Inoue & Havard, 2014; Wann et al., 2015, 2011). In fact, the volume of this literature is now so extensive it warranted publication of a separate text titled *Sport and Social Capital* (Nicholson & Hoye, 2008).

Thus, it appears that what we may well be witnessing is a gradual shift in locale for the satisfaction of social needs. No longer do traditional institutions such as the family, workplace, and neighborhood fully satisfy our need for social interaction and engagement. Instead, people now turn to less intimate, more public locales for association and to connect with one another (e.g., singles bars, personal columns in newspapers and magazines, dating services, and cruises). The list of such places likely includes those at which sport fans congregate and commune.

Socialization Through Sport Fandom

In Chapter 2, we detailed the extensive process through which people are socialized into fandom and to follow specific teams. However, there is an equally (if not more) important relationship between fandom and socialization processes. Specifically, not only can individuals be socialized *into* sport fandom, they may also be **socialized *through* sport fandom** (Delaney, 2015; Lewis, 2007). It may well be that no functional imperative is more important to a society's survival than successfully teaching its structure of action to each generation of new members. Each individual must be taught the appropriate modes for dealing with everyday life circumstances and situations. This socialization involves teaching each of the following: (1) shared cognitive orientations, (2) articulated sets of goals, and (3) the prescription of means for attaining those socially formulated goals (Aberle et al., 1950). It is essential for members of any society to become effectively integrated into its core belief system and acquire the appropriate behavioral patterns (Stevenson, 1974).

For the current discussion, we are interested in what role, if any, sport fandom plays in teaching members of a society information that can assist their ability to successfully navigate their way through the vicissitudes of everyday living. That is, we are concerned here with the extent to which sport fandom contributes to the adoption of shared cognitions, articulated goals, and opportunities for obtaining those goals. Although the extent to which an individual is directly socialized via fandom is difficult to assess empirically, Edwards (1973) was certainly of the opinion that sport effectively performs this socializing function. He observed that "sport is a social institution which has primary functions in disseminating and reinforcing the values regulating behavior and goal attainment and determining acceptable solutions to problems in the secular spheres of life" (p. 90).

Directing his attention specifically to sport fans, Edwards (1973) also noted, "As an institution having primarily socialization and value maintenance functions, sport affords the fan an opportunity to reaffirm the established values and beliefs defining acceptable means and solutions to central problems in the secular realm of everyday societal life" (p. 243). Consistent with Edwards' remarks, recall that we previously noted how sport has the potential to influence the value systems of fans, in both positive and negative ways (see Chapter 10).

Thus, however imperfect, sport typically offers fans demonstrable evidence of the ideological elements that constitute the dominant value structure in society (Loy, 1978). In fact, even those watching sport on television can access the important value lessons sport teaches. For instance, Bailey and Sage (1988) conducted a content analysis of sportscasters' commentary during a Super Bowl contest and found that the dominant values communicated were the prototypical American values of individualism and achievement. They concluded that "the salience of the sportscasters' specific comments provides a vehicle for value transmission" (p. 126).

Sport Fandom and Religiosity

When considering the intersection between **sport fandom and religiosity**, the notion that following sport can be sacred and share the same societal functions provided by religious institutions is likely to border on blasphemy for some. In fandom, we have mass entertainment that sometimes appears crude, vulgar, and profane. And yet, at least by analogy, the similarities between sport fandom and organized religion are striking (Bain-Selbo, 2008; Bain-Selbo & Sapp, 2016; Groeneman, 2017). For instance, consider the vocabulary associated with both: faith, devotion, worship, ritual, dedication, sacrifice, commitment, spirit, prayer, suffering, festival, and celebration. Given the linguistic commonality between sport and religion, further investigation of the potential relationship between the two is warranted.

A number of works have been published that can help inform our understanding of the intersection between religion and sport (e.g., Hoffman, 1992; Novak, 1976; Prebish, 1993; Price, 2004). For example, Bain-Selbo (2012) conducted an extensive review of the literature and found a great number of commonalities between sport and religion. A partial list of these appears in Table 11.4. McGee (1975) noted that one of the key societal functions of religious institutions is to assist in defining, rationalizing, and coping with the crises that people experience (e.g., birth, childbearing, death, etc.). These crises represent organizational problems for society because they threaten to disrupt interpersonal relationships. Thus, one purpose of religious institutions from a sociological perspective is to help maintain social cohesion, a critical imperative facing any society. Put more succinctly, what religious institutions do for society is bind people together through ritual and belief by offering common values and goals toward which they may strive. Could a similar case be made for the binding, integrating, and organizing functions of sport fandom?

Although not everyone accepts the view of sport fandom as religion (e.g., Edwards, 1973; Higgs, 1995; Higgs & Braswell, 2004), it is clear that fandom and religiosity share much in common. Sport has "godlike" figures, such as Paul "Bear" Bryant, former head coach for the University of Alabama (St. John, 2004). Sport rituals, such as tailgating prior to a game or camping out for tickets, certainly have the fervor and devotion commonly associated with religious ceremonies. Smith et al. (2012) found that individuals reported a greater sense of attachment to their favorite sport team than to their religion. In fact, devoted fans even appear to have a form of brand evangelism (Dwyer, Greenhalgh, &

TABLE 11.4 Similarities Between Sport and Religion

Both sport and religion have:
1. Holy days
2. Temples and sacred places
3. Sacred rituals
4. Myths and legends
5. Symbols and sacred objects
6. Artifacts and relics from the past
7. Sacred music
8. Social components
9. Taboos
10. Active participation by those involved
11. Sharing meals among participants
12. The ability to provide a sense of understanding and meaning to life
13. The ability to provide a sense of belonging
14. Deities, saints, and patriarchs
15. Violent components
16. Sacrifice
17. Affective experience
18. Traditions
19. Socialization at an early age
20. Devotion

Note: Adapted from Bain-Selbo (2012).

LeCrom, 2015). Ultimately, the extent to which sport fandom is a religious experience may come down to one's operational definition of religion, of which there are many (Bain-Selbo, 2012). However, it certainly seems reasonable that for many fans, sport assists in the satisfaction of this societal imperative.

Sport Fandom and Societal Integration

Commonly referred to as unification, solidarity, or social cohesion, the integration of the masses presents every society with the formidable challenge of generating common interests, loyalty, and enthusiasm among its members. **Societal integration** is a critically important social imperative because it serves as a counterpoint to the potentially disruptive conflicts, cleavages, and antagonistic factions that are the inevitable consequences of scarce means, unfulfilled expectations, and imperfections in the socialization process (Lever, 1983; Lewis, 2007; Shin, 2007). The integrative powers of sport were nicely captured by Markovits and Albertson (2012), who noted that through "inclusiveness and ubiquity, sports have created ties across class, ethnic, regional, cultural, religious, and age lines that few, if any, other forces could even approximate" (pp. 2–3). Evidence of this can be found at each of the following levels of social organization: interpersonal, community/metropolitan (city), state, national, and global.

Integration at the Interpersonal Level With respect to **integration at the interpersonal level**, attending a sporting event can facilitate encounters with strangers and provide opportunities for casual sociability (Wann et al., in press). In analyzing interactions between two strangers at a sporting event, we find a number of potentially positive elements present. For instance, both parties are likely to know and understand the expectations associated with the role of sport fan. Also, the temporal boundaries of the encounter are clear-cut and implicitly understood, thereby guaranteeing the safety of any exchange. Further, both parties are likely willing to share relevant information about players and home teams. And finally, the safety, comfort, and ambience of the ecological setting facilitate attempts at social interaction (Melnick, 1993).

Integration at the Community/Metropolitan Level The Chicago Cubs' 2016 World Series championship celebration was attended by an estimated five million individuals, which would rank it as the seventh-largest gathering in human history (Flosi, 2016). This massive congregation of like-minded individuals stands as perhaps the ultimate example of the ability of sport fandom to foster **integration at the community/metropolitan level**. The notion that sport fandom promotes connections at the community and metropolitan levels has empirical support (Kim & Walker, 2012; Zhang, Pease, & Hui, 1996). For example, Wilkerson and Dodder (1987) tested the proposition that "sport holds the potential to activate collective conscience and group affirmation by linking the identity of individuals to a common community orientation" (p. 36). They surveyed public school teachers in nine communities and found a significant relationship between attendance at high school football games and scores on a collective conscience scale. Interestingly, the better the team's winning percentage, the higher the scores. The researchers concluded that participation and winning can interact to "provide a basis for shared identity, common focus, and, consequently, collective conscience" (p. 40).

Governing bodies have taken notice of the possibility that sport can integrate otherwise diverse members of a community (Hoye & Nicholson, 2008). Indeed, perhaps Groeneman (2017) said it best when he wrote

> Not to sound Pollyannaish, but the way I see it the positive contributions of fandom in building community and solidarity, especially among people of diverse backgrounds and differing points of view, far outweigh its being a source of social conflict and disunity.
>
> (p. 131)

For instance, in an attempt to establish a national policy on sport, researchers from England concluded that "Sport contributed to strengthening community cohesion, engagement and capacity building—sport activities and events contribute to the development of stronger social networks and more cohesive communities" (Sport England, 2005, p. 8). Likewise, a similar governmental report from Australia (Commonwealth of Australia, 1999) concluded that "Sport is an inclusive social phenomenon and provides opportunities for specific groups to feel a part of a community" (p. 55). Given that community cohesion is an important component of social psychological health (Inoue et al., 2015; Keyes, 1998), the ability of sport to facilitate cohesion at this level cannot be overstated.

Integration at the State Level There are numerous examples of sport fandom facilitating **integration at the state level**, including college teams such as University of Kentucky men's basketball (Kelley & Tian, 2004) and University of Nebraska football (Aden, 2008). At the high school level, the Indiana state boys' basketball tournament provides an excellent example of how fandom can unify an entire state. Because high school basketball in Indiana is a central component in the identities of many persons living in the state (Johnson, 1996), virtually all Hoosiers turn their attention to basketball at tournament time. Immortalized in the movie classic *Hoosiers*, the tournament has, until recently, been open to every school in the state, regardless of enrollment or record. However, beginning with the 1997–1998 season, school administrators voted to do away with the one-class tournament in favor of four boys' and four girls' tournaments based on school size. Interestingly, in its first year of operation, total attendance was down 22 percent from the previous year (Hoosier Rebellion, 1998). Remarked the Indiana University sports information director, "They are ruining one of the great traditions in the history of Indiana athletics" (cited in White, 1996).

Integration at the National Level The "Miracle on Ice" U.S. men's ice hockey gold medal victory in the 1980 Winter Olympic Games demonstrates the ability of sport fandom to encourage **integration at the national level**. Many Americans can recall what they were doing or where they were on that special day. The 100 million or more television viewers who tune into the Super Bowl every year provide us with another example of how a major sporting event can integrate an entire country.

As with integration at the community/metropolitan level, governing bodies have addressed the issue of national integration via sport (Hoye & Nicholson, 2008). For example, officials from Australia concluded that "Sport fosters the social cohesiveness and unity that reinforces our sense of being an Australian" (Commonwealth of Australia, 1999, p. 55). The government of Canada came to a similar conclusion, stating that "Sport is considered an essential tool for nation building and can lead to the promotion of national identity, and enhancing our sense of community and citizenship" (Government of Canada, 2001, pp. 5–6).

Integration at the Global Level Finally, in terms of **integration at the global level**, it's hard to think of any event, short of a major war, that can capture the world stage like international sporting events. Competitions such as the

Global Sporting Events Such as the Olympics May Lead to Integration and Facilitate World Peace, Although Some Research Casts Doubt on These Processes

Summer and Winter Olympics and the FIFA World Cup soccer tournament are expected to assist in the integration of persons from a wide variety of countries (Allison & Monnington, 2002). Indeed, part of the "Olympic Ideal" is to use sport to unite otherwise different people (the Olympic rings symbolize the unity of five continents) and Pierre de Coubertin's vision for renewing the Olympics was, in part, to promote peace among nations (The Olympic Rings, 2017). More recently, the notion of sport facilitating peace was promoted by the United Nations through the establishment of April 6, 2014, as the first annual International Day of Sport for Development and Peace (United Nations, 2014).

However, Wertheim and Sommers (2016) challenge the notion that global sport leads to peace, writing, "Do global events—the World Cup in particular—truly lead to world peace? In a word: No" (p. 225). Based on research by Bertoli (in press), Wertheim and Sommers appear to have justification for their skepticism. Bertoli examined the national aggression (i.e., militarized interstate disputes) for countries whose national soccer team either barely qualified for or missed the World Cup tournament. He reasoned that if participation in international sporting events facilitates peace, then those teams qualifying for the Word Cup should exhibit lower levels of national aggression subsequent to making the tournament. Interestingly, this is not what Bertoli found. Rather, although qualifiers and non-qualifiers had similar levels of national aggression prior to the tournament, those countries whose teams qualified exhibited *greater* levels of post-qualifying aggression. This pattern of effects is in direct opposition to the belief that international sporting events facilitate peace among nations.

So, should we lobby to eliminate such events in the name of peace and tranquility? Can international sports, at least in some contexts, bring people together? In all likelihood, they can. In fact, even Wertheim and Sommers (2016) seem to soften their view of such events, stating that "To be clear: We are not diminishing the positive role that sports can play in international relations and peace-making initiatives" (p. 227). Their argument, and they are likely correct, is simply that getting everyone together at a sporting event will not solve all of the world's ills. It might help, but it is just one of many strategies needed to promote international peace and goodwill.

Sport Fandom, Integration, and Suicide One of the most intriguing lines of inquiry regarding the integrative possibilities of sport fandom is the potential relationship between **fandom and suicide.** Durkheim (1951) was one of the first social scientists to propose a relationship between participation in ritualized, ceremonial activities and suicide rates. His thinking is captured in the following syllogism (a syllogism is a logical formula used to test the validity of reasoning and consists of a major premise, a minor premise, and a conclusion):

Major Premise: Participation in collective ceremonies is related to a high degree of integration of the social group.

Minor Premise: A high degree of integration of the social group is related to lower suicide rates.

Conclusion: Participation in collective ceremonies is related to lower suicide rates.

This line of deductive reasoning has served as the theoretical basis for much of the research on sport fandom and suicide. That is, it has been hypothesized that fandom and the consumption of popular sporting events leads to a sense of greater connectedness and belonging, which is likely to discourage thoughts of self-destruction, at least in the short term (a pattern of effects consistent with the Team Identification–Social Psychological Health Model discussed in Chapter 10). Andriessen and Krysinska (2011) captured the logic being suggested here by stating "Being a sports fan creates camaraderie, a sense of belongingness and being cared for and can result in sports-related 'pulling together' which might protect against suicide" (p. 180).

A number of researchers have examined the relationship between fandom and suicide rates. Some studies indicate that suicide rates appear to be associated with fandom (Masterson & Mander, 1990). For example, Fernquist (2001) found that the relocation of professional sport teams (e.g., when the Brooklyn Dodgers left for Los Angeles) was associated with increased suicide rates in those locales. In a separate study, Fernquist (2000) examined suicide rates in 30 metropolitan areas and found that suicide rates dropped in those areas when their professional teams made the playoffs. Joiner, Hollar, and Van Orden (2006) examined a series of data sets and found consistent support for the hypothesis that fandom is associated with lower suicide rates. Their data revealed lower suicide rates in college towns housing a successful collegiate football team and lower rates in the U.S. on the day of the "Miracle on Ice" 1980 Olympic hockey victory as well as on Super Bowl Sundays.

Other researchers, however, have failed to find that sport fandom was related to suicide rates (Fernquist, 2002; Trovato, 1998). For instance, Curtis, Loy, and Karnilowicz (1986) investigated two sport ceremonial days (the last day of the World Series and the Super Bowl) and two civil holidays (July 4th and Thanksgiving Day), reviewing suicide incidence rates three days before and after these days for the years 1972–1978. Although net declines in suicides were found for the three days leading up to the two sport days, the effect was much stronger for these two civil holidays. The researchers concluded that the integrative effects of sport ceremonial days were considerably weaker than those of civil holidays. Lester (1988) replicated the above study but examined a time period (1972–1984) twice as long as the earlier study. He also found no significant deviation in suicide rates from chance expectations for the two sport ceremonial days.

Thus, although some work appears to substantiate the relationship between sport fandom and lower rates of suicide, other studies have failed to find such an effect. Andriessen and Krysinska (2011) conducted a review of this research and concluded that fandom may indeed have an influence on suicide but that the

> impact seems to depend on mediating variables such as characteristics of the spectator, including gender, age, and marital status, and characteristics of the sport event, such as outcome (victory versus defeat) and the importance of the game (playoff versus championship).
>
> (p. 182)

Thus, as with most fan behaviors and reactions, the relationship between fandom and suicide is highly complex and in need of additional research.

Critiquing the Structural-Functionalist Perspective

Although the structural-functionalist view can help us gain insight into the role of sport fandom in contemporary society, the perspective is not without limitations. In particular, Coakley (1998) articulated three major problems with the functionalist approach. First, the functionalist approach can lead to an overstatement of the positive impact of sport fandom. The fact that an aspect of culture (e.g., sport) is popular does not guarantee that it is valuable or useful. Just because fandom has been around for many centuries does not insure that it is "functional" and satisfies important societal imperatives.

Second, there is the tendency when using functional analysis to "overlook cases where sports benefit some groups more than others within a community or society" (Coakley, 1998, pp. 34–35). For example, although the case was previously made that sport fandom can make important contributions to affective expression, communication, and integration into society, a class analysis suggests that fandom likely benefits some socioeconomic groups more than others. For example, the cost of attending professional sporting events in the U.S. strongly discourages the lower and lower-middle socioeconomic classes from participating. If sport fandom is an important contributor to small talk, affect production, and social cohesion, then clearly these positive consequences are not equally distributed among all strata in society.

And third, because functionalists are not especially concerned with how sport might be "created and defined by members of society to promote their own interests and the interests of the groups to which they belong," advocates are likely to overlook how sport "might promote the interests of those with power and wealth, and thereby contribute to disruptive forms of social inequality in societies" (Coakley, 1998, p. 35). Instead of serving the basic needs of society, Coakley argues that sport may actually perpetuate social inequalities based on race/ethnicity, class, and gender, a view that is consistent with the feminist critique discussed earlier.

Some Final Thoughts

As one can see from the discussions in this chapter, social scientists have very different views as to the societal impact of sport fandom. On the one hand, the conflict, feminist, cultural elitist, and moralist critiques argue that fandom has a net negative impact on society at large. From any of these perspectives, fandom may be perceived dysfunctional from society's vantage point. On the other hand, the structural-functionalist perspective paints a more positive picture of the societal impacts of sport fandom, viewing the activity as beneficial to society. In fact, seven different imperatives were identified for sport fandom, each addressing a particular societal function.

Although each of the theories and perspectives identified and discussed were supported with the most relevant research available, the fact remains that the formal study of sport fandom from institutional and popular-culture perspectives continues to be an understudied phenomenon. Consequently, several of the observations offered must remain informed speculations until such time as more qualitative and quantitative data become available. In the absence of a significant research literature bearing on the question proposed at the beginning of this chapter, the reader is challenged to weigh the strengths and weaknesses of each of the theories and critiques discussed and arrive at his or her own answers to the question "What is the relationship between sport fandom and society?"

And finally, it seems appropriate to note that there is always the danger of engaging in over-analysis when attempting to make sense of something commonplace, like sport fandom. After all, we are not talking about rocket science! Maybe the importance of sport fandom to a society is more obvious than researchers and theorists would have us believe. The growing popularity and increasing importance of spectator sports throughout the world may simply reflect a collective need on the part of spectators and fans to add a bit of zest to their everyday lives (Shames, 1989). Sporting events provide followers with an opportunity to take a break from their daily routines and responsibilities, whether to watch a daughter participate in a youth soccer game, attend a minor league baseball game, or take up a comfortable position on the living room couch for a Sunday date with the NFL. Maybe we should view sport fandom as a nutritional supplement, a tropical spice, a spiritual, emotional substitute. In the same way that herbs and spices can improve the taste of a bland main dish, sport fandom can add a dash of excitement, wonder, and meaning to our lives and society as a whole. Despite all the socio-babble the subject attracts, it would truly be ironic if we discover, when all is said and done, that the major societal function of sport fandom is to provide fans with a time-out institution, one that allows them to temporarily reinvigorate their emotional, spiritual, and social lives.

PART FOUR

Summary and Conclusion

CHAPTER 12

The Future of Sport Fandom: Gazing Into the Crystal Ball

When one reflects back on the content of this text, it becomes clear that a great deal of work has targeted sport fandom, particularly in the last two decades. This work has not been confined to a single discipline. Rather, scholars from a wide variety of fields have added to the literature on sport fans, including persons with a background in psychology, sociology, marketing/management, history, religious studies, and biology. As a result, we now have a more comprehensive understanding of the psychological and societal impact of sport fandom.

However, there is still much work to be done. In this final chapter, we peer into the future and discuss two related topics. First, we examine a few issues that we believe will change the landscape of the sport fan experience. We follow this with our thoughts about several topics that should be targeted by future investigators.

The Ever-Changing Sport Fan Experience

History tells us that, ironically, one of the greatest constants in life is change. This is most certainly true for the lives and experiences of sport fans. Past changes that altered fandom include nighttime sporting events, greater acceptance of female sport spectators, racial integration of leagues, televised sport (and primetime sporting events such as Monday Night Football), cable television (in particular ESPN), pay-per-view events, leagues starting (e.g., the United States Football League, Major League Soccer) and leagues ending (e.g., the United States Football League, the American Basketball League), and most recently, the Internet. In the following paragraphs, we speculate about a few changes that are happening now or we believe will happen in the coming years that should alter how fans experience sport, what that experience means, and how sport fandom impacts society.

Changing Technology

In his discussion of the future of sport fandom, Groeneman (2017) writes that **technological advancements** may have the greatest impact on changes to the pastime. He very well may be right. Both changes to existing technology and technologies yet to be introduced are almost certain to alter what fans do and how they do it. Researchers have already begun to examine the impact of changing technology on the sport fan experience (Sanderson, 2011; Seo & Green, 2008). This includes Twitter (Delia et al., 2017; Watanabe, Yan, & Soebbing, 2016; Witkemper, Lim, & Waldburger, 2012), Facebook (Moyer, Pokrywczynski, & Griffin, 2015; Stavros et al., 2014), blogging (Norman, 2014), message boards (Cleland, 2014), and sport-related mobile phone applications (Kang et al., 2015).

Technological advancements will likely require changes to current theories of fan behavior. For example, consider the Psychological Continuum Model (Funk & James, 2001, 2006, 2016) and the Team Identification–Social Psychological Health Model (Wann, 2006c). One commonality between these two approaches is their focus on connections gained via sport fandom. However, new technologies often have an impact on our relationships (especially social media). For example, both sport bloggers (Hardin & Whiteside, 2012) and Twitter users (Norman, 2012) engage in these activities in part to build communities and gain connections with other fans. Consequently, these and similar

Technological Advancements Will Continue to Change the Experiences of Sport Fans

theoretical approaches to sport fandom may need to be adjusted to include new media through which fans consume sport and interact with other fans.

The Impact of the Increased Legalization of Sport Wagering

Another potential change in sport fandom involves the **increased legalization of sport wagering**. Sport gambling is a popular activity among fans and can be a critical motivator for some (Wann, 1995; Wann & Ensor, 1999; Wann et al., 1999). Estimates of the amount of money bet on sport in the U.S. can be staggering; it is thought that over $100 billion is wagered on sporting events each year (Purdam,2017). In fact, it was estimated that over $4 billion was gambled just on Super Bowl 50 (American Gaming Association, 2016).

Due to the 1992 Professional and Amateur Sports Protection Act, only a handful of states are legally permitted to accept sport wagers (the vast majority of this activity occurs in Nevada). Several states have become interested in joining the list of those allowed to offer sport gambling. Led by New Jersey, these states hope to increase revenue via legalized sport wagering. Initially, professional sport leagues and the NCAA resisted the increased legalization of sport gambling, arguing their brand would be damaged by the change. Although they shared several concerns about increasing access to legalized sport gambling (e.g., decreased league integrity, greater criminal activity), at the forefront was the belief that legalized sport wagering would negatively affect the sport fan experience (Tuohy, 2013). For example, sport leagues argued that fans would begin to care more about their bets than their favorite teams. Historical team loyalties would decrease; fans' loyalty would now reside with whichever team they had wagered to win. Interestingly, sport leagues (and the commissioners running them) have softened their stance in recent years. Some have even shown interest in increasing access to sport gambling in the hopes that it may prove beneficial for their leagues by generating fan interest (Nuckols, 2017).

In late 2017, the U.S. Supreme Court heard arguments in a case involving the increased legalization of sport gambling. Many believe they will vote in favor of allowing all states to offer legalized sport wagering (Waldron, 2017). Thus, fans may have increased access to this activity. Wann and his colleagues conducted a pair of studies to determine how the increased availability of legalized sport gambling might impact the sport fan experience. In the first study, Wann, Zapalac, Grieve, Partridge, and Lanter (2015) examined the impact of sport fandom and **economic motivation** (one's interest in sport fandom due to the opportunity to bet on games). Participants completed a questionnaire assessing their fandom, economic motivation, and expectations for how their fandom would be impacted by the increased legalization of sport wagering. Wann and his colleagues found that, should legal sport gambling become more accessible, persons higher in fandom and economic motivation would be more likely to gamble on sporting events. These persons also expected to have a greater level of interest in and consumption of sport.

In the second study, Wann, Zapalac, Grieve, Lanter, and Peetz (2017) extended the earlier work by investigating the impact of additional motives. As

TABLE 12.1 The Impact of Motivation on Reactions to the Increased Legalization of Sport Wagering

Motive	Expected Impact of Increased Legalization of Sport Wagering
Persons with higher levels of . . .	
Self-esteem	Expect higher amounts of sport wagering Expect higher levels of interest in sport
Eustress	Expect higher amounts of sport wagering Expect higher levels of sport attendance Expect higher levels of sport television viewing
Aesthetic	Expect lower amounts of sport wagering Expect lower levels of interest in sport Expect lower levels of sport attendance Expect lower levels of sport television viewing
Escape	Expect lower amounts of sport wagering Expect lower levels of sport television viewing

discussed in Chapter 4, there are a number of motivating factors driving involvement in sport fandom. Wann et al. (2017) examined the potential impact of these additional motives on fan reactions to the increased legalization of sport wagering. Using items from the previous study, Wann and his associates (2017) assessed participants' expectations of the impact of increased availability of legalized gambling and the extent to which other motives played a role in their perceptions. Several motives (including economic) were significant predictors of expected reactions to legalized sport wagering. Table 12.1 summarizes the impact of these motives. Looking at the table, it appears that, for some persons, the sport experience would be enhanced by sport gambling (i.e., self-esteem, eustress), while those high on other motives would be negatively affected (i.e., eustress, escape). It will be interesting to see how the increased legalization of sport wagering plays out and, ultimately, how it impacts the sport landscape and experiences of fans.

Maintaining the Safety and Security of Athletes and Fans

A final issue that may lead to changes involves the **safety and security of athletes and fans.** With respect to athletes, sport leagues and teams want to provide safe competitive environments. In some instances, however, the safety of players can be called into question. A prime example of this is football and the long-term negative consequences of repeatedly suffering a blow to the head (e.g., concussions). Deubert, Cohen, and Lynch (2016) published a comprehensive report on the concussion issue in the NFL. Their report examined a number of groups impacted by the safety (or lack thereof) of NFL players. The list of affected parties included the players themselves, coaches, team medical staff, club employees, and equipment managers. An additional group discussed by Deubert and his colleagues were fans of the NFL. The authors discussed a number of ways fans can be impacted by player safety. For instance, the perception that a sport is not safe for players may lead some fans to turn their attention elsewhere. Similarly, parents may not allow their children to participate in football if they believe that it is too dangerous, preferring instead to steer their children to safer options. These outcomes could lead to reduced interest in and consumption of football. In fact, the NFL saw a dramatic drop in television ratings during the 2017 season (Rapaport, 2018). Although there were multiple reasons behind the decline in viewership (e.g., bickering owners, player protests), the violence of the game was also a contributing factor (Grossman, 2017). However, as mentioned previously in this text, many fans enjoy the violent content of sporting events. Thus, governing bodies in sport must walk a fine line between being viewed as "too soft" and "too violent." How leagues walk that line will impact the sport fan experience.

As for the safety and security of fans, persons attending sporting events will also experience changes as teams, leagues, and sporting-event organizers implement strategies designed to safeguard the attendees. For example, based on recommendations from a league study and in response to spectator injuries, Major League Baseball teams have increased the amount of netting separating fans from the playing field (Bieler, 2017; Hagen, 2015). The netting may serve as a distraction to some fans and may decrease their enjoyment of the game.

There is also concern with the safety and security of fans from external threats, particularly from various types of terrorism. Examples include the attack on the Summer Olympics in 1972 in Munich, Germany; the bombing at the Atlanta Olympic Games in 1996; and the bombing at the Boston Marathon in 2013. Terrorist activities are often regarded as the number one security issue at large sporting events (Taylor & Toohey, 2015). Reviewing the literature between 1996 and 2016 results in well over 150 articles published on the subject of terrorism and security at sporting events. These articles focus on topics such as terrorism and risk management practices at NCAA football stadiums (Baker, Connaughton, Zhang, & Spengler, 2007), the impact of terror alert levels on sporting event attendance (Kalist, 2010), the impact of safety and security measures at major sporting events (Taylor & Toohey, 2005), and security, perceived safety, and event attendee enjoyment at mega sporting events (Taylor & Toohey, 2006). The examples listed above illustrate there are a variety of issues to address when considering sport fans' safety and security. Future researchers may want to investigate media portrayals of terrorism at sporting events, the perceptions of terrorism and sense of safety of attendees, and the consequences of increased security and surveillance.

Advancing Research and Theory on Sport Fandom

Having discussed some potential changes to the experiences of fans, we now turn our focus to topics that would benefit from increased consideration from sport scholars. In the sections that follow, we highlight a handful of areas we believe are in need of additional examination. It is our hope that the paragraphs to follow will stimulate further discussion about sport fandom and that these conversations lead to additional empirical and theoretical work.

Cross-Cultural Research

Although sport fandom is a global phenomenon (sport fans are *everywhere*), this is not the case with research on fandom. Rather, the overwhelming majority of research has been conducted in only a handful of (usually English-speaking) countries. However, cultures differ in many ways, and these differences can have a profound impact on persons within them (Hofstede, 2001). Given this, it is likely that persons from different cultures have different experiences within sport (Bhalla & Weiss, 2010). Indeed, there is growing evidence that culture plays a role in the lives of fans. For instance, as noted in Chapter 2, there are cultural differences in the process of socialization into sport fandom (e.g., Melnick & Wann, 2011; Parry et al., 2014; Theodorakis et al., 2017).

Research indicates that cross-cultural differences are not limited to the process of becoming a fan but, rather, also impact individuals once their fandom is established (Gau & Kim, 2011). That is, framed within the Psychological Continuum Model (Funk & James, 2001, 2006, 2016), cross-cultural differences are not simply found at the Awareness stage. Instead, differences are found at the later stages of the model as well (e.g., Attachment and Allegiance). In the future, researchers should expand their work on the impact of culture on sport fandom and highlight critical cross-cultural differences and similarities.

Positive Sport Fandom

At the conclusion of Chapter 6, we noted that most of the work examining the affective reactions of fans has targeted negative emotions such as sadness, anger, and anxiety. Fewer studies have investigated positive affective reactions. We suggested that researchers should increase their attention on the positive emotional reactions of fans. However, this call for research on the positive aspects of fandom should go out to all areas of fandom research. Most sport fan experiences and behaviors are positive rather than negative. For instance, most fans are not violent. Nor does their interest in sport lead to the loss of friends, loved ones, or jobs. Most people who gamble on sport do so responsibly and within a budget.

We are suggesting that sport scholars balance their research; we need to understand both the positive and negative impact sport has on individuals and society. Essentially, research on the psychology of sport fandom needs to follow the positive psychology movement (Seligman, 2011; Seligman & Csikszentmihalyi, 2000). **Positive psychology** is the belief that social scientists should not simply study the abnormal (e.g., violence, problematic relationships, psychological disturbances) but also investigate what makes life worth living (e.g., well-being, positive affect, healthy relationships with others). There have been studies conducted that target the more positive aspects of being a sport fan, or what Wann et al. (in press) termed "**positive sport fandom.**" It is our contention that more of this type of research is needed.

One example of emerging research pertaining to positive sport fandom is work from Kim, Kim, and Kim (2017), who studied the impact of sport media viewing on sport consumer well-being. Kim et al. measured the well-being of sport consumers and fandom for a national soccer team prior to the team competing in qualifying matches for the World Cup. Participants then watched the qualifying match via a media source (e.g., television or Internet broadcast). Immediately after the match, participants completed a post-event survey. The researchers reported that, "hedonic, eudaimonic, and social values experienced in sport event viewing fully or partially led to improved well-being" (p. 317). They also noted that global well-being was influenced most by hedonic need fulfillment. In other words, viewing the match of a favorite team satisfied the participants' hedonic need, which then contributed to an improvement in general well-being. Researchers are encouraged to continue down this path, the result of which will further our understanding of the beneficial ways in which fandom impacts individuals and society at large.

Sport Fandom Across the Lifespan

Another area of investigation that should receive increased research attention involves changes in **fandom across the lifespan**. The vast majority of research investigating the emotions, attitudes, and actions of fans is cross-sectional, simply providing a snapshot of their current state as a sport enthusiast. What is also needed is longitudinal work that tracks persons over extended periods of time to determine the impact of life changes in their fandom (Harrington & Bielby, 2010). For example, how does moving away from home, getting married, having children, and/or having an empty nest impact one's fandom? These changes impact other aspects of daily living (Feldman, 2018), and there is no reason to believe that sport fandom would be immune from these effects.

A handful of studies suggest that we should be increasing our focus on the impact of life changes on fandom. For instance, Hyatt and Foster (2015) found that one of the key factors accounting for hockey fans' decrease in interest were life changes such as moving to a different city. Grieve, Wann, Zapalac, Cyr, and Lanter (in press) specifically examined this lifespan change by investigating the impact of moving away to college. They found that college freshman had higher levels of identification with their high school football team than those who had been away longer (e.g., college seniors). A third study on life events included an investigation of the impact of parenthood on one's fandom; the researchers reported that having children often leads to lowered interest in sport fandom due to the time constraints needed to raise a family (Tinson, Sinclair, & Kolyperas, 2017). Taken together, these studies suggest that life-changing events (e.g., moving, having children) can influence one's fandom. Additional research (particularly of a longitudinal nature) is needed to shed light on the impact of other life events.

Assessment of Previous Ideas and Advancement of Theory

When updating a work such as this book, an important part of the process is reviewing previous work and thinking about what has been done well and where there is room for improvement. As illustrated in Chapter 3, although there has been a substantial amount of research with team identification, we are still learning about this important construct. We highlighted the thought-provoking work by Lock and Heere (2017) challenging those interested in team identification to further develop our understanding of the theoretical bases of team identification. We also presented information on the revised Sport Spectator Identification Scale (SSIS-R; James et al., in press), which came about after the realization that many scholars (the authors included) had misinterpreted the extent to which individuals may have a low level of team identification versus no team identification.

The work with the SSIS-R is a good illustration of the importance of reviewing research and our understanding of concepts to insure we have a sound basis from which to work and that the work is accurate and rigorous. In this same vein, a retrospective review of the research on sport consumer motives merits attention. We have written in several chapters about sport fan motives, particularly Chapters 4 and 5. Although there has been a substantial amount of research in this area, much of it has simply focused on the development of scales to measure motives. Unfortunately, much of the work is disjointed, and a comprehensive study of sport fan motives research is a project that merits attention.

Making the effort to study previous research and striving to improve upon it contributes to the advancement of theory and our knowledge of sport fandom. We have written extensively about the use of the PCM in this book and believe the theory provides an important basis for studying fandom. At the same time, we should continue to test this framework and consider opportunities for improvement. One prospective advancement is addressing the misplacement of individuals into the stages of the PCM. Funk and James (2016) suggest that as many as 20 percent of participants in empirical studies could be staged incorrectly. There are different approaches to consider in trying to improve the staging of individuals within the PCM. One approach would be to develop a screening process to identify misplaced individuals by establishing statistical thresholds at different stages on particular outcome measures such as identification or satisfaction. Such an approach would allow for the designation of outliers and provide an opportunity to assess why individuals fall outside the expected parameters.

Another approach would be to consider revisions to the staging protocol developed by Beaton et al. (2009) discussed in Chapter 5. For example, Kota, Du, James, Kennedy, and Funk (2018) presented a rationale for the inclusion of **risk** as another facet to assess psychological connection to a sport object. In the initial presentation of the PCM, Funk and James (2001) discussed risk as a facet of involvement and provided observations about measuring perceived risk to differentiate among the stages. This included the assessment of risk probability

TABLE 12.2 Five Dimensions of Risk

Dimension	Definition
Financial	A consumer's perception as to whether she or he is getting her or his "money's worth" (Selin, 1986).
Performance	A consumer's perception that the product may have something wrong with it or be unsafe (Stone & Gronhaug, 1993).
Physical	A consumer's perception of the possibility of physical danger or bodily harm (Stone & Gronhaug, 1993).
Social	A consumer's perception that consuming a product may change the views others have of the consumer (Cheron & Ritchie, 1982).
Time	A consumer's perception that consuming a product will be a waste of one's time (Brooker, 1984).

and risk consequence, both of which were originally conceptualized in consumer behavior scholarship (Havitz & Dimanche, 1997; Laurent & Kapferer, 1985). Beaton et al. (2009) found problems with and a lack of empirical support for these two dimensions of risk, resulting in their omission from the staging tool. Kota et al. have proposed that five dimensions of risk be considered as potential modifiers of an individual's involvement level and included in the staging process: **financial, performance, physical, social**, and **time**. The five dimensions are presented in Table 12.2.

Operationalizing and including five dimensions of risk would increase the complexity of the measurement of an individual's involvement with a sport object. Adding other factors will necessitate a change to the way individuals are staged within the PCM. Accordingly, Beaton et al.'s (2009) algorithm and staging matrix could be modified to include the risk dimensions. Concerns with such an approach include the increasing complexity associated with staging individuals and continuing to limit the PCM's utility by transforming continuous data into categorical data.

Another approach to staging individuals along the PCM would involve the use of **latent profile analysis** (LPA) rather than the approach pioneered by Beaton and his associates (2009). LPA is a deductive statistical approach designed to segment individuals into theoretically sound and distinctive groups. Analogous to other Structural Equation Modeling analyses, the technique provides a series of fit indices and tests to determine the optimal number of latent groups and examination of the quality of membership classification based on theoretical justification, interpretability, intergroup heterogeneity, intragroup homogeneity, and statistical parsimony. Instead of using 27 (or more) combinations of involvement profiles based on selected cutoff points, LPA would utilize an individual's original scores for the involvement facets to calculate the probabilities associated with an individual being positioned among the PCM stages. Regardless of whether the existing staging mechanism is altered, other facets of involvement are included, or different techniques for staging are introduced, it is clear we can and should continue to improve the PCM.

Integration of Research Streams

Our next suggested topic for additional research does not target a specific area of investigation but, rather, concerns how research is conducted on sport fandom. Historically, research has been fragmented. We believe that greater integration will lead to a more well-rounded understanding of the individual and societal impacts of fandom. Two areas of increased integration are needed. First, although work on fandom originates from a variety of areas, in many instances work conducted in one area remains unknown to researchers working within a different discipline (Butryn, LaVoi, Kauer, Semerjian, & Waldron, 2014; Thorpe, Ryba, & Denison, 2014). As a result, entire literatures can go unnoticed and unused (your authors have frequently reviewed papers submitted for publication in journals in which this was the case). Thus, we need more integration and collaboration **across social scientific disciplines**. Such a multidisciplinary approach will result in the sharing of knowledge across areas and a better understanding of fandom.

Second, researchers studying sport fandom may be able to improve their work by incorporating research and theory from studies that examine **fans of non-sport domains**. Persons investigating different fan groups (e.g., fans of sport versus fans of other forms of pop culture) are often unaware of research in other areas (Schimmel, Harrington, & Bielby, 2007). Certainly, fans of sport and non-sport pastimes are different (Gantz, Wang, Paul, & Potter, 2006). Yet in spite of these differences, we may be able to learn vital information by comparing the two. Such comparisons would highlight both similarities and differences between fans of sport and fans of other forms of pop culture, leading to a better understanding of both groups. Interestingly, the integration of these domains appears to have begun. There is even a new journal, the *Journal of Fandom Studies*, that welcomes research on both sport and non-sport fans.

Sport Fandom and Evolutionary Processes

A final topic that could use additional interest from scholars is the extent to which sport fandom can be understood from an **evolutionary perspective**. Can the global popularity of sport be understood within an evolutionary framework? A few authors believe it can (Simons, 2013). For example, Apostolou and Zacharia (2015) suggest that centuries ago men may have been interested in watching other men compete in athletic arenas to help identify potential spouses for their daughters. Lombardo (2012) hypothesizes that individuals were interested in sport fandom to evaluate potential allies and rivals. Taking a somewhat different perspective, Winegard (2010) argues that, because fandom and spectating are social activities, interest in sport likely assisted in the building of coalitions. Each of these processes and outcomes have clear evolutionary advantages (e.g., persons who were able to build stronger coalitions were more likely to survive, reproduce, and pass on the genetic makeup for caring about coalitions).

Interestingly, research supports each of these (and other) predictions based on evolutionary psychology. For example, consistent with the logic developed by Apostolou and Zacharia (2015), men with daughters are particularly interested in watching sport. And consistent with the importance of coalitions discussed by Winegard (2010), team identification is positively correlated with coalitional activities, such as loyalty and authority. However, research on the evolutionary significance of sport fandom and spectating is still very new, and the topic has attracted little attention from researchers (Lombardo, 2012). The truth is we are just now beginning to understand the precise mechanisms through which evolutionary forces shaped and influenced our interest in following and viewing sport. Additional work is needed to paint a more complete picture of the relationship between fandom and evolution.

Some Final, Final Thoughts

We have covered a great deal in this text—who knew there was so much to being a sport fan! We close this book with an acknowledgement that the subjects we examined may seem to be somewhat fragmented. This often happens when writing a comprehensive book, particularly when the topic has been examined by multiple disciplines. However, we feel there is a unifying theme running throughout the chapters of this book: the importance of connections. We believe that in many ways connections are at the heart of being a sport fan. Whether it is connections fans feel with teams and sports, connections they feel with one another, or connections they feel with society, it seems that being a sport fan involves gaining and maintaining associations with someone or something. It is our hope that you found the information in this book interesting and enlightening and that, just perhaps, you formed a connection with it as well!

REFERENCES

Aberle, D. F., Cohen, A. K., Davis, A. K., Levy, M. J., & Sutton, F. S. (1950). The functional prerequisites of a society. *Ethics*, *60*, 100–111.

Aden, R. C. (2008). *Huskerville: A story of Nebraska Football, fans, and the power of place*. Jefferson, NC: McFarland.

Aden, R. C., & Titsworth, S. (2012). Remaining rooted in a sea of red: Agrarianism, place attachment, and Nebraska Cornhusker football fans. In A. C. Earnheardt, P. M. Haridakis, & B. S. Hugenberg (Eds.), *Sports fans, identity and socialization: Exploring the fandemonium* (pp. 9–23). Lanham, MD: Lexington.

Adubato, B. (2016). The promise of violence: Televised, professional Football games and domestic violence. *Journal of Sport and Social Issues*, *40*, 22–37.

Aiken, K. D., Campbell, R. M., Jr., & Sukhdial, A. (2010). An investigation of *old school* Values in the Arena Football League. *Sport Marketing Quarterly*, *19*, 125–131.

Aiken, K. D., & Koch, E. C. (2009). A conjoint approach investigating factors in initial team preference formation. *Sport Marketing Quarterly*, *18*, 81–91.

Aiken, K. D., & Sukhdial, A. (2004). Exploring the old school concept: Adding definition to a "new" market segmentation dimension. *Sport Marketing Quarterly*, *13*, 173–181.

Ajzen, I. (1985). From intentions to actions: A theory of planned behavior. In J. Kuhl & J. Beckmann (Eds.), *Action control: SSSP Springer series in social psychology*. Berlin, Germany: Springer-Verlag.

Alderfer, C. P. (1972). *Existence, relatedness, and growth*. New York, NY: Free Press.

Alexandris, K., Du, J., Funk, D., & Theodorakis, N. D. (2017). Leisure constraints and the psychological continuum model: A study among recreational mountain skiers. *Leisure Studies*, *36*, 670–683.

Allen, J. J., & Anderson, C. A. (in press). General aggression model. In P. Roessler, C. A. Hoffner, & L. van Zoonen (Eds.), *International encyclopedia of media effects*. Hoboken, NJ: Wiley-Blackwell.

Allen, J. T., Drane, D., & Byon, K. K. (2010). Gender differences in sport spectatorship among college baseball fans. *International Journal of Sport Management*, *11*, 418–439.

Allison, L., & Monnington, T. (2002). Sport, prestige, and international relations. *Government and Opposition*, *37*, 106–134.

Allon, F. (2012). The ladies stand. In K. Toffoletti & P. Mewett (Eds.), *Sport and its female fans* (pp. 28–45). New York, NY: Routledge.

Allport, G. W. (1937). *Personality: A psychological interpretation*. New York, NY: Holt.

Allport, G. W. (1961). *Pattern and growth in personality*. New York, NY: Holt.

Al-Suqri, M. N., & Al-Kuarusi, R. M. (1980). Ajzen and Fishbein's Theory of Reasoned Action (TRA). In M. Al-Suqri & A. Al-Aufi (Eds.), *Information seeking behavior and technology adoption: Theories and trends* (pp. 188–204). Hershey, PA: IGI Global.

American Gaming Association. (2016). *Americans to bet $4.2 billion on super bowl 50*. Retrieved from www.americangaming.org/newsroom/press-releasess/americans-bet-42-billion-super-bowl-50

Amiot, C. E., Sansfacon, S., & Louis, W. R. (2014). How normative and social identification processes predict self-determination to engage in derogatory behaviours against outgroup hockey fans. *European Journal of Social Psychology*, *44*, 216–230.

Anderson, C. A., & Bushman, B. J. (2002). Human aggression. *Annual Review of Psychology*, *53*, 27–51.

Anderson, C. A., & Carnagey, N. L. (2004). Violent evil and the general aggression model. In A. Miller (Ed.), *The social psychology of good and evil* (pp. 168–192). New York, NY: Guilford Press.

Anderson, C. A., & Carnagey, N. L. (2009). Causal effects of violent sports video games on aggression: Is it competitiveness or violent content? *Journal of Experimental Social Psychology*, *45*, 731–739.

Anderson, C. A., & DeNeve, K. M. (1992). Temperature, aggression, and the negative affect escape model. *Psychological Bulletin*, *111*, 347–351.

Anderson, C. A., Deuser, W. E., & DeNeve, K. M. (1995). Hot temperatures, hostile affect, hostile cognition, and arousal: Tests of a general theory of affective aggression. *Personality and Social Psychology Bulletin*, *21*, 434–448.

Anderson, D., & Stone, G. P. (1981). Responses of male and female metropolitans to the commercialization of professional sport 1960 to 1975. *International Review of Sport Sociology*, *16*(3), 5–20.

Andrew, D. P. S., Koo, G-Y., Hardin, R., & Greenwell, T. C. (2009). Analyzing motives of minor league hockey fans: The introduction of violence as a spectator motive. *International Journal of Sport Management and Marketing*, *5*, 73–89.

Andriessen, K., & Krysinska, K. (2011). Spectators' involvement in sports and suicidal behavior: Review of current evidence. In B. D. Geranto (Ed.), *Sport psychology* (pp. 175–185). Hauppauge, NY: Nova.

Andrijiw, A. M., & Hyatt, C. G. (2009). Using optimal distinctiveness theory to understand identification with a nonlocal professional hockey team. *Journal of Sport Management*, *23*, 156–181.

Angyal, A. (1941). *Foundations for a science of personality*. New York, NY: Commonwealth Fund.

Antonen, M. (2004, September 15). MLB investigating player-fan clash. *USA Today*, p. 1C.

Apostolou, M., & Zacharia, M. (2015). The evolution of sports: Exploring parental interest in watching sport. *Evolutionary Psychological Science*, *1*, 155–162.

Appelbaum, L. G., Cain, M. S., Darling, E. F., Stanton, S. J., Nguyen, M. T., & Mitroff, S. R. (2012). What is the identity of a sports spectator? *Personality and Individual Differences*, *52*, 422–427.

Arai, A., Ko, Y. J., & Kaplanidou, K. (2013). Athlete brand image: Scale development and model test. *European Sport Management Quarterly*, *13*, 383–403.

Arai, A., Ko, Y. J., & Ross, S. (2014). Branding athletes: Exploration and conceptualization of athlete brand image. *Sport Management Review*, *17*, 97–106.

Armour, N. (2002, September 21). Attacking fans charge coach provoked them. *The Paducah Sun*, p. 3B.

Arms, R. L., & Russell, G. W. (1997). Impulsivity, fight history and camaraderie as predictors of a willingness to escalate a disturbance. *Current Psychology: Research & Reviews*, *15*, 279–285.

Arms, R. L., Russell, G. W., & Sandilands, M. L. (1979). Effects on the hostility of spectators viewing aggressive sports. *Social Psychology Quarterly*, *42*, 275–279.

Armstrong, K. L. (2002a). An examination of the social psychology of blacks' consumption of sport. *Journal of Sport Management*, *16*, 267–288.

Armstrong, K. L. (2002b). Race and sport consumption motivations: A preliminary investigation of a Black Consumers' Sport Market Motivation Scale. *Journal of Sport Behavior*, *25*, 309–330.

Armstrong, K. L. (2008). Consumers of color and the "culture" of sport attendance: Exploratory insights. *Sport Marketing Quarterly*, *17*, 218–231.

Armstrong, K. L., & Peretto Stratta, T. M. (2004). Market analysis of race and sport consumption. *Sport Marketing Quarterly*, *13*, 7–16.

Aronson, E., & Mills, J. (1959). The effect of severity of initiation on liking for a group. *Journal of Abnormal and Social Psychology*, *59*, 177–181.

Ashforth, B. E., & Mael, F. (1989). Social identity theory and the organization. *Academy of Management Review*, *14*, 20–39.

Ashley, F. B., Dollar, J., Wigley, B., Gillentine, J. A., & Daughtrey, C. (2000). Professional wrestling fans: Your next door neighbors? *Sport Marketing Quarterly*, *9*, 140–148.

Ashmore, R. D., Deaux, K., & McLaughlin-Volpe, T. (2004). An organizing framework for collective identity: Articulation and significance of multidimensionality. *Psychological Bulletin*, *130*, 80–114.

Auburn Tree Poisoning. (2013, March 25). Auburn tree poisoning: Harvey Updyke, Jr., sentenced to 3 years for poisoning beloved trees. *Crimesider*. Retrieved from www.cbsnews.com/news/auburn-tree-poisoning-harvey-updyke-jr-sentenced-to-3-years-for-poisoning-beloved-trees/

Averill, L. A. (1950). The impact of a changing culture upon pubescent ideals. *School and Society*, *72*, 49–53.

Baade, R. A., & Tiehen, L. J. (1990). An analysis of Major League Baseball attendance, 1969–1987. *Journal of Sport & Social Issues*, *14*(1), 14–32.

Babb, K., & Rich, S. (2016, October 28). A quietly escalating issue for the NFL: Fan violence and how to contain it. *The Washington Post*. Retrieved from www.washingtonpost.com/sports/redskins/a-quietly-escalating-issue-for-nfl-fan-violence-and-how-to-contain-it/2016/10/28/4ec37964–39470–394 11e6-bb29-bf2701dbe0a3_story.html?utm_term=.9f6292a0c452

Bahk, C. M. (2000). Sex differences in sport spectator involvement. *Perceptual and Motor Skills*, *91*, 79–83.

Bailey, C. I., & Sage, G. H. (1988). Values communicated by a sports event: The case of the Super Bowl. *Journal of Sport Behavior*, *11*, 126–143.

Bain-Selbo, E. (2008). Ecstasy, joy, and sorrow: The religious experience of southern college Football. *The Journal of Religion and Popular Culture*, *20*, 1–9.

Bain-Selbo, E. (2012). *Game day and god: Football, faith, and politics in the American South*. Macon, GA: Mercer University Press.

Bain-Selbo, E., & Sapp, D. G. (2016). *Understanding sport as a religious phenomenon: An introduction*. New York, NY: Bloomsbury.

Bairner, A. (1996). Sportive Nationalism and Nationalist politics: A comparative analysis of Scotland, the Republic of Ireland, and Sweden. *Journal of Sport & Social Issues*, *23*, 314–334.

Bairner, A. (2001). *Sport, Nationalism and globalization: European and North American perspectives*. Albany, NY: State University of New York Press.

Baker, T. A., III, Connaughton, D., Zhang, J. J., & Spengler, J. O. (2007). Perceived risk of terrorism and related risk management practices of NCAA Division 1A football stadium managers. *Journal of Legal Aspects of Sport*, *17*, 27–51.

Balch, M. J., & Scott, D. (2007). Contrary to popular belief, refs are people too! Personality and perceptions of officials. *Journal of Sport Behavior*, *30*, 3–20.

Ballouli, K., Trail, G. T., Koesters, T. C., & Bernthal, M. J. (2016). Differential effects of motives and points of attachment on conative loyalty of Formula 1 U.S. Grand Prix attendees. *Sport Marketing Quarterly*, *25*, 166–181.

Balmer, N. J., Nevill, A. M., & Williams, A. M. (2003). Modelling home advantage in the Summer Olympic games. *Journal of Sport Sciences*, *21*, 469–478.

Balswick, J., & Ingoldsby, B. (1982). Heroes and heroines among American adolescents. *Sex Roles*, *8*, 243–249.

Bandura, A. (1973). *Aggression: A social learning analysis*. Englewood Cliffs, NJ: Prentice Hall.

Bandura, A. (1986). *Social foundations of thought and action*. Englewood Cliffs, NJ: Prentice Hall.

Baron, R. A., & Richardson, D. R. (1994). *Human aggression* (2nd ed.). New York, NY: Plenum.

Bartholow, B. D., & Heinz, A. (2006). Alcohol and aggression without consumption: Alcohol cues, aggressive thoughts, and hostile perception bias. *Psychological Science*, *17*, 30–37.

Bartholow, B. D., Pearson, M. A., Gratton, G., & Fabiani, M. (2003). Effects of alcohol on person perception: A social cognitive neuroscience approach. *Journal of Personality and Social Psychology*, *85*, 627–638.

Bass, J. R., Gordon, B. S., & Kim, Y. K. (2013). University identification: A conceptual framework. *Journal of Contemporary Athletics*, *7*, 13–25.

Baumeister, R. F. (2012). Need-to-belong theory. In R. A. M. Van Lange, A. W. Kruglanski, & E. T. Higgins (Eds.), *Handbook of theories of social psychology* (Vol. 2, pp. 121–140). Los Angeles, CA: Sage Publishers.

Baumeister, R. F., & Leary, M. R. (1995). The need to belong: Desire for interpersonal attachments as a fundamental human motivation. *Psychological Bulletin, 117*, 497–529.

Baumeister, R. F., Twenge, J. M., & Nuss, C. K. (2002). Effects of social exclusion on cognitive processes: Anticipated aloneness reduces intelligent thought. *Journal of Personality and Social Psychology, 83*, 817–827.

Beaton, A. A., Funk, D. C., & Alexandris, K. (2009). Operationalizing a theory of participation in physically active leisure. *Journal of Leisure Research, 41*, 177–203.

Beaton, A. A., Funk, D. C., Ridinger, L., & Jordan, J. (2011). Sport involvement: A conceptual and empirical analysis. *Sport Management Review, 14*, 126–140.

Begue, L., Bushman, B. J., Giancola, P. R., Subra, B., & Rosset, E. (2010). "There is no such thing as an accident," especially when people are drunk. *Personality and Social Psychology Bulletin, 36*, 1301–1304.

Beisser, A. R. (1967). *The madness in sports: Psychosocial observations on sports*. New York, NY: Appleton-Century-Crofts.

Bell, D. E. (1985). Disappointment in decision making under uncertainty. *Operations Research, 33*, 1–27.

Belmi, P., Barragan, R. C., Neale, M. A., & Cohen, G. L. (2015). Threats to social identity can trigger social deviance. *Personality and Social Psychology Bulletin, 41*, 467–484.

Benedict, J., & Yaeger, D. (1998). *Pros and cons: The criminals who play in the NFL*. New York, NY: Warner Books.

Benjamin, A. J., Jr., Kepes, S., & Bushman, B. J. (in press). Effects of weapons on aggressive thoughts, angry feelings, hostile appraisals, and aggressive behavior: A meta-analytic review of the weapons effect literature. *Personality and Social Psychology Review*.

Bergkvist, L. (2012). The flipside of the sponsorship coin: Do you still by the beer when the brewer underwrites a rival team? *Journal of Advertising Research, 52*, 65–73.

Berkman, L. F., & Syme, L. (1979). Social networks, host resistance, and mortality: A nine-year follow-up study of Alameda County residents. *American Journal of Epidemiology, 109*, 186–204.

Berkowitz, L. (1989). Frustration-aggression hypothesis: Examination and reformulation. *Psychological Bulletin, 106*, 59–73.

Berkowitz, L. (1993). *Aggression: Its causes, consequences, and control.* Philadelphia, PA: Temple University Press.

Bernache-Assollant, I., Bouchet, P., & Lacassagne, M-F. (2007). Spectators' identification with French sports teams: A French adaptation of the sport spectator identification scale. *Perceptual and Motor Skills, 104*, 83–90.

Bernache-Assollant, I., & Chantal, Y. (2011). Fans' reactions to the team victories: An exploratory look at the COFFing process in elite sport fandom. *Sport Science Review, 20*, 161–173.

Bernache-Assollant, I., Laurin, R., Bouchet, P., Bodet, G., & Lacassagne, M-F. (2010). Refining the relationship between ingroup identification and identity management strategies in the sport context: The moderating role of gender and the mediating role of negative mood. *Group Processes & Intergroup Relations*, *13*, 639–652.

Bernhardt, P. C., Dabbs, J. M., Fielden, J. A., & Lutter, C. D. (1998). Testosterone changes during vicarious experiences of winning and losing among fans at sporting events. *Physiology and Behavior*, *65*, 59–62.

Bertoli, A. (in press). Nationalism and conflict: Lessons from International sports. *International Studies Quarterly*.

Bhalla, J. A., & Weiss, M. R. (2010). A cross-cultural perspective of parental influence on female adolescents'' achievement beliefs and behaviors in sport and school domains. *Research Quarterly for Exercise and Sport*, *81*, 494–505.

Bhattacharjee, A., Berman, J. Z., & Reed, A. (2013). Tip of the hat, wag of the finger: How moral decoupling enables consumers to admire and admonish. *Journal of Consumer Research*, *39*, 1167–1184.

Bhattacharya, C. B., Rao, H., & Glynn, M. A. (1995). Understanding the bond of identification: An investigation of its correlates among art museum members. *The Journal of Marketing*, *59*, 46–57.

Bieler, D. (2017, September 22). Four MLB teams announce plans for more safety netting after young girl's injury. *The Washington Post*. Retrieved from www.washingtonpost.com/news/early-lead/wp/2017/09/22/four-mlb-teams-announce-plans-for-more-safety-netting-after-young-girls-injury/?utm_term=.38653e1f6fea

Billings, A. C., & Ruihley, B. J. (2013). Why we watch, why we play: The relationship between fantasy sport and fanship motivations. *Mass Communication and Society*, *16*, 5–25.

Bilyeu, J. K., & Wann, D. L. (2002). An investigation of racial differences in sport fan motivation. *International Sports Journal*, *6*(2), 93–106.

Biscaia, R., Correia, A., Rosado, A., Maroco, J., & Ross, S. (2012). The effects of emotions on football spectators' satisfaction and behavioural intentions. *European Sport Management Quarterly*, *12*, 227–242.

Bizman, A., & Yinon, Y. (2002). Engaging in distancing tactics among sport fans: Effects on self-esteem and emotional responses. *The Journal of Social Psychology*, *142*, 381–392.

Bloss, H. (1970). Sport and vocational school pupils. *International Review of Sport Sociology*, *5*, 25–58.

Boen, F., Vanbeselaere, N., Pandelaere, M., Schutters, K., & Rowe, P. (2008). When your team is not really your team anymore: Identification with a merged basketball club. *Journal of Applied Sport Psychology*, *20*, 165–183.

Bormann, C. A., & Stone, M. H. (2001). The effects of eliminating alcohol in a college stadium: The Folsom Field beer ban. *Journal of American College Health*, *50*, 81–88.

Bouchet, P., Bodet, G., Bernache-Assollant, I., & Kada, F. (2011). Segmenting sport spectators: Construction and preliminary validation of the Sporting Event Experience Search (SEES) scale. *Sport Management Review*, *14*, 42–53.

Boyle, B. A., & Magnusson, P. (2007). Social identity and brand formation: A comparative study of collegiate sports fans. *Journal of Sport Management*, *21*, 497–520.

Brandon-Lai, S. A., Funk, D. C., & Jordan, J. S. (2015). The stage-based development of behavioral regulation within the context of physically active leisure. *Journal of Leisure Research*, *47*, 401–424.

Branscombe, N. R., & Baron, R. A. (2017). *Social psychology* (14th ed.). New York, NY: Pearson.

Branscombe, N. R., Ellemers, N., Spears, R., & Doosje, B. (1999). The context and content of social identity threat. In N. Ellemers, R. Spears, & B. Doosje (Eds.), *Social identity* (pp. 35–58). Oxford: Wiley-Blackwell.

Branscombe, N. R., & Wann, D. L. (1991). The positive social and self-concept consequences of sport team identification. *Journal of Sport & Social Issues*, *15*, 115–127.

Branscombe, N. R., & Wann, D. L. (1992a). Physiological arousal and reactions to outgroup members that implicate an important social identity. *Aggressive Behavior*, *18*, 85–93.

Branscombe, N. R., & Wann, D. L. (1992b). Role of identification with a group, arousal, categorization processes, and self-esteem in sports spectator aggression. *Human Relations*, *45*, 1013–1033.

Branscombe, N. R., & Wann, D. L. (1994). Collective self-esteem consequences of outgroup derogation when a valued social identity is on trial. *European Journal of Social Psychology*, *24*, 641–657.

Braun, R., & Vliegenthart, R. (2008). The contentious fans: The impact of repression, media coverage, grievances, and aggressive play on supporters' violence. *International Sociology*, *23*, 795–818.

Brewer, M. B. (1979). In-group bias in the minimal group situation: A cognitive motivational analysis. *Psychological Bulletin*, *86*, 307–324.

Brewer, M. B. (1991). The social self: On being the same and being different at the same time. *Personality and Social Psychology Bulletin*, *17*, 475–482.

Brewer, M. B. (2012). Optimal distinctiveness theory: Its history and development. In R. A. M. Van Lange, A. W. Kruglanski, & E. T. Higgins (Eds.), *Handbook of theories of social psychology* (Vol. 2, pp. 81–98). Los Angeles, CA: Sage Publishers.

Brill, A. A. (1929). The why of the fan. *North American Review*, *228*, 429–434.

Brohm, J. M. (1978). *Sport-A prison of measured time*. London: Ink Links.

Brook, A. T., Garcia, J., & Fleming, M. (2008). The effects of multiple identities on psychological well-being. *Personality and Social Psychology Bulletin*, *34*, 1588–1699.

Brooker, G. (1984). An assessment of an expanded measure of perceived risk. *Advances in Consumer Research*, *11*, 439–441.

Brooks, C. M. (1994). *Sport marketing: Competitive business strategies for sports*. Englewood Cliffs, NJ: Prentice Hall.

Brown, B., & Bennett, G. (2015). "Baseball is whack!" Exploring the lack of African American baseball consumption. *Journal of Sport and Social Issues*, *39*, 287–307.

Brown, W. J., Basil, M. D., & Bocarnea, M. C. (2003). The influence of famous athletes on health beleifs and practices: Mark McGwire, child abuse prevention, and androstenedione. *Journal of Health Communication*, *8*, 41–57.

Brown, T. J., Sumner, K. E., & Nocera, R. (2002). Understanding sexual aggression against women: An examination of the role of men's athletic participation and related variables. *Journal of Interpersonal Violence*, *17*, 937–952.

Brummett, B., & Duncan, M. C. (1990). Theorizing without totalizing: Specularity and televised sports. *Quarterly Journal of Speech*, *76*, 227–246.

Bryant, J. (1989). Viewers' enjoyment of televised sports violence. In L. A. Wenner (Ed.), *Media, sports, and society* (pp. 270–289). Newbury Park, CA: Sage Publishers.

Bryant, J., Comisky, P. W., & Zillmann, D. (1981). The appeal of rough-and-tumble play in televised professional Football. *Communication Quarterly*, *29*, 256–262.

Bryant, J., & Raney, A. A. (2000). Sports on the screen. In D. Zillmann & P. Vorderer (Eds.), *Media entertainment: The psychology of its appeal* (pp. 153–174). Hillsdale, NJ: Lawrence Erlbaum Associates.

Bryant, J., Rockwell, S. C., & Owens, J. W. (1994). "Buzzer beaters" and "barn burners": The effects on enjoyment of watching the game go "down to the wire." *Journal of Sport & Social Issues*, *18*, 326–339.

Bryant, J., & Zillmann, D. (1983). Sports violence and the media. In J. H. Goldstein (Ed.), *Sports violence* (pp. 195–211). New York, NY: Springer-Verlag.

Bryson, L. (1987). Sport and the maintenance of masculine hegemony. *Women's Studies International Forum*, *10*, 340–361.

Bushman, B. J., & Anderson, C. A. (2001). Is it time to pull the plug on the hostile versus instrumental aggression dichotomy? *Psychological Review*, *108*, 273–279.

Bushman, B. J., & Cooper, H. M. (1990). Effects of alcohol on human aggression: An integrative research review. *Psychological Bulletin*, *107*, 341–354.

Buss, A. H. (1961). *The psychology of aggression*. New York, NY: Wiley-Blackwell.

Butryn, T. M., LaVoi, N. M., Kauer, K. J., Semerjian, T. Z., & Waldron, J. J. (2014). We walk the line: An analysis of the problems and possibilities of work at the sport psychology-sport sociology nexus. *Sociology of Sport Journal*, *31*, 162–184.

Byon, K. K., Cottingham, M., & Carroll, M. S. (2010). Marketing murderball: The influence of spectator motivation factors on sports consumption behaviors of wheelchair rugby spectators. *International Journal of Sports Marketing and Sponsorship*, *12*, 71–89.

Byrne, D. (1971). *The attraction paradigm*. New York, NY: Academic Press.

Byrne, D., Clore, G. L., & Smeaton, G. (1986). The attraction hypothesis: Do similar attitudes attract anything? *Journal of Personality and Social Psychology*, *51*, 1167–1170.

Campbell, R. M., Aiken, D., & Kent, A. (2004). Beyond BIRGing and CORFing: Continuing the exploration of fan behavior. *Sport Marketing Quarterly*, *13*, 151–157.

Card, D., & Dahl, G. B. (2011). Family violence and football: The effect of unexpected emotional cues on violence behavior. *The Quarterly Journal of Economics*, *126*, 103–143.

Carlson, B. D., & Donavan, D. T. (2013). Human brands in sport: Athlete brand personality and identification. *Journal of Sport Management*, *27*, 193–206.

Carroll, D., Ebrahim, S., Tilling, K., Macleod, J., & Smith, G. D. (2002). Admissions for myocardial infarction and World Cup Football: Database survey. (Evidence that really matters). *British Medical Journal*, *325*, 1439–1447.

Carron, A. V., Loughhead, T. M., & Bray, S. R. (2005). The home advantage in sport competitions: Courneya and Carron's (1992) conceptual framework a decade later. *Journal of Sports Sciences*, *23*, 395–407.

Casper, J. M., & Menefee, W. C. (2010a). The impact of socialization on current and retrospective adolescent sport consumption with college students. *International Journal of Sport Management*, *11*, 541–560.

Casper, J. M., & Menefee, W. C. (2010b). Prior sport participation and spectator sport consumption: Socialization and soccer. *European Sport Management Quarterly*, *10*, 595–611.

Caspi, A., Herbener, E. S., & Ozer, D. J. (1992). Shared experiences and the similarity of personalities: A longitudinal study of married couples. *Journal of Personality and Social Psychology*, *62*, 281–291.

Castine, S. C., & Roberts, G. C. (1974). Modeling in the socialization process of the black athlete. *International Review of Sport Sociology*, *9*, 59–74.

Chalip, L. (2006). Toward a distinctive sport management discipline. *Journal of Sport Management*, *20*, 1–21.

Chang, Y., Wann, D. L., & Inoue, Y. (in press). The effects of implicit team identification on revisit and word-of-mouth intentions: A moderated mediation of emotions and flow. *Journal of Sport Management*.

Chen, C-H., Lin, Y-H., & Chiu, H-T. (2013). Development of psychometric evaluation of sport stadium atmosphere scale in spectator sport events. *European Sport Management Quarterly*, *13*, 200–215.

Cheron, E. J., & Ritchie, J. R. B. (1982). Leisure activities and perceived risk. *Journal of Leisure Research*, *14*, 139–154.

Chien, C-I., & Ross, S. (2012). Spectator anxiety and internalization: A case of the Chinese Professional Baseball League. *International Journal of Sport Management*, *13*, 59–72.

Churchill, G. A. (1999). *Marketing research methodological foundations* (7th ed.). London: Dryden Press.

Cialdini, R. B., Borden, R. J., Thorne, A., Walker, M. R., Freeman, S., & Sloan, L. R. (1976). Basking in reflected glory: Three (football) field studies. *Journal of Personality and Social Psychology*, *34*, 366–375.

Cialdini, R. B., & De Nicholas, M. E. (1989). Self-presentation by association. *Journal of Personality and Social Psychology*, *57*, 626–631.

Cikara, M., Botvinick, M. M., & Fiske, S. T. (2011). Us versus them: Social identity shapes neural responses to intergroup competition and harm. *Psychological Science*, *22*, 306–313.

Clark, L., Lawrence, A. J., Astley-Jones, F., & Gray, N. (2009). Gambling near-misses enhance motivation to gamble and recruit win-related brain circuitry. *Neuron*, *61*, 481–490.

Clark, D. M. T., Loxton, N. J., & Tobin, S. J. (2015). Declining loneliness over time: Evidence from American colleges and high schools. *Personality and Social Psychology Bulletin*, *41*, 78–89.

Cleland, C. J., & Cashmore, E. (2016). Football fans' views of the violence in British football: Evidence of a sanitized and gentrified culture. *Journal of Sport & Social Issues*, *40*, 124–142.

Cleland, J. (2014). Racism, football fans, and online message boards: How social media has added a new dimension to racist discourse in English football. *Journal of Sport and Social Issues*, *38*, 415–431.

Clopton, A. W. (2008). College sports on campus: Uncovering the link between fan identification and sense of community. *International Journal of Sport Management*, *9*, 343–362.

Clopton, A. W. (2012). Re-examining the role of antecedent orientation in social psychological well-being through team identification. *Journal of Contemporary Athletics*, *6*, 97–111.

Clotfelter, C. T. (2015). Die-hard fans and the ivory tower's ties that bind. *Social Science Quarterly*, *96*, 381–399.

Coakley, J. J. (1998). *Sport in society: Issues and controversies* (6th ed.). St. Louis: Times Mirror/Mosby.

Coates, D., & Humphreys, B. R. (2002). The economic impact of postseason play in professional sports. *Journal of Sports Economics*, *3*, 291–299.

Cohen, A. (2017). Fans' identification with teams: A field study of Israeli soccer fans. *Cogent Social Sciences*, *3*, 1–12.

Commonwealth of Australia. (1999). *Shaping up: A review of commonwealth involvement in sport and recreation in Australia*. Canberra, Australia: Commonwealth of Australia.

Compton, W. C. (2005). *An introduction to positive psychology*. Belmont, CA: Thomson Wadsworth.

Cook, K., & Mravic, M. (1999, August 16). Go figure. *Sports Illustrated*, p. 28.

Cooper, C. G. (2011). The motivational preferences of consumers attending multiple NCAA wrestling events. *Sport Marketing Quarterly*, *20*, 33–40.

Cooper, D., Livingood, A. B., & Kurz, R. B. (1981). Children's choice of sports heroes and heroines: The role of child-hero similarity. *Psychological Documents*, *11*, 85 (Ms. No. 2376).

Corbin, C. B. (1973). Among spectators, "trait" anxiety, and coronary risk. *Physician and Sports Medicine*, *1*(2), 55–58.

Corder, M. (2000, April 4). Aboriginals warn of violent protests during Olympics. *The Paducah Sun*, p. 4B.

Cormil, Y., & Chandon, P. (2013). From fan to fat? Vicarious losing increases unhealthy eating, but self-affirmation is an effective remedy. *Psychological Science*, *24*, 1936–1946.

Correia, A., & Esteves, S. (2007). An exploratory study of spectators' motivation in football. *International Journal of Sport Management and Marketing*, *2*, 572–590.

Cottingham, M., Chatfield, S., Gearity, B. T., Allen, J. T., & Hall, S. A. (2012). Using points of attachment to examine repatronage and online consumption of wheelchair rugby spectators. *International Journal of Sport Management*, *13*, 160–172.

Cottingham, M., Carroll, M. S., Phillips, D., Karadakis, K., Gearity, B. T., & Drane, D. (2014). Development and validation of the motivation scale for disability sport consumption. *Sport Management Review*, *17*, 49–64.

Cottingham, M. D. (2012). Interaction ritual theory and sports fans: Emotion, symbols, and solidarity. *Sociology of Sport Journal*, *29*, 168–185.

Cottingham, M. D., Phillips, D., Hall, S. A., Gearity, B. T., & Carroll, M. S. (2014). Application of the motivation scale for disability sport consumption: An examination of intended future consumption behavior of collegiate wheelchair basketball spectators. *Journal of Sport Behavior*, *37*, 117–133.

Courneya, K. S., & Carron, A. V. (1992). The home advantage in sport competitions: A literature review. *Journal of Sport & Exercise Psychology*, *14*, 13–27.

Courtney, J. J., & Wann, D. L. (2010). The relationship between sport fan dysfunction and bullying behaviors. *North American Journal of Psychology*, *12*, 191–198.

Crawford, G. (2001). Characteristics of a British ice hockey audience. *International Review for the Sociology of Sport*, *36*, 71–81.

Crawford, G. (2003). The career of the sport supporter: The case of the Manchester Storm. *Sociology*, *37*, 219–237.

Crawford, G. (2004). *Consuming sport: Fans, sport and culture*. New York, NY: Routledge.

Crawford, G., & Gosling, V. K. (2004). The myth of the 'Puck Bunny': Female fans and men's ice hockey. *Sociology*, *38*, 477–493.

Crawford, G., & Gosling, V. K. (2009). More than a game: Sports-themed video games and player narrative. *Sociology of Sport Journal*, *26*, 50–66.

Crisp, R. J., Heuston, S., Farr, M. J., & Turner, R. N. (2007). See red or feeling blue: Differentiated intergroup emotions and ingroup identification in soccer fans. *Group Processes and Intergroup relations*, *10*, 9–26.

Crocker, J., & Major, B. (1989). Social stigma and self-esteem: The self-protective properties of stigma. *Psychological Review*, *96*, 608–630.

Cullen, F. T. (1974). Attitudes of players and spectators toward norm violation in ice hockey. *Perceptual and Motor Skills*, *38*, 1146.

Curtis, J., Loy, J., & Karnilowicz, W. (1986). A comparison of suicide-dip effects of major sports events and civil holidays. *Sociology of Sport Journal*, *3*, 1–14.

Dalakas, V., & Melancon, J. P. (2012). Fan identification, schadenfreude toward hated rivals, and the mediating effects of IWIN (Importance of Winning Index). *Journal of Services Marketing*, *26*, 51–59.

Dalakas, V., Melancon, J. P., & Sreboth, T. (2015). A qualitative inquiry on schadenfreude by sport fans. *Journal of Sport Behavior*, *38*, 161–179.

Danielson, M. N. (1997). *Home team: Professional sports and the American metropolis*. Princeton, NJ: Princeton University Press.

Darrah, E. M. (1898, May). A study of children's ideals. *Popular Science Monthly*, *52*, 88–98.

Darrow, C., & Lewinger, P. (1968). The Detroit uprising: A psychological study. In J. Masserman (Ed.), *The dynamics of dissent: Science and psychoanalysis* (Vol. 13). New York, NY: Grune & Stratton.

Daughtrey, C., & Stotlar, D. (2000). Donations: Are they affected by a football championship? *Sport Marketing Quarterly*, *9*, 185–193.

Davis, M. C., & End, C. M. (2010). A winning proposition: The economic impact of successful National Football League franchises. *Economic Inquiry*, *48*, 39–50.

Davis, M. H., & Harvey, J. C. (1992). Declines in Major League batting performance as a function of game pressure: A drive theory analysis. *Journal of Applied Social Psychology*, *22*, 714–735.

de Groot, M., & Robinson, T. (2008). Sport fan attachment and the psychological continuum model: A case study of an Australian Football League fan. *Leisure/Loisir*, *32*, 117–138.

Delaney, T. (2015). The functionalist perspective on sport. In R. Giulianotti (Ed.), *Routledge handbook of the sociology of sport* (pp. 18–28). New York, NY: Routledge.

Delia, E. B. (2015). The exclusiveness of group identity in celebrations of team success. *Sport Management Review*, *18*, 396–406.

Delia, E. B. (2017). March sadness: Coping with fan identity threat. *Sport Management Review*, *20*, 408–421.

Delia, E. B., Bass, J. R., & Wann, D. L. (2017). Tweets of self-presentation: Assessing in-game sport consumer behavior via twitter. *Applied Research in Coaching and Athletics Annual*, *32*, 33–62.

Delia, E. B., & James, J. D. (in press). The meaning of team in team identification. *Sport Management Review*.

Denham, B. E. (2010). Correlates of pride in the performance success of United States athletes competing on an international stage. *International Review for the Sociology of Sport*, *45*, 457–473.

Derbaix, C., Decrop, A., & Cabossart, O. (2002). Colors and scarves: The symbolic consumption of material possessions by soccer fans. *Advances in Consumer Research*, *29*, 511–518.

DeRossett, T., & Wann, D. L. (2018, April). *The few, the proud, the distinct: The relationship between belonging and distinctiveness on sport team choice*. Poster presented at the annual meeting of the Midwestern Psychological Association, Chicago, IL.

Deubert, C. R., Cohen, I. G., & Lynch, H. F. (2016). *Protecting and promoting the health of NFL player: Legal and ethical analysis and recommendations*. Cambridge, MA: Harvard Law School.

DeWall, C. N., Anderson, C. A., & Bushman, B. J. (2011). The general aggression model: Theoretical extensions to violence. *Psychology of Violence*, *1*, 245–258.

Dewar, C. K. (1979). Spectator fights at professional baseball games. *Review of Sport & Leisure*, *4*, 14–25.

Diener, E. (1980). Deindividuation: The absence of self-awareness and self-regulation in group members. In P. Paulas (Ed.), *The psychology of group influence* (pp. 209–242). Hillsdale, NJ: Lawrence Erlbaum Associates.

Diener, E., Suh, E. M., Lucas, R. E., & Smith, H. L. (1999). Subjective well-being: Three decades of progress. *Psychological Bulletin, 125*, 276–302.

Dietz-Uhler, B., End, C., Jacquemotte, L., Bentley, M., & Hurlbut, V. (2000). Perceptions of male and female fans. *International Sports Journal, 4*(2), 88–97.

Dietz-Uhler, B., Harrick, E. A., End, C., & Jacquemotte, L. (2000). Sex differences in sport fan behavior and reasons for being a sport fan. *Journal of Sport Behavior, 23*, 219–231.

Dietz-Uhler, B., & Lanter, J. R. (2008). The consequences of sports fan identification. In L. W. Hugenberg, P. M. Haridakis, & A. C. Earnheardt (Eds.), *Sports mania: Essays on fandom and the media in the 21st century* (pp. 103–113). Jefferson, NC: McFarland.

Dietz-Uhler, B., & Murrell, A. (1999). Examining fan reactions to game outcomes: A longitudinal study of social identity. *Journal of Sport Behavior, 22*, 15–27.

Dimanche, F., Havitz, M. E., & Howard, D. R. (1993). Consumer involvement profiles as a tourism segmentation tool. *Journal of Travel & Tourism Marketing, 1*, 33–52.

Dimmock, J. A., & Grove, J. R. (2005). Relationship of fan identification to determinants of aggression. *Journal of Applied Sport Psychology, 17*, 37–47.

Dimmock, J. A., & Grove, J. R. (2006). Identification with sport teams as a function of the search for certainly. *Journal of Sport Sciences, 24*, 1203–1211.

Dimmock, J. A., Grove, J. R., & Eklund, R. C. (2005). Reconceptualizing team identification: New dimensions and their relationship to intergroup bias. *Group Dynamics: Theory, Research, and Practice, 9*, 75–86.

Dimmock, J. A., & Gucciardi, D. F. (2008). The utility of modern theories of intergroup bias for research on antecedents to team identification. *Psychology of Sport and Exercise, 9*, 284–300.

Dittmore, S. W., Stoldt, G. C., & Greenwell, T. C. (2008). Use of an organizational weblog in relationship building: The case of Major League Baseball team. *International Journal of Sport Communication, 1*, 384–397.

Doczi, T. (2011). Gold fever(?) Sport and national identity—the Hungarian case. *International Review for the Sociology of Sport, 47*, 165–182.

Dollard, J., Doob, L. W., Miller, N. E., Mowrer, O. H., & Sears, R. R. (1939). *Frustration and aggression*. New Haven, CT: Yale University Press.

Donahue, T., & Wann, D. L. (2009). Perceptions of the appropriateness of sport fan physical and verbal aggression: Potential influences of team identification and fan dysfunction. *North American Journal of Psychology, 11*, 419–428.

Donavan, D. T., Carlson, B. D., & Zimmerman, M. (2005). The influence of personality traits on sport fan identification. *Sport Marketing Quarterly, 14*, 31–42.

Dosseville, F., Edoh, K. P., & Molinaro, C. (2016). Sports officials in home advantage phenomenon: A new framework. *International Journal of Sport and Exercise Psychology*, *14*, 250–254.

Doyle, J. P., Filo, K., Lock, D., Funk, D. C., & McDonald, H. (2016). Exploring PERMA in spectator sport: Applying positive psychology to examine the individual-level benefits of sport consumption. *Sport Management Review*, *19*, 506–519.

Doyle, J. P., Kunkel, T., & Funk, D. C. (2013). Sports spectator segmentation: Examining the differing psychological connections among spectators of leagues and teams. *International Journal of Sports Marketing & Sponsorship*, *15*, 95–111.

Drayer, J., & Dwyer, B. (2013). Perception of fantasy is not always reality: An exploratory examination into blacks' lack of participation in fantasy sports. *International Journal of Sport Management*, *14*, 81–102.

Durkheim, E. (1951). *Suicide*. (J. A. Spaulding & G. Simpson, Eds. and Trans.). Glencoe, IL: Free Press. (Original work published 1897).

Dwyer, B., Greenhalgh, G. P., & LeCrom, C. W. (2015). Exploring fan behavior: Developing a scale to measure sport eFANgelism. *Journal of Sport Management*, *29*, 642–656.

Dwyer, B., & Kim, Y. (2011). For love or money: Developing and validating a motivational scale for fantasy football participation. *Journal of Sport Management*, *25*, 70–83.

Dwyer, B., Mudrick, M., Greenhalgh, G. P., LeCrom, C. W., & Drayer, J. (2015). The tie that binds? Developing and validating a scale to measure emotional attachment to s sport team. *Sport Management Review*, *18*, 570–582.

Eagly, A. H., & Steffen, V. J. (1986). Gender and aggressive behavior: A meta-analytic review of the social psychological literature. *Psychological Bulletin*, *100*, 309–330.

Eastman, S. T., & Riggs, K. E. (1994). Televised sports and ritual: Fan experiences. *Sociology of Sport Journal*, *11*, 149–174.

eBIZMBA. (2017). Top 15 most popular sports websites. Retrieved from www.ebizmba.com/articles/sports-websites

Edmans, A., Garcia, D., & Norli, O. (2007). Sports sentiment and stock returns. *The Journal of Finance*, *62*, 1967–1998.

Edwards, H. (1973). *Sociology of sport*. Homewood, IL: The Dorsey Press.

Elias, N., & Dunning, E. (1970). The quest for excitement in unexciting societies. In G. Luschen (Ed.), *The cross-cultural analysis of sport and games*. Champaign, IL: Stipes.

Elison, J. (2005). Shame and guilt: A hundred years of apples and oranges. *New Ideas in Psychology*, *23*, 5–32.

Elling, A., van Hilvoorde, I., & Van Den Dool, R. (2014). Creating or awakening national pride through sporting success: A longitudinal study on macro effect in the Netherlands. *International Review for the Sociology of Sport*, *49*, 129–151.

End, C. M., Davis, M. C., Kretschmar, J. M., Campbell, J., Mueller, D. G., & Worthman, S. S. (2009). Missed call? Reexamination of sport fans' and nonfans' alcohol usage and alcohol-related experiences. *Sociological Spectrum*, *29*, 649–658.

End, C. M., Dietz-Uhler, B., Harrick, E. A., & Jacquemotte, L. (2002). Identifying with winners: A reexamination of sport fans' tendency to BIRG. *Journal of Applied Social Psychology*, *32*, 1017–1030.

End, C. M., Kretschmar, J., Campbell, J., Mueller, D. G., & Dietz-Uhler, B. (2003). Sport fans' attitudes toward war analogies as descriptors for sport. *Journal of Sport Behavior*, *26*, 356–367.

End, C. M., Kretschmar, J. M., & Dietz-Uhler, B. (2004). College students' perceptions of sports fandom as a social status determinant. *International Sports Journal*, *8*(1), 114–123.

End, C. M., Worthman, S. S., Foster, N. J., & Vandemark, A. P. (2009). Sports and relationships: The influence of game outcome on romantic relationships. *North American Journal of Psychology*, *11*, 37–48.

End, C. M., Meinert, J. L., Jr., Worthman, S. S., & Mauntel, G. J. (2009). Sport fan identification in obituaries. *Perceptual and Motor Skills*, *109*, 551–554.

Entertainment Software Association. (2012). *Essential facts about the computer and video game industry*. Retrieved from www.theesa.com/facts/pdfs/esa_ef_2012.pdf

Erickson, D. J., Toomey, T. L., Lenk, K. M., Kilian, G. R., & Fabian, L. E. (2011). Can we assess blood alcohol levels at attendees leaving professional sporting events? *Alcoholism: Clinical and Experimental Research*, *35*, 689–694.

Esmonde, K., Cooky, C., & Andrews, D. L. (2015). "It's supposed to be about the love of the game, not about the love of Aaron Rodgers' eyes: Challenging the exclusions of women's sports fans. *Sociology of Sport Journal*, *32*, 22–48.

Etzioni, A. (1993). *The spirit of community: Rights, responsibilities, and communitarian agenda*. New York, NY: Crown.

Evaggelinou, C., & Grekinis, D. (1998). A survey of spectators at the International Stoke Mandeville Wheelchair Games. *Adapted Physical Education Quarterly*, *15*, 25–35.

Evans, M. D. R., & Kelley, J. (2002). National pride in the developed world: Survey data from 24 nations. *International Journal of Public Opinion Research*, *14*, 303–338.

Farred, G. (2002). Long distance love: Growing up a Liverpool Football Club fan. *Journal of Sport & Social Issues*, *26*, 6–24.

Farrell, A., Fink, J., & Fields, S. (2011). Women's sport spectatorship: An exploration of men's influence. *Journal of Sport Management*, *25*, 190–201.

Feldman, R. S. (2018). *Discovering the life span* (4th ed.). New Yok, NY: Pearson.

Fenz, W. D. (1988). Learning to anticipate stressful events. *Journal of Sport & Exercise Psychology*, *10*, 223–228.

Ferguson, C. J., & Dyck, D. (2012). Paradigm change in aggression research: The time has come to retire the general aggression model. *Aggression and Violent Behavior*, *17*, 220–228.

Ferguson, J. D. (1981). Emotions in sport sociology. *International Review of Sport Sociology*, *16*, 15–23.

Fernquist, R. M. (2000). An aggregate analysis of professional sports, suicide, and homicide rates: 30 U.S. metropolitan areas, 1971–1990. *Aggression and Violent Behavior*, *5*, 329–341.

Fernquist, R. M. (2001). Geographical location, suicide, and homicide: An exploratory analysis of geographic relocation of professional sports teams in three U.S. areas and the impact on suicide and homicide rates. *Sociology of Sport On-line*, *4*, 1–12.

Fernquist, R. M. (2002). The 1994–1995 baseball and hockey strikes and their impact on suicide and homicide rates in the United States. *Archives of Suicide Research*, *6*, 103–110.

Ferreira, M., & Armstrong, K. L. (2004). An exploratory examination of attributes influencing students' decisions to attend college sport events. *Sport Marketing Quarterly*, *13*, 194–208.

Festinger, L., & Carlsmith, J. M. (1959). Cognitive consequences of forced compliance. *Journal of Abnormal and Social psychology*, *58*, 203–210.

Festinger, L., Pepitone, A., & Newcomb, T. (1952). Some consequences of deindividuation in a group. *Journal of Abnormal and Social Psychology*, *47*, 382–389.

Field, R. (2012). Stoic observers or fanatic fans? Women ice hockey spectators in 1930s North America. In K. Toffoletti & P. Mewett (Eds.), *Sport and its female fans* (pp. 13–27). New York, NY: Routledge.

FIFA.com. (2015). 2014 FIFA World Cup™ reached 3.2 billion viewers, one billion watched final. Retrieved from www.fifa.com/worldcup/news/y=2015/m=12/news=2014-fifa-world-cuptm-reached-3-2-billion-viewers-one-billion-watched-2745519.html

Filo, K., Chen, N., King, C., & Funk, D. C. (2013). Sport tourists' involvement with a destination: A stage-based examination. *Journal of Hospitality & Tourism Research*, *37*, 100–124.

Filo, K., Funk, D. C., & Alexandris, K. (2008). Exploring the impact of brand trust on the relationship between brand associations and brand loyalty in sport and fitness. *International Journal of Sport Management and Marketing*, *3*, 39–57.

Filo, K., Funk, D. C., & Hornby, G. (2009). The role of web site content on motive and attitude change for sport events. *Journal of Sport Management*, *23*, 21–40.

Fink, J. S. (2016). Hiding in plain sight: The embedded nature of sexism is sport. *Journal of Sport Management*, *30*, 1–7.

Fink, J. S., & Parker, H. M. (2009). Spectator motives: Why do we watch when our favorite team is not playing? *Sport Marketing Quarterly*, *18*, 210–217.

Fink, J. S., Parker, H. M., Brett, M., & Higgins, J. (2009). Off-field behavior of athletes and team identification: Using social identity theory and balance theory to explain fan reactions. *Journal of Sport Management*, *23*, 142–155.

Fink, J. S., Trail, G. T., & Anderson, D. F. (2002). An examination of team identification: Which motives are most salient to its existence? *International Sports Journal, 6*, 195–207.

Fischer, S., Anderson, K. G., & Smith, G. T. (2004). Coping with distress by eating or drinking: Role of trait urgency and expectancies. *Psychology of Addictive Behaviors, 18*, 269–274.

Fisher, R. J. (1998). Group-derived consumption: The role of similarity and attractiveness in identification with a favorite sports team. *Advances in Consumer Research, 25*, 283–288.

Fisher, R. J., & Wakefield, K. (1998). Factors leading to group identification: A field study of winners and losers. *Psychology & Marketing, 15*, 23–40.

Flosi, N. (2016, November 16). Cubs World Series celebration ranks as 7th largest gathering in human history. *Fox 32*. Retrieved from www.fox32chicago.com/news/local/cubs-world-series-celebration-ranks-as-7th-largest-gathering-in-human-history

Foran, H. M., & O'Leary, K. D. (2008). Alcohol and intimate partner violence: A meta-analytic review. *Clinical Psychology Review, 28*, 1222–1234.

Foster, W. M., Hyatt, C. G., & Julien, M. (2012). "Pronger you ignorant ape . . . I hope you fall off space mountain!" A study of the institutional work of sport fans. In A. C. Earnheardt, P. M. Haridakis, & B. S. Hugenberg (Eds.), *Sports fans, identity and socialization: Exploring the fandemonium* (pp. 119–133). Lanham, MD: Lexington.

Foundation for Child Development. (1977). *National survey of children*. New York, NY: Foundation for Child Development.

Franco, F. M., & Maass, A. (1996). Implicit versus explicit strategies of out-group discrimination: The role of intentional control in biased language use and reward allocation. *Journal of Language and Social Psychology, 15*, 335–359.

Frank, M. G., & Gilovich, T. (1988). The dark side of self- and social perception: Black uniforms and aggression in professional sports. *Journal of Personality and Social Psychology, 54*, 74–85.

Frankl, V. E. (1963). *Man's search for meaning: An introduction to logotherapy*. New York, NY: Washington Square Press.

Frawley, S., & Cush, A. (2011). Major sport events and participation legacy: The case of the 2003 Rugby World Cup. *Managing Leisure, 16*, 65–76.

Freischlag, J., & Hardin, D. (1975). The effects of social class and school achievement on the composition of sport crowds. *Sport Sociology Bulletin, 4*, 36–46.

Fromm, E. (1941). *Escape from freedom*. New York, NY: Holt, Rinehart, & Winston.

Funk, D. C. (1998). *Fan loyalty: The structure and stability of an individual's loyalty toward an athletic team* (Electronic Thesis or Dissertation). Retrieved from https://etd.ohiolink.edu/

Funk, D. C., Beaton, A., & Alexandris, K. (2012). Sport consumer motivation: Autonomy and control orientations that regulate fan behaviors. *Sport Management Review, 15*, 355–367.

Funk, D. C., Beaton, A., & Pritchard, M. (2011). The stage-based development of physically active leisure: A recreational golf context. *Journal of Leisure Research*, *43*, 268–289.

Funk, D. C., Filo, K., Beaton, A. A., & Pritchard, M. (2009). Measuring the motives of sport event attendance: Bridging the academic-practitioner divide to understanding behavior. *Sport Marketing Quarterly*, *18*, 126–138.

Funk, D. C., & James, J. D. (2001). The psychological continuum model: A conceptual framework for understanding an individual's psychological connection to sport. *Sport Management Review*, *4*, 119–150.

Funk, D. C., & James, J. D. (2006). Consumer loyalty: The meaning of attachment in the development of sport team allegiance. *Journal of Sport Management*, *20*, 189–217.

Funk, D. C., & James, J. D. (2016). The psychological continuum model: An evolutionary perspective. In G. B. Cunningham, J. S. Fink, & A. Doherty (Eds.), *Routledge handbook of theory in sport management* (pp. 247–261). New York, NY: Routledge.

Funk, D. C., Mahony, D. F., Nakazawa, M., & Hirakawa, S. (2001). Development of the Sport Interest Inventory (SII): Implications for measuring unique consumer motives at team sporting events. *International Journal of Sports Marketing and Sponsorship*, *3*, 38–63.

Funk, D. C., Mahony, D. F., & Ridinger, L. L. (2002). Characterizing consumer motivation as individual difference factors: Augmenting the Sport Interest Inventory (SII) to explain level of spectator support. *Sport Marketing Quarterly*, *11*, 33–43.

Funk, D. C., Ridinger, L. L., & Moorman, A. M. (2003). Understanding consumer support: Extending the Sport Interest Inventory (SII) to examine individual differences among women's professional sport consumers. *Sport Management Review*, *6*, 1–32.

Gaines, C. (2015, May 22). The NFL and Major League Baseball are the most attended sports leagues in the world. *Business Insider*. Retrieved from www.businessinsider.com/attendance-sports-leagues-world-2015-5

Galanis, S. (2015, October 15). Fan shot in AT&T stadium parking lot after Cowboys-Patriots game dies. *NESN*. Retrieved from http://nesn.com/2015/10/fan-shot-in-att-stadium-parking-lot-after-cowboys-patriots-game-dies/

Game plans. (1997, September). *Reader's Digest*, p. 91.

Gan, S-L., Tuggle, C. A., Mitrook, M. A., Coussement, S. H., & Zillmann, D. (1997). The thrill of a close game: Who enjoys it and who doesn't? *Journal of Sport & Social Issues*, *21*, 53–64.

Gantz, W. (1981). An exploration of viewing motives and behaviors associated with television sports. *Journal of Broadcasting*, *25*, 263–275.

Gantz, W., Wang, Z., & Bradley, S. D. (2006). Televised NFL games, the family, and domestic violence. In A. A. Raney & J. Bryant (Eds.), *Handbook of sports and media* (pp. 365–381). Mahwah, NJ: Lawrence Erlbaum Associates.

Gantz, W., Wang, Z., Paul, B., & Potter, R. F. (2006). Sports versus all comers: Comparing TV sports fans with fans of other programming genres. *Journal of Broadcasting & Electronic Media*, *50*, 95–118.

Gantz, W., & Wenner, L. A. (1995). Fanship and the television sports viewing experience. *Sociology of Sport Journal*, *12*, 56–74.

Gantz, W., Wenner, L. A., Carrico, C., & Knorr, M. (1995a). Assessing the football widow hypothesis: A co-orientation study of the role of televised sports in long-standing relationships. *Journal of Sport & Social Issues*, *19*, 352–376.

Gantz, W., Wenner, L. A., Carrico, C., & Knorr, M. (1995b). Televised sports and marital relationships. *Sociology of Sport Journal*, *12*, 306–323.

Gargone, D. (2016). A study of the fan motives for varying levels of team identity and team loyalty of college football fans. *The Sport Journal*, *19*.

Gau, L-S., & Kim, J-C. (2011). The influences of cultural values on spectators' sport attitudes and team identification: An east-west perspective. *Social Behavior and Personality*, *39*, 587–596.

Gayton, W. F., Coffin, J. L., & Hearns, J. (1998). Further validation of the sports spectator identification scale. *Perceptual and Motor Skills*, *87*, 1137–1138.

Geen, R. G. (1990). *Human aggression*. Pacific Grove, CA: Brooks/Cole.

Geen, R. G., & McCown, E. J. (1984). Effects of noise and attack on aggression and physiological arousal. *Motivation and Emotion*, *8*, 231–241.

Gencer, R., Kiremitci, O., & Boyacioglu, H. (2011). Spectator motives and points of attachment: An investigation on professional basketball. *Journal of Human Kinetics*, *30*, 189–196.

Giamatti, A. B. (1989). *Take time for paradise: Americans and their games*. New York, NY: Summit.

Gilbert, B., & Twyman, L. (1984). Violence: Out of hand in the stands. In D. S. Eitzen (Ed.), *Sport in contemporary society* (pp. 112–212). New York, NY: St. Martin's Press.

Gilbert, D. T., Driver-Linn, E., & Wilson, T. D. (2002). The trouble with Vronsky: Impact bias in the forecasting of future affective states. In L. F. Barrett & P. Salovey (Eds.), *The wisdom in feeling: Psychological processes in emotional intelligence* (pp. 114–143). New York, NY: Guilford Press.

Giuliano, T. A., Turner, K. L., Lundquist, J. C., & Knight, J. L. (2007). Gender and the selection of public athlete role models. *Journal of Sport Behavior*, *30*, 161–198.

Giulianotti, R. (2002). Supporters, followers, fans, and flaneurs: A taxonomy of spectator identities in football. *Journal of Sport & Social Issues*, *26*, 25–46.

Gkorezis, P., Bellou, V., Xanthopolou, D., Bakker, A. B., & Tsiftsis, A. (2016). Linking football team performance to fans' work engagement and job performance: Test of a spillover model. *Journal of Occupational and Organizational Psychology*, *89*, 791–812.

Gloster, R. (1999, November 24). Player cited, fans arrested after snowball attack. *The Paducah Sun*, p. 4B.

Glover, T. D., Parry, D. C., & Shinew, K. J. (2005). Building relationships, accessing resources: Mobilizing social capital in community garden contexts. *Journal of Leisure Research*, *37*, 450–474.

Gmelch, G., & San Antonio, P. M. (1998). Groupies and American baseball. *Journal of Sport & Social Issues*, *22*, 32–45.

Goldberg, D. T. (1998). Sports, talk radio, and the death of democracy. *Journal of Sport & Social Issues*, *22*, 212–223.

Goldman, M. M., Chadwick, S., Funk, D. C., & Wocke, A. (2016). I am distinctive when I belong: Meeting the need for optimal distinctiveness through team identification. *International Journal of Sport Management and Marketing*, *16*, 198–220.

Goldstein, J. H., & Arms, R. L. (1971). Effects of observing athletic contests on hostility. *Sociometry*, *34*, 83–90.

Goodger, J. M., & Goodger, B. C. (1989). Excitement and representation: Toward a sociological explanation of the significance of sport in modern society. *Quest*, *41*, 257–272.

Goranson, R. E. (1980). Sports violence and the catharsis hypothesis. In P. Klavora (Ed.), *Psychological and sociological factors in sport* (pp. 131–138). Toronto: University of Toronto Press.

Gordon, B. S., & Arney, J. (2017). Investigation the negative fan behaviors of a branded collegiate basketball student section. *Journal of Amateur Sport*, *3*(2), 82–108.

Government of Canada. (2001). *Building Canada through sport: Towards a Canadian sport policy*. Quebec, Canada: Government of Canada.

Green, C. D. (2009). Colemean Roberts Griffith: "Father" of North American sport psychology. In C. D. Green & L. T. Benjamin (Eds.), *Psychology gets in the game: Sport, mind, and behavior, 1880–1960*. Lincoln, NB: University of Nebraska Press.

Greenwood, P. B., Kanters, M. A., & Casper, J. M. (2006). Sport fan team identification formation in mid-level professional sport. *European Sport Management Quarterly*, *6*, 253–265.

Grieve, F. G., Shoenfelt, E. L., Wann, D. L., & Zapalac, R. K. (2009). The puck stops here: A brief report of National Hockey League fans' reactions to the 2004–2005 lockout. *International Journal of Sport Management and Marketing*, *5*, 101–114.

Grieve, F. G., Wann, D. L., Zapalac, R. K., Cyr, C. Y., & Lanter, J. R. (in press). Factors associated with college students' identification with high school football teams. *Journal of Sport Behavior*.

Grieve, F. G., Zapalac, R. K., Visek, A. J., Wann, D. L., Parker, P. M., Partridge, J., & Lanter, J. R. (2009). Identification with multiple sporting teams: How many teams do sport fans follow? *Journal of Contemporary Athletics*, *3*, 283–294.

Grieve, P. G., & Hogg, M. A. (1999). Subjective uncertainty and intergroup discrimination in the minimal group situation. *Personality and Social Psychology Bulletin*, *25*, 926–940.

Griffith, C. R. (1938). *General report, Coleman Roberts Griffith papers*. Urbana & Champaign, IL: University of Illinois.

Griggs, G., Leflay, K., & Groves, M. (2012). "Just watching it again now still gives me goose bumps!" Examining the mental postcards of sport spectators. *Sociology of Sport Journal*, *29*, 89–101.

Groeneman, S. (2017). *American's sports fans and their teams: Who roots for whom and why*. Lexington, KY: Seabird Press.

Grossman, E. (2017, December 6). NFL violence, on full display Monday night, should be more off-putting to fans than players kneeling during national anthem. *New York Daily News*. Retrieved from www.nydailynews.com/sports/football/nfl-violence-off-putting-anthem-kneeling-article-1.3678673

Grove, J. R., Hanrahan, S. J., & McInman, A. (1991). Success/failure bias in attributions across involvement categories in sport. *Personality and Social Psychology Bulletin*, *17*, 93–97.

Grove, S. J., Pickett, G. M., & Dodder, R. A. (1982). Spectatorship among a collegiate sample: An exploratory investigation. In M. Etzel & J. Gaski (Eds.), *Applying marketing technology to spectator sports* (pp. 26–40). South Bend, IN: University of Notre Dame Press.

Gunter, B. (2006). Sport, violence, and the media. In A. A. Raney & J. Bryant (Eds.), *Handbook of sports and media* (pp. 353–364). Mahwah, NJ: Lawrence Erlbaum Associates.

Guttmann, A. (1980). On the alleged dehumanization of the sports spectator. *Journal of Popular Culture*, *14*, 275–282.

Guttmann, A. (1986). *Sports spectators*. New York, NY: Columbia University Press.

Guttmann, A. (1996). *The erotic in sports*. New York, NY: Columbia University Press.

Gwinner, K., & Swanson, S. R. (2003). A model of fan identification: Antecedents and sponsorship outcomes. *Journal of Services Marketing*, *17*, 275–294.

Haag, P. (1996). The 50,000-watt sports bar: Talk radio and the ethic of the fan. *South Atlantic Quarterly*, *95*, 453–470.

Hagen, P. (2015, December 9). MLB recommends netting between dugouts. *MLB.com*. Retrieved from www.mlb.com/news/mlb-issues-recommendations-on-netting/c-159233076

Hallmann, K., Breuer, C., & Kuhnreich, B. (2013). Happiness, pride, and elite sporting success: What population segments gain most from national athletic achievements? *Sport Management Review*, *16*, 226–235.

Hansen, H., & Gauthier, R. (1989). Factors affecting attendance at professional sport events. *Journal of Sport Management*, *3*, 15–32.

Hardaway, F. (1976). Foul play: Sports metaphors as public doublespeak. *College English*, *38*, 78–82.

Hardin, M., & Whiteside, E. (2012). How do women talk sports? Women sports fans in a blog community. In K. Toffoletti & P. Mewett (Eds.), *Sport and its female fans* (pp. 152–168). New York, NY: Routledge.

Hare, R. D. (1993). *Without conscience: The disturbing world of the psychopaths among us*. New York, NY: Pocket Books.

Harrington, C. L., & Bielby, D. D. (2010). A life course perspective on fandom. *International Journal of Cultural Studies*, *13*, 429–450.

Harris, J. C. (1986). Athletic exemplars in context: General exemplar selection patterns in relation to sex, race, and age. *Quest*, *38*, 95–115.

Harris, J. C. (1994). *Athletes and the American hero dilemma*. Champaign, IL: Human Kinetics.

Harris, J. C. (1998). Civil society, physical activity, and the involvement of sport sociologists in the preparation of physical activity professionals. *Sociology of Sport Journal*, *15*, 138–153.

Harris, S. J. (1981, November 3). Sport is new opium of the people. *Democrat and Chronicle*, p. 3B.

Harrison, L. K., Carroll, D., Burns, V. E., Corkill, A. R., Harrison, C. M., Ring, C., & Drayson, M. (2000). Cardiovascular and secretory immunoglobulin A reactions in humorous, exciting, and didactic film presentations. *Biological Psychology*, *52*, 113–126.

Hart, J. (2016, October 28). Addicted to losing: Some Cubs fans want their team to lose World Series, survey shows. *Yahoo Sports*. Retrieved from https://sports.yahoo.com/news/addicted-to-losing-some-cubs-fans-want-their-team-to-lose-world-series-survey-shows-161752141.html

Harter, S. (1993). Causes and consequences of low self-esteem in children and adolescents. In R. F. Baumeister (Ed.), *Self-esteem: The puzzle of low self-regard* (pp. 87–116). New York, NY: Plenum.

Hartmann, D. (1996). The politics of race and sport: Resistance and domination in the 1968 African American Olympic protest movement. *Ethnic and Racial Studies*, *19*, 548–566.

Hastorf, A. H., & Cantril, H. (1954). They saw a game: A case study. *Journal of Abnormal and Social Psychology*, *49*, 129–134.

Havard, C. T. (2014). Glory out of reflected failure: The examination of how rivalry affects sport fans. *Sport Management Review*, *17*, 243–253.

Havard, C. T., Gray, D. P., Gould, J., Sharp, L. A., & Schaffer, J. J. (2013). Development and validation of the Sport Rivalry Fan Perception Scale (SRFPS). *Journal of Sport Behavior*, *36*, 45–65.

Havard, C. T., Shapiro, S. L., & Ridinger, L. L. (2016). Who's our rival? Investigating the influence of a new intercollegiate football program on rivalry perceptions. *Journal of Sport Behavior*, *39*, 385–408.

Havard, C. T., Wann, D. L., & Grieve, F. G. (in press). Rivalry versus hate: Measuring the influence of promotional titles and logos on fan rival perceptions. *Journal of Applied Sport Management*.

Havard, C. T., Wann, D. L., & Ryan, T. D. (2013). Investigating the impact of conference realignment on rivalry in intercollegiate athletics. *Sport Marketing Quarterly*, *22*, 224–234.

Havard, C. T., Wann, D. L., & Ryan, T. D. (2017). Reinvestigating the impact of conference realignment on rivalry in intercollegiate athletics. *Journal of Applied Sport Management*, *9*(2), 25–36.

Havard, C. T., Wann, D. L., & Ryan, T. D. (2018). I love seeing them lose: Investigating fan perceptions and behaviors toward rival teams. In L. Wang (Ed.), *Exploring the rise of fandom in contemporary consumer culture* (pp. 102–125). Hershey, PA: IGI Global.

Havitz, M. E., & Dimanche, F. (1997). Leisure involvement revisited: Conceptual conundrums and measurement advances. *Journal of Leisure Research*, *29*, 245–278.

Hawkins, D. I., Best, R. J., & Coney, K. A. (2004). Consumer behavior and marketing strategy. In D. I. Hawkins, R. J. Best, & K. A. Coney (Eds.),

Consumer behavior: Building marketing strategy (pp. 5–35). New York, NY: McGraw-Hill Irwin.

Hay, R. D., & Rao, C. P. (1982). Factors affecting attendance at football games. In M. Etzel & J. Gaski (Eds.), *Applying marketing technology to spectator sports* (pp. 65–76). South Bend, IN: University of Notre Dame Press.

Healy, A. J., Malhotra, N., & Mo, C. H. (2010). Irrelevant events affect voters' evaluation of government performance. *Proceedings of the National Academy of Science, 107*, 12804–12809.

Heere, B., & James, J. D. (2007). Sports teams and their communities: Examining the influence of external group identities on team identity. *Journal of Sport Management, 21*, 319–337.

Heere, B., & Katz, M. (2014). Still undefeated: Exploring the dimensions of team identity among fans of a new college football team. *Journal of Applied Sport Management, 6*, 25–47.

Heinegg, P. (1985). Philosopher in the playground: Notes on the meaning of sport. In D. L. Vanderwerken & S. K. Wertz (Eds.), *Sport inside out* (pp. 455–458). Fort Worth, TX: Christian University Press.

Hemphill, D. A. (1995). Revisioning sport spectatorism. *Journal of the Philosophy of Sport, 22*, 48–60.

Hennessy, D. A., & Schwartz, S. (2007). Personal predictors of spectator aggression at Little League Baseball games. *Violence and Victims, 22*, 205–215.

Hennessy, D. A., & Schwartz, S. (2012). The influence of instrumental motives and daily hassles on spectator aggression at Little league Baseball games. In B. M. O'Connor (Ed.), *Social and psychological issues in sports* (pp. 95–114). Hauppauge, NY: Nova.

Higgs, R. J. (1982). *Sports: A reference guide*. Westport, CT: Greenwood Press.

Higgs, R. J. (1995). *God in the stadium: Sports and religion in America*. Lexington, KY: University Press of Kentucky.

Higgs, R. J., & Braswell, M. C. (2004). *An unholy alliance: The sacred and modern sports*. Macon, GA: Mercer University Press.

High school team opts to take forfeit to protect students. (1991, November 1). *Democrat and Chronicle*, p. D4.

Hillmann, C. H., Cuthbert, B. N., Bradley, M. M., & Lang, P. J. (2004). Motivated engagement to appetitive and aversive fanship cues: Psychophysiological responses of rival sport fans. *Journal of Sport and Exercise Psychology, 26*, 338–351.

Hillmann, C. H., Cuthbert, B. N., Cauraugh, J., Schupp, H. T., Bradley, M. M., & Lang, P. J. (2000). Psychophysiological responses of sport fans. *Motivation and Emotion, 24*, 13–28.

Hirt, E. R., Zillmann, D., Erickson, G. A., & Kennedy, C. (1992). Costs and benefits of allegiance: Changes in fans' self-ascribed competencies after team victory versus defeat. *Journal of Personality and Social Psychology, 63*, 724–738.

Hoch, P. (1972). *Rip off the big game: The exploitation of sport by the power elite*. New York, NY: Anchor Books.

Hockey dad found guilty. (2002, July). *CBS*. Retrieved from www.cbsnews.com/news/hockey-dad-found-guilty/

Hofacre, S. (1994). The women's audience in professional indoor soccer. *Sport Marketing Quarterly*, *3*, 25–27.

Hoffman, S. J. (Ed.). (1992). *Sport and religion*. Champaign, IL: Human Kinetics.

Hofstede, G. (2001). *Culture's consequences: Comparing values, behaviors, institutions, and organizations across nations*. Thousand Oaks, CA: Sage Publishers.

Hogg, M. A., & Abrams, D. (1988). *Social identifications: A social psychology of intergroup relations and group processes*. New York, NY: Routledge.

Hogg, M. A., & Abrams, D. (1993). Towards a single-process uncertainly-reduction model of social motivation in groups. In M. A. Hogg & D. Abrams (Eds.), *Group motivation: Social psychological perspectives* (pp. 173–190). Hemel Hempstead, UK: Harvester Wheatsheaf.

Holt, D. B. (1995). How consumers consume: A typology of consumption practices. *Journal of Consumer Research*, *22*, 1–16.

Holt-Lunstad, J., Smith, T. B., & Layton, J. B. (2010). Social relationships and mortality risk: A meta-analytic review. *PLOS Medicine*, *7*, 1–20.

Hong, E. (2011). Elite sport and nation-building in South Korea: South Korea as the dark horse in global elite sport. *The International Journal of the History of Sport*, *28*, 977–989.

Hong, J., McDonald, M. A., Yoon, C., & Fujimoto, J. (2005). Motivation for Japanese baseball fans' interest in Major League Baseball. *International Journal for Sport Management and Marketing*, *1*, 141–154.

Hoogland, C. E., Schurtz, D. R., Cooper, C. M., Combs, D. J. Y., Brown, E. G., & Smith, R. H. (2015). The joy or pain and the pain of joy: In-group identification predicts schadenfreude and gluckschmerz following rival groups' fortunes. *Motivation and Emotion*, *39*, 260–281.

Hooligans sour World Cup. (1998, June 23). *Democrat and Chronicle*, p. A1.

Hoosier rebellion? (1998, May 7). *USA Today*, p. C7.

Hornsey, M. J., & Jetten, J. (2004). The individual within the group: Balancing the need to belong with the need to be different. *Personality and Social Psychology Review*, *8*, 248–264.

Howard, G. E. (1912). Social psychology of the spectator. *American Journal of Sociology*, *18*, 33–50.

Howard, J. W., & Rothbart, M. (1980). Social categorization and memory for ingroup and out-group behavior. *Journal of Personality and Social Psychology*, *38*, 301–310.

Howlett, D. (1998, June 12). Chicago cops know the drill for Bulls titles. *USA Today*, p. C4.

Hoye, R., & Nicholson, M. (2008). Locating social capital in sport policy. In M. Nicholson & R. Hoye (Eds.), *Sport and social capital* (pp. 69–91). New York, NY: Elsevier.

Huang, K., & Dixon, M. A. (2013). Examining the financial impact of alcohol sales on football game days: A case study of a major football program. *Journal of Sport Management*, *27*, 207–216.

Hughes, R. H. (1987). Response to "An Observer's View of Sport Sociology". *Sociology of Sport Journal*, *4*, 137–139.

Hunt, K. A., Bristol, T., & Bashaw, R. E. (1999). A conceptual approach to classifying sports fans. *Journal of Services Marketing, 13*, 439–452.

Hyatt, C. G., & Andrijiw, A. M. (2008). How people raised and living in Ontario became fans of a non-local National Hockey League team. *International Journal of Sport Management and Marketing, 4*, 338–355.

Hyatt, C. G., & Foster, W. M. (2015). Using identity work theory to understand the de-escalation of fandom: A study of former fans of National Hockey League teams. *Journal of Sport Management, 29*, 443–460.

Hyatt, C. G., Kerwin, S., Hoeber, L., & Sveinson, K. (2017, June). *Understanding the intersection between sport fandom and parenting.* Paper presented at the annual meeting of the North American Society for Sport Management, Denver, CO.

Inoue, Y., Berg, B. K., & Chelladurai, P. (2015). Spectator sport and population health: A scoping study. *Journal of Sport Management, 29*, 705–725.

Inoue, Y., Funk, D. C., Wann, D. L., Yoshida, M., & Nakazawa, M. (2015). Team identification and postdisaster social well-being: The mediating role of social support. *Group Dynamics: Theory, Research, and Practice, 19*, 31–44.

Inoue, Y., & Havard, C. T. (2014). Determinants and consequences of the perceived social impact of a sport event. *Journal of Sport Management, 28*, 295–310.

Inoue, Y., Sato, M., Filo, K., Du, J., & Funk, D. C. (in press). Sport spectatorship and life satisfaction: A multicountry investigation. *Journal of Sport Management.*

Investigators. (2017, April 6). Investigators looking into hundreds of threats against official who worked Kentucky loss. *ESPN*. Retrieved from www.espn.com/mens-college-basketball/story/_/id/19087341/investigator-eyeing-100s-threats-ncaa-official

Irwin, J. (1977). *Scenes.* Beverly Hills, CA: Sage Publishers.

Irwin, R. L., Southall, R. M., & Sutton, W. A. (2007). Pentagon of sport sales training: A 21st century sport sales training model. *Sport Management Education Journal, 1*, 18–39.

Iso-Ahola, S. E., & Hatfield, B. (1986). *Psychology of sports: A social psychological approach.* Dubuque, IA: Brown.

Ito, T. A., Miller, N., & Pollock, V. E. (1996). Alcohol and aggression: A meta-analysis on the moderating effects of inhibitory cues, triggering events, and self-focused attention. *Psychological Bulletin, 120*, 60–82.

Iwasaki, Y., & Havitz, M. E. (1998). A path analytic model of the relationships between involvement, psychological commitment, and loyalty. *Journal of Leisure Research, 30*, 256–280.

Izod, J. (1996). Television sport and the sacrificial hero. *Journal of Sport & Social Issues, 22*, 173–193.

Jackson, S. J., & Andrews, D. L. (2004). Aggressive marketing: Interrogating the use of violence in sport-related advertising. In L. R. Kahle & C. Riley (Eds.), *Sports marketing and the psychology of marketing communication* (pp. 307–325). Mahwah, NJ: Lawrence Erlbaum Associates.

Jaffe, Y., & Yinon, Y. (1983). Collective aggression: The group-individual paradigm in the study of collective antisocial behavior. In H. H. Blumberg et al.

(Eds.), *Small groups and social interaction* (pp. 267–275). London: John Wiley & Sons Ltd.

James, J. D. (1997). *Becoming a sports fan: Understanding cognitive development and socialization in the development of fan loyalty* (Electronic Thesis or Dissertation). Retrieved from https://etd.ohiolink.edu/

James, J. D. (2001). The role of cognitive development and socialization in the initial development of team loyalty. *Leisure Sciences*, *23*, 233–262.

James, J. D. (2002). Women's and men's Basketball: A comparison of sport consumption motivations. *Women in Sport and Physical Activity Journal*, *11*, 141–170.

James, J. D. (2016). Sport fan socialization: Becoming loyal to a team. In G. B. Cunningham, J. S. Fink, & A. Doherty (Eds.), *Routledge handbook of theory in sport management* (pp. 263–271). New York, NY: Routledge.

James, J. D., Delia, E. B., & Wann, D. L. (in press). "No" is not "Low": Improving the assessment of sport team identification. *Sport Marketing Quarterly*.

James, J. D., Fujimoto, J., Ross, S. D., & Matsuoka, H. (2009). Motives of United States and Japanese professional baseball consumers and level of team identification. *International Journal of Sport Management and Marketing*, *6*, 351–366.

James, J. D., Kolbe, R., & Trail, G. (2002). Psychological connection to a new sport team: Building or maintaining the consumer base. *Sport Marketing Quarterly*, *11*, 215–225.

James, J. D., & Ridinger, L. (2002). Female and male sport fans: A comparison of sport consumption motives. *Journal of Sport Behavior*, *25*, 260–278.

James, J. D., & Ross, S. D. (2004). Comparing sport consumer motivations across multiple sports. *Sport Marketing Quarterly*, *13*, 17–25.

James, J., & Trail, G. T. (2008). The relationship between team identification and sport consumption intentions. *International Journal of Sport Management*, *9*, 427–440.

James, J., Trail, G., Wann, D., Zhang, J., & Funk, D. (2006, June). *Bringing parsimony to the study of sport consumer motivations: Development of the Big 5*. Paper presented annual meeting of the North American Society for Sport Management, Kansas City, MO.

Jamieson, J. P. (2010). The home field advantage in athletics: A meta-analysis. *Journal of Applied Social Psychology*, *40*, 1819–1848.

Jang, W., Ko, Y. J., Wann, D. L., & Kim, D. (in press). Does spectatorship increase happiness? The energy perspective. *Journal of Sport Management*.

Jang, W., Wann, D. L., & Ko, Y. J. (in press). Influence of team identification, game outcome, and game process on sport consumer's happiness. *Sport Management Review*.

Jang, W., Ko, Y. J., Wann, D. L., & Chang, Y. (in press). The relative effects of game outcome and process on fans' media consumption experiences. *European Sport Management Quarterly*.

Jensen, J. A., Turner, B. A., Delia, E., James, J., Greenwell, T. C., McEvoy, C., Ross, S., Seifried, C., & Walsh, P. (2016). Forty years of BIRGing: New perspectives on Cialdini's seminal studies. *Journal of Sport Management, 30*, 149–161.

Jetten, J., Haslam, C., & Haslam, S. A. (Eds.). (2012). *The social cure: Identity, health, and well-being*. New York, NY: Psychology Press.

Jewell, R. T. (2012). Aggressive play and demand for English Premier League football. In R. T. Jewell (Ed.), *Violence and aggression in sporting contests: Economics, history and policy* (pp. 113–131). New York, NY: Springer-Verlag.

Jewell, R. T., Moti, A., & Coates, D. (2012). A brief history of violence and aggression in spectator sports. In R. T. Jewell (Ed.), *Violence and aggression in sporting contests: Economics, history and policy* (pp. 11–26). New York, NY: Springer-Verlag.

Jhaveri, H. (2017, May 30). Nashville Predators fan who threw catfish on the ice arrested for 'possessing instruments of a crime'. *USA Today Sports*. Retrieved from http://ftw.usatoday.com/2017/05/nashville-predators-fan-who-threw-catfish-on-the-ice-arrested-for-possessing-instruments-of-a-crime

Johnson, K. (1996, January 23). Hoosier hoop dreams. *USA Today*, pp. 1A–2A.

Joiner, T. E., Jr., Hollar, D., & Van Orden, K. (2006). On Buckeyes, Gators, Super Bowl Sunday, and the Miracle on Ice: "Pulling together" is associated with lower suicide rates. *Journal of Social and Clinical Psychology, 25*, 179–195.

Jones, I. (1997). A further examination of the factors influencing current identification with a sports team, a response to Wann et al. (1996). *Perceptual and Motor Skills, 85*, 257–258.

Jones, J. M. (2015, June 17). As industry grows, percentage of U.S. sports fans steady. *Gallup*. Retrieved from www.gallup.com/poll/183689/industry-grows-percentage-sports-fans-steady.aspx

Jones, K. W. (2008). Female fandom: Identity, sexism, and men's professional football in England. *Sociology of Sport Journal, 25*, 516–537.

Jones, M. B. (2013). The home advantage in individual sports: An augmented review. *Psychology of Sport and Exercise, 14*, 397–404.

Jones, M. V., Coffee, P., Sheffield, D., Yanguez, M., & Barker, J. B. (2012). Just a game? Changes in English and Spanish soccer fans' emotions in the 2010 World Cup. *Psychology of Sport and Exercise, 13*, 162–169.

Jones, R. P., Cox, D., & Navarro-Rivera, J. (2014, January 16). Half of American fans see supernatural forces at play in sports. *PRRI*. Retrieved from www.prri.org/research/jan-2014-sports-poll/

Judson, K. M., & Carpenter, P. (2005). Assessing a university community's identification to sport in a changing climate. *Sport Marketing Quarterly, 14*, 217–226.

Kagan, J. (1958). The concept of identification. *Psychological Review, 65*, 296–305.

Kain, E. (2015, January 15). The top ten best-selling video games of 2014. *Forbes*. Retrieved from www.forbes.com/sites/erikkain/2015/01/19/the-top-ten-best-selling-video-games-of-2014/#7a5bc2cf82cf

Kalist, D. E. (2010). Terror alert levels and Major League Baseball attendance. *International Journal of Sport Finance*, *5*, 181.

Kang, C., Lee, J., & Bennett, G. (2014). Comparative analysis of sport consumer motivation affecting sport consumption behavior between American and Asian international students. *International Journal of Sport Management*, *15*, 286–310.

Kang, S. J., Ha, J-P., & Hambrick, M. E. (2015). A mixed method approach to exploring the motives of sport-related mobile applications among college students. *Journal of Sport Management*, *29*, 272–290.

Karg, A. J., & McDonald, H. (2011). Fantasy sport participation as a complement to traditional sport consumption. *Sport Management Review*, *14*, 327–346.

Katz, M., & Heere, B. (2016). New team, new fans: A longitudinal examination of team identification as a driver of university identification. *Journal of Sport Management*, *30*, 135–148.

Keaton, S. A., & Gearhart, C. C. (2014). Identity formation, identify strength, and self-categorization as predictors of affective and psychological outcomes: A model reflecting sport team fans' responses to highlights and lowlights of a college football season. *Communication & Sport*, *2*, 363–385.

Keaton, S. A., Gearhart, C. C., & Honeycutt, J. M. (2014). Fandom and psychological enhancement: Effects of sport team identification and imagined interactions on self-esteem and management of social behaviors. *Imagination, Cognition, and Personality*, *33*, 251–269.

Keaton, S. A., Watanabe, N. M., & Gearhart, C. C. (2015). A comparison of college football and NASCAR consumer profiles: Identity formation and spectatorship motivation. *Sport Marketing Quarterly*, *24*, 43–55.

Kelley, S. W., & Tian, K. (2004). Fanatical consumption: An investigation of the behavior of sports fans through textual data. In L. R. Kahle & C. Riley (Eds.), *Sports marketing and the psychology of marketing communication* (pp. 27–65). Mahwah, NJ: Lawrence Erlbaum Associates.

Kenyon, G. S. (1968). A conceptual model for characterizing activity. *Research Quarterly*, *39*, 96–105.

Kenyon, G. S., & McPherson, B. D. (1974). An approach to the study of sport socialization. *International Review of Sport Sociology*, *1*, 127–138.

Kermer, D. A., Driver-Linn, E., Wilson, T. D., & Gilbert, D. T. (2006). Loss aversion is an affective forecasting error. *Psychological Science*, *17*, 649–653.

Kerr, J. H. (1994). *Understanding soccer hooliganism*. Buckingham, England: Open University Press.

Kerr, J. H., Wilson, G. V., Nakamura, I., & Sudo, Y. (2005). Emotional dynamics of soccer fans at winning and losing games. *Personality and Individual Differences*, *38*, 1855–1866.

Kerstetter, D. L., & Kovich, G. M. (1997). An involvement profile of Division I women's basketball spectators. *Journal of Sport Management*, *11*, 234–249.

Kessler, M., & Brady, E. (2004, September 15). Tension mounts with fans. *USA Today*, p. 3C.

Ketturat, C., Frisch, J. U., Ullrich, J., Hausser, J. A., van Dick, R., & Mojzisch, A. (2016). Disaggregating within and between-person effects of social identification on subjective and endocrinological stress reactions in a real-life stress situation. *Personality and Social Psychology Bulletin*, *42*, 147–160.

Keyes, C. L. M. (1998). Social well-being. *Social Psychology Quarterly*, *61*, 121–140.

Kian, E. M., Clavio, G., Vincent, J., & Shaw, S. D. (2011). Homophobic and sexist yet uncontested: Examining football fan postings on Internet message boards. *Journal of Homosexuality*, *58*, 680–699.

Kilduff, G. J., Elfenbein, H. A., & Staw, B. M. (2010). The psychology of rivalry: A relationally dependent analysis of competition. *Academy of Management Journal*, *53*, 943–969.

Kim, J. H., Allison, S. T., Eylon, D., Goethals, G. R., Markus, M. J., Hindle, S. M., & McGuire, H. A. (2008). Rooting for (and then abandoning) the underdog. *Journal of Applied Social Psychology*, *38*, 2550–2573.

Kim, J. W., James, J. D., & Kim, Y. K. (2013). A model of the relationship among sport consumer motives, spectator commitment, and behavioral intentions. *Sport Management Review*, *16*, 173–185.

Kim, S., Greenwell, T. C., Andrew, D. P. S., Lee, J., & Mahony, D. F. (2008). An analysis of spectator motives in an individual combat sport: A study of mixed martial arts fans. *Sport Marketing Quarterly*, *17*, 109–119.

Kim, J., Kim, Y. K., & Kim, D. H., (2017). Improving well-being through hedonic, eudaimonic, and social needs fulfillment in sport media consumption. *Sport Management Review*, *20*, 309–321.

Kim, W., & Walker, M. (2012). Measuring the social impacts associated with Super Bowl XLIII: Preliminary development of a psych income scale. *Sport Management Review*, *15*, 91–108.

Kim, Y., & Kim, S. (2009). The relationships between team attributes, team identification and sponsor image. *International Journal of Sports Marketing and Sponsorship*, *10*, 18–32.

Kim, Y., & Ross, S. (2015). The effect of sport video gaming on sport brand attitude, attitude strength, and attitude-behavior relationship. *Journal of Sport Management*, *29*, 657–671.

Kim, Y. K., Trail, G. T., & Magnusen, M. J. (2013). Transition from motivation to behavior: Examining the moderating role of identification (ID) on the relationship between motives and attendance. *International Journal of Sports Marketing and Sponsorship*, *14*, 35–56.

Kimble, C. E., & Cooper, B. P. (1992). Association and dissociation by football fans. *Perceptual and Motor Skills*, *75*, 303–309.

King, A. (1995). Outline of a practical theory of football violence. *Sociology*, *29*, 635–651.

Kirkup, W., & Merrick, D. W. (2003). A matter of life and death: Population mortality and football results. *Journal of Epidemiol Community Health*, *57*, 429–432.

Klapp, O. E. (1972). *Currents of unrest: An introduction to collective behavior*. New York, NY: Holt, Rinehart & Winston.

Kloner, R. A., McDonald, S., Leeka, J., & Poole, W. K. (2009). Comparison of total and cardiovascular death rates in the same city during a losing versus wining Super Bowl championship. *The American Journal of Cardiology*, *103*, 1647–1650.

Knecht, R. S., & Zenger, B. R. (1985). Sports spectator knowledge as a predictor of spectator behavior. *International Journal of Sport Psychology*, *16*, 270–279.

Knobloch-Westerwick, S., David, P., Eastin, M. S., Tamborini, R., & Greenwood, D. (2009). Sports spectators' suspense: Affect and uncertainly in sports entertainment. *Journal of Communication*, *59*, 750–767.

Koch, K., & Wann, D. L. (2013). Fans' identification and commitment to a sport team: The impact of self-selection versus socialization processes. *Athletic Insight*, *5*, 129–143.

Koch, K., & Wann, D. L. (2016). Team identification and sport fandom: Gender differences in relationship-based and recognition-based perceived antecedents. *Journal of Sport Behavior*, *39*, 278–300.

Koenigstorfer, J., Groeppel-Klein, A., & Schmitt, M. (2010). "You'll never walk alone"—how loyal are soccer fans to the clubs when they are struggling against relegation? *Journal of Sport Management*, *24*, 649–675.

Koenigstorfer, J., & Uhrich, S. (2009). Riding a rollercoaster: The dynamics of sports fans' loyalty after promotion and relegation. *Marketing Journal of Research and Management*, *31*, 71–83.

Kolbe, R. H., & James, J. D. (2000). An identification and examination of influences that shape the creation of a professional team fan. *International Journal of Sports Marketing & Sponsorship*, *2*, 21–37.

Konrath, S. H., Chopik, W. J., Hsing, C. K., & O'Brien, E. (2014). Changes in adult attachment styles in American college students over time: A meta-analysis. *Personality and Social Psychology Review*, *18*, 326–248.

Konrath, S. H., O'Brien, E. H., & Hsing, C. (2011). Changes in dispositional empathy in American college students over time: A meta-analysis. *Personality and Social Psychology Review*, *14*, 180–198.

Koo, G. Y., Andrew, D. P. S., Hardin, R., & Greenwell, T. C. (2009). Classification of sport consumers on the basis of emotional attachment: A study of minor league hockey fans and spectators. *International Journal of Sport Management*, *10*, 307–329.

Koo, G. Y., & Hardin, R. (2008). Difference in interrelationship between spectators' motives and behavioral intentions based on emotional attachment. *Sport Marketing Quarterly*, *17*, 30–43.

Koss, M. P., & Gaines, J. A. (1993). The prediction of sexual aggression by alcohol use, athletic participation, and fraternity affiliation. *Journal of Interpersonal Violence*, *8*, 94–108.

Kota, R., Du, J., James, J. D., Kennedy, H., & Funk, D. C. (2018, June). *Advancing the psychological continuum model: Dealing with risk and misclassification.* Paper presented at the North American Society for Sport Management Annual Conference, Halifax, Nova Scotia.

Kota, R., Reid, C., James, J. D., & Kim, A. C. H. (in press). Development and assessment of a scale to measure daily fantasy sport motives. *Sport Marketing Quarterly*.

Krohn, F. B., Clarke, M., Preston, E., McDonald, M., & Preston, B. (1998). Psychological and sociological influences on attendance at small college sporting events. *College Student Journal*, *32*, 277–288.

Kuenzel, S., & Yassim, M. (2007). The effect of joy on the behaviour of cricket spectators: The mediating role of satisfaction. *Managing Leisure*, *12*, 43–57.

Kunkel, T., Doyle, J. P., & Funk, D. C. (2014). Exploring sport brand development strategies to strengthen consumer involvement with the product—the case of the Australian A-League. *Sport Management Review*, *17*, 470–483.

Kwon, H. H., & Armstrong, K. L. (2002). Factors influencing impulse buying of sport team licensed merchandise. *Sport Marketing Quarterly*, *11*, 151–163.

Kwon, H. H., Lee, C., & Lee, S. (2008). Can spectators' mood be manipulated and maintained in a losing game?: Interaction between team identification and pre-game mood. *Contemporary Athletics*, *3*, 11–31.

Kwon, H. H., Trail, G., & James, J. D. (2007). The mediating role of perceived value: Team identification and purchase intention of team-licensed apparel. *Journal of Sport Management*, *21*, 540–554.

Kwon, H. H., Trail, G. T., & Anderson, D. F. (2005). Are multiple points of attachment necessary to predict cognitive, affective, conative, or behavioral loyalty? *Sport Management Review*, *8*, 255–270.

Kwon, H. H., Trail, G. T., & Lee, D. (2008). The effects of vicarious achievement and team identification on BIRGing and CORFing. *Sport Marketing Quarterly*, *17*, 209–217.

Kwon, H., & Trail, G. (2001). Sport fan motivation: A comparison of American students and international students. *Sport Marketing Quarterly*, *10*, 147–155.

Lam, K. C. H., Buehler, R., McFarland, C., Ross, M., & Cheung, I. (2005). Cultural differences in affective forecasting: The role of focalism. *Personality and Social Psychology Bulletin*, *31*, 1296–1309.

Lambert, N. M., Stillman, T. F., Hicks, J. A., Kamble, S., Baumeister, R. F., & Fincham, F. D. (2013). To belong is to matter: Sense of belonging enhances meaning in life. *Personality and Social Psychology Bulletin*, *39*, 1418–1427.

Lambird, K. H., & Man, T. (2006). When do ego threats lead to self-regulation failure? Negative consequences of defensive high self-esteem. *Personality and Social Psychology Bulletin*, *32*, 1177–1187.

Landers, D. M., Brawley, L. R., & Hale, B. D. (1978). Habit strength differences in motor behavior: The effects of social facilitation paradigms and subject sex. In D. M. Landers & R. W. Christina (Eds.), *Psychology of motor behavior and sport-1977* (pp. 420–433). Champaign, IL: Human Kinetics.

Lanter, J. R. (2011). Spectator identification with the team and participation in celebratory violence. *Journal of Sport Behavior*, *34*, 268–280.

Lanter, J. R. (2013). "But it's Joe Pa!" The effects of social identification on sport fan perceptions of the Penn State case. *Journal of Issues in Intercollegiate Athletics*, *6*, 58–69.

Lanter, J. R., & Blackburn, J. Z. (2015). The influence of athletic success on the self-esteem of first-year college students. *Journal for the Study of Sports and Athletes in Education*, *9*, 1–11.

Lasch, C. (1989). The degradation of sport. In W. J. Morgan & K. V. Meier (Eds.), *Philosophic inquiry in sport* (pp. 403–417). Champaign, IL: Human Kinetics.

Lau, R. R. (1984). Dynamics of the attribution process. *Journal of Personality and Social Psychology*, *46*, 1017–1028.

Laurent, G., & Kapferer, J-N. (1985). Measuring consumer involvement profiles. *Journal of Marketing Research*, *22*, 41–53.

Laverie, D. A., & Arnett, B. A. (2000). Factors affecting fan attendance: The influence of identity salience and satisfaction. *Journal of Leisure Research*, *32*, 225–246.

Lavigne, G. L., Vallerand, R. J., & Crevier-Braud, L. (2011). The fundamental need to belong: On the distinction between growth and deficit-reduction orientations. *Personality and Social Psychology Bulletin*, *37*, 1185–1201.

Lazarsfeld, P. F., & Merton, R. K. (1948). Mass communication, popular taste, and organized social action. In L. Bryson (Ed.), *The communication of ideas: A series of addresses* (pp. 95–118). New York, NY: Harper & Row.

Le Bon, G. (1946). *The crowd: A study of the popular mind*. New York, NY: Palgrave Macmillan. (Original work published 1896).

Leach, C. W., Spears, R., Branscombe, N. R., & Doosje, B. (2003). Malicious pleasure: Schadenfreude at the suffering of another group. *Journal of Personality and Social Psychology*, *84*, 932–943.

Leary, M. R. (1992). Self-presentational processes in exercise and sport. *Journal of Sport & Exercise Psychology*, *14*, 339–351.

Leary, M. R. (1995). *Self-presentation: Impression management and interpersonal behavior*. Dubuque, IA: Brown & Benchmark.

Lee, B. A., & Zeiss, C. A. (1980). Behavioral commitment to the role of sport consumer: An exploratory analysis. *Sociology and Social Research*, *64*, 405–419.

Lee, D., Trail, G. T., & Anderson, D. F. (2008). Differences in motives and points of attachment by season ticket status: A case study of ACHA. *International Journal of Sport Management and Marketing*, *5*, 132–150.

Lee, H. K. (2007, January 12). A's fan injured by flying chair settles lawsuit against Texas Rangers. *SFGATE*. Retrieved from www.sfgate.com/sports/article/A-s-fan-injured-by-flying-chair-settles-lawsuit-2624561.php

Lee, J., & Ferreira, M. (2011). Cause-related marketing: The role of team identification in consumer choice of team licensed products. *Sport Marketing Quarterly*, *20*, 157–169.

Lee, J. S., & Kang, J-H. (2015). Effects of sport event satisfaction on team identification and revisit intention. *Sport Marketing Quarterly*, *24*, 225–234.

Lee, J. S., Kwak, D. H., & Braunstein-Minkove, J. R. (2016). Coping with athlete endorsers' immoral behavior: Roles of athlete identification and moral emotions on moral reasoning strategies. *Journal of Sport Management*, *30*, 176–191.

Lee, J. S., Kwak, D. H., & Moore, D. (2015). Athletes' transgressions and sponsor evaluations: A focus on consumers' moral reasoning strategies. *Journal of Sport Management*, *29*, 672–687.

Lee, M. J. (1985). From rivalry to hostility among sports fans. *Quest*, *37*, 38–49.

Lee, R. M., & Robbins, S. B. (1998). The relationship between social connectedness and anxiety, self-esteem, and social identity. *Journal of Counseling Psychology*, *45*, 338–345.

Lee, S. P., Cornwell, T. B., & Babiak, K. (2013). Developing an instrument to measure the social impact of sport: Social capital, collective identities, health literacy, well-being and human capital. *Journal of Sport Management*, *27*, 24–42.

Lee, S., Heere, H., & Chung, K. (2013). Which senses matter more? The impact of our sense on team identity and team loyalty. *Sport Marketing Quarterly*, *22*, 203–213.

Lee, S., Seo, W. J., & Green, B. C. (2013). Understanding why people play fantasy sport: Development of the Fantasy Sport Motivation Inventory (Fan SMI). *European Sport Management Quarterly*, *13*, 166–199.

Lee, S., Shin, H., & Schinchi, T. (2010). Identifying sociological motivation of Hispanic/Latino sport consumers attending sporting events. *Sport Management International Journal*, *6*, 79–94.

Lehr, S. A., Ferreira, M. L., & Banaji, M. R. (in press). When outgroup negativity trumps ingroup positivity: Fans of the Boston Red Sox and New York Yankees place greater value on rival losses than own-team games. *Group Processes & Intergroup Relations*.

Lenk, H. (1982). Tasks of the philosophy of sport: Between publicity and anthropology. *Journal of the Philosophy of Sport*, *9*, 94–106.

Leonard, K. E. (1989). The impact of explicit aggressive and implicit nonaggressive cues on aggression in intoxicated and sober males. *Journal of Personality and Social Psychology*, *15*, 390–400.

Lester, D. (1988). Suicide and homicide during major sports events 1972–1984: Comment on Curtis, Loy and Karnilowicz. *Sociology of Sport Journal*, *5*, 285.

Levenson, M. R. (1990). Risk taking and personality. *Journal of Personality and Social Psychology*, *58*, 1073–1080.

Lever, J. (1983). *Soccer madness*. Chicago, IL: The University of Chicago Press.

Levin, A. M., Beasley, F., & Gilson, R. L. (2008). NASCAR fans' responses to current and former NASCAR sponsors: The effect of perceived group norms and fan identification. *International Journal of Sports Marketing and Sponsorship*, *9*, 35–46.

Lewis, J. M. (1980). The structural dimensions of fan violence. In P. Klavora & K. A. Wipper (Eds.), *Psychological and sociological factors in sport* (pp. 148–155). Toronto: University of Toronto Press.

Lewis, J. M. (1989). A value-added analysis of the Heysel Stadium riot. *Current Psychology: Research & Reviews*, *8*, 15–29.

Lewis, J. M. (2007). *Sports fan violence in North America*. New York, NY: Rowman & Littlefield.

Lieberman, S. (1991, September/October). The popular culture: Sport in America-A look at the avid sports fan. *The Public Perspective: A Roper Center Review of Public Opinion and Polling*, 2(6), 28–29.

Lisjak, M., Lee, A. Y., & Gardner, W. L. (2012). When a threat to the brand is a threat to the self: The importance of brand identification and implicit self-esteem in predicting defensiveness. *Personality and Social Psychology Bulletin*, *38*, 1120–1132.

Lock, D., Darcy, S., & Taylor, T. (2009). Starting with a clean slate: An analysis of member identification with a new sports team. *Sport Management Review*, *12*, 15–25.

Lock, D. J., & Funk, D. C. (2016). The multiple in-group identity framework. *Sport Management Review*, *19*, 85–96.

Lock, D., & Heere, B. (2017). Identity crisis: A theoretical analysis of 'team identification' research. *European Sport Marketing Quarterly*, *17*, 413–435.

Lock, D., Taylor, T., & Darcy, S. (2011). In the absence of achievement: The formation of new team identification. *European Sport Management Quarterly*, *11*, 171–192.

Lock, D., Taylor, T., Funk, D., & Darcy, S. (2012). Exploring the development of team identification. *Journal of Sport Management*, *26*, 283–294.

Lombardo, M. P. (2012). On the evolution of sport. *Evolutionary Psychology*, *10*, 1–28.

Loomes, G., & Sugden, R. (1986). Disappointment and dynamic consistency in choice under uncertainly. *Review of Economic Studies*, *53*, 271–282.

Loy, J. W., Jr. (1978). The cultural system of sport. *Quest*, *29*, 73–102.

Luellen, T. B., & Wann, D. L. (2010). Rival salience and sport team identification. *Sport Marketing Quarterly*, *19*, 97–106.

Luker, R. (2014, January 6–12). Survey says: Twenty insights from poll's 20 years. *Sports Business Journal*. Retrieved from www.sportsbusinessdaily.com/Journal/Issues/2014/01/06/Research-and-Ratings/Up-Next.aspx

Madrigal, R. (1995). Cognitive and affective determinants of fan satisfaction with sporting event attendance. *Journal of Leisure Research*, *27*, 205–227.

Madrigal, R. (2003). Investigating an evolving leisure experience: Antecedents and consequences of spectator affect during a live sporting event. *Journal of Leisure Research*, *35*, 23–48.

Madrigal, R. (2004). A review of team identification and its influence on consumer's responses toward corporate sponsors. In L. R. Kahle & C. Riley (Eds.), *Sports marketing and the psychology of marketing communication* (pp. 241–255). Mahwah, NJ: Lawrence Erlbaum Associates.

Madrigal, R. (2006). Measuring the multidimensional nature of sporting event performance consumption. *Journal of Leisure Research*, *38*, 267–292.

Madrigal, R., & Chen, J. (2008). Moderating and mediating effects of team identification in regard to causal attributions and summary judgments following a game outcome. *Journal of Sport Management*, *22*, 717–733.

Maehr, M. L., & Braskamp, L. A. (1986). *The motivation factor: A theory of personal investment*. Lexington, MA: Lexington Books.

Mael, F. A., & Ashforth, B. E. (2001). Identification in work, war, sports, and religion: Contrasting the benefits and risks. *Journal for the Theory of Social Behavior*, *31*, 197–222.

Magdol, L., & Bessel, D. R. (2003). Social capital, social currency, and portable assets: The impact of residential mobility on exchanges of social support. *Personal Relationships*, *10*, 149–169.

Mahony, D. F., Nakazawa, M., Funk, D. C., James, J. D., & Gladden, J. D. (2002). Motivational factors influencing the behaviour of J. League spectators. *Sport Management Review*, *5*, 1–24.

Mandelbaum, M. (2004). *The meaning of sports*. New York, NY: PublicAffairs.

Mann, L. (1979). Sports crowds viewed from the perspective of collective behavior. In J. H. Goldstein (Ed.), *Sports, games, and play: Social and psychological viewpoints* (1st ed., pp. 337–369). Hillsdale, NJ: Lawrence Erlbaum Associates.

Mann, L. (1989). Sports crowds and the collective behavior perspective. In J. H. Goldstein (Ed.), *Sports, games, and play: Social and psychological viewpoints* (2nd ed., pp. 299–331). Hillsdale, NJ: Lawrence Erlbaum Associates.

Mann, L., Newton, J. W., & Innes, J. M. (1982). A test between deindividuation and emergent norm theories of crowd aggression. *Journal of Personality and Social Psychology*, *42*, 260–272.

Mann, L., & Pearce, P. (1978). Social psychology of the sports spectator. In D. J. Glencross (Ed.), *Psychology and sport* (pp. 173–201). New York, NY: McGraw-Hill Irwin.

Mariscal, J. (1999). Chicanos and Latinos in the jungle of sports talk radio. *Journal of Sport & Social Issues*, *23*, 111–117.

Markman, K. D., & Hirt, E. R. (2002). Social prediction and the "allegiance bias". *Social Cognition*, *20*, 58–86.

Markovits, A. S., & Albertson, E. K. (2012). *Sportista: Female fandom in the United States*. Philadelphia, PA: Temple University Press.

Martens, R. (1981). Sport personology. In G. R. F. Luschen & G. H. Sage (Eds.), *Handbook of social science in sport* (pp. 492–508). Champaign, IL: Stipes.

Marx, G. T. (1972). Issueless riots. In J. F. Short, Jr. & M. E. Wolfgang (Eds.), *Collective violence* (pp. 46–59). Chicago, IL: Adline-Atherton.

Mashiach, A. (1980). A study to determine the factors which influence American spectators to go see the Olympics in Montreal, 1976. *Journal of Sport Behavior*, *3*, 17–26.

Maslow, A. H. (1970). *Motivation and personality* (2nd ed.). New York, NY: Harper & Row.

Masterson, G., & Mander, A. J. (1990). Psychiatric emergencies, Scotland, and the World Cup finals. *British Journal of Psychiatry*, *156*, 475–478.

Matsuoka, H., Chelladurai, P., & Harada, M. (2003). Direct and interaction effects of team identification and satisfaction on intention to attend games. *Sport Marketing Quarterly*, *12*, 244–253.

Matsuoka, H., & Fujimoto, J. (2002, May). *Foci of fan's psychological commitment*. Meeting of the North American Society of Sport Management, Canmore, AB, Canada.

McCabe, C. (2008). Gender effects of spectators' attitudes toward WNBA basketball. *Social Behavior and Personality*, *36*, 347–358.

McCallum, J., & Hersch, H. (1997, December 1). Courtside at the Eagles' game. *Sports Illustrated*, *24*, 29.

McCrae, R. R., & Costa, P. T., Jr. (1987). Validation of the five-factor model of personality across instruments and observers. *Journal of Personality and Social Psychology*, *52*, 81–90.

McCrae, R. R., & Costa, P. T., Jr. (2008). The five-factor model of personality. In O. P. John, R. W. Robbins, & L. A. Pervin (Eds.), *Handbook of personality: Theory and research* (Vol. 3, pp. 159–181). New York, NY: Guilford Press.

McDaniel, S. R. (2002). An exploration of audience demographics, personal values, and lifestyle: Influences on viewing network coverage of the 1996 Summer Olympic games. *Journal of Sport Management*, *16*, 117–131.

McDaniel, S. R. (2003). Reconsidering the relationship between sensation seeking and audience preferences for viewing televised sports. *Journal of Sport Management*, *17*, 13–36.

McDonald, M. A., Milne, G. R., & Hong, J. (2002). Motivational factors for evaluating sport spectator and participant markets. *Sport Marketing Quarterly*, *11*, 100–113.

McGee, R. (1975). *Points of departure: Basic concepts in sociology*. Hinsdale, IL: The Dryden Press.

McGinnis, L., Chun, S., & McQuillan, J. (2003). A review of gendered consumption in sport and leisure. *Academy of Marketing Science Review*, *5*, 1–24.

McGinnis, L., McQuillan, J., & Chapple, C. L. (2005). "I just want to play": Women, sexism, and persistence in golf. *Journal of Sport & Social Issues*, *29*, 313–337.

McGuire, M. (1994, June). Baseball played a special role during World War II. *Baseball Digest*, 66–70.

McHoul, A. (1997). On doing "we's": Where sport leaks into everyday life. *Journal of Sport & Social Issues*, *21*, 315–320.

McIntyre, N. (1989). The personal meaning of participation: Enduring involvement. *Journal of Leisure Research*, *21*, 167–179.

McNair, D., Lorr, M., & Droppleman, L. (1971). *Manual for the profile of mood states*. San Diego: Educational and Industrial Testing Service.

McNeil, E. B. (1968). The ego and stress-seeking in man. In S. Z. Klausner (Ed.), *Why man takes chances* (pp. 171–192). Garden City, NY: Doubleday/Anchor.

McPherson, B. (1975). Sport consumption and the economics of consumerism. In D. W. Ball & J. W. Loy (Eds.), *Sport and social order: Contributions to the sociology of sport* (pp. 243–275). Reading, MA: Addison-Wesley.

McPherson, B. (1976). Socialization into the role of sport consumer: A theory and causal model. *Canadian Review of Sociology and Anthropology*, *13*, 165–177.

McPherson, B. D. (1968). *Unpublished study*. Madison: University of Wisconsin.

Mean, L. (2012). Empowerment through sport? Female fans, women's sports, and the construction of gendered fandom. In K. Toffoletti & P. Mewett (Eds.), *Sport and its female fans* (pp. 169–192). New York, NY: Routledge.

Medvec, V. H., Madley, S. F., & Gilovich, T. (1995). When less is more: Counterfactual thinking and satisfaction among Olympic medalists. *Journal of Personality and Social Psychology*, *69*, 603–610.

Mehus, I. (2005). Distinction through sport participation: Spectators of soccer, basketball, and ski-jumping. *International Review for the Sociology of Sport*, *40*, 321–333.

Mehus, I. (2005). Sociability and excitement motives of spectators attending entertainment sport events: Spectators of soccer and ski-jumping. *Journal of Sport Behavior*, *28*, 333–350.

Mehus, I., & Kolstad, A. (2011). Football team identification in Norway: Spectators of local and national football matches. *Social Identities*, *17*, 833–845.

Meier, H. E., & Leinwather, M. (2012). Women as 'armchair audience'? Evidence from German National Team football. *Sociology of Sport Journal*, *29*, 365–384.

Meier, K. V. (1989). The ignoble sports fan. *Journal of Sport & Social Issues*, *13*, 111–119.

Melnick, M. J. (1993). Searching for sociability in the stands: A theory of sports spectating. *Journal of Sport Management*, *7*, 44–60.

Melnick, M. J., & Wann, D. L. (2004). Sport fandom influences, interests, and behaviors among Norwegian university students. *International Sports Journal*, *8*(1), 1–13.

Melnick, M. J., & Wann, D. L. (2011). An examination of sport fandom in Australia: Socialization, team identification, and fan behavior. *International Review for the Sociology of Sport*, *46*, 456–470.

Meyers, B. (1997, August 28). Feminine touches planned but blood and guts remain. *USA Today*, pp. A1, A2.

Mihoces, G. (1998, May 7). Women checking in more as NHL fans. *USA Today*, pp. C1, C2.

Miller, N. E. (1941). The frustration-aggression hypothesis. *Psychological Review*, *48*, 337–342.

Miller, S. (1976). Personality correlates of football fandom. *Psychology*, *14*(4), 7–13.

Monfarde, F. T., Tojari, F., & Nikbakhsh, R. (2014). Constraints and motivators of sport consumption behavior. *Bulletin of Environment, Pharmacology and Life Sciences*, *3*, 308–312.

Montgomery, S. S., & Robinson, M. D. (2006). Take me out to the opera: Are sports and arts complements? Evidence from the performing arts research coalition data. *International Journal of Arts Management*, *8*, 24–37.

Moon, J. H., & Sung, Y. (2015). Individuality within the group: Testing the optimal distinctiveness principle through brand consumption. *Social Behavior and Personality*, *43*, 15–26.

Moore, J. C., & Brylinsky, J. A. (1993). Spectator effect on team performance in college basketball. *Journal of Sport Behavior*, *16*, 77–84.

Morgan, W. P. (1980). The trait psychology controversy. *Research Quarterly for Exercise and Sport*, *51*, 50–76.

Moskowitz, T. J., & Wertheim, L. J. (2011). *Scorecasting: The hidden influences behind how sports are played and games are won*. New York, NY: Crown Archetype.

Moyer, C., Pokrywczynski, J., & Griffin, R. J. (2015). The relationship of fans' sports-team identification and Facebook usage to purchase team products. *Journal of Sports Media*, *10*, 31–49.

Mullin, B. J., Hardy, S., & Sutton, W. (2014). *Sport marketing* (4th ed.) Champaign, IL: Human Kinetics.

Mumford, L. (1937). *Ends and means*. New York, NY: Harper & Row.

Murphy, N. M., & Bauman, A. (2007). Mass sporting and physical activity events: Are they bread and circuses or public health interventions to increase population levels of physical activity? *Journal of Physical Activity and Health*, *4*, 193–202.

Murrell, A. J., & Dietz, B. (1992). Fan support of sports teams: The effect of a common group identity. *Journal of Sport and Exercise Psychology*, *14*, 28–39.

Mustonen, A., Arms, R. L., & Russell, G. W. (1996). Predictors of sports spectators' proclivity for violence in Finland and Canada. *Personality and Individual Differences*, *21*, 519–525.

Mutter, F., & Pawlowski, T. (2014). The monetary value of the demonstration effect of professional sports. *European Sport Management Quarterly*, *14*, 129–152.

Nassis, P., Theodorakis, N. D., Alexandris, K., Tsellou, A., & Afthinos, Y. (2012). Testing the role of team identification on the relationship between sport involvement and sponsorship outcomes in the context of professional soccer. *International Journal of Sport Management*, *13*, 385–401.

Nathanson, D. L. (1992). *Shame and pride*. New York, NY: Norton.

National Conference. (2003, November). *National conference addressing issues related to celebratory riots*.

Neal, L., & Funk, D. (2006). Investigation motivation, attitudinal loyalty and attendance behavior with fans of Australian Football. *International Journal of Sports Marketing & Sponsorship*, *7*, 307–319.

Nelson, K. (2004). Identification with sports teams by fans of women's sports. *Perceptual and Motor Skills*, *99*, 575–576.

Nelson, M. B. (1994). *The stronger women get, the more men love Football*. New York, NY: Harcourt Brace & Company.

Nelson, T. F., & Wechsler, H. (2003). School spirits: Alcohol and collegiate sports fans. *Addictive Behaviors*, *28*, 1–11.

Nevill, A. M., Newell., S. M., & Gale, S. (1996). Factors associated with home advantage in English and Scottish soccer matches. *Journal of Sports Sciences*, *14*, 181–186.

The New Columbia. (2016, December 11). *CBS 60 Minutes*.

Newell, S. J., Henderson, K. V., & Wu, B. Y. (2001). The effects of pleasure and arousal on recall of advertisements during the Super Bowl. *Psychology & Marketing*, *18*, 1135–1153.

NFL Notebook. (1997, December 1). Briefly. *USA Today*, p. 5C.

Nicholson, M., & Hoye, R. (Eds.). (2008). *Sport and social capital*. New York, NY: Elsevier.

Norman, M. (2012). Saturday night's alright for tweeting: Cultural citizenship, collective discussion, and the new media consumption/production of *Hockey Day in Canada*. *Sociology of Sport Journal*, *29*, 306–324.

Norman, M. (2014). Online community or electronic tribe? Exploring the social characteristics and spatial production of an Internet hockey fan culture. *Journal of Sport and Social Issues*, *38*, 395–414.

Norris, J. I., Wann, D. L., & Zapalac, R. K. (2015). Sport fan maximizing: Following the best team or being the best fan? *Journal of Consumer Marketing*, *32*, 157–166.

Novak, M. (1976). *The joy of sports*. New York, NY: Basic Books, Inc.

Nuckols, B. (2017, November 27). US sports leagues are hedging their bets on legal gambling. *Chicago Tribune*. Retrieved from www.chicagotribune.com/news/sns-bc-us-sports-gambling-conflicted-leagues-20171127-story.html

Number of dedicated sports radio stations grew each year from '02–10. (2012, February 14). *SportsBusiness Daily*. Retrieved from www.sportsbusinessdaily.com/Daily/Issues/2012/02/14/Research-and-Ratings/Sports-radio.aspx

Nyadzayo, M. W., Leckie, C., & McDonald, H. (2016). CSR, relationship quality, loyalty and psychological connection in sports. *Marketing Intelligence & Planning*, *34*, 883–898.

Nylund, D. (2003). Taking a slice out of sexism: The controversy over the exclusionary membership practices of the Augusta National Golf Club. *Journal of Sport & Social Issues*, *27*, 195–202.

Oglesby, C. A. (1989). Women and sport. In J. H. Goldstein (Ed.), *Sports, games, and play: Social and psychological viewpoints* (2nd ed., pp. 129–145). Hillsdale, NJ: Lawrence Erlbaum Associates.

Oldenburg, R., & Brissett, D. (1982). The third place. *Qualitative Sociology*, *5*, 265–284.

Olweus, D. (1987). Testosterone and adrenaline: Aggressive antisocial behavior in normal adolescent males. In S. A. Mednick, T. E. Moffitt, & S. A. Stacks (Eds.), *The causes of crime: New biological approaches* (pp. 263–282). New York, NY: Cambridge University Press.

The Olympic Rings. (2017). *The International Olympic Committee*. Retrieved from www.olympic.org/olympic-rings

Ostrowsky, M. K. (2014). The social psychology of alcohol use and violent behavior among sports spectators. *Aggression and Violent Behavior*, *19*, 303–310.

Ouwerkerk, J. W., Ellemes, N., & De Gilder, D. (1999). Group commitment and individual effort in experimental and organizational contexts. In N. Ellemers, R. Spears, & B. Doosje (Eds.), *Social identity* (pp. 184–204). Malden, MA: Wiley-Blackwell.

Özer, A., & Argan, M. (2006). Licensed team merchandise buying behavior: A study on Turkish fans. *Innovative Marketing*, 2, 117–130.

Packers Fan. (1997, December 1). Packers fan, barber swap some unkind cuts. *USA Today*, p. 5C.

Pallerino, M. (2003, March/April). Survey says: End the madness-now. *Sporting Kid*, pp. 13–14.

Palmatier, R. A., & Ray, H. L. (1989). *Sports talk: A dictionary of sports metaphors*. Westport, CT: Greenwood Press.

Palmer, C., & Thompson, K. (2007). The paradoxes of football spectatorship: On-field and online expressions of social capital among the "Grog Squad". *Sociology of Sport Journal*, *24*, 187–205.

Pan, D. W., & Baker, J. A. W. (1999). Mapping of intercollegiate sports relative to selected attributes as determined by a product differentiation strategy. *Journal of Sport Behavior*, *22*, 69–82.

Pan, D. W., & Baker, J. A. W. (2005). Factors, differential marketing effects, and marketing strategies in the renewal of season tickets for intercollegiate football games. *Journal of Sport Behavior*, *28*, 351–377.

Pan, D. W., Gabert, T. E., McGaugh, E. C., & Branvold, S. E. (1997). Factors and differential demographic effects on purchases of season tickets for intercollegiate basketball games. *Journal of Sport Behavior*, *20*, 447–464.

Park, S. H., Andrew, D. P. S., & Mahony, D. F. (2008). Exploring the relationship between trait curiosity and initial interest in sport spectatorship. *International Journal of Sport Management*, *9*, 1–17.

Park, S. H., Mahony, D. F., & Greenwell, T. C. (2010). The measurement of sport fan exploratory curiosity. *Journal of Sport Management*, *24*, 434–455.

Park, S. H., Mahony, D., & Kim, Y. K. (2011). The role of sport fan curiosity: A new conceptual approach to the understanding of sport fan behavior. *Journal of Sport Management*, *25*, 46–56.

Park, S. H., Mahony, D., Kim, Y. K., & Kim, Y. D. (2015). Curiosity generating advertisements and their impact of sport consumer behavior. *Sport Management Review*, *18*, 359–369.

Parker, H. M., & Fink, J. S. (2010). Negative sponsor behavior, team response and how this impacts fan attitudes. *International Journal of Sports Marketing and Sponsorship*, *11*, 17–28.

Parry, K. D. (2009). Search for the hero: An investigation into the sports heroes of British sports fans. *Sport in Society*, *12*, 212–226.

Parry, K. D., Jones, I., & Wann, D. L. (2014). An examination of sport fandom in the United Kingdom: A comparative analysis of fan behaviors, socialization processes, and team identification. *Journal of Sport Behavior*, *37*, 251–267.

Parsons, T. (1951). *The social system*. New York, NY: Free Press.

Partridge, J. A., & Wann, D. L. (2015). Exploring the shame coping experiences of youth sport parents. *Journal of Sport Behavior*, *38*, 288–305.

Partridge, J. A., Wann, D. L., & Elison, J. (2010). Understanding college sport fans' experiences of and attempts to cope with shame. *Journal of Sport Behavior*, *33*, 160–175.

Pease, D. G., & Zhang, J. J. (2001). Socio-motivational factors affecting spectator attendance at professional basketball games. *International Journal of Sport Management*, *2*, 31–59.

Peetz, T. B., Parks, J. B., & Spencer, N. E. (2004). Sport heroes as sport product endorsers: The role of gender in the transfer of meaning process for selected undergraduate students. *Sport Marketing Quarterly*, *13*, 141–150.

Perks, T. (2007). Does sport foster social capital? The contribution of sport to a lifetime of community participation. *Sociology of Sport Journal*, *24*, 378–401.

Pettersson-Lidbom, P., & Priks, M. (2010). Behavior under social pressure: Empty Italian stadiums and referee bias. *Economics Letters*, *108*, 212–214.

Phares, E. J. (1991). *Introduction to personality* (3rd ed.). New York, NY: Harper Collins.

Phetrasuwan, S., Miles, M. S., Mesibov, G. B., & Robinson, C. (2009). Defining autism spectrum disorders. *Journal for Specialists in Pediatric Nursing*, *14*, 206–209.

Phillips, D. P. (1986). Natural experiments on the effects of mass media violence on fatal aggression: Strengths and weaknesses of a new approach. In L. Berkowitz (Ed.), *Advances in experimental social psychology* (Vol. 19, pp. 207–250). New York, NY: Academic Press.

Phua, J. (2012). Use of social networking sites by sports fans. *Journal of Sports Media*, *7*, 109–132.

Pickett, C. L., Gardner, W. L., & Knowles, M. (2004). Getting a cue: The need to belong and enhanced sensitivity to social cues. *Personality and Social Psychology Bulletin*, *30*, 1095–1107.

Pilz, G. A. (1989). Social factors influencing sport and violence: On the "problem" of football fans in West Germany. *Concilium-International Review of Theology*, *5*, 32–43.

Pinnuck, M., & Potter, B. (2006). Impact of on-field football success on the off-field financial performance of AFL football clubs. *Accounting and Finance*, *46*, 499–517.

Polansky, N., Lippitt, R., & Redl, F. (1950). An investigation of behavioral contagion in groups. *Human Relations*, *3*, 319–348.

Pope, S. (2013). "The love of my life": The meaning and importance of sport for female fans. *Journal of Sport and Social Issues*, *37*, 176–195.

Popp, N., Barrett, H., & Weight, E. (2016). Examining the relationship between age of fan identification and donor behavior at an NCAA Division I athletics department. *Journal of Issues in Intercollegiate Athletics*, *9*, 107–123.

Porter, R. (2016, December 27). 2016: Super Bowl 50 leads by a mile. *Screener*. Retrieved from http://tvbythenumbers.zap2it.com/more-tv-news/the-100-most-watched-tv-programs-of-2016-super-bowl-50-leads-by-a-mile/

Potter, R. F., & Keene, J. R. (2012). The effect of sports fan identification on the cognitive processing of sports news. *International Journal of Sport Communication*, *5*, 348–367.

Prebish, C. S. (1993). *Religion and sport: The meeting of sacred and profane*. Westport, CT: Greenwood Press.

Preston, F. W. (1978). Hucksters at the circus. *Urban Life*, *7*, 205–212.

Price, J. L. (1991). The Final Four as final judgment: The cultural significance of the NCAA Basketball championship. *Journal of Popular Culture*, *24*, 49–58.

Price, J. L. (Ed.). (2004). *From season to season: Sports as American religion.* Macon, GA: Mercer University Press.

Price, S. L. (2016, December 5). Purpose pitch. *Sports Illustrated*, pp. 17–18.

Prisuta, R. H. (1979). Televised sports and political values. *Journal of Communication*, *29*, 94–102.

Pritchard, M. P., & Stinson, J. L. (2014). Building loyal consumers in sport business. In M. P. Pritchard & J. L. Stinson (Eds.), *Leveraging brands in sport business* (pp. 123–141). New York, NY: Routledge.

Pritchard, M. P., Stinson, J., & Patton, E. (2010). Affinity and affiliation: The dual-carriage way to team identification. *Sport Marketing Quarterly*, *19*, 67–77.

Pu, H., & James, J. D. (2017). The distant fan segment: Exploring motives and psychological connection of international National Basketball Association fans. *International Journal of Sports Marketing and Sponsorship*, *18*, 418–438.

Purdam, D. (2017, September 14). Sports betting legalization: Where do we stand right now? *ESPN*. Retrieved from www.espn.com/chalk/story/_/id/20704273/gambling-where-does-sports-betting-legalization-us-stand-right-now

Putnam, R. D. (1995). Bowling alone: America's declining social capital. *Journal of Democracy*, *6*, 65–78.

Rainey, D. W., & Duggan, P. (1998). Assaults on basketball referees: A statewide survey. *Journal of Sport Behavior*, *21*, 113–120.

Rainey, D. W., Larsen, J., & Yost, J. H. (2009). Disappointment theory and disappointment among baseball fans. *Journal of Sport Behavior*, *32*, 339–356.

Rainey, D. W., Yost, J. H., & Larsen, J. (2011). Disappointment theory and disappointment among football fans. *Journal of Sport Behavior*, *34*, 175–187.

Raney, A. A., & Depalma, A. J. (2006). The effect of viewing varying levels and contexts of violent sports programming on enjoyment, mood, and perceived violence. *Mass Communication & Society*, *9*, 321–338.

Rapaport, D. (2018, January 4). NFL TV ratings down roughly 10% from last season. *Sports Illustrated*. Retrieved from www.si.com/tech-media/2018/01/04/nfl-tv-ratings-decline-ten-percent-colin-kaepernick-thursday-night-football

Reams, L., Eddy, T., & Cork, B. C. (2015). Points of attachment and sponsorship outcomes in an individual sport. *Sport Marketing Quarterly*, *24*, 159–169.

Reding, F. N., Grieve, F. G., Derryberry, W. P., & Paquin, A. R. (2011). Examining the team identification of football fans at the high school level. *Journal of Sport Behavior*, *34*, 378–391.

Rees, D. I., & Schnepel, K. T. (2009). College football games and crime. *Journal of Sports Economics*, *10*, 68–87.

Reese, C. (1994, November 5). Game's over if sports fans stop playing the fools. *Democrat and Chronicle*, p. 12A.

Reifman, A. S., Larrick, R. P., & Fein, S. (1991). Temper and temperature on the diamond: The heat-aggression relationship in Major League Baseball. *Personality and Social Psychology Bulletin, 17*, 580–585.

Reiss, A. J., & Roth, J. A. (Eds.). (1993). *Understanding and preventing violence* (Vol. 1). Washington, DC: National Academic Press.

Remillard, A. (2015). The shrines of sport: Sacred space and the world's athletic venues. In S. D. Brunn (Ed.), *The changing world religion map* (pp. 2881–2892). Dordrecht: Springer-Verlag.

Reysen, S., & Branscombe, N. R. (2010). Fanship and fandom: Comparisons between sport and non-sport fans. *Journal of Sport Behavior, 33*, 176–192.

Reysen, S., Plante, C. N., Roberts, S. E., & Gerbasi, K. C. (2017). Anime fans to the rescue: Evidence of Daniel Wann's team identification-social psychological health model. *The Phoenix Papers, 3*, 237–247.

Rhoads, T. A., & Gerking, S. (2000). Educational contributions, academic quality, and athletic success. *Contemporary Economic Policy, 18*, 248–258.

Ridinger, L. L., & Funk, D. C. (2006). Looking at gender differences through the lens of sport spectators. *Sport Marketing Quarterly, 15*, 155–166.

Rinehart, R. (1996). Dropping hierarchies: Toward the study of a contemporary sporting avant-garde. *Sociology of Sport Journal, 13*, 159–175.

Riskind, J. H., Moore, R., & Bowley, L. (1995). The looming of spiders: The fearful perception distortion of movement and menace. *Behaviour Research and Therapy, 33*, 171–178.

Roadburg, A. (1980). Factors precipitating fan violence: A comparison of professional soccer in Britain and North America. *The British Journal of Sociology, 31*, 265–275.

Robinson, M. J., & Trail, G. T. (2005). Relationships among spectator gender, motives, points of attachment, and sport preference. *Journal of Sport Management, 19*, 58–80.

Robinson, M. J., Trail, G. T., Dick, R. J., & Gillentine, A. J. (2005). Fans vs. spectators: An analysis of those who attend intercollegiate football games. *Sport Marketing Quarterly, 14*, 43–53.

Robinson, M. J., Trail, G. T., & Kwon, H. (2004). Motives and points of attachment of professional golf spectators. *Sport Management Review, 7*, 167–192.

Roloff, M. E., & Solomon, D. H. (1989). Sex typing, sports interests, and relational harmony. In L. A. Wenner (Ed.), *Media, sports, and society* (pp. 290–311). Newbury Park, CA: Sage Publishers.

Rosenfeld, M. J. (1997). Celebrating, politics, selective looting and riots: A micro level study of the Bulls riot of 1992 in Chicago. *Social Problems, 44*, 483–502.

Ross, L., Greene, D., & House, P. (1977). The "false consensus effect": An egocentric bias in social perception and attributional processes. *Journal of Experimental Social Psychology, 13*, 279–301.

Ross, S. D. (2007). Segmenting sport fans using brand associations: A cluster analysis. *Sport Marketing Quarterly, 16*, 15–26.

Rosset, E. (2008). It's no accident: Our bias for intentional explanations. *Cognition, 108*, 771–780.

Roy, D. P., Goss, B. D., & Jubenville, C. B. (2010). Influences on event attendance decisions for stock car racing fans. *International Journal of Sport Management and Marketing, 8*, 73–92.

Rudd, A., & Gordon, B. S. (2010). An exploratory investigation of sportsmanship attitudes among college student basketball fans. *Journal of Sport Behavior, 33*, 466–486.

Ruihley, B. J., Runyan, R. C., & Lear, K. E. (2010). The use of sport celebrities in advertising: A replication and extension. *Sport Marketing Quarterly, 19*, 132–142.

Russell, G. W. (1979). Hero selection by Canadian ice hockey players: Skill or aggression? *Canadian Journal of Applied Sport Sciences, 4*, 309–313.

Russell, G. W. (1981). Spectator moods at an aggressive sports event. *Journal of Sport Psychology, 3*, 217–227.

Russell, G. W. (1993). *The social psychology of sport.* New York, NY: Springer-Verlag.

Russell, G. W. (1995). Personalities in the crowd: Those who would escalate a sports riot. *Aggressive Behavior, 21*, 91–100.

Russell, G. W. (2004). Sport riots: A social—psychological review. *Aggression and Violent Behavior, 9*, 353–378.

Russell, G. W. (2008). *Aggression in the sports world: A social psychological perspective.* New York, NY: Oxford University Press.

Russell, G. W., & Arms, R. L. (1995). False consensus effect, physical aggression, anger, and a willingness to escalate a disturbance. *Aggressive Behavior, 21*, 381–386.

Russell, G. W., & Arms, R. L. (1998). Toward a social psychological profile of would-be rioters. *Aggressive Behavior, 24*, 219–226.

Russell, G. W., & Arms, R. L. (1999). Calming troubled waters: Peacemakers in a sports riot. *Aggressive Behavior, 27*, 292–296.

Russell, G. W., & Arms, R. L. (2002). The sport widow hypothesis: A research note. *North American Journal of Psychology, 4*, 249–252.

Russell, G. W., Arms, R. L., & Mustonen, A. (1999). When cooler heads prevail: Peacemakers in a sports riot. *Scandinavian Journal of Psychology, 40*, 153–155.

Russell, G. W., & Goldstein, J. H. (1995). Personality differences between Dutch football fans and nonfans. *Social Behavior and Personality, 23*, 199–204.

Russell, G. W., & Mustonen, A. (1998). Peacemakers: Those who intervene to quell a sports riot. *Personality and Individual Differences, 24*, 335–339.

Ryan, R. M., & Frederick, C. (1997). On energy, personality, and health: Subjective vitality as a dynamic reflection of well-being. *Journal of Personality, 65*, 529–565.

Sabo, D., Jansen, S. C., Tate, D., Duncan, M. C., & Leggett, S. (1996). Televising international sport: Race, ethnicity, and nationalistic bias. *Journal of Sport & Social Issues, 21*, 7–21.

Sack, A. L., Singh, P., & DiPaola, T. (2009). Spectator motives for attending professional women's tennis events: Linking marketing and Maslow's hierarchy of needs. *International Journal of Sport Management and Marketing*, *9*, 1–16.

Sadlock, J. (2016). Cubs parade was 7th largest gathering in human history. *Fansided*. Retrieved from http://fansided.com/2016/11/04/cubs-parade-7th-largest-gathering-human-history/

Sanderson, J. (2011). *It's a whole new ball-game*. New York, NY: Hampton.

Sandstrom, G. M., & Dunn, E. W. (2014a). Is efficiency overrated? Minimal social interactions lead to belonging and positive affect. *Social Psychology and Personality Science*, *5*, 437–442.

Sandstrom, G. M., & Dunn, E. W. (2014b). Social interactions and well-being: The surprising power of weak ties. *Personality and Social Psychology Bulletin*, *40*, 910–922.

Sani, F. (2012). Group identification, social relationships, and health. In J. Jetten, C. Haslam, & S. A. Haslam (Eds.), *The social cure: Identity, health, and well-being* (pp. 21–37). New York, NY: Psychology Press.

Sapolsky, B. S. (1980). The effect of spectator disposition and suspense on the enjoyment of sport contests. *International Journal of Sport Psychology*, *11*, 1–10.

Sargent, S. L., Zillmann, D., & Weaver, J. B., III. (1998). The gender gap in the enjoyment of televised sports. *Journal of Sport & Social Issues*, *22*, 46–64.

Sarstedt, M., Ringle, C. M., Raithel, S., & Gudergan, S. P. (2014). In pursuit of understanding what drives fan satisfaction. *Journal of Leisure Research*, *46*, 5419–5447.

Sassenberg, A. (2015). Effects of sport celebrity transgressions: An exploratory study. *Sport Marketing Quarterly*, *24*, 78–90.

Sato, S., Ko, Y. J., Park, C., & Tao, W. (2015). Athlete reputation crisis and consumer evaluation. *European Sport Management Quarterly*, *15*, 434–453.

Schimmel, K. S., Harrington, C. L., & Bielby, D. D. (2007). Keep you fans to yourself: The disjuncture between sport studies' and pop culture studies' perspectives on fandom. *Sport in Society*, *10*, 580–600.

Schlegel, A., Pfitzner, R., & Koenigstorfer, J. (2017). The impact of atmosphere in the city on subjective well-being of Rio de Janeiro residents during (vs. before) the 2014 World Cup. *Journal of Sport Management*, *31*, 605–619.

Schoetz, D. (2008, May 5). Red Sox-Yankees rivalry turns fatal. *ABC News*. Retrieved from http://abcnews.go.com/US/story?id=4790887

Schofield, J. A. (1983). Performance and attendance at professional team sports. *Journal of Sport Behavior*, *6*, 196–206.

Schreyer, D., Schmidt, S. L., & Torgler, B. (in press). Game outcome uncertainty in the English Premier League: Do German fans care? *Journal of Sports Economics*.

Schurr, K. T., Ruble, V. E., & Ellen, A. S. (1985). Myers-Briggs type inventory and demographic characteristics of students attending and not attending a college basketball game. *Journal of Sport Behavior*, *8*, 181–194.

Schurr, K. T., Wittig, A. F., Ruble, V. E., & Ellen, A. S. (1988). Demographic and personality characteristics associated with persistent, occasional, and nonattendance of university male basketball games by college students. *Journal of Sport Behavior*, *11*, 3–17.

Schurr, K. T., Wittig, A. F., Ruble, V. E., & Henriksen, L. W. (1993). College graduation rates of student athletes and students attending college male basketball games: A case study. *Journal of Sport Behavior*, *16*, 33–41.

Schwartz, J. M. (1973). Causes and effects of spectator sports. *International Review of Sport Sociology*, *8*, 25–45.

Schwarz, N., Strack, F., Kommer, D., & Wagner, D. (1987). Soccer, rooms, and the quality of your life: Mood effects on judgments of satisfaction with life in general and with specific domains. *European Journal of Social Psychology*, *17*, 69–79.

Schweitzer, K., Zillmann, D., Weaver, J. B., & Luttrell, E. S. (1992). Perception of threatening events in the emotional aftermath of a televised college football game. *Journal of Broadcasting & Electronic Media*, *36*, 75–82.

Scibetti, R. (2017, February 14). Interactive analysis of fan cost index. *The Business of Sports*. Retrieved from www.thebusinessofsports.com/2017/02/14/interactive-analysis-of-fan-cost-index/

Security Check. (2001, September 29). Security check threatens real thing. *SportBusiness International*. Retrieved from www.sportbusiness.com/sport-news/security-check-threatens-real-thing

Segrave, J. (1994). The perfect 10: "Sportspeak" in the language of sexual relations. *Sociology of Sport Journal*, *11*, 95–113.

Segrave, J. O. (1997). A matter of life and death: Some thoughts on the language of sport. *Journal of Sport & Social Issues*, *21*, 211–220.

Seligman, M. E. P. (2011). *Flourish: A visionary new understanding of happiness and well- being*. New York, NY: Atria.

Seligman, M. E. P., & Csikszentmihalyi, M. (2000). Positive psychology: An introduction. *American Psychologist*, *55*, 5–14.

Selin, S. W. (1986). *A two-stage test of selected causal antecedents of recreation program loyalty: A consumer behavior model* (Unpublished doctoral dissertation), University of Oregon, Eugene, OR.

Semyonov, M., & Farbstein, M. (1989). Ecology of sports violence: The case of Israeli soccer. *Sociology of Sport Journal*, *6*, 50–59.

Seo, W. J., & Green, B. C. (2008). Development of the Motivation Scale for Sport Online Consumption. *Journal of Sport Management*, *22*, 82–109.

Shames, L. (1989, January 2). America's icon. *Sports Inc*, p. 52.

Shank, M. D., & Beasley, F. M. (1998). Fan or fanatic: Refining a measure of sports involvement. *Journal of Sport Behavior*, *21*, 435–443.

Shapiro, S. L., Drayer, J., & Dwyer, B. (2014). Exploring fantasy baseball consumer behavior: Examining the relationship between identification, fantasy participation, and consumption. *Journal of Sport Behavior*, *37*, 77–93.

Shepperd, J. A., & McNulty, J. K. (2002). The affective consequences of expected and unexpected outcomes. *Psychological Sciences*, *13*, 85–88.

Shepperd, J. A., Quellette, J. A., & Fernandez, J. K. (1996). Abandoning unrealistic optimism: Performance estimates and the temporary proximity of self-relevant feedback. *Journal of Personality and Social Psychology, 70,* 844–855.

Sherman, E., Mathur, A., & Smith, R. B. (1997). Store environment and consumer purchase behavior: Mediating role of consumer emotions. *Psychology & Marketing, 14,* 361–378.

Shin, E. H. (2007). State, society, and economic development in sports life cycles: The case of boxing in Korea. *East Asia, 24,* 1–22.

Shuster, R. (1994, June 15). Female athletes, fans need not justify passion. *USA Today*, p. 3C.

Siemaszco, C. (2010, May 4). Phillies fan Tasered after running across field: 17-yr.-old hit with stun gun. *Daily News.* Retrieved from www.nydailynews.com/news/national/video-phillies-fan-tasered-running-field-17-yr-old-hit-stun-gun-article-1.444313

Silva, J. M., III. (1984). Personality and sport performance: Controversy and challenge. In J. M. Silva & R. S. Weinberg (Eds.), *Psychological foundations of sport* (pp. 59–69). Champaign, IL: Human Kinetics.

Simon, D. (2016, May 13). Bryan Stow, attacked for being a baseball fan, finds his new calling. *CNN.* Retrieved from www.cnn.com/2016/05/13/health/bryan-stow-san-francisco-giants-fan-rewind/

Simons, E. (2013). *The secret lives of sports fans: The science of sports obsession.* New York, NY: Overlook Duckworth.

Simons, Y., & Taylor, J. (1992). A psychosocial model of fan violence in sports. *International Journal of Sport Psychology, 23,* 207–226.

Sipes, R. (1996). Sports as a control for aggression. In D. S. Eitzen (Ed.), *Sport in contemporary society* (pp. 154–160). New York, NY: St. Martin's Press.

Sivarajasingam, V., Corcoran, J., Jones, D., Ware, A., & Shepherd, J. (2004). Relations between violence, calendar events and ambient conditions. *Injury, International Journal of the Care of the Injured, 35,* 467–473.

Skinner, J., Zakus, D. H., & Cowell, J. (2008). Development through sport: Building social capital in disadvantaged communities. *Sport Management Review, 11,* 253–275.

Skowronski, J. J., & Carlston, D. E. (1989). Negativity and extremity biases in impression formation: A review of explanations. *Psychological Bulletin, 105,* 131–142.

Sloan, L. R. (1989). The motives of sports fans. In J. D. Goldstein (Ed.), *Sports, games, and play: Social and psychosocial viewpoints* (2nd ed., pp. 175–240). Hillsdale, NJ: Lawrence Erlbaum Associates.

Sloan, L. R., & Van Camp, D. (2008). Advances in theories of sport fans' motives. In L. W. Hugenberg, P. Haridakis, & A. Earnheardt (Eds.), *Sports Mania: Essays on fandom and the media in the 21st century* (pp. 129–157). Jefferson, NC: McFarland.

Smelser, N. J. (1968). Social and psychological dimensions of collective behavior. In N. J. Smelser (Ed.), *Essays in sociological explanation* (pp. 92–121). Upper Saddle River, NJ: Prentice Hall.

Smith, E. R., & Henry, S. (1996). An in-group becomes part of the self: Response time evidence. *Personality and Social Psychology Bulletin, 22,* 635–642.

Smith, G. J. (1976). An examination of the phenomenon of sports hero worship. *Canadian Journal of Applied Sport Sciences*, *1*, 259–270.

Smith, G. J. (1988). The noble sports fan. *Journal of Sport & Social Issues*, *12*, 54–65.

Smith, G. J. (1989). The noble sports redux. *Journal of Sport & Social Issues*, *13*, 121–130.

Smith, G. J., Patterson, B., Williams, T., & Hogg, J. (1981). A profile of the deeply committed male sports fan. *Arena Review*, *5*, 26–44.

Smith, M. D. (1976). Precipitants of crowd violence. *Sociological Inquiry*, *48*, 121–131.

Smith, M. D. (1983). *Violence in sport*. Toronto: Butterworth.

Smith, S. E., Grieve, F. G., Zapalac, R. K., Derryberry, W. P., & Pope, J. (2012). How does sport team identification compare to identification with other social institutions? *Journal of Contemporary Athletics*, *6*, 69–82.

Sniehotta, F. F., Presseau, J., & Araújo-Soares, V. (2014). Time to retire the theory of planned behavior. *Health Psychology Review*, *8*, 1–7.

Snyder, C. R. (1999). Coping: Where have you been? In C. R. Snyder (Ed.), *Coping: The psychology of what works* (pp. 3–19). New York, NY: Oxford University Press.

Snyder, C. R., Lassegard, M., & Ford, C. E. (1986). Distancing after group success and failure: Basking in reflected glory and cutting off reflected failure. *Journal of Personality and Social Psychology*, *51*, 382–388.

Snyder, E. A., & Spreitzer, E. E. (1973). Family influence and involvement in sports. *Research Quarterly*, *44*, 249–255.

Snyder, M. A. (1993). The new competition: Sports careers for women. In G. L. Cohen (Ed.), *Women in sport: Issues and controversies* (pp. 264–274). Newbury Park, CA: Sage Publishers.

Solomon, R. L. (1980). The opponent-process theory of acquired motivation: The costs of pleasure and the benefits of pain. *American Psychology*, *35*, 691–712.

Solomon, R. L., & Corbit, J. D. (1974). An opponent-process theory of motivation: Temporal dynamics of affect. *Psychological Review*, *81*, 119–145.

Spies, K., Hesse, F., & Loesch, K. (1997). Store atmosphere, mood and purchasing behavior. *International Journal of Research in Marketing*, *14*, 1–17.

Spinda, J. S., & Haridakis, P. M. (2008). Exploring the motives of fantasy sports: A uses-and-gratifications approach. In L. W. Hugenberg, P. M. Haridakis, & A. C. Earnheardt (Eds.), *Sports mania: Essays on fandom and the media in the 21st century* (pp. 187–199). Jefferson, NC: McFarland.

Spinda, J. S. W. (2011). The development of basking in reflected glory (BIRGing) and cutting off reflected failure (CORFing) measures. *Journal of Sport Behavior*, *34*, 392–420.

Spinda, J. S. W., Wann, D. L., & Hardin, R. (2016). Attachment to sports conferences: An expanded model of points of attachment among professional, collegiate, and high school football fans. *Communication and Sport*, *4*, 347–362.

Spinda, J., Wann, D. L., & Sollitto, M. (2012). Cards, dice, and male bonding: A case study examination of Strat-O-Matic baseball motives. *International Journal of Sport Communication*, *5*, 246–284.

Spink, C. C. (1978, June 10). We believe. *The Sporting News*, p. 2.

Sport England. (2005). *Sport playing its part: The contribution of sport to community priorities and the improvement agenda*. London: Sport England.

Sporteology. (n.d.). *Top 10 most popular sports in the world*. Retrieved from http://sporteology.com/top-10-popular-sports-world/

St. John, W. (2004). *Rammer jammer yellow hammer: A journey into the heart of fan mania*. New York, NY: Crown.

Statista. (2016). *Average ticket prices in the major sports leagues in North America in 2015/2016*. Retrieved from www.statista.com/statistics/261588/average-ticket-price-major-us-sports-leagues/

Statista. (2017a). *Facts on the video game industry*. Retrieved from www.statista.com/topics/868/video-games/

Statista. (2017b). *Number of Olympic Games TV viewers worldwide from 2002 to 2014 (in billions)*. Retrieved from www.statista.com/statistics/287966/olympic-games-tv-viewership-worldwide/

Statista. (2017c). *TV viewership of the Super Bowl in the United States from 1990 to 2017 (in millions)*. Retrieved from www.statista.com/statistics/216526/super-bowl-us-tv-viewership/

Stavros, C., Meng, M. D., Westberg, K., & Farrelly, F. (2014). Understanding fan motivation for interacting on social media. *Sport Management Review*, *17*, 455–469.

Steele, C. M., & Josephs, R. A. (1990). Alcohol myopia: Its prized and dangerous effects. *American Psychologist*, *45*, 921–933.

Steger, M. F., Frazier, P., Oishi, S., & Kaler, M. (2006). The meaning in life questionnaire: Assessing the presence of and search for meaning in life. *Journal of Counseling Psychology*, *53*, 80–93.

Steinberg, D. (2013, November 1). Matthew McConaughey and the redskins. *The Washington Post*. Retrieved from www.washingtonpost.com/news/dc-sports-bog/wp/2013/11/01/matthew-mcconaughey-and-the-redskins/?utm_term=.4b0d67032eec

Stevens, J. A., Lathrop, A. H., & Bradish, C. L. (2003). "Who is your hero?" Implications for athlete endorsement strategies. *Sport Marketing Quarterly*, *12*, 103–110.

Stevenson, C. L. (1974). Sport as a contemporary social phenomenon: A functional explanation. *International Journal of Physical Education*, *11*, 8–13.

Stewart, A. L., Hayes, R. D., & Ware, J. E., Jr. (1992). Health perceptions, energy/fatigue, and health distress measures. In A. L. Stewart & J. E. Ware, Jr. (Eds.), *Measuring functioning and well-being: The medical outcomes study approach* (pp. 143–172). Durham, NC: Duke University Press.

Stewart, B., Smith, A. C. T., & Nicholson, M. (2003). Sport consumer typologies: A critical review. *Sport Marketing Quarterly*, *12*, 206–216.

Stieger, S., Gotz, F. M., & Gehrig, F. (2015). Soccer results affect subjective well-being, but only briefly: A smartphone study during the 2014 FIFA World Cup. *Frontiers of Psychology*, *6*, 1–8.

Stone, R. N., & Grønhaug, K. (1993). Perceived risk: Further considerations for the marketing discipline. *European Journal of Marketing*, *27*, 39–50.

Stott, C., & Reicher, S. (1998). Crowd actions as intergroup processes: Introducing the police perspective. *European Journal of Social Psychology, 28*, 509–529.

Straub, B. (1995). Die Messung der Identifikation mit einer Sportmannschaft: Eine deutsche adaptation der "Team Identification Scale" von Wann und Branscombe [A measure of identification with a sport team: A German adaptation of the "Team Identification Scale" by Wann and Branscombe]. *Psychologie und Sport, 4*, 132–145.

Strinati, D. (1995). *An introduction to theories of popular culture*. London: Routledge.

Stryker, S. (1968). Identity salience and role performance: The relevance of symbolic interaction theory for family research. *Journal of Marriage and the Family, 30*, 558–564.

Student Summit. (2003). *Student summit: Promoting responsible celebrations held at the University of New Hampshire*.

Subra, B., Muller, D., Begue, L., Bushman, B. J., & Delmas, F. (2010). Automatic effects of alcohol and aggressive cues on aggressive thoughts and behaviors. *Personality and Social Psychology Bulletin, 36*, 1052–1057.

Suh, Y. I., Ahn, T., & Eagleman, A. N. (2013). Comparisons of gender and team identification on web motivations and web characteristics in the official athletic department website: Uses and gratifications perspectives. *International Journal of Sport Management, 14*, 317–337.

Suh, Y. I., Lim, C., Kwak, D. H., & Pedersen, P. M. (2010). Examining the psychological factors associated with involvement in fantasy sports: An analysis of participants' motivations and constraints. *International Journal of Sport Management, Recreation and Tourism, 5*, 1–28.

Sukhdial, A., Aiken, D., & Kahle, L. (2002). Are you old school? A scale for measuring sport fans' old-school orientation. *Journal of Advertising Research, 42*, 71–81.

Sullivan, R. (1986, January 6). Foxboro flow. *Sports Illustrated*, p. 7.

Sumino, M., & Harada, M. (2004). Affective experience of J. League fans: The relationship between affective experience, team loyalty, and intention to attend. *Managing Leisure, 9*, 181–192.

Sun, T. (2010). Antecedents and consequences of parasocial interaction with sport athletes and identification with sport teams. *Journal of Sport Behavior, 33*, 194–217.

Sun, T., Youn, S., & Wells, M. D. (2004). Exploration of consumption and communication communities in sports marketing. In L. R. Kahle & C. Riley (Eds.), *Sports marketing and the psychology of marketing communication* (pp. 3–26). Mahwah, NJ: Lawrence Erlbaum Associates.

Sutton, W. A., McDonald, M. A., Milne, G. R., & Cimperman, J. (1997). Creating and fostering fan identification in professional sports. *Sport Marketing Quarterly, 6*, 15–22.

Sveinson, K., & Hoeber, L. (2016). Female sport fans' experiences of marginalization and empowerment. *Journal of Sport Management, 30*, 8–21.

Swanson, S. R., Gwinner, K., Larson, B. V., & Janda, S. (2003). Motivations of college student game attendance and word-of-mouth behavior: The impact of gender differences. *Sport Marketing Quarterly, 12*, 151–162.

Sweeney, D. R., & Nguyen, S. N. (2012). Identification and its impact on attitudes toward corporation social responsibility: The "internal/external" stakeholder perspective. *International Journal of Sport Management, 13*, 402–422.

Swyers, H. (2005). Community America: Who owns Wrigley Field? *The International Journal of the History of Sport, 22*, 1086–1105.

Tajfel, H. (1978). Social categorization, social identity and social comparison. In H. Tajfel (Ed.), *Differentiation between social groups: Studies in the social psychology of intergroup relations* (pp. 61–76). London: Academic Press.

Tajfel, H., & Turner, J. (1979). An integrative theory of intergroup conflict. In W. Austin & S. Worchel (Eds.), *The social psychology of intergroup relations* (pp. 33–47). Monterey, CA: Brooks/Cole.

Tangney, J. P., Miller, R. S., Flicker, L., & Barlow, D. B. (1996). Are shame, guilt, and embarrassment distinct emotions? *Journal of Personality and Social Psychology, 70*, 1256–1269.

Tannenbaum, P. H., & Noah, J. E. (1959). Sportugese: A study of sports page communication. *Journalism Quarterly, 36*, 163–170.

Tanner, J., Sev'er, A., & Ungar, S. (1989). Explaining the steroid scandal: How Toronto students interpret the Ben Johnson case. *International Journal of Sport Psychology, 20*, 297–308.

Taute, H. A., Sierra, J. J., & Heiser, R. S. (2010). Team loving and loathing: Emotional determinants of consumption in collegiate football. *Journal of Intercollegiate Sport, 3*, 182–199.

Taylor, S. P., Gammon, C. B., & Capasso, D. R. (1976). Aggression as a function of the interaction of alcohol and threat. *Journal of Personality and Social Psychology, 34*, 938–941.

Taylor, S. P., & Leonard, K. E. (1983). Alcohol and human physical aggression. In R. G. Geen & E. I. Donnerstein (Eds.), *Aggression: Theoretical and empirical reviews* (Vol. 2, pp. 77–101). New York, NY: Academic Press.

Taylor, T., & Toohey, K. (2005). Impacts of terrorism-related safety and security measures at a major sport event. *Event Management, 9*, 199–209.

Taylor, T., & Toohey, K. (2006). Security, perceived safety, and event attendee enjoyment at the 2003 Rugby World Cup. *Tourism Review International, 10*, 257–267.

Taylor, T., & Toohey, K. (2015). The security agencies' perspective. In M. M. Parent & J. L. Chappelet (Eds.), *Handbook of sports event management* (pp. 373–396). New York, NY: Routledge.

Tedeschi, J. T., & Felson, R. B. (1994). *Violence, aggression, and coercive actions*. Washington, DC: American Psychological Association.

Telander, R. (1993, November 8). Violent victory. *Sports Illustrated*, 60–64.

Texas Football Fan. (2007, September 12). Texas football fan nearly castrated in bar fight in Oklahoma bar. *Fox News*. Retrieved from www.foxnews.com/story/2007/09/12/texas-football-fan-nearly-castrated-in-bar-fight-in-oklahoma-bar.html

Theberge, N. (1985). Toward a feminist alternative to sport as a male preserve. *Quest, 37*, 193–202.

Theodorakis, N. D., Kousetelios, A., Robinson, L., & Barlas, A. (2009). Moderating role of team identification on the relationship between service quality and repurchase intentions among spectators of professional sports. *Managing Service Quality*, *19*, 456–473.

Theodorakis, N. D., & Wann, D. L. (2008). An examination of sport fandom in Greece: Influences, interests, and behaviors. *International Journal of Sport Management and Marketing*, *4*, 356–374.

Theodorakis, N. D., Wann, D. L., Akindes, A., & Chadwick, S. (2017). *A comparative analysis of Football fans' attitudes and consumption behaviors in the Middle East.* Manuscript submitted for publication.

Theodorakis, N. D., Wann, D. L., Carvalho, M., & Sarmento, P. (2010). Translation and initial validation of the Portuguese version of the sport spectator identification scale. *North American Journal of Psychology*, *12*, 67–80.

Theodorakis, N. D., Wann, D. L., Lianopoulos, Y., Foudouki, A., & Al-Emadi, A. (2017). An examination of levels of fandom, team identification, socialization processes, and fan behaviors in Qatar. *Journal of Sport Behavior*, *40*, 87–107.

Theodorakis, N. D., Wann, D. L., Nassis, P., & Luellen, T. B. (2012). The relationship between sport team identification and the need to belong. *International Journal of Sport Management and Marketing*, *12*, 25–38.

Thomas, W. E., Brown, R., Easterbrook, M. J., Vignoles, V. L., Manzi, C., D'Angelo, C., & Holt, J. J. (2017). Social identification in sports teams: The role of personal, social, and collective identity motives. *Personality and Social Psychology Bulletin*, *43*, 508–523.

Thompson, C. Y., & Forsyth, C. J. (2012). Women fans of the rodeo. In K. Toffoletti & P. Mewett (Eds.), *Sport and its female fans* (pp. 61–80). New York, NY: Routledge.

Thompson, W. (2011, November 28). "The Pittsburgh we're from isn't there anymore": For many displaced NFL fans, their teams are their only way back home. *ESPN The Magazine*, pp. 120–122, 124, 126.

Thorpe, H., Ryba, T., & Denison, J. (2014). Toward new conversations between sociology and psychology. *Sociology of Sport Journal*, *31*, 131–138.

Timmor, Y., & Katz-Navon, T. (2008). Being the same and different: A model explaining new product adoption. *Journal of Consumer Behavior*, *7*, 249–262.

Tinson, J., Sinclair, G., & Kolyperas, D. (2017). Sport fandom and parenthood. *European Sport Management Quarterly*, *17*, 370–391.

Tobar, D. A. (2006). Affect and purchase intentions of Super Bowl XL television spectators: Examining the influence of sport fandom, age, and gender. *Sport Marketing Quarterly*, *15*, 243–252.

Toffoletti, K., & Mewett, P. (2012). *Sport and its female fans.* New York, NY: Routledge.

Tokmak, G., & Aksoy, R. (2016). Factors affecting brand loyalty in football: An application on "The Big Four" football clubs in Turkish Super League. *International Review of Economics and Management*, *4*, 84–106.

Tolman, E. C. (1943). Identification and the post-war world. *Journal of Abnormal and Social Psychology*, *38*, 141–148.

Tomlinson, T. (2011, August 15). Something went very wrong at Toomer's corner. *Sports Illustrated*, 59–63.

Topend Sports. (n.d.). *Top 10 list of the world's most popular sports*. Retrieved from www.topendsports.com/world/lists/popular-sport/fans.htm

Townsend, K. C., & McWhirter, B. T. (2005). Connectedness: A review of the literature with implications for counseling, assessment, and research. *Journal of Counseling and Development*, *83*, 191–201.

Trail, G., & James, J. (2001). The Motivation Scale for Sport Consumption: Assessment of the scale's psychometric properties. *Journal of Sport Behavior*, *24*, 108–127.

Trail, G. T., Anderson, D. F., & Lee, D. (2016). A longitudinal study of past attendance behavior and preseason loyalty on actual attendance, post-season loyalty, and end-of-year loyalty. *Journal of Amateur Sport*, *2*(3), 1–23.

Trail, G. T., Anderson, D., & Fink, J. S. (2005). Consumer satisfaction and identity theory: A model of sport spectator conative loyalty. *Sport Marketing Quarterly*, *14*, 98–111.

Trail, G., & James, J. D. (2015). *Sport consumer behavior*. Sport Consumer Research Consultants.

Trail, G. T., Robinson, M. J., Dick, R. J., & Gillentine, A. J. (2003). Motives and points of attachment: Fans versus spectator in intercollegiate athletics. *Sport Marketing Quarterly*, *12*, 217–227.

Triplett, N. (1898). The dynamogenic factors in pacemaking and competition. *American Journal of Psychology*, *9*, 507–533.

Trovato, F. (1998). The Stanley Cup of hockey and suicide in Quebec. *Social Forces*, *77*, 105–127.

Tuohy, B. (2013, October 15). *Sport on earth: Why sports gambling should be legal*. Retrieved from www.sportsonearth.com/article/62954908/

Turner, R. H., & Killian, L. M. (1972). *Collective behavior* (2nd ed.). Englewood Cliffs, NJ: Prentice Hall.

Tykocinski, O. E., Pick, D., & Kedmi, D. (2002). Retroactive pessimism: A different kind of hindsight bias. *European Journal of Social Psychology*, *32*, 577–588.

Tyler, B. D., & Cobbs, J. B. (2015). Rival conceptions of rivalry: Why some competitions mean more than others. *European Sport Management Quarterly*, *15*, 227–248.

Tzoumaka, E., Tsiotsou, R. H., & Siomkos, G. (2016). Delineating the role of endorser's perceived qualities and consumer characteristics on celebrity endorsement effectiveness. *Journal of Marketing Communications*, *22*, 307–326.

Uemukai, K., Takenouchi, T., Okuda, E., Matsumoto, M., & Yamanaka, K. (1995). Analysis of the factors affecting spectators' identification with professional football teams in Japan. *Journal of Sport Sciences*, *13*, 522.

Uhlman, B. T., & Trail, G. T. (2012). An analysis of the motivators of Seattle Sounders FC season ticket holders: A case study. *Sport Marketing Quarterly*, *21*, 243–252.

Uhrich, S., & Benkenstein, M. (2010). Sport stadium atmosphere: Formative and reflective indicators for operationalizing the construct. *Journal of Sport Management*, *24*, 211–237.

Uhrich, S., & Benkenstein, M. (2012). Physical and social atmospheric effects in hedonic service consumption: Customers' roles at sporting events. *The Service Industries Journal*, *32*, 1741–1757.

Underwood, R., Bond, E., & Baer, R. (2001). Building service brands via social identity: Lessons from the sports marketplace. *Journal of Marketing Theory and Practice*, *9*, 1–13.

United Nations. (2014). International Day of Sport for Development and Peace 2014. *United Nations: Office on Sport for Development and Peace*. Retrieved from www.un.org/sport/

Unkelbach, C., & Memmert, D. (2010). Crowd noise as a cue in referee decisions contributes to the home advantage. *Journal of Sport & Exercise Psychology*, *32*, 483–498.

Unruh, D. R. (1983). *Invisible lives: Social worlds of the aged*. Beverly Hills, CA: Sage Publishers.

Vaish, A., Grossmann, T., & Woodward, A. (2008). Not all emotions are created equal: The negativity bias in social-emotional development. *Psychological Bulletin*, *134*, 383–403.

van der Meij, L., Almela, M., Hidalgo, V., Villada, C., IJzerman, H., van Lange, P. A. M., & Salvador, A. (2012). Testosterone and cortisol release among Spanish soccer fans watching the 2010 World Cup Final. *PLOS One*, *7*, e34814.

Van Dijk, W. W. (2009). How do you feel? Affective forecasting and the impact bias in track athletics. *The Journal of Social Psychology*, *149*, 243–248.

Van Dijk, W. W., & van der Pligt, J. (1997). The impact of probability and magnitude of outcome on disappointment and elation. *Organizational Behavior and Human Decision Processes*, *69*, 277–284.

van Hilvoorde, I., Elling, A., & Stokvis, R. (2010). How to influence national pride: The Olympic medal index as a unifying narrative. *International Review for the Sociology of Sport*, *54*, 87–102.

Vander Velden, L. (1986). Heroes and bad winners: Cultural differences. In L. Vander Velden & J. H. Humphrey (Eds.), *Psychology and sociology of sport* (pp. 205–220). New York, NY: AMS Press.

Vignoles, V. L., Regalia, C., Manzi, C., Golledge, J., & Scabini, E. (2006). Beyond self-esteem: Influence of multiple motives on identity construction. *Journal of Personality and Social Psychology*, *90*, 308–333.

Vilanova, F., Beria, F. M., Costa, A. B., & Koller, S. H. (2017). Deindividuation: From Le Bon to the social identity model of deindividuation effects. *Cogent Psychology*, *4*, 1–21.

Vildiz, Y. (2016). The relationship between fan identification and moral disengagement of physical education and sports students. *Education and Research Reviews*, *11*, 402–410.

von Allmen, P., & Solow, J. (2012). The demand for aggressive behavior in American stock car racing. In R. T. Jewell (Ed.), *Violence and aggression in sporting contests: Economics, history and policy* (pp. 79–95). New York, NY: Springer-Verlag.

Wakefield, K. L. (1995). The pervasive effects of social influence on sporting event attendance. *Journal of Sport & Social Issues*, *19*, 335–351.

Wakefield, K. L., & Wann, D. L. (2006). An examination of dysfunctional sport fans: Method of classification and relationships with problem behaviors. *Journal of Leisure Research*, *38*, 168–186.

Waldron, T. (2017, December 5). Supreme Court appears ready to legalize sports gambling. *Huffpost*. Retrieved from www.huffingtonpost.com/entry/supreme-court-sports-gambling_us_5a25ffa8e4b07324e84022a5

Walker, J. R. (2012). Foreward. In A. C. Earnheardt, P. M. Haridakis, & B. S. Hugenberg (Eds.), *Sports fans, identity and socialization: Exploring the fandemonium* (pp. ix–xi). Lanham, MD: Lexington.

Wallis, C. (1999, July 5). The kids are alright. *Time*, pp. 26–28.

Walters, J. (1999, January 25). SI view: The week in TV sports. *Sports Illustrated*, p. 31.

Walzer, M. (1991). The idea of civil society: A path to social reconstruction. *Dissent*, *38*, 293–304.

Wang, C., & Matsuoka, H. (2014). Motives of sport spectators in China: A case study of the Chinese Super League. *International Journal of Sport Management and Marketing*, *15*, 57–74.

Wang, F., Orpana, H. M., Morrison, H., de Groh, M., Dai, S., & Luo, W. (2012). Long-term association between leisure-time physical activity and changes in happiness: Analysis of the prospective national population health survey. *American Journal of Epidemiology*, *176*, 1095–1100.

Wang, M., & Wong, M. C. S. (2014). Happiness and leisure across countries: Evidence from International survey data. *Journal of Happiness Studies*, *15*, 85–118.

Wang, R. T., & Kaplanidou, K. (2013). I want to buy more because I feel good: The effect of sport-induced emotion on sponsorship. *International Journal of Sports Marketing & Sponsorship*, *15*, 52–66.

Wang, R. T., Zhang, J. J., & Tsuji, Y. (2011). Examining fan motives and loyalty for the Chinese Professional Baseball League of Taiwan. *Sport Management Review*, *14*, 347–360.

Wann, D. L. (1993). Aggression among highly identified spectators as a function of their need to maintain positive social identity. *Journal of Sport & Social Issues*, *17*, 134–143.

Wann, D. L. (1994a). Biased evaluations of highly identified sport spectators: A response to Hirt and Ryalls. *Perceptual and Motor Skills*, *79*, 105–106.

Wann, D. L. (1994b). The "noble" sports fan: The relationships between team identification, self-esteem, and aggression. *Perceptual and Motor Skills*, *78*, 864–866.

Wann, D. L. (1995). Preliminary validation of the sport fan motivational scale. *Journal of Sport & Social Issues*, *19*, 377–396.

Wann, D. L. (1996). Seasonal changes in spectators' identification and involvement with and evaluations of college basketball and football teams. *The Psychological Record*, *46*, 201–215.

Wann, D. L. (1997). *Sport psychology*. Upper Saddle River, NJ: Prentice Hall.

Wann, D. L. (1998). A preliminary investigation of the relationship between alcohol use and sport fandom. *Social Behavior and Personality: An International Journal*, *26*, 287–290.

Wann, D. L. (2000). Further exploration of seasonal changes in sport fan identification: Investigating the importance of fan expectations. *International Sports Journal*, *4*, 119–123.

Wann, D. L. (2001, June). *Encouraging positive adult behavior at youth sporting events: Changing to a culture of FUN*. Invited address presented at the National Alliance for Youth Sport Summit, Chicago, IL.

Wann, D. L. (2002). Preliminary validation of a measure for assessing identification as a sport fan: The Sport Fandom Questionnaire. *International Journal of Sport Management*, *3*, 103–115.

Wann, D. L. (2006a). The causes and consequences of sport team identification. In A. A. Raney & J. Bryant (Eds.), *Handbook of sports and media* (pp. 331–352). Mahwah, NJ: Lawrence Erlbaum Associates.

Wann, D. L. (2006b). Examining the potential causal relationship between sport team identification and psychological well-being. *Journal of Sport Behavior*, *29*, 79–95.

Wann, D. L. (2006c). Understanding the positive social psychological benefits of sport team identification: The team identification—social psychological health model. *Group Dynamics: Theory, Research, and Practice*, *10*, 272–296.

Wann, D. L., Allen, B., & Rochelle, A. R. (2004). Using sport fandom as an escape: Searching for relief from under-stimulation and over-stimulation. *International Sports Journal*, *8*(1), 104–113.

Wann, D. L., Bayens, C., & Driver, A. K. (2004). Likelihood of attending a sporting event as a function of ticket scarcity and team identification. *Sport Marketing Quarterly*, *13*, 209–215.

Wann, D. L., Bilyeu, J. K., Brennan, K., Osborn, H., & Gambouras, A. F. (1999). An exploratory investigation of the relationship between sport fan motivation and race. *Perceptual and Motor Skills*, *88*, 1081–1084.

Wann, D. L., & Branscombe, N. R. (1990). Person perception when aggressive or nonaggressive sports are primed. *Aggressive Behavior*, *16*, 27–32.

Wann, D. L., & Branscombe, N. R. (1992). Emotional responses to the sports page. *Journal of Sport & Social Issues*, *16*, 49–64.

Wann, D. L., & Branscombe, N. R. (1993). Sports fans: Measuring degree of identification with the team. *International Journal of Sport Psychology*, *24*, 1–17.

Wann, D. L., & Branscombe, N. R. (1995). Influence of identification with a sports team on objective knowledge and subjective beliefs. *International Journal of Sport Psychology*, *26*, 551–567.

Wann, D. L., Brasher, M., Thomas, D. L., & Scheuchner, H. L. (2015). Generalizing the team identification—social psychological health model for adolescents. *Journal of Sport Behavior*, *38*, 339–355.

Wann, D. L., Brewer, K. R., & Royalty, J. L. (1999). Sport fan motivation: Relationships with team identification and emotional reactions to sporting events. *International Sports Journal*, *3*, 8–18.

Wann, D. L., Carlson, J. D., Holland, L. C., Jacob, B. E., Owens, D. A., & Wells, D. D. (1999). Belief in symbolic catharsis: The importance of involvement with aggressive sports. *Social Behavior and Personality: An International Journal*, *27*, 155–164.

Wann, D. L., Carlson, J. D., & Schrader, M. P. (1999). The impact of team identification on the hostile and instrumental verbal aggression of sport spectators. *Journal of Social Behavior and Personality*, *14*, 279–286.

Wann, D. L., & Craven, L. (2014). Further support for the team identification—social psychological health model: Relationships between identification of college sport teams, vitality, and social avoidance/distress among college students. *Journal of Issues in Intercollegiate Athletics*, *7*, 352–366.

Wann, D. L., Culver, Z., Akanda, R., Daglar, M., De Divitiis, C., & Smith, A. (2005). The effects of team identification and game outcome on willingness to consider anonymous acts of hostile aggression. *Journal of Sport Behavior*, *28*, 282–294.

Wann, D. L., Dimmock, J. A., & Grove, J. R. (2003). Generalizing the team identification—psychological health model to a different sport and culture: The case of Australian Rules Football. *Group Dynamics: Theory, Research, and Practice*, *7*, 289–296.

Wann, D. L., & Dolan, T. J. (1994a). Attributions of highly identified sport spectators. *The Journal of Social Psychology*, *134*, 783–792.

Wann, D. L., & Dolan, T. J. (1994b). Influence of spectators' identification on evaluation of the past, present, and future performance of a sports team. *Perceptual and Motor Skills*, *78*, 547–552.

Wann, D. L., & Dolan, T. J. (1994c). Spectators' evaluations of rival and fellow fans. *The Psychological Record*, *44*, 351–358.

Wann, D. L., Dolan, T. J., McGeorge, K. K., & Allison, J. A. (1994). Relationships between spectator identification and spectators' perceptions of influence, spectators' emotions, and competition outcome. *Journal of Sport & Exercise Psychology*, *16*, 347–364.

Wann, D. L., Dunham, M. D., Byrd, M. L., & Keenan, B. L. (2004). The five-factor model of personality and the psychological health of highly identified sport fans. *International Sports Journal*, *8*(2), 28–36.

Wann, D. L., & Ensor, C. L. (1999). Further validation of the economic subscale of the sport fan motivation scale. *Perceptual and Motor Skills*, *88*, 659–660.

Wann, D. L., & Ensor, C. L. (2001). Family motivation and a more accurate classification of preferences for aggressive sports. *Perceptual and Motor Skills*, *92*, 603–605.

Wann, D. L., Ensor, C. L., & Bilyeu, J. K. (2001). Intrinsic and extrinsic motives for originally following a sport team and team identification. *Perceptual and Motor Skills*, *93*, 451–454.

Wann, D. L., Fahl, C. L., Erdmann, J. B., & Littleton, J. D. (1999). The relationship between identification with the role of sport fan and trait levels of aggression. *Perceptual and Motor Skills*, *88*, 1296–1298.

Wann, D. L., Friedman, K., McHale, M., & Jaffe, A. (2003). The Norelco Sport Fanatics Survey: Understanding the behaviors of avid sport fans. *Psychological Reports*, *92*, 930–936.

Wann, D. L., & Goeke, M. E. (2017). Relationships among dysfunctional fandom, sport fandom, team identification and perceptions of sport and war terminology. *Journal of Sport Behavior*, *40*, 231–243.

Wann, D. L., & Goeke, M. E. (in press). Sport fan superstition: The importance of team identification, sport fandom, and fan dysfunction. *Journal of Sport Behavior*.

Wann, D. L., & Grieve, F. G. (2005). Biased evaluations of ingroup and outgroup spectator behavior at sporting events: The importance of team identification and threats to social identity. *Journal of Social Psychology, 145*, 531–545.

Wann, D. L., & Grieve, F. G. (2007). Use of proactive pessimism as a coping strategy for sport fans: The importance of team identification. *Journal of Contemporary Athletics*, 2, 341–356.

Wann, D. L., Grieve, F. G., End, C., Zapalac, R. K., Lanter, J. R., Pease, D. G., . . . Wallace, A. (2013). Examining the superstitions of sport fans: Types of superstitions, perceptions of impact, and relationship with team identification. *Athletic Insight, 5*, 21–44.

Wann, D. L., Grieve, F. G., Havard, C. T., Zapalac, R. K., Peetz, T. B., & Lanter, J. R. (2017). Sport fan evaluations of a Major League Baseball season: Key predictors and influence on future evaluations and consumption behaviors. *Journal of Global Sport Management, 3*, 143–161.

Wann, D. L., Grieve, F. G., Waddill, P. J., & Martin, J. (2008). Use of retroactive pessimism as a method of coping with identity threat: The impact of group identification. *Group Processes & Intergroup Relations, 11*, 439–450.

Wann, D. L., Grieve, F. G., Zapalac, R. K., Lanter, J. R., Partridge, J. A., Short, S. E., Parker, P. M., & Short, M. (2011). What would you do for a championship: Willingness to consider acts of desperation among Major League Baseball fans. In B. D. Geranto (Ed.), *Sport psychology* (pp. 161–173). Hauppauge, NY: Nova.

Wann, D. L., Grieve, F. G., Zapalac, R. K., & Pease, D. G. (2008). Motivational profiles of sport fans of different sports. *Sport Marketing Quarterly, 17*, 6–19.

Wann, D. L., Grieve, F. G., Zapalac, R. K., Visek, A. J., Partridge, J. A., & Lanter, J. R. (2012). The importance of team identification in perceptions of trust of fellow and rival sport fans. In A. C. Earnheardt, P. M. Haridakis, & B. S. Hugenberg (Eds.), *Sports fans, identity and socialization: Exploring the fandemonium* (pp. 79–90). Lanham, MD: Lexington.

Wann, D. L., & Hackathorn, J. (in press). Audience effects in sport: The reciprocal flow of influence. In M. Anshel, T. Petrie, F. Gardner, S Petruzzello, & E. Labbe-Coldsmith (Eds.), *Handbook of sport and exercise psychology*. New York, NY: American Psychological Association.

Wann, D. L., Hackathorn, J., & Sherman, M. R. (in press). Testing the team identification—social psychological health model: Mediational relationships among team identification, sport fandom, sense of belonging and meaning in life. *Group Dynamics: Theory, Research, and Practice*.

Wann, D. L., & Hamlet, M. A. (1995). Author and subject gender in sports research. *International Journal of Sport Psychology, 26*, 225–232.

Wann, D. L., Hamlet, M. A., Wilson, T., & Hodges, J. A. (1995). Basking in reflected glory, cutting off reflected failure, and cutting off future failure:

The importance of identification with a group. *Social Behavior and Personality: An International Journal*, *23*, 377–388.

Wann, D. L., Havard, C. T., Grieve, F. G., Lanter, J. R., Partridge, J. A., & Zapalac, R. K. (2016). Investigating sport rivals: Number, evaluations, and relationship with team identification. *Journal of Fandom Studies*, *4*, 71–88.

Wann, D. L., Haynes, G., McLean, B., & Pullen, P. (2003). Sport team identification and willingness to consider anonymous acts of hostile aggression. *Aggressive Behavior*, *29*, 406–413.

Wann, D. L., Inman, S., Ensor, C. L, Gates, R. D., & Caldwell, D. S. (1999). Assessing the psychological well-being of sport fans using the Profile of Mood States: The importance of team identification. *International Sports Journal*, *3*, 81–90.

Wann, D. L., Hunter, J. L., Ryan, J. A., & Wright, L. A. (2001). The relationship between team identification and willingness of sport fans to illegally assist their team. *Social Behavior and Personality: An International Journal*, *29*, 531–536.

Wann, D. L., Keenan, B., & Page, L. (2009). Testing the team identification—social psychological health model: Examining non-marquee sports, seasonal differences, and multiple teams. *Journal of Sport Behavior*, *32*, 112–124.

Wann, D. L., Koch, K., Knoth, T., Fox, D., Aljubaily, H., & Lantz, C. D. (2006). The impact of team identification on biased predictions of player performance. *The Psychological Record*, *56*, 55–66.

Wann, D. L., Lane, T. M., Duncan, L. E., & Goodson, S. L. (1998). Family status, preference for sport aggressiveness, and sport fan motivation. *Perceptual and Motor Skills*, *86*, 1319–1422.

Wann, D. L., & Martin, J. (2008). The positive relationship between sport team identification and social psychological well-being: Identification with favorite teams versus local teams. *Journal of Contemporary Athletics*, *3*, 81–91.

Wann, D. L., Martin, J., Grieve, F. G., & Gardner, L. (2008). Social connections at sporting events: Attendance and its positive relationship with state social psychological well-being. *North American Journal of Psychology*, *10*, 229–238.

Wann, D. L., Metcalf, L. A., Adcock, M. L., Choi, C. C., Dallas, M. B., & Slaton, E. (1997). Language of sport fans: Sportugese revisited. *Perceptual and Motor Skills*, *85*, 1107–1110.

Wann, D. L., Melnick, M. J., Russell, G. W., & Pease, D. G. (2001). *Sport fans: The psychology and social impact of spectators* (1st ed.). New York, NY: Routledge Press.

Wann, D. L., & Ostrander, A. (2017). The relationship between dysfunctional sport fandom and assertiveness. *Contemporary Athletics*, *11*, 189–197.

Wann, D. L., Peterson, R. R., Cothran, C., & Dykes, M. (1999). Sport fan aggression and anonymity: The importance of team identification. *Social Behavior and Personality: An International Journal*, *27*, 597–602.

Wann, D. L., & Pierce, S. (2005). The relationship between sport team identification and social well-being: Additional evidence supporting the Team

Identification—Social Psychological Health Model. *North American Journal of Psychology*, *7*, 117–124.

Wann, D. L., Pierce, S., Padgett, B., Evans, A., Krill, K., & Romay, A. (2003). Relations between sport team identification and optimism. *Perceptual and Motor Skills*, *97*, 803–804.

Wann, D. L., & Polk, J. (2007). The positive relationship between sport team identification and belief in the trustworthiness of others. *North American Journal of Psychology*, *9*, 251–256.

Wann, D. L., Polk, J., & Franz, G. (2011). Examining the state social psychological health benefits of identifying with a distant sport team. *Journal of Sport Behavior*, *34*, 188–205.

Wann, D. L., Roberts, A., & Tindall, J. (1999). The role of team performance, team identification, and self-esteem in sport spectators' game preferences. *Perceptual and Motor Skills*, *89*, 945–950.

Wann, D. L., & Robinson, T. R., III. (2002). The relationship between sport team identification and integration into and perceptions of a university. *International Sports Journal*, *6*, 36–44.

Wann, D. L., Rogers, K., Dooley, K., & Foley, M. (2011). Applying the team identification—social psychological health model to older sport fans. *The International Journal of Aging and Human Development*, *72*, 303–315.

Wann, D. L., Royalty, J. L., & Roberts, A. R. (2000). The self-presentation of sport fans: Investigating the importance of team identification and self-esteem. *Journal of Sport Behavior*, *23*, 198–206.

Wann, D. L., Royalty, J. L., & Rochelle, A. R. (2002). Using motivation and team identification to predict sport fans' emotional responses to team performance. *Journal of Sport Behavior*, *25*, 207–216.

Wann, D. L., & Runyon, C. F. (2010). Team identification, fan dysfunction, and social psychological well-being: Further investigation of the team identification—social psychological health model. *Journal of Contemporary Athletics*, *4*, 227–235.

Wann, D. L., Schinner, J., & Keenan, B. L. (2001). Males' impressions of female fans and nonfans: There really is "Something About Mary". *North American Journal of Psychology*, *3*, 183–192.

Wann, D. L., & Schrader, M. P. (1996). An analysis of the stability of sport team identification. *Perceptual and Motor Skills*, *82*, 322.

Wann, D. L., & Schrader, M. P. (1997). Team identification and the enjoyment of watching a sporting event. *Perceptual and Motor Skills*, *84*, 954.

Wann, D. L., & Schrader, M. P. (2000). Controllability and stability in the self-serving attributions of sport spectators. *Journal of Social Psychology*, *140*, 160–168.

Wann, D. L., Schrader, M. P., & Adamson, D. R. (1998). The cognitive and somatic anxiety of sport spectators. *Journal of Sport Behavior*, *21*, 322–337.

Wann, D. L., Schrader, M. P., & Carlson, J. D. (2000). The verbal aggression of sport spectators: A comparison of hostile and instrumental motives. *International Sports Journal*, *4*, 56–63.

Wann, D. L., Schrader, M. P., & Wilson, A. M. (1999). Sport fan motivation: Questionnaire validation, comparisons by sport, and relationship to athletic motivation. *Journal of Sport Behavior*, *22*, 114–139.

Wann, D. L., Shelton, S., Smith, T., & Walker, R. (2002). The relationship between team identification and trait aggression: A replication. *Perceptual and Motor Skills, 94*, 595–598.

Wann, D. L., Tucker, K. B., & Schrader, M. P. (1996). An exploratory examination of the factors influencing the origination, continuation, and cessation of identification with sports teams. *Perceptual and Motor Skills, 82*, 995–1101.

Wann, D. L., & Waddill, P. J. (2007). Examining reactions to the Dale Earnhardt crash: The importance of identification with NASCAR drivers. *Journal of Sport Behavior, 30*, 94–109.

Wann, D. L., & Waddill, P. J. (2014). Predicting sport fans' willingness to consider anonymous acts of aggression: Importance of team identification and fan dysfunction. In C. Mohiyeddini (Ed.), *Contemporary topics and trends in the psychology of sports* (pp. 139–151). Hauppauge, NY: Nova.

Wann, D. L., Waddill, P. J., Bono, D., Scheuchner, H., & Ruga, K. (2017). Sport spectator verbal aggression: The impact of team identification and fan dysfunction on fans' abuse of opponents and officials. *Journal of Sport Behavior, 40*, 423–443.

Wann, D. L., Waddill, P. J., Brasher, M., & Ladd, S. (2015). Examining sport team identification, social connections, and social well-being among high school students. *Journal of Amateur Sport, 1*(2), 27–50.

Wann, D. L., Waddill, P. J., & Dunham, M. D. (2004). Using sex and gender role orientation to predict level of sport fandom. *Journal of Sport Behavior, 27*, 367–377.

Wann, D. L., Walker, R. G., Cygan, J., Kawase, I., & Ryan, J. (2005). Further replication of the relationship between team identification and psychological well-being: Examining non-classroom settings. *North American Journal of Psychology, 7*, 361–366.

Wann, D. L., Waddill, P. J., Polk, J., & Weaver, S. (2011). The team identification—social psychological health model: Sport fans gaining connections to others via sport team identification. *Group Dynamics: Theory, Research, and Practice, 15*, 75–89.

Wann, D. L., & Weaver, S. (2009). Understanding the relationship between sport team identification and dimensions of social well-being. *North American Journal of Psychology, 11*, 219–230.

Wann, D. L., Weaver, S., Belva, B., Ladd, S., & Armstrong, S. (2015). Investigating the impact of team identification on the willingness to commit verbal and physical aggression by youth baseball spectators. *Journal of Amateur Sport, 1*(1), 1–28.

Wann, D. L., & Wiggins, M. S. (1999). A preliminary investigation of the confidence of sport spectators: The importance of time, game features, and team identification. *Perceptual and Motor Skills, 89*, 305–310.

Wann, D. L., & Wilson, A. M. (1999). The relationship between aesthetic fan motivation and preferences for aggressive and nonaggressive sports. *Perceptual and Motor Skills, 89*, 931–934.

Wann, D. L., & Zaichkowsky, L. (2009). Sport team identification and belief in team curses: The case of the Boston Red Sox and the curse of the Bambino. *Journal of Sport Behavior, 32*, 489–502.

Wann, D. L., Zapalac, R. K., Grieve, F. G., Lanter, J. R., & Peetz, T. B. (2017). The influence of fan motives on perceptions of legalizing sport wagering. In A. M. Columbus (Ed.), *Advances in psychology research* (Vol. 130, pp. 89–121). New York, NY: Nova.

Wann, D. L., Zapalac, R. K., Grieve, F. G., Partridge, J. A., & Lanter, J. R. (2015). An examination of sport fans' perceptions of the impact of the legalization of sport wagering on their fan experience. *UNLV Gaming Research and Review Journal*, *19*(2), 21–40.

Warde, A., Tampubolon, G., & Savage, M. (2005). Recreation, informal social networks and social capital. *Journal of Leisure Research*, *37*, 402–425.

Watanabe, N. W., Yan, G., & Soebbing, B. P. (2016). Consumer interest in Major League Baseball: An analytic modeling of Twitter. *Journal of Sport Management*, *30*, 207–220.

Waterhouse, L. (2013). *Rethinking autism: Variation and complexity*. Waltham, MA: Academic Press.

Watkins, B. A. (2014). Revisiting the social identity—brand equity model: An application to professional sports. *Journal of Sport Management*, *28*, 471–480.

Weiller, K. H., & Higgs, C. T. (1997). Fandom in the 40's: The integrating functions of All American Girls Professional Baseball League. *Journal of Sport Behavior*, *20*, 211–231.

Wenger, J. L., & Brown, R. O. (2014). Sport fans: Evaluating the consistency between implicit and explicit attitudes toward a favorite and rival teams. *Psychological Reports: Mental & Physical Health*, *114*, 572–584.

Wenner, L. A., & Gantz, W. (1989). The audience experience with sports on television. In L. A. Wenner (Ed.), *Media, sports, and society* (pp. 241–268). Newbury Park, CA: Sage Publishers.

Wenner, L. A., & Gantz, W. (1998). Watching sports on television: Audience experience, gender, fanship, and marriage. In L. A. Wenner (Ed.), *Media sport*. New York, NY: Routledge.

Wertheim, L. J., & Apstein, S. (2016, November 14). Sports and autism. *Sports Illustrated*, 52–59.

Wertheim, L. J., & Sommers, S. (2016). *This is your brain on sports*. New York, NY: Three Rivers Press.

Westerbeek, H. M. (2000). The influence of frequency of attendance and age on 'place'-specific dimensions of service quality at Australian Rules Football matches. *Sport Marketing Quarterly*, *9*, 194–202.

Westerman, D., & Tamborini, R. (2010). Scriptedness and televised sports: Violent consumption and viewer enjoyment. *Journal of Language and Social Psychology*, *29*, 321–337.

Wheeler, L., & Caggiula, A. R. (1966). The contagion of aggression. *Journal of Experimental Social Psychology*, *2*, 1–10.

White, C. (1996, April 30). Multiclass opponents consider strategy. *USA Today*, p. 4C.

White, G. F. (1989). Media and violence: The case of professional football championship games. *Aggressive Behavior*, *15*, 423–433.

White, G. F., Katz, J., & Scarborough, K. E. (1992). The impact of professional football games upon violent assaults on women. *Violence and Victims*, *7*, 157–171.

White, P., & Wilson, B. (1999). Distinctions in the stands. *International Review for the Sociology of Sport*, *34*, 245–264.

Wiid, J. A., & Cant, M. C. (2015). Sport fan motivation: Are you going to the game? *International Journal of Academic Research in Business and Social Sciences*, *5*, 383–398.

Wilbert-Lampen, U., Leistner, D., Greven, S., Pohl, T., Sper, S., Volker, C., . . . Steinbeck, G. (2008). Cardiovascular events during World Cup soccer. *New England Journal of Medicine*, *358*, 475–483.

Wilkerson, M., & Dodder, R. A. (1987). Collective conscience and sport in modern society: An empirical test of a model. *Journal of Leisure Research*, *19*, 35–40.

Wilson, S. A., Grieve, F. G., Ostrowski, S., Mienaltowski, A., & Cyr, C. (2013). Roles of team identification and game outcome in sport fan superstitious behaviors. *Journal of Sport Behavior*, *36*, 417–431.

Wilson, T. D., & Gilbert, D. T. (2005). Affective forecasting: Knowing what to want. *Current Directions in Psychological Science*, *14*, 131–134.

Wilson, T. D., Wheatley, T., Meyers, J. M., Gilbert, D. T., & Axsom, D. (2000). Focalism: A source of durability bias in affective forecasting. *Journal of Personality and Social Psychology*, *78*, 821–836.

Wine, S. (1996, July 29). Cops called to quell angry net fans who demand audience with Andre. *The Paducah Sun*, p. 2B.

Winegard, B. (2010). The evolutionary significance of Red Sox Nation: Sport fandom as a by-product of coalitional psychology. *Evolutionary Psychology*, *8*, 432–446.

Witkemper, C., Lim, C. H., & Waldburger, A. (2012). Social media and sports marketing: Examining the motivations and constraints of Twitter users. *Sport Marketing Quarterly*, *21*, 170–183.

Witte, D. R., Bots, M. L., Hoes, A. W., & Grobbee, D. E. (2000). Cardiovascular mortality in Dutch men during 1996 European Football Championship: Longitudinal population study. *British Medical Journal*, *321*, 23–30.

Wohl, M. J. A., Branscombe, N. R., & Reysen, S. (2010). Perceiving your group's future to be in jeopardy: Extinction threat induces collective angst and the desire to strengthen the ingroup. *Personality and Social Psychology Bulletin*, *36*, 898–910.

Wolff, A. (2016, December 12). The revolution will not be televised. *Sports Illustrated*, 112–118, 120.

Wolff, A., & O'Brien, R. (1994, December 19). Thrown out. *Sports Illustrated*, p. 19.

Wolfson, S., Wakelin, D., & Lewis, M. (2005). Football supporters' perceptions of their role in the home advantage. *Journal of Sports Sciences*, *23*, 365–374.

Won, J., & Kitamura, K. (2007). Comparative analysis of sport consumer motivations between South Korea and Japan. *Sport Marketing Quarterly*, *16*, 93–105.

Woo, B., Trail, G. T., Kwon, H. H., & Anderson, D. (2009). Testing models of motives and points of attachment among spectators in college football. *Sport Marketing Quarterly*, *18*, 38–53.

Wood, S., McInnes, M. M., & Norton, D. A. (2011). The bad thing about good games: The relationship between close sporting events and game day traffic fatalities. *Journal of Consumer Research*, *38*, 611–621.

Wright, S. (1978). *Crowds and riots*. Beverly Hills, CA: Sage Publishers.

Wu, S-H., Tsai, C-Y. D., & Hung, C-C. (2012). Toward a team or player? How trust, vicarious achievement motive, and identification affect fan loyalty. *Journal of Sport Management*, *26*, 177–191.

Xiao, Y. J., & Van Bavel, J. J. (2012). See your friends close and your enemies closer: Social identity and identity threat shape the representation of physical distance. *Personality and Social Psychology Bulletin*, *38*, 959–972.

Yergin, M. L. (1986). Who goes to the game? *American Demographics*, *8*, 42–43.

Yoh, T., Pai, H-T., & Pedersen, P. M. (2009). The influence of socialization agents on the fan loyalty of Korean teens. *International Journal of Sport Management and Marketing*, *6*, 404–416.

Yoshida, M., Gordon, B., Heere, B., & James, J. D. (2015). Fan community identification: An empirical examination of its outcomes in Japanese professional sport. *Sport Marketing Quarterly*, *24*, 105–119.

Yoshida, M., & James, J. D. (2010). Consumer satisfaction with game and service experiences: Antecedents and consequences. *Journal of Sport Management*, *24*, 338–361.

Yost, J. H., & Rainey, D. W. (2014). The consequences of disappointment in team performance among Baseball fans. *Journal of Sport Behavior*, *37*, 407–425.

Young, K. (2002). Standard deviations: An update on North American sports crowd disorder. *Sociology of Sport Journal*, *19*, 237–275.

Zaharia, N., Biscaia, R., Gray, D., & Stotlar, D. (2016). No more "good" intentions: Purchase behaviors in sponsorship. *Journal of Sport Management*, *30*, 162–175.

Zajonc, R. B. (1965). Social facilitation: A solution is suggested for an old unresolved social psychological problem. *Science*, *149*, 269–274.

Zani, B., & Kirchler, E. (1991). When violence overshadows the spirit of sporting competition: Italian football fans and their clubs. *Journal of Community and Applied Social Psychology*, *1*, 5–21.

Zembura, P., & Zysko, J. (2015). Testing relationships between spectator's motives and points of attachment in mixed martial arts in Poland. *Journal of Combat Sports and Martial Arts*, *2*, 67–75.

Zhang, J. J., Pease, D. G., & Hui, S. C. (1996). Value dimensions of professional sport as viewed by spectators. *Journal of Sport & Social Issues*, *21*, 78–94.

Zillmann, D., Bryant, J., & Sapolsky, B. S. (1989). Enjoyment from sports spectatorship. In J. H. Goldstein (Ed.), *Sports, games, and play: Social and psychological viewpoints* (2nd ed., pp. 241–278). Hillsdale, NJ: Lawrence Erlbaum Associates.

Zillmann, D., & Paulas, P. B. (1993). Spectators: Reactions to sports events and effects on athletic performance. In R. N. Singer, M. Murphey, & L. K. Tennant (Eds.), *Handbook of research on sport psychology* (pp. 600–619). New York, NY: Palgrave Macmillan.

Zuckerman, M. (1979). *Sensation-seeking: Beyond the optimal level of arousal.* Hillsdale, NJ: Lawrence Erlbaum Associates.

Zuckerman, M. (1984). Sensation seeking: A comparative approach to a human behavior. *The Behavioral and Brain Sciences*, *7*, 413–471.

Zurcher, L. A., & Meadow, A. (1967). On bullfights and baseball: An example of interaction of social institutions. *The International Journal of Comparative Sociology*, *8*, 99–117.

INDEX

Note: Page numbers in italic indicate figures; those in bold indicate tables.

CPSIA information can be obtained
at www.ICGtesting.com
Printed in the USA
FSHW020841120420
69087FS